THE KING ARTHUR CONSPIRACY

HOW A SCOTTISH PRINCE BECAME A MYTHICAL HERO

SIMON ANDREW STIRLING

An ART & WILL Book

To
William Arthur Stanley – 'Art'
&
Campbell-Godley, who made me an honorary member of the clan

In Memoriam

Map outlines courtesy of d-map.com.
All artwork by Simon Andrew Stirling.

First published 2012

The History Press
The Mill, Brimscombe Port
Stroud, Gloucestershire, GL5 2QG
www.thehistorypress.co.uk

© Simon Andrew Stirling, 2012

The right of Simon Andrew Stirling to be identified as the Author
of this work has been asserted in accordance with the
Copyrights, Designs and Patents Act 1988.

British Library Cataloguing in Publication Data.
A catalogue record for this book is available from the British Library.

ISBN 978 0 7524 7685 8

Typesetting and origination by The History Press
Printed in Great Britain

CONTENTS

Three   Twilight of the Gods

LIST OF ILLUSTRATIONS

Maps

Figures

ACKNOWLEDGEMENTS

KEEPING IT brief: thanks, first and most of all, to Kim and Kiri for their unflagging patience and encouragement. Thanks also to my parents, Norman and Brenda, for introducing me to the Arthurian realms, to the inimitable Campbell of Barcaldine Castle – sorely missed – for inspiring me, and to Charbel Mattar for accompanying me on my first proper research trip. Special thanks go to Rev. Richard Armitage, for making the journey to Avalon for a very special ceremony; to Joyce and Lindsay, our guides to the island, and to Bruce Wall for additional information; to Jim Kilcullen and the *Charna* for the early island-hopping jaunts; and to Phil and Ness for taking me to ancient sites.

Fond thanks to Mike Southworth, history teacher extraordinaire; to Professor Edwin Barrett, for instilling an interest in the Greeks; to my tutors at the University of Glasgow; to An Comunn Gàidhealach and the Birmingham Cymmrydorion (Welsh) Society. A huge thanks also to my friends in the Authonomy community, especially N. Gemini Sasson, Maria Bustillos, Richard Dowling, Shayne Parkinson and Richard Pierce-Sanderson, for all their enthusiasm and advice; to Simon Young for the books; to Andrew Lownie and Ian Drury for helping to shape the project; to Michael Birkett for arguing with me about it; and to John Gist for the kind words. Heartfelt thanks to my editor Lindsey Smith and to all at The History Press for their outstanding help and support. Finally, thanks to Sue and Martin Grantham and Melissa Cother, who did their bit to make sure that I found the road's end.

AUTHOR'S NOTE

ANY CREATIVE endeavour involves making choices. One choice I have made is not to include footnotes or endnotes. This was a conscious decision. Footnotes clutter up the page and distract the eye of the reader; endnotes would add extra bulk and little else. I suspect that too many numbers intruding on the text can detract from the simple pleasure of reading, and if the information isn't important enough to be included in the narrative then it arguably has no place in the book – and besides, the bibliography indicates where most of the references came from.

Most readers will, I hope, forgive me for not attempting to write a quasi-academic tome and for concentrating on being a storyteller rather than a scholar. There are hurdles enough as it is in the story of Arthur, two of the main ones being language and nomenclature.

Some of the names and places in this book will be familiar; many will not. To make matters worse, many of the individuals encountered in these pages were known by more than one name. Different regions, speaking different tongues, evolved different names and titles for Arthur and his confederates. The poets of the time specialised in devising descriptive ways of referring to well-known people. At each new stage of life a person could be awarded a new name. Keeping track of all these name changes can be quite a challenge.

The problem is compounded by the fact that place names and personal names could switch from one language to another. For example, what appears to have been a Welsh name, and is generally treated by scholars as such, can in fact make more sense when it is seen as an attempt to replicate a Gaelic term – or, to put it another way, the Britons took an Irish word and reproduced it, more or less phonetically, in their own language. Though these terms originated in the Gaelic language of the Irish, they settled into the Welsh language of the Britons and over time their initial meanings were forgotten. Only by tracing these odd terms back to their roots can we hope to reveal their original meanings.

The Celtic languages of the Atlantic littoral of Europe are grouped into two branches. The Goidelic or 'Q-Branch' languages are Irish, Scottish Gaelic and Manx. The Brythonic or 'P-Branch' languages are Welsh, Cornish and Breton. The principal difference between the two groups is that words which begin or end with a 'C' in one branch (e.g. *ceann* and *mac* – 'head' and 'son' in Gaelic) tend to have a corresponding 'P' or 'B' in the other (e.g. *pen* and *mab* – 'head' and 'son' in Welsh).

The world of Arthur incorporated both branches. He straddled the Brythonic and Goidelic worlds and probably had a command of several languages. More to the point, the story of Arthur takes in names, places and literature deriving from P-Branch and Q-Branch sources, and so we will come up against words and phrases from both, with translations immediately provided (for the sake of clarity I shall generally refer to the languages of the Britons and the Irish Scots as 'Welsh' and 'Gaelic' respectively; 'Scots', when it occurs, relates to the Lowland dialect which evolved from the same Germanic tongue as English).

A comprehensive guide to the pronunciation of every consonant, vowel and diphthong in Welsh and Gaelic would be of minimal benefit. Few readers would want to keep flicking back to consult it whenever they came across a new character, place name or quotation. Now and then, an approximate pronunciation is offered in the text – for example: *Gwenddolau* (pronounced 'gwen-thol-eye').

There are, however, two sounds which deserve a short note of their own. These are the Gaelic 'ch' and the Welsh 'll'. The 'c-h' combination is in fact present and sounds the same in both languages. As with the name of the German composer J.S. Bach, the sound is made by the tongue very nearly forming a hard 'k' while forcing air up past the back of the tongue. The uniquely Welsh 'l-l' is fairly similar, only the tongue should be flatter and the air forced around its sides. Thus, the 'ch' sound can be formed by softening and extending the 'k' sound, making a hard, rasping 'h', while the 'll' effect can be achieved by softening and prolonging an 'l' sound.

In the crude pronunciation guides I include in the text, the 'ch' sound is designated 'ch' and the 'll' sound is given as 'd' – examples: *Culhwch* (pronounced 'kil-hooch') and *Gwyddbwyll* (pronounced 'gwith-boo-ud').

I have translated most of the early poems in this book myself. It follows that any inaccuracies or infelicities are mine as well.

Alas! there exists an order of minds so sceptical that they deny the possibility of any fact as soon as it diverges from the commonplace.
It is not for them that I write.

André Gide

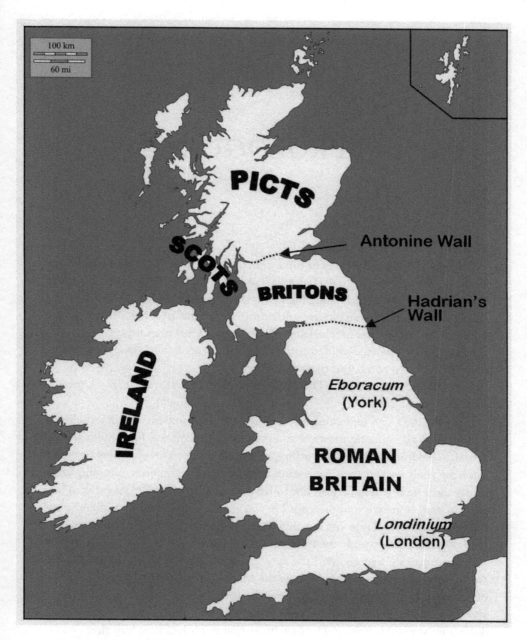

Map 1 Britain, Fourth Century AD

PROLOGUE

THE WINTER had been hard.

Hidden away in the depths of the forest, the crazy man had shivered and gibbered his way through the dark months; snow up to his thighs, ice in his beard. Bitterly, he imagined the feasting halls with their bright choking fires, their music, stories and laughter. More bitterly still, he thought of the great hall of Dumbarton, where his enemy would have celebrated the foreign Christmas feast.

Once, he had worn a golden torque around his neck. Girls swarmed around him like bees to a comb. But that was before.

In his dreams he saw them. Their hollow faces floated above him: black mouths spewing accusations.

Only the wolf kept him company, sharing his hunger and his mountain solitude.

He cut an alarming figure; short and emaciated, his hair was long and matted at the back, the front of his scalp bristling with stubble. When his eyes were not starting from their sockets they were sunk deep inside their cavities, contemplating things most men would be glad not to have seen. Blue-black tattoos pricked into his skin with iron awls told his story. He was a poet, a shouter, one of the inspired ones; he was also a battle-horseman and an enchanter. He was the madman, the wild prophet of the woods, the myrddin.

For months he had guarded the spring which burst through the side of the world (it was the earth's wound, where the Mother made water). From the summit of his forest hideaway he could glimpse the great hills of Bryneich and Rheged and the mountains to the north, even those beyond Dumbarton. He could look down on the ruin of Britain. The metallic spring water had kept him alive.

Alone with the wolf and the wraiths he kept watch on the skies, waiting for a sign. He knew it would come. The world had not ended. Men would polish their armour.

All winter long, when the madness was not upon him, he had thought ahead. The tang of iron was in his mouth. Sometimes the spring water made him retch. It tasted of blood and weapons. And then the visions came again.

The battle-fog, the cries of confusion, the killing.

The voices that whispered.

All winter long, up to his thighs in snow.

On the first day of spring, the serpent came from the mound. That was the way of things.

He was a serpent, coiled inside the cavern where the spring trickled out of the Mother like a running wound. The men of Rhydderch had not found him. The stars had turned: the stream froze in its rocky gully – a terrible winter.

It was time for the serpent to emerge from its mound, sloughing its skin like an old garment.

Spring brought the youth up the mountain. He rode from the lake where he had passed the winter, safe on an island of stones, and left his pony down in the valley where the river was young. There was still ice in the gully, and the peaks were white.

The boy was a man now. At the battle, he became a man; now the years had caught up.

The Wildman greeted him. It was a sorrowful reunion. Though moons had passed the youth still wore the battle on him. But unlike the myrddin, who heard voices in the trees, the boy suffered his own recriminations. The madman was blamed by everybody, the youth only by himself.

They could not talk of plans and purposes until ghosts had been laid to rest. The man they called Little-Shout, who could talk with the birds, had readied himself for this meeting through endless frosty nights. He spoke: '*Peiryan faban*, cease your weeping. Áedán will come across the wide sea. And from Manau a host of excellent hundreds. On the islands on the way to the hill of the Irish, a series of bloody encounters, like a race.'

He was seeing now, just as he had seen by the winter moonlight. Long-headed spears, many long lances. Many red swords, stern troops, shining shields, lively steeds.

'*Peiryan faban*, fewer tears. The encounter of Rhydderch and Áedán by the bright Clyde will resound from the northern border to the south.'

The young man listened. Ahead of him was his sixteenth summer, a season of battles, and beyond that more battles – a lifetime of war, perhaps. Would they all be as awful as the one at which his friend had gone mad?

'*Peiryan faban*, try to rest.'

The young warrior gazed down the hillside, his eyes following the course of the water through its rocky gully. He was taller than his crazy friend but he wore his hair the same way, long at the back. It streamed from the top of his head like reddish gold. His forehead was speckled with dark spots. He had brought the eagle with him.

His name was already famous among the tribes. Druids had prophesied that he was the longed-for one and a brilliant poet had spent the winter spreading the word.

Last summer, he had fought his first battle. This summer, he would lead the armies of the North. He had become a dragon, a champion, a leader of men. The Romans had a word for such things, but his crazy friend had just given him a new title: Little-Shout called him *peiryan faban*. He was the Commanding Youth.

Though the people knew him as Arthur.

ONE

BIRTH OF A DRAGON

'This Arthur of whom the idle tales of the Britons rave
even to this day is a man worthy to be celebrated
not in the foolish dreams of the deceitful fables,
but in truthful histories.'

William of Malmesbury, *History of the Kings of England*, 1125

I

Dragon of the Island

AVALON, THE blessed island on which Arthur was buried. Where is it?

Had it not been for centuries of obfuscation, misdirection, make-believe and propaganda, that question would not need to be asked. Finding Avalon is much the same as finding Arthur: it cannot be done unless prejudices are eschewed and myths laid bare. The facts are that Arthur did exist and the island of his burial can be visited. That is the good news. The bad news is that all this was hidden for so many years because of a conspiracy: a conspiracy that began during Arthur's lifetime; a conspiracy, moreover, which led directly to the fall of Britain.

Such conspiracy talk can often seem far-fetched – by the end of this book the reader will be able to judge for themselves whether or not there was a conspiracy to overthrow him and hand power to his enemies. That conspiracy was of its time; in the case of Arthur, though, we are actually dealing with two conspiracies. The second continues to this day, appropriating his legacy and seeking to turn Arthur into something he was not. For evidence of the latter one has only to visit the county of Somerset in south-west England.

Approaching the town of Glastonbury, the visitor is greeted by a road sign proudly announcing that Glastonbury is the 'ANCIENT ISLE OF AVALON'. Once a thriving religious community, Glastonbury has now become a centre of the New Age movement. The town is dominated by a steep, conical hill known as the Tor, which has attracted more than its fair share of legend. But the association of Glastonbury with Arthur's Isle of Avalon rests on nothing more than an act of deception.

The abbey at Glastonbury was established 300 or 400 years after the death of Arthur. Then, in 1184, disaster struck: the old church was destroyed by fire. Money was urgently needed to build a more durable structure, and the principal source of money was pilgrims. The monks had to come up with a plan to lure pilgrims in their thousands to Glastonbury. It was King Henry II who threw the monks a lifeline by wondering out loud whether the grave of Arthur might not be found in the abbey precinct.

Henry II died in 1189 and was succeeded by his son Richard, nicknamed 'Lionheart'. Richard's overriding interest was the Third Crusade, for which he too needed funds, and so he summoned Henri de Sully, the Abbot of Fécamp in Normandy, over to Glastonbury to work a miracle. Henri de Sully had already turned the abbey at Fécamp into a profitable enterprise by making the most of its holy relics, which supposedly included a bone from the arm of Mary Magdalene and a quantity of Christ's own blood. In their different ways, both of these relics would magically reappear at Glastonbury, the latter in the form of the mysterious receptacle known as the Holy Grail.

The monks of Glastonbury began their excavations in 1191. In no time at all they had unearthed a grave 'between two stone pillars that were erected long ago in that holy place'. The grave contained two skeletons 'hidden very deep in the earth in an oak-hollow', one being that of a large man with a damaged skull, the other belonging to a woman whose golden hair crumbled to dust when it was grasped by one of the monks.

There is no evidence that a Christian settlement existed at Glastonbury in Arthur's time, and if one did it was not significant enough to be mentioned in Bede's eighth-century *Ecclesiastical History of the English People*. Equally, there were no strong grounds at all for believing that Arthur was buried there, and perhaps a certain amount of scepticism greeted the claims that Arthur's grave had been discovered. To overcome these doubts a propagandist by the name of Giraldus Cambrensis ('Gerald of Wales') was brought in to provide an 'eye-witness account' of the discovery and to add a few details of his own. Writing in 1193, Giraldus went into overdrive:

> What is now called Glastonbury was, in antiquity, called the Isle of Avalon; it is like an island because it is entirely hemmed in by swamps. In Welsh it is called *Inis Avallon*, that is *insula pomifera*, 'The Island of Apples', because the apple, which is called *aval* in the Welsh tongue, was once abundant in this place …

Giraldus was right, insofar as the Welsh word for an 'apple' is *afal*. In all other regards, though, he was wrong. Almost certainly, Giraldus had misidentified the kind of apples for which Avalon was famous, and his claim that Glastonbury was the Isle of Avalon had no basis in fact.

Giraldus Cambrensis was on a roll, however. He described a leaden cross he claimed had been discovered on the underside of the gravestone. The cross bore a Latin inscription, which read:

HERE LIES ENTOMBED KING ARTHUR,
WITH GUENEVERE HIS SECOND WIFE,
IN THE ISLE OF AVALON

It does not appear to have occurred to Giraldus that 'Guenevere' was a medieval French version of the name of Arthur's queen and, therefore, not quite authentic. The leaden cross vanished many years ago, but William Camden made a sketch of it in 1607. Camden's sketch shows no reference whatsoever to Arthur's 'second wife'. Giraldus, it would seem, had dreamt that bit up.

Still, the 'discovery' of the grave, along with the publicity campaign undertaken by Giraldus Cambrensis, did the trick. Pilgrims flocked to Glastonbury (rather like their latter-day counterparts, now known as tourists) and their cash paid for the reconstruction of the abbey and for the Lionheart's military adventures in the Holy Land. As an added benefit, the rebellious Welsh were thoroughly discomfited. For years they had predicted the return of their glorious culture hero. Once his bones had been found mouldering in an English grave, the prospect of him riding forth again seemed much less likely.

The 'discovery' of Arthur's remains had been engineered to boost the fortunes of Glastonbury Abbey, but the effects would be far-reaching. In the summer of 2008, an exhibition entitled *King Arthur: A Legend in the Making* opened at the French university of Rennes. The event's curator, Sarah Toulouse, told the world's press, 'King Arthur is a mythical character who was invented at a certain point in history for essentially political reasons.'

There is, sadly, some truth in that statement, but it is not the full story. Ms Toulouse continued: 'If [King Arthur] had really existed there would be more concrete historical traces of him.' Those historical traces are not difficult to find, if one is prepared to look in the right direction. A hero named Arthur undoubtedly existed, but his legend was stolen, uprooted from its proper place and time and transplanted to another country. Few acts of cultural appropriation can compare with this flagrant theft. Quoted in the BBC's *Radio Times* magazine in 2011, author Peter Ackroyd described one of the more famous versions of the Arthur legend as 'a story of Englishness'. But Arthur was never English. England did not exist in his day. Ackroyd's statement offers proof of the fact that the cult of Arthur was commandeered by his enemies.

The scam of Arthur's grave and the subsequent myth that Glastonbury was the Isle of Avalon formed a major part of the conspiracy to reinvent Arthur as an English paragon. Not for nothing has Glastonbury been described by one writer as a 'factory of fraud' and a 'laboratory of forgeries'. The same manipulative cynicism was brought into play more than three centuries after the faked discovery of Arthur's grave, when Glastonbury's interests were once again threatened. On this occasion it was another King Henry – the eighth of that name – who had set his sights on the vast wealth of the Church. His officers were standing by to 'suppress' the monasteries and seize their assets for the Crown.

With exquisite timing, at that precise moment – 1536 – a manuscript appeared; known to scholars as the Hafod MS 19, it also goes by the more enticing title of *The Greal*.

The manuscript contained an account of the life of St Collen, an obscure British saint more commonly associated with the parish of Llangollen in Wales. The tale, as told by the Glastonbury monks, had St Collen inhabiting a primitive hovel at the foot of Glastonbury Tor. One day, Collen overheard two men outside who were talking about Gwyn ap Nudd (pronounced 'gwin ap nith') and saying that he was the 'King of Annwn and of the fairies'. Collen stuck his head out of the door and reprimanded the men with the words: 'Hold your tongues quickly, those are but Devils.' The men replied that it was Collen who should hold his tongue, lest he receive a rebuke from the mighty Gwyn.

A little later, a messenger knocked on the door to Collen's hut, inviting him to a meeting with Gwyn ap Nudd on the Tor at noon. For two days, Collen ignored the summons. On the third day, he armed himself with a flask of holy water and climbed the hill to meet with the 'King of Annwn'.

On the summit of the Tor, Collen saw 'the fairest castle he had ever beheld', surrounded by the 'best-appointed troops', the most talented minstrels and 'maidens of elegant aspect'. Courteously, Collen was ushered into the castle, where the king was seated on a throne of gold. Gwyn ap Nudd offered the saint an abundance of sweetmeats and entertainments, to which Collen responded with a fit of righteous fury and a well-aimed dash of holy water, instantly sending Gwyn and his court back to the realm of everlasting fire and interminable cold.

The story, as told in 1536, was a thinly veiled parable: such was the sanctity of Glastonbury that it could withstand the blandishments of luxury-loving kings like Gwyn ap Nudd, and like Henry VIII. The propaganda machine had swung into action once more, but this time it failed in its mission. Three years after *The Greal* appeared, the king's officers swooped. The walls of the abbey were torn down, its library plundered and burnt; even the black marble tomb to which the supposed remains of Arthur and his queen had been transferred was destroyed, and the last Abbot of Glastonbury was marched up to the top of the Tor and cruelly butchered.

The myth, however, refused to die. Along with the fabricated legend of the Holy Grail at Glastonbury, the notion that the Tor was the dwelling place of the king of the fairies, Gwyn ap Nudd, is regularly trotted out in books of British folklore. Glastonbury had not only laid claim to having been the Isle of Avalon – it was now also Annwn (pronounced 'an-noon'), the Celtic Otherworld. And all this on the basis of a tale concocted simply to preserve the abbey from the greed of King Henry VIII and his supporters.

On the face of it, there is little to link the Glastonbury legend of St Collen and Gwyn ap Nudd with the historical Arthur. But the fact is that Glastonbury had again turned to the traditions of Arthur and his people in an attempt to bolster its spiritual reputation. St Collen, as we shall discover, was implicated in the assassination of Arthur, while Gwyn ap Nudd was one of Arthur's closest companions.

Gwyn ap Nudd – the name meant 'Blessed son of Mist' – is traditionally thought of as a very British sort of Devil: a lord of the underworld who rides out on stormy nights at the head of his pack of spectral hounds. A fourteenth-century manuscript preserves an invocation uttered by Welsh magicians:

> *ad regum Eumenidium et regina eius: Gwynn ap Nudd qui es ultra in silva pro amore concubine tue permitte nos venire domum*

> to the king of the Fates and his queen: Gwyn son of Nudd, who is far off in the forest, for the love of your lover permit us to enter your domain

The assumption, then, is that Gwyn was some sort of British god. But the gods of today tend to be the heroes of yesteryear, and before he was demonised in Christian fables the original Gwyn was a princely poet and a prophet. It is he who will eventually lead us to the true place of Arthur's burial.

His story was transcribed by Llewellyn Sion, a Welsh bard of the sixteenth century, who introduced him as Gwion Bach or Little Gwyn. He was raised by a foster-father named Gwreang (meaning 'page' or 'squire') and, at an early age, made the short journey from the old Roman fort at Caereinion to the lake of Llyn Tegid in the kingdom of Gwynedd.

Llyn Tegid is better known in English as Bala Lake. It is a long, deep stretch of water, hemmed in by mountains and cleansed by the River Dee, which runs the entire length of the lake on its way, via Llangollen (the parish of Gwyn's persecutor), to its junction with the sea near Liverpool. The lake is also the home of a supernatural water-monster affectionately known as 'Teggie'.

In Gwyn's day, Llyn Tegid was the site of a finishing school for the British nobility. Central to the cultic nature of this school was a remarkable cauldron, which dispensed what Gwyn would refer to as the 'liquor of science and inspiration'. The divine patron of the cauldron was a sow-goddess called Ceridwen. The goddess was said to be the spiritual partner of Tegid the Bald, who was perhaps none other than 'Teggie', the resident monster of the lake.

On arrival at the Llyn Tegid college, Little Gwyn was given the task of tending the fire that warmed the sacred cauldron of inspiration. The cauldron was being prepared for a lad named Morfrân (meaning 'Cormorant'), who was so hideously ugly that he was also known as Afagddu (from *afanc*, a 'water-monster', and *du*, meaning 'black'). The cauldron's gift of poetic inspiration was intended to compensate Morfrân for his ghastly appearance. But where Morfrân was horrible to look at, his sister was the absolute opposite. She was a striking beauty known as Creirwy.

Morfrân is mentioned elsewhere in early British literature as one of the few survivors of Arthur's last battle; he was also the father of the original Merlin. Creirwy, meanwhile, was even more crucial to the story of Arthur. Her name (pronounced 'cray-ir-ooy') seems to have drawn on *crëyr*, the Welsh word for a 'heron'. The lovely Creirwy would, therefore, appear to have had something in common with the grey, ghostly and elegant bird – perhaps because the heron stands on one leg, which was also the stance adopted by Celtic seers. The likelihood is that Creirwy, as a senior priestess of the cauldron cult, was a prophetess. She was also destined to give birth to the most famous hero of them all.

Creirwy and Morfrân were lined up to play the parts of goddess and consort in what would have been a joint initiation. But, according to legend, fate intervened to ensure that it was Little Gwyn who received the blessing of the cauldron. Three droplets of the mystical brew splashed onto his hand. Gwyn thrust his smarting fingers into his mouth and instantly gained wisdom and enlightenment. The cauldron gave a shriek and broke into pieces, spilling its remaining contents into a stream and poisoning the horses of the local magnate.

With his newly acquired knowledge, Gwyn realised that he was in trouble. As the goddess Ceridwen lumbered towards him, furious that the cauldron's goodness had been stolen, Gwyn turned himself into a hare and gambolled away. The goddess transformed herself into a greyhound and chased after him. Gwyn leapt into a river, becoming a fish. Ceridwen took on the form of an otter. Next, Gwyn flew up into the air as a bird, but the goddess transformed herself into a hawk. Finally, Gwyn spied a farmyard and dropped down into the middle of it, disguised as a grain of wheat. Ceridwen changed her shape into that of a great crested hen and swallowed him whole.

Gwyn's transformations find their echo in the Scottish legend of Tam Lin. Abducted by the Queen of Elfland, Tam Lin was rescued by his lover Janet, who had to hold him fast while he took on a variety of menacing forms. Such shape-shifting seems to have been an integral part of a poet's visit to the Otherworld, and it was Creirwy's task to hold Gwyn still as he wrestled with the demons of his imagination.

The 'liquor of science and inspiration' almost certainly contained hallucinogens which, once imbibed, gave the initiate the sensation of being chased and of passing through different states. Writing in the person of Merlin, a churchman of the twelfth century clearly grasped what the ritual was all about:

> I was taken out of my true self, I was as a spirit and knew the history of people long past and could foretell the future. I knew then the secrets of nature, bird flight, star wanderings and the way fish glide.

The story of Little Gwyn suggests that he jumped the queue for this trippy experience, inadvertently taking the place of the ugly Morfrân. In reality, Gwyn's preferential treatment was probably the result of blood ties and politics.

The horses that were poisoned when the cauldron shrieked and fell apart belonged to one Gwyddno Garanhir, whose epithet meant 'Tall-Crane'; like

Creirwy, Gwyddno was associated with the sacred bird of letters and foresight. Gwyddno (pronounced 'gwi-th-no') governed the province of Meirionydd, a subdivision of the Welsh kingdom of Gwynedd. His roots were in the North, however: he was a descendant of the venerable Dyfnwal, onetime overlord of the British kingdom of Strathclyde. The sons of Dyfnwal the Old had spread out to occupy most of what we now think of as the Scottish Lowlands. One of Dyfnwal's grandsons was Clydno, the ruler of Lothian (Clydno's epithet, 'Eidyn', indicates that he controlled the citadel of Din Eidyn – Edinburgh). Clydno Eidyn had at least two children: a son known as Cynon and a daughter named Creirwy.

Another grandson of Dyfnwal the Old was Nudd the Generous, who held the tribal lands of the Selgovae in what are now the Scottish Borders. As the son of Nudd, Little Gwyn was himself a prince of Strathclyde and a cousin to Creirwy daughter of Clydno, as well as being related to Gwyddno Tall-Crane, the chieftain whose domain embraced the site of the cauldron cult at Llyn Tegid.

Morfrân belonged to a different British dynasty. He was descended from Coel the Old, the last Romanised *dux Britanniarum* ('Duke of Britain') and the 'Old King Cole' of the children's rhyme. To all intents and purposes, Morfrân the Speckled came from another tribe, and so his place in the queue for the cauldron initiation was taken by the better-connected Gwyn son of Nudd as the children of Strathclyde asserted their dominance. Morfrân would just have to wait his turn.

For nine months Gwyn gestated in the belly of the goddess, until the time came for him to be reborn. The goddess was so struck by his beauty that she decided not to kill him after all – he was not yet forgiven for his theft of the cauldron's bounty. Instead, she placed him inside a wicker coracle and cast him adrift like Moses in the bulrushes. The date, so we are told, was 29 April.

The proper name for a wicker coracle with a leather canopy, like the one in which Little Gwyn was placed, is a Dovey coracle, after the River Dovey on which these simple fishing boats were seen. The same kind of vessel was said to have carried St Collen to his parish at Llangollen, a short distance downriver from Llyn Tegid. The irascible Collen was seemingly another graduate of the cauldron cult – his Druidic-sounding name, 'Hazel', would certainly suggest as much – who later embraced Christianity and turned on his former associates with all the fiery zeal of the convert.

Gwyddno Tall-Crane now re-enters the story. He had a hapless and highly strung son named Elffin. On the first of May, Gwyddno instructed his son to go down to the weir on the river near his court and to bring back 100 pounds worth of salmon.

Elffin son of Gwyddno came to the salmon weir on the river and found it devoid of fish. There was, however, a Dovey coracle trapped in the weir. Elffin pulled back the leather canopy to reveal a youth whose forehead had been shaved in the Druidic manner, across the top of the head from ear to ear, and had probably been tattooed with salmon-like speckles. With a gasp, Elffin exclaimed, 'Behold, a beautiful brow!'

And so Little Gwyn acquired his new name, Taliesin (*tal iesin* – 'beautiful brow'), and he sprang from the coracle spouting verses. With his own personal bard by his side, Elffin son of Gwyddno grew in confidence. He became a favourite of his uncle Maelgwyn, the 'tall, fair prince' of Gwynedd.

It is at the court of King Maelgwyn that we next find Taliesin. Maelgwyn's chief seat was at Deganwy, on a pair of fortified hilltops overlooking the mouth of the River Conwy on the coast of North Wales. Taliesin had prepared his protégé, Elffin son of Gwyddno, for his own cauldron ordeal, part of which involved a form of ritual imprisonment. The bard went to Maelgwyn's stronghold to release Elffin from his enchanted prison. Hiding himself in a corner of Maelgwyn's hall, Taliesin first played a trick on the king's twenty-four bards by making them bow to their lord while playing '*Blerwm, blerwm!*' on their lips with their fingers. The bard then leapt to his feet and delivered a typically cocksure performance:

> Primary Chief Bard am I to Elffin,
> And my native realm is the place of the summer stars.
> Other bards have called me Myrddin,
> But soon all kings shall call me Taliesin.
> Nine months in the womb of Ceridwen,
> Before I was Gwyn, but now I am Taliesin …

His song charmed the fetters from Elffin's feet, and the bard then presented his student with a cauldron full of gold. Elffin, it would seem, had passed his own initiation ordeal.

The legend of Little Gwyn – or Taliesin, as we must now call him – the son of Nudd the Generous, has given us our first glimpse of the item that came to be thought of as the Holy Grail. It has also introduced us to certain individuals who would play major roles in the story of Arthur. The presence of Maelgwyn the Tall in the story allows us to put a rough date to the proceedings. According to the *Annales Cambriae*, or *Welsh Annals*, Maelgwyn of Gwynedd succumbed to the 'yellow plague', which swept through Britain like a veil of mist in the middle of the sixth century. He died, near his Deganwy court, in about the year AD 547.

The death of Maelgwyn the Tall set in motion a chain of events which would lead to the birth of a boy named Arthur.

Maelgwyn's kingdom of Gwynedd had been established about a century earlier. Cunedda, a warlord responsible for defending Manau Gododdin (the Stirling region of the River Forth), was transferred to North Wales in order to drive out Irish settlers. Along with his sons, Cunedda forced the Irish back into the Lleyn Peninsula, so called after the people of Leinster, and took control of north-west Wales, founding the kingdom of Gwynedd. One of Cunedda's sons, Einion, gave his name to the Roman fort where Taliesin was raised. The lake of Llyn Tegid, meanwhile, was named after one of Cunedda's predecessors, Tacitus, who had previously defended Manau Gododdin against violent incursions by the Picts and the Scots.

As a descendant of Cunedda of Manau, Maelgwyn the Tall had northern roots, which helps to explain why so many noble youths of North Britain had flocked to Gwynedd for their education. Maelgwyn allowed the cauldron school to flourish at Llyn Tegid. This provided him with a steady supply of bards and ensured that the princes of Strathclyde studied the arts of verse and vision in Maelgwyn's realm. It also earned him a place in history, thanks to a scabrous open letter penned by a man of the Church.

Gildas Sapiens – 'Gildas the Wise' – was himself a child of the North, born and raised near the edge of Britain. St Gildas left his native region, presumably to study Christianity, and according to one (highly suspect) account of his life he ended his days at Street in Somerset, a stone's throw from the town of Glastonbury. His *De Excidio et Conquestu Britanniae* – '*Of the Ruin and Conquest of Britain*' – is a document of enormous historical importance; in it, Gildas outlined the history of Britain after the Roman withdrawal and fired off a savage critique of his contemporary kings.

Even before the Romans left, Gildas wrote, the Britons had grown painfully accustomed to the 'cruelty of two foreign nations – the Scots from the north-west and the Picts from the north'. These were not the only enemies of Britain, but they were the ones with whom Gildas had been most familiar. With the departure of the last Roman legion in AD 409, the Picts and their Scottish neighbours, 'differing from one another in manners but inspired by the same avidity for blood, and all the more eager to shroud their villainous faces in bushy hair than to cover with decent clothing those parts of their bodies which required it', resumed their assaults on the Romanised Britons. When a welcome respite came, the Britons failed to prepare themselves for future attacks. Britain was 'deluged with a most extraordinary plenty of things,' stated Gildas, 'greater than was known before, and with it grew up every kind of luxury and licentiousness.' But rumours of an impending invasion from the North, coupled with a fresh outbreak of plague, forced the Britons to take defensive measures.

A 'proud tyrant' – Gildas called him Gurthrigen, but he is more widely known as Vortigern – made the mistake of inviting, 'like wolves into the sheep-fold, the fierce and impious Saxons, a race hateful both to God and men' to wage war on the troublesome Picts and Scots on the Britons' behalf. Germanic mercenaries were recruited by the British High King to drive the Picts and Scots back into their homelands beyond the River Forth – it was at about this time that Cunedda of Manau was transferred from Stirling to North Wales, clearing the way for the Germanic warriors to tackle the northern barbarians head-on.

As a reward for their efforts, the mercenaries of Jutland, Angeln and Saxony received land on the eastern seaboard of Britain. They sent word back to their compatriots on the Baltic shores that the Britons were incapable of defending themselves. More and more settlers crossed the North Sea to join the Germanic communities in Britain. Finally, the immigrants complained that their 'monthly supplies' were not being 'furnished in sufficient abundance' by their British hosts and ran amok.

'[The] fire of vengeance spread from sea to sea,' wrote Gildas. 'Lamentable to behold, in the midst of streets lay the tops of lofty towers, tumbled to the ground, stones of high walls, holy altars, fragments of human bodies, covered with livid clots of coagulated blood, looking as if they had been squeezed together in a press.'

All was not lost – not yet, at any rate. The Britons rallied under the leadership of one Ambrosius Aurelianus, a 'modest man' born into the Romano-British nobility. Under Ambrosius the Britons fought back against the Germanic marauders and 'sometimes our countrymen, sometimes the enemy, won the field'. This continued up until 'the year of the siege of Badon Hill, when took place the last almost, though not the least slaughter of our cruel foes', which was, St Gildas was sure, 'forty-four years and one month after the landing of the Saxons, and also the time of my nativity'.

If, as seems likely, Gildas had in mind the *adventum Saxonum* or 'coming of the Saxons', which the Venerable Bede dated to the year 449, then the British triumph at the siege of Badon Hill must have taken place in about 493, which, as Gildas observed, was also the year of his own birth.

The reference to a 'siege of Badon Hill' (*obsessionis Badonici montis*) is one of the banes of Arthurian research. Another early source lists a battle on Mount Badon as the twelfth and last of Arthur's famous victories, and many historians have assumed that the Battle of Mount Badon and the 'siege of Badon Hill' must have been one and the same. This has required some tortured explanations for the fact that St Gildas made no mention of Arthur in his *De Excidio*. The real reason is simple enough: Arthur had not yet been born when St Gildas wrote his lengthy open letter. Arthur's Battle of Mount Badon and the 'siege of Badon Hill' referred to by Gildas were two completely different occasions. But by trying to shoehorn Arthur into a battle at which he could not possibly have fought, historians have persisted in placing him in the wrong part of Britain and in the wrong century.

The British victory at Badon Hill in roundabout 493 heralded a period of peace. The Britons were still plagued by 'civil troubles' but their 'foreign wars' had come to a temporary end. The Germanic intruders, known collectively as Saxons, retreated to their east-coast settlements while the Britons recovered from the traumas of the fifth century and, if Gildas is to be believed, fell back into their bad old ways.

The *De Excidio et Conquestu Britanniae* is an extremely partisan piece of work. It represents the view of an early churchman. Christianity had taken root in Britain during the latter years of the Roman occupation. The collapse of the Roman administration in Britain left the natives to fend for themselves. Inevitably, many Britons returned to the customs and beliefs of their forebears, and even the Christians in Britain demonstrated their independence from Rome by supporting the heretic Pelagius, who rejected the orthodox belief in Original Sin. Two continental bishops were despatched to combat this heresy, and these bishops almost certainly colluded in a rebellion against the High King of Britain. In short, many Britons were fighting to preserve not only their land but their political and religious freedoms as well. They were opposed in this by those Britons who looked upon the Church of Rome as the natural successor to the Roman Empire and welcomed its influence. There were, in effect, two factions in Britain: the hairy pagans and the Romanised Christians. St Gildas was writing exclusively from the point of view of the latter. He was dismissive of anyone who did not accept the Church as the ultimate authority in all things, and carefully avoided admitting that the 'civil troubles' to which Britain was prone were often the result of hectoring and intransigence on the part of the Christians.

Gildas seems to have considered the British triumph at Badon Hill as a success for the Romanised party, led by Ambrosius Aurelianus. To the saint's dismay, though, the Britons did not all rush to join the Church. In the aftermath of the Badon Hill siege his fellow countrymen allowed 'all the laws of truth and justice' to be 'shaken and subverted'. They were hurtling 'headlong down to hell'. So Gildas unleashed a vicious attack on the kings of Britain.

Starting in the extreme south-west, with Devon and Cornwall and their chieftain Constantine, the 'tyrannical whelp of the unclean lioness', Gildas the Wise worked his way up through the western kingdoms, spewing his bile with abandon, until he came to the imposing figure of Maelgwyn, Lord of Gwynedd. Gildas dubbed him Maglocunus – 'Hound-Prince':

> And likewise, O thou dragon of the island, who hast deprived many tyrants, as well of their kingdoms as their lives, and though the last-mentioned in my writing, the first in mischief, exceeding many in power, and also in malice, more liberal than others in giving, more licentious in sinning, strong in arms, but stronger in working thine own soul's destruction, Maglocune, why art thou (as if soaked in the Sodomitical grape) foolishly rolling in the black pool of thine offences? Why dost thou willfully heap like a mountain, upon thy kingly shoulders, such a load of sins?

It was into this world that Taliesin, the Primary Chief Bard, had burst like a supernova. Like the twenty-four bards of Maelgwyn's court, Taliesin was a product of the school at Llyn Tegid – the 'black pool' of Maelgwyn's 'offences'. Maelgwyn's kingdom included the Isle of Anglesey, which had been the site of a major Druidic college until it was destroyed by the Roman army. Druidism was enjoying something of a renaissance under Maelgwyn of Gwynedd and, therefore, in the eyes of St Gildas, Maelgwyn was damned.

The designation 'dragon of the island' provides a hint as to how far Maelgwyn was embroiled with the Druidic elite. The Welsh *draig* can mean either a 'dragon' or a 'lord', just as the Gaelic equivalent, *drèagan*, can mean 'dragon' or 'champion' (as late as the sixteenth century one MacDougall of Dunollie was described in the *Book of the Dean of Lismore* as 'the dear dragon from Connel'). By branding him 'dragon of the island', St Gildas might have been acknowledging that Maelgwyn was the Chief Warlord of Britain, although it is more likely that Gildas was thinking of a specific island where the Druidic intelligentsia still held sway.

Maelgwyn's first marriage was to a princess identified as Gwallwen ferch Afallach. The Welsh term *Afallach* compares with the Gaelic *ubhalach*, meaning 'apple-bearing', and was an early form of the more familiar *Avalon*. As we shall see, Arthur was reportedly buried 'in a hall on the island of Afallach'. Maelgwyn's first wife, then, was a 'daughter of Avalon' – one of only two we shall meet in these pages, the other being Arthur's half-sister. The tradition that the isle of the apple trees was guarded by a 'dragon' or champion can be traced back to deepest antiquity; it also accounts for the fact that Arthur's father – another 'dragon of the island' – came to be thought of as the Pendragon. By marrying Gwallwen, a 'daughter' of the island of apples, Maelgwyn might well have taken on the responsibility of defending the Druidic isle, thereby becoming the 'dragon' of the sacred island.

The Christian community refused to accept the validity of such a pagan marriage and the product of the union – a boy named Rhun – was summarily declared by the Church to be illegitimate. In an attempt to placate his critics, Maelgwyn next married a British princess of the Pennines. The ceremony was presumably conducted along Christian lines because the clergy were happy with it. Maelgwyn upset the Christian fraternity again, however, by taking for his third wife a princess of the Picts.

To the Christians of North Britain, such as Gildas and St Patrick, the Picts of the far north were barely human. They were tattooed savages; the bogeymen of the Roman world. But Maelgwyn's decision to marry a Pictish princess was canny. Pictish society was matrilineal: power and prestige were handed down from mother to son. This meant that a male child born to Maelgwyn and his royal Pictish bride would automatically become the next in line to the Pictish throne. In fact, Maelgwyn's Pictish queen provided him with at least two children: a boy named Bridei or Bruide, who did indeed become King of the Picts a few years after his father's death, and a girl named Domelch, who would grow up to marry the father of Arthur.

Arthur's mother, meanwhile, was happily settled in North Wales where, under Maelgwyn's protection, she had initiated her cousin Gwyn, who became Taliesin, the Primary Chief Bard in Britain. She was helping to educate a new generation of warrior-poets, preparing them for their cauldron initiation, much to the chagrin of churchmen like Gildas the Wise.

But the death of Maelgwyn the Tall in the late 540s sparked a crisis, setting Briton against Briton and forcing Creirwy to return to her Lothian homeland, where a warrior-prince was waiting to deprive her of her sacred virginity.

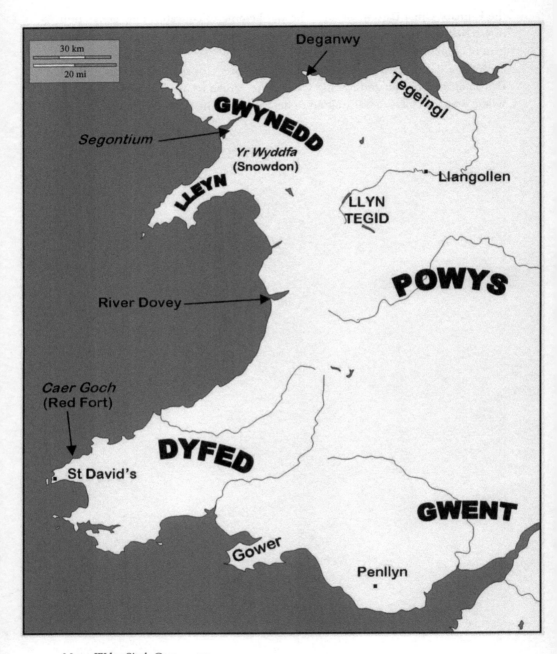

Map 2 Wales, Sixth Century AD

2

THE SEA-KINGDOM

THE YEAR was 498. Three brothers set sail from the north coast of Ireland.

They crossed the Moyle and came to the peninsula of Kintyre. Following the shoreline they arrived at the bay of Loch Crinan, where the winding River Add empties into the Atlantic. Ahead of them, standing out from the surrounding plain, a double-crested rocky outcrop rose 50m above the sodden peat of the Big Moss. Capping the hill was the stronghold of *Dùn Add* – 'Dunadd'. First fortified many centuries earlier, it would continue to function as a seat of royal power in the region for a 1,000 years to come.

The brothers climbed to the lower summit of Dunadd where, by placing his right foot inside a footprint carved into the rock of the hill, the eldest of the three was proclaimed king of the Irish colony of Dalriada. His name was Fergus Mór mac Eirc. He was the great-great-grandfather of Arthur.

His brother Loarn proceeded northwards as far as the Little Haven, or *an t-Òban*, where he established his headquarters at the hill fort of Dunollie – the future home of a 'dear dragon from Connel'. From there, Loarn's kindred patrolled the land and seaways which still bear his name: 'Lorne'. Oenghus, the youngest of the three, sailed for the island of Islay so that his clansmen could guard the maritime approaches to the colony.

The sons of Erc thus took control of the 'Coastland of the Gael' – *Airer Gáidel*, or Argyll as it is known today – the sea-kingdom of the Scots.

They had done so in line with a prophecy uttered by the British-born evangelist who called himself Patricius; the Irish knew him as Pádraig. The *Tripartite Life of St Patrick* relayed the words spoken by the saint to Fergus Mór:

> Though today thy brother hath little esteem of thee, yet thou shalt be king, and from thee shall come the kings in this country and over Fortriu for ever.

By 'this country', Patrick meant the Irish province of Ulster. 'Fortriu' referred to the tribal lands of the southern Picts in the great central plain of what we now call Scotland. St Patrick had promised Fergus the Great that his descendants would govern both the north of Ireland and the fertile realm of the southern Picts. In staking their claim to the Irish colony in Argyll, the sons of Erc were pursuing their manifest destiny.

The origins of Arthur's Scottish ancestors are shrouded in myth. Irish tradition records a series of invasions, beginning with the arrival of Noah's granddaughter; she fled to Ireland to escape the Flood and there married one Fintan, who alone survived the deluge by turning himself into a salmon. Fintan thereby became the original 'salmon of wisdom' and the first in a long line of Druids.

The last of the conquests, as outlined in the medieval *Book of the Taking of Ireland*, was that of the Milesians, who were also known as the Gaels. They wrested control of Ireland from the magicians of the *Tuatha dé Danann*, 'Children of Danu', a race of poets and prophets (a collective term for artists is still *aois-dàna* or 'people of Danu'). During their earlier period of exile the *Tuatha dé Danann* had wandered as far as ancient Greece, where they settled at Thebes and performed acts of magic on behalf of the Athenians. Their skills reputedly included reviving the fallen warriors of Athens. If certain classical authors are to be believed, the Druids of the Children of Danu also tutored the mathematical genius Pythagoras of Samos, who established a secret sect of vegetarian mystics and was associated with a mystery cult devoted to the death-and-rebirth process of initiation.

The Children of Danu eventually moved on, turning homewards in search of their Land of Promise. The legends argue that they spent some time in the Northern Isles of Scotland and, when they finally reached Ireland, brought with them four magical objects from their cities in the North. The sacred objects were a cauldron, a sword, a spear and a stone. Each one has a role to play in the story of Arthur.

Despised by the Church, these cultic hallows vanished into the European underground, only to return as the suits of the Tarot pack and the familiar hearts, spades, clubs and diamonds of the ordinary deck of playing cards.

The priestly Children of Danu were no match for the militaristic elite that swept them from power and seized Ireland. Folklore would claim that the *Tuatha dé Danann* retreated into their burial mounds and lonely places, becoming those ancestral spirits known as the *Sìdhe* (pronounced 'shee'), the Shining Ones, the Fair Folk and the Gentry. But reports of their demise were somewhat exaggerated. Their influence would linger among the natives of Britain and their Pictish cousins, as well as their Irish counterparts, the Cruithne. The Welsh legends often refer to Arthur's British relatives as the 'Children of Dôn', for in Arthur the blood of the *Tuatha dé Danann* mingled with that of the Gaels.

Two origin myths account for the Milesians who became the Gaels of Ireland and Scotland. The first is to be found in the eleventh-century *Book of the Taking of Ireland*. It states that one Míl Éspáine – 'Soldier of Spain' – fought for the King of Scythia before moving to Egypt, where he married the daughter of a pharaoh named Nectanebus. The Egyptian princess was known as Scota and she was the progenitor of the Scots.

The alternative myth concerns the father of the Gaelic peoples, a figure referred to as Gathelus or Gáedal Glas. According to some accounts he was a Scythian king who was bitten by a snake in Egypt. His friend Moses cured the wound, leaving a pale grey-green scar, and told Gathelus that no snakes would infest the land in which his people settled; he also advised the king to escape from Egypt ahead of the coming plagues. Gathelus duly sailed from the Nile to Spain.

The historian Hector Boece recorded a version of this story in 1527:

> Gathelus, an Athenian or Argive, travelled from Greece to Egypt, where he married Scota, daughter of Pharaoh. At the Exodus, Gathelus fled with Scota to Iberia, where he founded a kingdom at Brigantium, now Santiago de Compostella. There, Gathelus reigned in the marble chair, or fatal stone like a chair: wherever it was found would be the kingdom of the Scots. Simon Breck, a descendant of Gathelus, then took the chair from Spain to Ireland, and was crowned King of Ireland in it.

Quite clearly, the two myths – those of Míl Éspáine and Gáedal Glas – are almost identical, in that both involve a King of Greece (or Scythia) who visited Egypt, married the pharaoh's daughter and then travelled west to Spain and the Galician city of Brigantium (now La Coruña), a traditional launching pad for migrations to Britain and Ireland. The twin myths seem to revolve around the same person, and the key to identifying who that might have been lies in the name of the Egyptian pharaoh, Nectanebus.

There were two pharaohs of the Thirtieth Dynasty who bore the name Nectanebo. The latter of the two, Nectanebo II, would be the last native Egyptian to rule the kingdom of the Nile until Egypt regained its independence in the 1950s.

Nectanebo II came to the Egyptian throne in about 360 BC. His reign lasted for some twenty years and during that time he enjoyed an unrivalled reputation as a magical adept. C.J.S. Thompson – who, in his *Mysteries and Secrets of Magic*, referred to the pharaoh as 'Nectanebus' – noted that the pharaoh was 'profoundly learned in astrology, in the interpretation of omens, in casting horoscopes and in magical practice', being able to 'rule all kings by his magical powers'. One of his skills involved a bowl of water, into which he would place wax models of enemy ships and warriors along with miniatures of his own forces. Putting on an 'Egyptian prophet's cloak', he would then take up his ebony wand and pronounce 'words of power':

the figures of the men in wax would come to life, and the ships began to engage in battle. He contrived that the models representing his own navy should vanquish the enemy and sink their ships to the bottom of the bowl, as did his real ships sink the enemy's vessels on the sea. Thus Nectanebus fought his battles by aid of magical art.

Magical battles aside, Nectanebo might never have secured the Egyptian throne had it not been for the support of a mercenary army commanded by the lame King of Sparta, Agesilaus II. Described by Plutarch as 'by far the most famous Greek of his time', Agesilaus had achieved the Spartan throne in 401 BC in defiance of a prophecy that Sparta would suffer an irreversible decline if a lame man became king. The oracle turned out to be right: Sparta never did recover its former glory after it was defeated by the Thebans during the reign of Agesilaus. The memory of a lame king and his effect on the fortunes of his kingdom would resurface, hundreds of years later, in the Arthurian legends of the Waste Land.

Five years into his reign, Agesilaus led a large army into Anatolia to defend Greek interests in what is now Turkey. It is conceivable that during his Anatolian campaign Agesilaus recruited Celtic soldiers of fortune from the Bronze Age city of Miletus. Situated on the Ionian coast near the mouth of the River Maeander, Miletus was the birthplace of Greek science and philosophy; Pythagoras of Samos had studied there. The people of the city were known as Milesians.

When he later sailed to Egypt, Agesilaus was accompanied by mercenaries who found a new god to worship in the form of the royal magician of the Nile. Agesilaus and his army reached Egypt in 361 BC and helped Nectanebo to the throne (the Nile cobra, which adorned the headdress of the pharaoh, might account for the 'snake bite' which gave Gathelus his distinctive green scar). Agesilaus was then sent home with a sizeable reward, but he died at Cyrene in Libya and Nectanebo issued instructions that the lame king's body should be embalmed in honey for the rest of its journey. Coincidence or not, the Old Irish word for 'honey' was *mil*. The people who would go on to colonise Ireland were called the Milesians, or 'Sons of Míl'.

Agesilaus II would appear to have been the historical model for those legendary founding fathers of the Gaels, Gathelus (or Gáedal Glas) and Míl Éspáine. Those who had fought under his command were aware that their world was changing: Sparta's glory days were over; Egypt was about to be conquered by Alexander the Great. The followers of Agesilaus decided to take ship and travel, via Spain, towards the sunset and the green isle at the edge of the world, where they would continue to worship the last of the Egyptian pharaohs.

They were a warrior caste, steeped in the religious practices of Greece and Egypt and influenced, no doubt, by the militarism of Sparta. From this stock came Arthur's people.

St Isidore of Seville, an exact contemporary of Arthur, made the observation that *Scotia eadem et Hibernia* – 'Scotland and Ireland are the same place'. A healthy trade in goods, ideas and people criss-crossed the narrow sea between the north of Ireland and the west coast of Scotland, and once they had taken control of the Emerald Isle the Milesian Gaels soon set their sights on the lands across the Moyle.

The Irish colony in Argyll had already existed for many years when Fergus and his brothers arrived there in AD 498. It became known as Dalriada, the original kingdom of the Scots, although initially it was just an offshoot of an Irish tribe, the Dál Riata.

Back in the first century BC the High King of Ireland, Conaire Mór, had three sons, all named Cairpre. After his death all three drifted southwards. Cairpre Bascháin and Cairpre Músc founded the subservient Déisi tribes of Munster, but the third son of Conaire Mór chose to lead his people back to the north, where two separate tribes were feuding over land and resources. One of these tribes, the Dál Fiatach, was also known as the *Ulaid*, from which we get the name of Ulster. The people of the rival Dál nAraidne tribe were also referred to as *Cruithne*, meaning 'Britons' or 'Picts'.

The Picts of Britain were those native tribes of the far north that had never yielded to Roman rule. Roman soldiers coined the term *pictii* – 'painted' – as a label for the tattooed aboriginals who lived beyond the River Forth. The Irish counterparts of these Picts were referred to by Diodorus Siculus in about 50 BC as 'those of the Pretani who inhabit the country called Iris' – that is, those Britons who inhabited Ireland. The word *Cruithne* compares with the *Prydyn* of Britain, in that both *cruth* and *pryd* meant 'form' or 'design'. All three native groups – the Britons, the Picts and the Cruithne of Ireland – were distinguished by their fondness for body art.

The tribe of Riata split into two halves, one remaining in Ulster and forming an alliance with the Cruithne, the rest following Cairpre Riata across the sea to Scotland. The breakaway tribe gained a foothold in the territory of the Epidii ('Horse-people') of Kintyre, and so, on both sides of the Moyle, Riata's people showed a willingness to join forces with their Pictish neighbours. Ultimately, the Scottish people would emerge from this mixture of Gaelic and Pictish blood.

The movement of Riata's people from Ireland to Scotland roughly coincided with a Druidic migration. The religion of the Gaels was transported across the Moyle and took root in the Highlands and Islands. At the same time a legend was spawned: the bittersweet story of Deirdre of the Sorrows.

Conchobar mac Nessa was the King of Ulster when Conaire Mór, the father of Cairpre Riata, was the King of all Ireland. The wife of Conchobar's bard was pregnant and the child in her womb was heard to scream. Conchobar summoned his Druid, who declared that the unborn child would be a woman of supreme loveliness but would bring sorrow and destruction to Ulster. The Druid's advice was that the child should be smothered at birth. Conchobar resolved instead that the girl would be raised in isolation until she was of an age to become the king's bedfellow.

The girl was born and given the name Deirdre, or *Dearshul* – 'Sunshine' – though she was also known as Darthula – the 'sorrowful' or 'raging' woman. She was raised by a nurse and grew up to be every bit as beautiful as the Druid had predicted.

One winter's day, Deirdre happened to see a raven land in the snow and gorge itself on the blood of a freshly slaughtered calf. She announced that the only man she could love would have hair as black as the raven's wing, skin like snow and lips as red as blood. Her nurse told her that there was such a youth: his name was Naoise. Deirdre demanded to be introduced to Naoise in secret, and the moment she saw him she fell in love. She clapped her hands over his ears and laid a solemn *geas*, or injunction, on him: 'Ears of sorrow and shame shall these be, unless you go off with me!' Naoise gathered his brothers, Ardan and Ainle, and together they smuggled Deirdre away to the Scottish coast.

Naoise and his brothers were collectively known as the Sons of Uisnech, after the hill which stood at the sacred centre of Ireland. The hill was the site of a spring called the Well of Life, which was home to an ancient salmon – one of the Druidic descendants of the original 'Wise Salmon' and Flood-survivor, Fintan. When the Milesians invaded Ireland the hill was rededicated to Nechtán, a god of water, healing and the underworld whose relationship to the goddess Boand replicated that of the pharaoh Nectanebo to Hathor, the cow-goddess of the Nile. The Gaels had brought their worship of Nectanebo to the west and taken the sacred hill at the centre of Ireland in the name of their god.

Three cup bearers – the Sons of Uisnech – alone had access to the Well of Life. When the goddess approached the well it overflowed, creating the River Boyne; Boand lost an arm, a leg, an eye and ultimately her life to the river, and when this happened 'all wisdom flowed out of Ireland'.

Deirdre herself was something of a cow-goddess, and the legend of the goddess who caused the Well of Life to overflow stands as a parallel to the tale of Deirdre and the Sons of Uisnech. The Milesian Druids who worshipped Nechtán had merged with the goddess–cult of the Picts (in some accounts, Deirdre is the daughter of a Pictish king) and turned their backs on King Conchobar and his warrior caste.

The Druids migrated to Scotland, where they settled first near the mouth of the River Etive in Argyll. At the village of Benderloch stand the remains of a vitrified hill fort known as *Dùn Mhic Uisneachan* – the 'Fort of the Sons of Uisnech'. The Irish *Book of Ballymote* states that it was one 'Manannan, son of Agnoe, who settled the sons of Uisnech in Alba [Scotland]. Sixteen years they were in Alba, and they took possession of Alba from Man northwards.' For 'Man' we should read *Manau* – the British-held bastion on the River Forth in central Scotland – especially since the name *Manannán* means 'dear one of Manau'. The *Book of Ballymote* indicates that the Sons of Uisnech 'took control' of the whole of Scotland north of the Forth, and there is indeed evidence that the Picts warmed to their religion. Numerous Pictish kings would bear the name Nechtan, and the deep stretch of water known as Loch Ness, which boasts its own Teggie-like monster, took its name from Naoise, the chief of the Druids.

After a while, Deirdre and the Sons of Uisnech relocated to an 'island in the sea'. This was the island which in time came to be thought of as Avalon, although Deirdre and her friends had another name for it:

Beloved is Draigen,
Dear the white sand beneath its waves ...

It was the island of *draigen* – 'blackthorn' – which was guarded by a Druidic champion or 'dragon'.

The legend of Deirdre ends in tragedy. She and her Druidic companions were lured back to Ireland under a false amnesty and the jealous King Conchobar had the Druids beheaded. Deirdre was kept as a royal plaything until she succeeded in throwing herself from the back of a chariot and dashing her brains out against a rock. Her followers then took sides against Conchobar of the Ulaid. As the king's Druid had foreseen, the raging woman brought sorrow and destruction to the kingdom of Ulster.

Deirdre and her Druids had refused to be subjugated by the warlike kings of Ireland. Like the people of Riata, they migrated to Scotland, where they founded a religion based on the living-god of the Nile and his cow-goddess consort. Their religion was still going strong in Arthur's day.

The Irish immigrants of Dalriada and their Pictish neighbours formed a fearsome alliance. By AD 297, according to the orator Eumenius, the people of Roman Britain were 'already accustomed to the Picti and Hiberni [Irish] as enemies'. Seventy years later, the situation had worsened dramatically for the Romanised Britons. The year 367 witnessed a 'barbarian conspiracy' in which the Picts and the Scots participated in a general assault on the Roman province. Britain was attacked from all sides. The tribes of the north ranged 'far and wide' and 'made great ravaging'. Order was restored, but Rome's grip on the Island of Britain was slipping.

Throughout the Roman Empire it was acknowledged that the wild lands immediately to the north of Roman Britain were a kind of hell on earth. Writing just before Arthur blazed his trail across the north, Procopius of Caesarea imagined the realm of the Picts as riddled with 'countless snakes and serpents and every other kind of wild creature', adding that it was 'actually impossible for a man to survive there even a half-hour'. It was thought that the souls of the dead were transported to those savage lands of the Picts.

Attitudes towards the Picts hardened under the Church of Rome. As the Roman occupation of Britain was drawing to its end, the court poet Claudian described a personified Britannia as being 'clothed in the skin of some Caledonian beast, her cheeks tattooed, and an azure cloak, rivalling the swell of ocean, sweeping to her feet'. This is a strikingly Pictish image of Britain and it suggests that Rome's civilising influence was barely skin-deep. The early Church was determined to restore Roman standards, regardless of the feelings of the natives.

Like St Gildas, who criticised the Picts and Scots for being hairy and naked, St Patrick had experience of the northern tribes. His prophecy to Arthur's great-great-grandfather Fergus Mór mac Eirc needs to be seen in the context of his loathing for the Picts, whom he referred to as 'apostate'. Since the barbarians had refused to yield to the Roman Empire and the Roman Church, they would have to be subjugated by St Patrick's Irish converts.

Fergus the Great was already well into his 60s when he claimed the throne of Dalriada in 498. He died five years later and was buried on the Isle of Iona where, according to Hector Boece, he had founded a church which became 'the burial place of the Scottish kings'. His son Domangart also reigned for just five years before retiring to a monastery in 508.

Domangart had two sons to succeed him. Comgall, the elder of the two, held the throne of Dalriada for thirty years before he retired, like his father before him, to a monastery. The throne then passed to his younger brother, who had already stamped his name on the map.

In about 525, Gabrán son of Domangart invaded the heartlands of the southern Picts and annexed the province of Fotla, which comprised the districts of Atholl ('New Ireland') and Gowrie. The latter derives from Gabrán, and so the Perthshire town of Blairgowrie, the fertile Carse of Gowrie along the north shore of the Tay estuary and the Dundee suburb of Invergowrie all owe their names to the paternal grandfather of Arthur.

Gabrán's bold move was a turning point in Scottish history. He had not acted alone. His advance into Perthshire came on the back of his marriage to a British princess.

After so many years of alliance with the Picts against the Britons, Gabrán had single-handedly reversed the trend. Now the Scots were allied with the Britons against the Picts. This allowed Gabrán to bring St Patrick's prophecy closer to fruition and won him the lasting respect of the Britons, who dubbed him *Greidiol* – 'Scorcher'. And from his marriage sprang the seeds of the Round Table.

Gabrán's new father-in-law was Brychan, the defender of the British-held redoubt of Manau Gododdin on the River Forth.

Precisely who this Brychan of Manau was has been obscured by the Church's tendency to rewrite history. There was a famous Brychan, born in Ireland to a

Pictish mother, who married a daughter of the British High King Vortigern and settled in south-east Wales. His name would imply that he was *brych* – 'speckled' – but the Church denied any Druidic associations and made him the father of an improbable number of saintly children. There were supposedly twenty-four sons of Brychan and an equal number of daughters. By a strange coincidence, there were also twenty-four horsemen in Arthur's Round Table alliance, and for each of those warriors there was a 'maiden' or female soul-partner. This raises the possibility that the Round Table of Arthur was modelled on an earlier cluster of interrelated warrior-princes, which had constellated around the figure known as Brychan.

The Church's meddling with history makes it difficult to determine whether it was Brychan himself or one of his sons – also named Brychan – who took on the defence of front line Britain. Whichever it was, a warlord named Brychan married a princess of Strathclyde and took charge of the Stirling region. Immediately to the west of Stirling lay the two fording places by means of which the Picts had repeatedly crossed the River Forth to raid deep into North Britain. The defence of those fords was entrusted only to a senior commander of impeccable lineage who was known as the *gwledig*, 'lord', of Manau.

Brychan of Manau brought together a network of British princes, which he forged into an extended family through a series of dynastic marriages. Among those involved was Clydno Eidyn, the Lord of Edinburgh, who married a daughter of Brychan named Goleudydd ('Bright-Day') and had two children by her: Cynon and Creirwy. Others who joined Brychan's coalition were the princes of North Rheged and South Rheged, neighbouring kingdoms on the west coast of North Britain – their sons would stand shoulder to shoulder with Arthur in the years to come.

It was a stroke of genius on Brychan's part to bring the Scottish prince Gabrán mac Domangairt into his web of alliances. Gabrán married a daughter of Brychan named Lleian or Lluan (perhaps from *lleu*, meaning 'light'), and it was she who would give birth to the father of Arthur.

Supported by his new British kinsmen, Gabrán marched into Perthshire, his father-in-law by his side. The southern Picts were vanquished. A poem attributed to Taliesin, the Chief Bard of Britain, reveals how the map had been altered:

Ravens shall wander
In Prydyn, in Eidyn …
In Gafran, in the region of Brecheiniog …

Prydyn was Britain – specifically 'Old' Britain, the land of the Picts. *Eidyn* referred to Edinburgh and its environs. *Gafran* was the Gowrie district, named after Gabrán, to the east of which lay the 'region of Brecheiniog' or Brychan's land, commemorated in the royal burgh of Brechin in Angus.

Gabrán's marriage was to have a profound and lasting impact on his kindred, the *Cenél nGabráin*. The Scots had aligned themselves with the Britons against their former allies and seized great swathes of Pictish territory. There was also the question of religion. It would appear that Fergus Mór and his brothers had brought Christianity to the kingdom of Dalriada. Gabrán, it seems, turned his back on the foreign faith. This almost certainly resulted from his union with a pagan princess whose father, Brychan, was 'speckled' with Druidic tattoos. There is evidence that Brychan was also known, in North Britain at least, as *Caw* – 'Skilful' – a term applied to those with noted magical abilities.

Gildas the Wise was one of the sons of Caw of North Britain. He rebelled against his father's pagan ways and distanced himself from the pagan revival in the North. It is worth noting that the open letter penned by St Gildas – *De Excidio et Conquestu Britanniae*, or '*Of the Ruin and Conquest of Britain*' – lambasted five British kings and culminated with the saint's denunciation of Maelgwyn of Gwynedd. St Gildas was careful, however, to avoid any overt criticism of the kings of North Britain, his father included. As the 'dragon of the island', Maelgwyn would have been one of Brychan's staunchest allies, and it is likely that the tall King of Gwynedd had provided a home for the cauldron cult when it was rejected by the Christian kings of Dalriada. The same cauldron cult, or something very like it, sustained Brychan's alliance of twenty-four princes in much the same way as it would cement Arthur's Round Table coalition. By venting his spleen against Maelgwyn the Tall, St Gildas indirectly attacked his father's allies, who were guilty by association, but he lacked the will or the courage to damn his father openly.

Gabrán, meanwhile, settled in his newly annexed territory with his British queen. They had a son who, being a child of two cultures, inevitably received more than one name. His Irish name was Áedán – from *áed*, meaning 'fire'; the addition of the diminutive suffix *–án* gave the name a familiar feel, like turning John into Johnny.

The Britons would call him many things over the years. But he is best remembered as Áedán mac Gabráin, the 'Fiery' son of the 'Scorcher' and the father of a boy named Arthur.

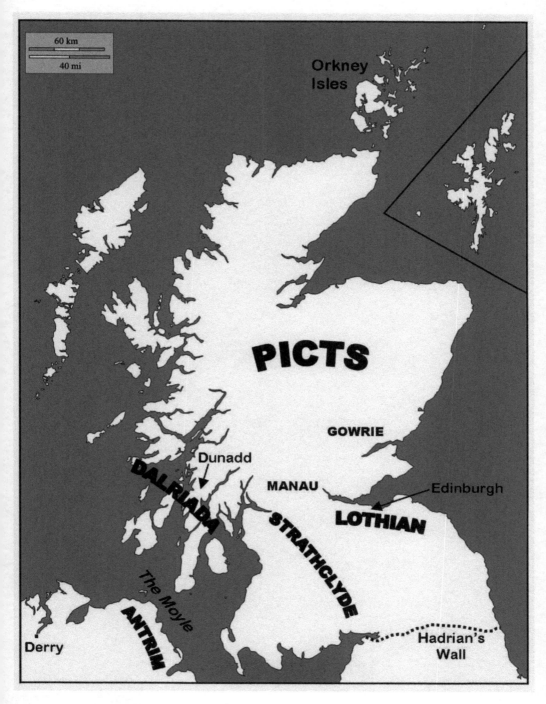

60 km
40 mi

Orkney
Isles

PICTS

GOWRIE

Dunadd

DALRIADA

MANAU

Edinburgh

LOTHIAN

STRATHCLYDE

The Moyle

ANTRIM

Derry

Hadrian's
Wall

Map 3 Scotland, Mid–Sixth Century AD

3

PRINCE OF THE FORTH

ARTHUR'S FATHER, Áedán mac Gabráin, was born sometime around the year 530. A curious poem, dating from the middle of the eleventh century, casts doubt on his paternity.

The *Birth of Áedán mac Gabráin* tells of an Irish prince named Eochu mac Muiredagh. Forced to leave his native Leinster, he travelled across the Moyle to stay at the court of the 'horse-rich' Gabrán. The wives of Eochu and Gabrán fell pregnant at the same time and went into labour while their husbands were out raiding. Eochu's wife was delivered of twin boys; Gabrán's wife gave birth to two daughters. Knowing that Gabrán was desperate for a son, the wives secretly agreed to swap two of the infants. And so, when Eochu returned to Leinster he took with him one of the boys, Brandub, leaving Áedán to be raised by Gabrán of the Scots.

The poem emphasises Áedán's Irish roots but provides no grounds for believing that he was anything other than the natural son of Gabrán mac Domangairt. If anything, the *Birth of Áedán mac Gabráin* points to Áedán and Brandub of Leinster having been foster-brothers. But the poem establishes that Áedán and his father were major historical characters – the sort about whom stories were being told hundreds of years later – and implies that the birth of Áedán was a crucial moment in Scottish history. It looked back from a time when the Gaelic influence over Scottish affairs was waning to a time when the kings of Dalriada were at their peak.

Áedán was still a child when his uncle Comgall renounced the throne of the Scots. A series of extreme weather events occurred during the second half of the 530s, initiated perhaps by a volcanic eruption: the sky grew dark and harvests failed. Whether this had anything to do with Comgall's decision to retire to a monastery is unknown. He had reigned for thirty years; perhaps the Scots felt that a change was due, especially as bread shortages might have been seen as an indictment of his kingship. The throne passed to Comgall's brother Gabrán who, in 538, became the king of a vastly expanded territory stretching from the islands of the west to the Tay estuary on the east coast.

The meteorological upsets of the 530s gave rise to a plague, which 'swept away the noblest third of the human race' in about 543. One of the victims of the contagion was quite possibly Gabrán's father-in-law, who died roundabout that time. An old manuscript held in the British Library and entitled *Cognatio de Brachan* states that Brychan was buried 'in the island which is called Ynysbrachan and which is next to Manau'. Brychan had demonstrated the efficacy of an extended family of warlords all working together. Arthur's Round Table alliance would follow Brychan's example and, as we shall see, there is a strong chance that the 'island' or green knoll standing in a water meadow, in which Brychan was buried, was the very place where Arthur and his twenty-four horsemen later held their councils of war.

The death of Brychan created a vacancy. There was a need for a new *gwledig* – the word (pronounced 'gu-ledig') came from *gwlad*, meaning 'land' – to hold the vital position of Stirling and the nearby fords on the River Forth. The post was awarded to Áedán mac Gabráin, who must have turned 15 at about that time. The fiery Áedán duly became the landholder of Manau Gododdin and was referred to accordingly as the 'Prince of the Forth'.

A prince was nothing without a princess, however. Though it was the chief who ruled the land, the land itself was personified by a woman. The contract between the law and the land was reflected in the sacred union of king and queen, and was contingent on the ability of both partners to fulfil their obligations. It was essentially a marriage of equals; the coming together of the sword of justice and the stone of sovereignty. A land without a virile king was barren; without a queen, a king's rule lacked sanction.

The bride chosen for Áedán was Domelch, the half-Pictish daughter of Maelgwyn of Gwynedd. Politically, the marriage had much to recommend it. Áedán's role as the Prince of the Forth required him to hold the fords across the river and safeguard North Britain from the depradations of the Picts. Marriage to Domelch ferch Maelgwyn made his task that much easier, since Domelch's brother Bruide was about to become King of the Picts. There were benefits, too, for Maelgwyn's kingdom of Gwynedd, the western spur of which had been settled by immigrants from Leinster. The poem of the *Birth of Áedán mac Gabráin* suggests that Áedán had strong ties to the ruling house of Leinster, and this must have given Maelgwyn some leverage in dealing with his Irish neighbours in North Wales.

There is a further factor to be considered. Domelch was the daughter of the 'dragon of the island', Maelgwyn the Tall, whose first marriage had been to a 'daughter of Afallach'. Áedán, meanwhile, was a prince of the Gaelic sea-kingdom – the 'companion of the western wave', as the poem of his birth described him – to which the Island of Afallach belonged. It could be said that the marriage of Áedán and Domelch was made in Avalon, and from it would spring the most famous of the daughters of that sacred isle: a girl who came to be thought of as Morgana or Morgan le Fay.

At least two children were born to Áedán and Domelch. The rules of Pictish succession ensured that their son, Gartnait, stood in line for the throne of the Picts. Gartnait son of Áedán would indeed follow his uncle Bruide onto the Pictish throne some forty years later.

The daughter of Áedán and Domelch is honoured by the Celtic Orthodox Church as a saint.

Established in 1866 as the Orthodox Church of the British Isles, and headed by the grandly titled Metropolitan of Dol and titular Bishop of Iona, the Celtic Orthodox Church has the following entry in its calendar for 27 January: 'My Lord loved Muirgein, a wondrous birth with victories!'

The entry draws on a much older record. The *Martyrology of Óengus the Culdee* was compiled in about AD 830 by a monk at the monastery of Tallaght in County Dublin. It notes the birth, on 27 January, of 'Muirgein, daughter of Áedán, in Bealach Gabráin'.

Her name meant 'Sea-Born'. Muirgein (pronounced 'myoor-gayne') bears comparison with the goddess of the Hebrides, *Brighid bhòidheach* – 'Brìde the beautiful' – who was also known as *Brighid Muirghin-na-tuine* – 'Sea-Birth-of-Wave'. Like the great goddess Venus, she emerged glistening and lovely from the sea. Muirgein was also the daughter of 'Sea' or 'Wave', insofar as these designations were bestowed on her father, the 'companion of the western wave'. Her 'Sea-Born' name, therefore, had something of a double meaning: she was a child of the goddess and a daughter of the mortal lord of the Gaelic sea-kingdom. The ocean stirred in her veins.

The place of her birth was identified by the Irish monk Óengus mac Óengobann as *Bealach Gabráin* – 'the Pass of Gabrán'. The likelihood is that this 'pass' or 'gorge' – *bealach* – lay in the Gowrie territory to which Gabrán gave his name.

Barry Hill stands a few miles to the north-east of Blairgowrie. The summit of the hill appears to be cratered. It was in fact the site of an Iron Age hill fort. The stronghold was surrounded by thick inner and outer walls, while two further ramparts suggest that extra precautions were taken to protect the enclosure against attack from the north and west. The name of the hill meant 'Summit of the King'. Standing on the edge of his Gowrie lands, and strongly defended against Pictish assaults, the hill fort was probably Gabrán's headquarters in Perthshire.

The Alyth Burn runs to the south of Barry Hill, where it becomes the Water of Quiech. The area between the hillside and the stream is known as Balloch, an alternative rendering of *bealach*, and the farmstead of North Balloch stands on the site of a long-lost castle; the Dovecote Well, which served the ruined castle of 'Belouch' in the 'lordship of Alicht' is still marked on the map. The site was reasonably well protected from the north wind and, with a ready supply of fresh water, would have offered some shelter to a woman giving birth during a Highland winter. It was in Scottish territory, and therefore under Gabrán's jurisdiction, but extremely close to the Pictish lands of which Domelch was a princess. The Water of Quiech, which runs through the Balloch, probably takes its name from *quaich* – a shallow drinking cup or bowl (Gaelic *cuach*); Muirgein, as we shall discover, was associated with one of the most famous bowls or drinking cups of all time.

The Balloch of Alyth near Blairgowrie is a strong candidate for the *Bealach Gabráin* in which Muirgein, the daughter of Áedán, was born. We shall return to this same spot at a later stage in our story, though in less happy circumstances.

The calendar of the Celtic Orthodox Church indicates that Muirgein shared her 27 January feast day with another 'abbess' known as St Agna (or Agnes, or Agnetis). Like Muirgein, whose 'wondrous' birth was associated with victories, the holy Agna was seen as a victorious Mother Superior: 'Agna with ten virgins won a pure victory before kings.'

The name Agna or Agnes was a variant form of Anna. It was pronounced rather like the Irish Eithne ('en-ya') and had much the same meaning: 'fire' (from *agni*, the Sanskrit word which also gave us the English *ignite*).

It is no coincidence that Geoffrey of Monmouth, in his *History of the Kings of Britain*, gave the name Anna to Arthur's sister. Even the fashionable 'Morgana' seems to combine both Muirgein and Anna into one convenient appellation. The names appear to have been interchangeable. Muirgein was the Gaelic form of her name, in which guise she was thought of as a representative of the Mórríghan, an Irish goddess of death and battle, or as a relative of the Mari-Morgan, a water-sprite of Brittany. By the late twelfth century, when the Welsh called her Morgen, she was dismissed as an 'imaginary goddess' (*dea phantastica*) by the propagandist Giraldus Cambrensis. She was not a goddess in the strict sense of the word, of course, but she was undoubtedly seen as the goddess in mortal form. As far as the Britons were concerned, that goddess was Ana or Dôn, the mother-goddess of the *Tuatha dé Danann* or 'Children of Danu'.

The goddess Anna was worshipped as the divine consort of the Sun-god Bel, or Beli Mawr. She gave her name to certain features of the landscape, such as the breast-shaped 'Paps of Anu' in County Kerry. In Britain, the goddess eventually morphed into the alarming figure of Black Annis (for protection against the 'evil-eye' one should resort to *aniseed*), but her origins lie far back in time. She compares with Agni Tara, the 'divine spark' of Tibet, and the Roman Diana, virginal huntress and goddess of the Moon; to the Greeks, she was Danäe who, impregnated by Zeus, gave birth to the hero Perseus. She was honoured in many a river name, including that of the Danube.

The time would come when Muirgein was fêted as Anna (or Agna), when she and her half-brother Arthur appeared in the roles of those heavenly siblings, Diana and Apollo, the Moon and the Sun. The place of her burial, which lies close to that of Arthur, gives her name as 'Little Anna'. Almost certainly, she was small in stature. Her beauty, however, was legendary.

She was born to be a priestess of great power, a noblewoman of mixed race and rare ability. Writing nearly 600 years after her birth, Geoffrey of Monmouth branded her 'the hottest and most lustful woman in all Britain', but in reality Muirgein was a sixth-century Scottish princess of Irish, Pictish and British blood who ruled over several regions and gave birth to heroes and saints. She was a healer, a power-broker and one of the most important female figures in British history.

We may never know whether Maelgwyn of Gwynedd lived to hear of the birth of his granddaughter. Muirgein was born sometime around the year 547, which is one of two dates given for the death of Maelgwyn the Tall.

Because Easter is a moveable feast, governed by the phases of the Moon, monasteries drew up tables to calculate when Easter would fall. The most notable events of any year were often recorded in the margins of these tables. These marginalia were later transcribed into chronological annals, some of which are relatively accurate. If in doubt, the scribes might hedge their bets, and so the *Welsh Annals* record the death of Maelgwyn twice, in 547 and again in 549.

Maelgwyn had offended the Church by engaging in pagan marriages and promoting the arts of poetry and prophecy, which were practiced by the bards. For a while at least, the principal bardic school in the whole of Britain had flourished under his protection. At the same time, Maelgwyn's dynastic ambitions had upset the Britons of Strathclyde. The most northerly of the British kingdoms, Strathclyde had occupied the buffer zone between Roman Britain and the Picts. The princes of Dumbarton (*Dùn Breatann* – 'Fort of the Britons') took Roman coin in return for policing the empire's border and embraced Roman manners with aplomb. Their love of all things Roman extended to the new religion of Christianity. Strathclyde would produce several leading evangelists, Ss Patrick and Gildas among them.

The Christians of Strathclyde had been agitating against Maelgwyn for years, largely because of his pagan inclinations. But it was Maelgwyn's death that sparked a full-blown crisis. His 'illegitimate' son, Rhun the Tall, inherited the throne of Gwynedd. Just a few years later, in 552, Bruide son of Maelgwyn became King of the northern Picts. Initially, Bruide ruled jointly with the King of the southern Picts, Galam Cennaleth, but by 553 the younger son of Maelgwyn had effectively taken control of the whole Pictish nation.

This gave the Britons of Strathclyde cause for concern. They found themselves sandwiched between two powerful kingdoms, both ruled by the pagan sons of Maelgwyn the Tall. On top of that, Áedán mac Gabráin, the Prince of the Forth, had married Bruide's sister, Domelch ferch Maelgwyn. The lords of Dumbarton feared that they were being enveloped and engulfed by Maelgwyn's offspring, and the Christians no doubt portrayed this as a pagan conspiracy to overwhelm the kingdom of the Clyde.

Maelgwyn's second marriage – the one approved of by the Christians – had produced a daughter who married a prince of Strathclyde. It fell to Elidyr the Wealthy, the prince who had married Eurgain daughter of Maelgwyn, to challenge the hegemony of Maelgwyn's sons. Elidyr assembled a fleet and sailed south from the Clyde. He landed near the old Roman fort of Segontium – now Caernarfon – where Rhun son of Maelgwyn was waiting with his army. The men of Gwynedd repelled the invaders and Elidyr was killed.

Elidyr's cousins then swung into action. Rhydderch of Dumbarton, Clydno of Edinburgh and Nudd of the Borders joined forces and mounted a blistering raid into Gwynedd. The fort of Segontium was razed to the ground. Rhun, however, survived.

The outbreak of hostilities naturally had consequences for those Strathclyde Britons who were based in Gwynedd. These included Gwyddno Tall-Crane, who had been granted the sub-kingdom of Meirionydd by King Maelgwyn. Elidyr of Strathclyde had landed his troops on the shore just north of Gwyddno's kingdom, and the men of Gwynedd must have suspected some level of collusion. According to legend, half of Gwyddno's kingdom was lost to the sea; more likely, he was stripped of some of his domains by a vengeful Rhun son of Maelgwyn.

The situation was even more fraught for the children of those princes who had launched the second assault on Gwynedd. These included Creirwy, the daughter of Clydno Eidyn, and Gwyn, the son of Nudd the Generous. They had both studied at Llyn Tegid under Maelgwyn's protection. Now, their fathers were at war with Maelgwyn's son. Neither Creirwy nor her cauldron-partner Taliesin could have remained safely in Gwynedd after the destruction of Segontium. When the armies of Strathclyde returned to the North, the Chief Bard and the priestess of the cauldron travelled with them.

Creirwy accompanied her father Clydno back to Lothian, where she was installed in a 'Castle of Maidens'. This was probably the *castellum puellarum* which, according to Geoffrey of Monmouth, occupied the volcanic outcrop that overlooks the city of Edinburgh. Taliesin almost certainly followed his 'sweetheart' like a faithful pet; he would later recall the days he had spent as a 'speckled white cock among the hens of Eidyn'.

Like the cauldron itself, which had a habit of falling apart, the Llyn Tegid cult had disintegrated and dispersed. The war between the Britons of Strathclyde and the children of Maelgwyn simmered on. The last blow had not yet been struck – that would come after the birth of Arthur.

The kingdom of Lothian stretched along the southern shore of the Firth of Forth and down the coast as far as the River Tweed. It had been the territory of a tribal federation known to the Romans as the Votadini. In common with the Damnonii tribes of Strathclyde, the Votadini had been paid for defending the northern border of Roman Britain.

The region had been overrun by Scots and Picts during the 'barbarian conspiracy' of 367. The emergency was dealt with by Flavius Theodosius, who 'restored to its former state a province which was recovered that he had previously abandoned to enemy rule'. This newly restored province was given the name *Valentia* in honour of the joint-emperors, Valens and Valentinian, and probably consisted of the dangerous zone between the Roman walls of Hadrian and Antoninus Pius, or what we would now term southern Scotland. A 'properly appointed governor' was installed to maintain order in the recovered territory. The name of the governor appointed by Rome was Tacitus, the 'Silent'. The Britons called him 'Tegid' and later gave his name to a long lake in North Wales.

The same region was swamped again after the departure of the last Roman legion in 409. The last Romano-British 'Duke of Britain', Coel the Old, attempted to smash the alliance of Picts and Scots that had caused so many problems for the North, only to be outwitted by his enemies and killed. So great was the threat posed by the Picts and the Scots that the High King of Britain brought in Germanic mercenaries to battle with the northern tribesmen. According to the *Kentish Chronicle*, the warriors from Germany 'sailed round against the Picts and plundered the Orkneys' before occupying 'several districts … as far as the borders of the Picts'.

In about 452, the Saxon mercenaries took Edinburgh, relinquishing it to the Britons in return for land further down the east coast. By the close of the fifth century, the royal family of Strathclyde had begun to extend its control over much of the region. The sons of the venerable Dyfnwal of Strathclyde laid claim to the various Lowland territories, while Dyfnwal's daughter married Brychan of Manau, the lord who united the North.

The tribal name of the Votadini of Lothian became *Guotodin* in Old Welsh, and then *Gododdin* ('god-o-thin'), which was how they were known in Arthur's day. The western spur of their territory, along the upper reaches of the River Forth, was Manau Gododdin. The fords to the west of Stirling were the backdoor into Britain.

When Creirwy returned with her father to Lothian, the defender of Manau and its fords was Áedán, the 'Prince of the Forth'. Áedán was the latest in a distinguished line of warriors to hold that post, beginning, as far as we know, with Tacitus or 'Tegid'. He owed allegiance as much to Clydno Eidyn, Lord of Lothian, as he did to his own father. Gabrán and Clydno had both married daughters of Brychan and so were equal partners in the defence of the North. Clydno must have been something of a father figure, as well as an uncle, to Áedán mac Gabráin.

Áedán was in a tricky position. He was related to the ruling house of Strathclyde by way of his father's marriage, but his own marriage to Domelch now meant that his brothers-in-law were the enemies of Strathclyde. His loyalties were divided and, worse, he was bored. He was the lynchpin of the North, but his marriage to the sister of Bruide of the Picts meant that he had no one to defend Manau against.

Áedán might have stood firm against Bruide, preventing his brother-in-law from sending a Pictish army to support Rhun in Gwynedd, but otherwise he was obliged to remain aloof from the struggle, a stance which went against his warlike nature. It must have been clear to him that the alliance which Brychan of Manau had knitted together was unravelling. Sooner or later, Áedán would have to pick sides.

The decision was made for him by the return of the lovely Creirwy to her father's Lothian kingdom.

A number of ancient Welsh tales drawn from two medieval sources, the *White Book of Rhydderch* and the *Red Book of Hergest*, were translated into English in the mid-nineteenth century by Lady Charlotte Guest and published as the *Mabinogion* – '*Tales of Youth*'. Centuries of oral storytelling and literary accretions had both blurred and enriched these tales by the time they were transcribed in the 1300s, but at heart they were the tales of Arthur's people.

Two dynasties dominate the legends of the *Mabinogion*: the Children of Dôn and the Children of Llyr. These two bloodlines met in the person of Arthur. He was descended, on his mother's side, from the Druidic Children of Danu who worshipped the goddess known variously as Anna and Dôn. His father, meanwhile, would become the lord of the isles and chief of the Gaelic sea-kingdom. The Britons would dub Áedán *Llyr* (meaning 'Sea' – Irish *Lir*), as in Llyr of the Hosts or, because they struggled to understand his Gaelic tongue, Llyr Half-Speech.

In the romantic tradition, Arthur's father is generally known as Uther Pendragon. The 'Pendragon' title is especially interesting and will be considered anon. 'Uther' originated in the Old Irish *athir*, meaning 'father', with an additional element, which we shall also come to in due course. But the name Uther, as we are familiar with it, reaches us via the Welsh *Gwythyr*.

A character named Gwythyr appears in one of the oldest tales of the *Mabinogion*. The legend tells of the adventures of Arthur and his heroes as they undertake a series of superhuman tasks on behalf his kinsman, Culhwch. At one point the action of *Culhwch and Olwen* is briefly held up by what seems like an irrelevant aside:

> A little while before this, Creiddylad the daughter of Lludd Llaw Ereint, and Gwythyr the son of Greidiol, were betrothed. And before she had become his bride, Gwyn ap Nudd came and carried her away by force; and Gwythyr the son of Greidiol gathered his host together, and went to fight with Gwyn ap Nudd.

Arthur duly heads into the North to make peace between Gwythyr son of Greidiol and Gwyn son of Nudd:

And this was the peace that was made: that the maiden should remain in her father's house, without advantage to either of them, and that Gwyn ap Nudd and Gwythyr the son of Greidiol should fight for her every first of May, and thenceforth until the day of Doom, and that whichever of them should then be the conqueror should have the maiden.

This episode has nothing to do with the story of Culhwch and is merely a repetition of something remarked upon earlier in the tale, when it is stated that Creiddylad:

> … was the most splendid maiden in the three islands of Britain, and in the three islands adjacent, and for her Gwythyr the son of Greidiol and Gwyn the son of Nudd fight every first of May until the day of doom.

Twice in the tale, then, the author of *Culhwch and Olwen* paused to introduce information that had no bearing on the story and which hardly needed to be mentioned twice. It is as if the storyteller was aware of a tradition concerning the eternal battle between Gwythyr and Gwyn for the 'most splendid maiden', but had no real idea what it meant. The legend was important enough to interrupt the story – twice! – even though it seems to have had no place in the narrative.

The twin references to this love triangle are the fragmentary remains of an older tradition and, as such, they have bemused scholars. Rather than accepting that the Britons told tales about genuine people, experts have chosen to interpret these fragments as part of a mythical scheme concerning the seasonal battle between the King of Summer and the King of Winter. The same scholarly condescension argues that Arthur and his comrades were not real historical individuals but cosmological culture heroes or 'gods' – as if the Britons had nothing much better to do with their time than fantasise about superheroes. We should at least entertain the possibility that their stories had a kernel of truth in them.

Gwyn son of Nudd became the poet known as Taliesin. In the *Black Book of Carmarthen* we find a poem, entitled *Ymddiddan Gwyn ap Nudd a Gwyddno Garanhir*, in which Taliesin and his kinsman Gwyddno Tall-Crane hold a slightly stilted conversation:

> Rough-hoofed my horse, turbulent in battle.
> Lo, I am named Gwyn son of Nudd,
> The sweetheart of Creiddlyad daughter of Lludd.

Creiddylad (pronounced 'cray-thuh-lad'), as we know from the tale of *Culhwch and Olwen*, was the 'most splendid maiden' over whom Gwyn and Gwythyr fought. The name of her father, Lludd ('dith'), compares with that of Clydno, otherwise Clyddno ('cluh-thno'), the chieftain of Edinburgh who joined with his cousins, Rhydderch and Nudd, in attacking Gwynedd in the 550s. Rhydderch and Nudd were fondly remembered for their liberality: they both bore the epithet *Hael*, meaning 'Generous'. This was also the meaning of *arianllaw* – literally, 'silver-handed'. Lludd, the father of Creiddylad, was *Llaw Ereint* or 'Silver Hand', putting him on a par with those other generous princes, Rhydderch and Nudd. Geoffrey of Monmouth would later convert Lludd into Loth, the titular Lord of Lothian.

A Welsh manuscript (Peniarth 16) names Creirwy as a daughter of Clydno of Edinburgh. Creirwy was also the priestess of the cauldron cult named in the story of Taliesin's poetic initiation, and it is probable that the daughter of Clydno acted as the soul-partner of her cousin Gwyn when he underwent his ordeal. She became his 'sweetheart', his consort of the cauldron, and just as Gwyn son of Nudd took a new name – Taliesin – at the culmination of the ritual, so the heron-like Creirwy was reborn as Creiddylad. Her new name would appear to have been formed by joining *crëydd*, meaning 'creator', to *dylad* meaning 'water'. She had become a veritable Lady of the Lake.

Creirwy daughter of Clydno and her sweetheart Taliesin, the poet formerly known as Gwyn son of Nudd, were now refugees from war-torn Gwynedd and had settled at Edinburgh, within easy range of the Prince of the Forth. Áedán's father had joined Brychan's alliance thirty years earlier, becoming a kinsman of Clydno of Edinburgh. Gabrán's passionate battle heat had so impressed the Britons that they thought of him as *Greidiol* – 'Scorcher'.

His son would earn the nickname *Gwythyr*. There are hints of 'Anger' or 'Wrath' (*gwyth*) in this alternative name for Áedán mac Gabráin, as would have been appropriate for the Fiery son of the Scorcher. Welsh grammar requires that the initial letter 'g' be dropped in certain circumstances. *Gwythyr* would then be contracted to *Wythyr*, from whence came the Welsh *Uthyr* and, eventually, Uther.

Gwythyr son of Greidiol was none other than Áedán mac Gabráin, and he was about to challenge Gwyn son of Nudd for the 'most splendid maiden' in the British Isles.

The tradition which kept nudging its way into the tale of *Culhwch and Olwen* concerned the eternal triangle of the Prince of the Forth, the Primary Chief Bard and the daughter of Clydno of Edinburgh. It was the story behind the conception of a boy whose birth would blow the North apart.

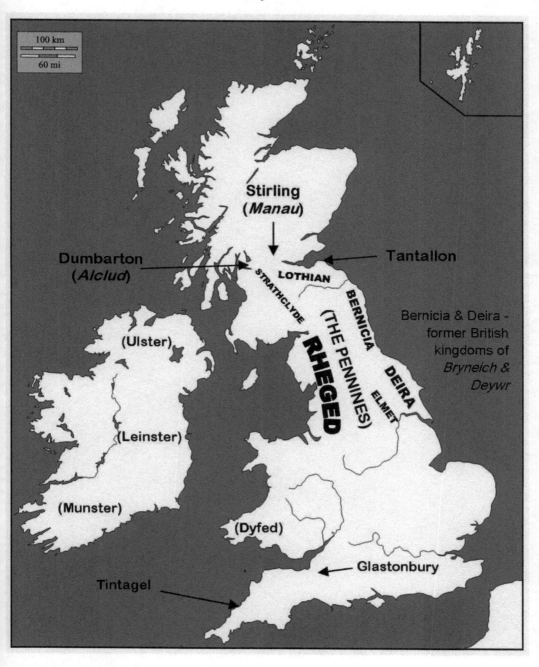

Map 4 The Old North, *c.* AD 560

4

THE BELTANE FIRES

MOST OF what we know – or think we know – about Arthur's conception came from the pen of one Geoffrey of Monmouth. His *Historia Regum Britanniae* ('*History of the Kings of Britain*') was a huge success when it first appeared in about 1137.

The tale, as Geoffrey told it, went like this:

King Utherpendragon [*sic*] developed an all-consuming lust for Ygerna, the wife of Gorlois, Duke of Cornwall. Gorlois grew jealous and retreated to his strong-hold at Tintagel Head on the stormy, windswept coast of south-west Britain. King Uther laid siege to Tintagel but his rival's fortress proved to be impregnable.

Despairing, Uther summoned Merlin the magician, who offered to make use of 'methods which are quite new and until now un-heard of in your day'. Merlin's drugs transformed Uther into the exact likeness of the Duke of Cornwall, and when Gorlois sallied forth from Tintagel to do battle with the king's army, Uther rode into the castle and, disguised as Gorlois, slept with Ygerna. That night, Arthur and his sister Anna were conceived and Gorlois was killed. King Uther then married Ygerna, the 'most beautiful woman in Britain'.

To visit the grey ruins of Tintagel Castle on the coast of north Cornwall is to feel as though one has stepped into world of Arthur. But that feeling is illusory. The castle did not exist when Geoffrey wrote his account of Arthur's birth. It was built by the brother of Geoffrey's patron, who thereby created a sort of Arthurian theme park in the wrong part of Britain.

With his story of Arthur's conception, Geoffrey did for Tintagel what Giraldus Cambrensis later did for Glastonbury: he created a myth. The myth owes a great deal of its success to the fact that it brought Arthur into England, cutting him free from his historical roots and helping to turn his legend into make-believe. It allowed the English to imagine that Arthur was one of their own; he became, as it were, a prototype Englishman.

Geoffrey's fabulous account of Arthur's conception quickly became the accepted version of events. It was, however, extremely wide of the mark.

Let us start with the names. Geoffrey called the mother of Arthur 'Ygerna'. Within a few hundred years, thanks to Sir Thomas Malory's *Le Morte d'Arthur*, this had become 'Igraine'. But the Ygerna of Geoffrey of Monmouth was merely a corruption of the Old Irish *tigerna*, meaning 'lady'. He might as well have called Arthur's mother 'Madonna'.

Geoffrey's story drew on the earlier legend of Gwythyr and Gwyn, those two powerful men who fought for the hand of the 'most splendid' Creiddylad. Gwythyr evolved into the familiar Uther, and so we might expect Gwyn son of Nudd to reappear in Geoffrey's story in the person of Gorlois, Duke of Cornwall. This would mean that Geoffrey had merely dramatised the love-triangle outlined in the old Welsh tale of *Culhwch and Olwen*.

In fact, Geoffrey seems to have muddled things up a little more than that. Gwyn ap Nudd became the Chief Bard of Britain, Taliesin, who later composed an elegy for 'Uther the Chief':

Am I not in a multitude making a tumult?
I would not cease host-splitting without blood.
Am I not he that is honoured as Gorlassar?
My belt was a rainbow to the enemy …

Taliesin was an old man when he composed his *Mawrnat Uthyr Pen*. He had known Arthur's father for many years and had seen him going into battle many times. The *Death-Song of Uther the Chief* was Áedán's petition to enter the Otherworldly hall of heroes. 'Am I not he that is honoured as Gorlassar?' sang the king. *Gorlassar* can be translated as 'bright blue' (in Welsh) or 'blue flame' (in Gaelic). Poets of the time generally thought of armour as being blue in colour, but Áedán mac Gabráin and his weaponry were 'super-blue'.

There is no record of a Duke of Cornwall by the name of Gorlois. But Áedán, whom the Britons came to know as *Gwythyr*, also went by the name of Gorlassar, the 'bright blue flame' of battle. From this we can deduce that Geoffrey of Monmouth, writing upwards of five centuries later, took the name Gorlassar and reproduced it in a suitably medieval form – Gorlois. He then applied this name to Áedán's love-rival, when it was actually another name for Áedán.

Geoffrey's account gives us one man going to war with himself over a 'lady'. What is more, he does so in a land he almost certainly never visited. For when Geoffrey decided to locate the scene of Arthur's conception at Tintagel in Cornwall he was out to the tune of 500 miles.

The Celtic year was divided by eight major festivals. Four of these festivals were determined by the status of the Sun during its annual progress: twice in the year, at the equinoxes, it achieved balance with the forces of darkness, while the solstices marked the moments when the Sun was at its weakest (Midwinter) and its strongest (Midsummer).

Between these four solar events fell four festivals which had more to do with the Sun's lunar partner. As the solar hero grew, was wounded, died, and was reborn, so the Moon underwent a process of transformation; changing from maiden to lover, to mother, to crone.

At Imbolc, the great spring festival, which took place around the start of February, the Moon-goddess appeared in her virginal form. At Beltane she became the Sun's nubile lover, his Flower-Bride. By the time of the Lughnasadh festivities in early August she had become a maternal figure of nourishment and plenty, and at Samhain or Hallowe'en, which was also the Celtic New Year, she took the form of a wizened hag.

Beltane stood at the opposite pole of the year from Samhain. It was the feast of the fires of the Sun-god Bel, or Belenos, or Beli Mawr. On the night of the full Moon around the last evening in April, huge bonfires were lit. Cattle were driven between the flames to cleanse the beasts of malign influences before they were moved to the summer pastures. The festival marked the beginning of summer and was one of the most important dates in the Celtic calendar.

It was at Beltane – May Day – that Little Gwyn was fished from his coracle on the River Dovey and reborn as the poet Taliesin. It was at Beltane, too, that he and Gwythyr fought their eternal battle for the hand of the lovely Creiddylad.

It was a night for lovers. The rules of marriage were relaxed so that the festival of fire and fertility could be celebrated with abandon. And it was on such a night that Arthur was conceived.

After the bellowing cattle had been led between the bonfires, the fire-leaping began. Women would jump over flaming brands to awaken the spark of life in their wombs. Men scooped up embers and rubbed them into their faces and bodies. Some no doubt practiced fire-walking to prove that, through fasting and sexual abstinence, they had won the blessings of the ancestral spirits, making them impervious to the scorching heat.

As the night wore on, the people disappeared into the neighbouring woods. In theory, they were gathering festive greenery to decorate the village, but the real reason they took to the shelter of the woods was to engage in procreation. That night, every hot-blooded male was Bel, the god of the Sun, and every fertile woman was his divine consort, Anna.

The ashes which had been rubbed into the faces of the men functioned as a kind of mask, rendering them anonymous. If a girl fell pregnant that night it was not the work of some local youth but the god himself who had blessed her.

(These pagan May Day rites would prove difficult to suppress: a thousand years later, an English Puritan complained that 'of forty, three-score, or a hundred maids going to the wood overnight, there have scarcely the third part of them returned home again undefiled.')

On a practical level, Beltane was a good time to conceive, for the child would emerge nine months later at around the time of Imbolc, which heralded the spring just as Beltane welcomed in the summer. Ewes started lactating around the time of the Imbolc festival and the plentiful months of summer lay ahead, giving the infant a better-than-average chance of survival. Muirgein, with her 27 January birthday, was in all probability a Beltane baby.

The British Sun-god Beli Mawr ('Great Bel') would live on in Arthurian romance as Pellinore, one of the names for the Rich Fisher or Maimed King. His roots were ancient: they can be traced all the way back to the Semitic Ba'al – 'lord, master, keeper and husband' – who was at one time equated with the Hebrew Yahweh, before being downgraded to one of the seven princes of Hell. In ancient Greece he was remembered as Belus, the father of the twins, Danaus and Aegyptus, who migrated from the Nile to the plain of Argos and founded the Greek nation known to Homer as the Danaans.

Christianity reviled Bel as Belial, the natural successor to Ba'al, and transferred many of the Sun-god's attributes to St Michael, the dragon-slaying archangel and forerunner of St George, the patron saint of England.

Returning to the Middle East, we find that the sister-consort of Ba'al was called 'Anat. She was both a virgin and a violent battle-goddess – traits she shared with the Roman Diana. 'Anat was worshipped in ancient Egypt, where Jewish refugees referred to her as 'Anat-Yahu or 'Anat-Yahweh (she was God's wife, no less), whilst in Mesopotamia she was known as Anu ('Sky'). On the island of Cyprus she was compounded with the bright-eyed Athena, another virginal war-goddess. Britain also adopted her, maintaining her sibling-lover relationship with Ba'al, whom the Britons called Bel, and revering the goddess as Anna or Danu.

The fire festival of Beltane at the very start of May celebrated the divine union of Bel and Anna – the sacred marriage of Sun and Moon – which brought new life into the tribe and fruitfulness to the fields.

On a Beltane night, late in the 550s, Áedán, the Prince of the Forth, rode to the fires of Bel like a spark to a flame. His intention that night was to sleep with the most beautiful woman in Britain, who just happened to be the 'sweetheart' of Gwyn son of Nudd.

In one regard, at least, Geoffrey of Monmouth's account of Arthur's conception had a grain of truth in it. The father of Arthur came to the beautiful 'Lady' in disguise. Whether he approached her in his blue battle-guise of Gorlassar or with his face smeared with the ashes of the Beltane fires, he was merely observing the Beltane protocol of hiding his true identity. He was neither Áedán nor Gwythyr nor Gorlassar: he was Beli Mawr, intent on spending the night in the arms of his Anna.

To figure out where this happened we must turn to a legend of Lothian which, on the face of it, has nothing to do with Arthur.

Creirwy, the daughter of Clydno of Edinburgh, had a brother called Cynon. His name meant 'Great-Hound'. Transmuted into Gaelic it became Kentigern – 'Hound-Lord'. As Kentigern, Cynon son of Clydno was destined to become the first bishop and patron saint of the City of Glasgow, known familiarly as Mungo ('Dear One').

The legends of St Kentigern associate him with several contemporaries of Arthur – including St Columba, Rhydderch of Strathclyde and the wild and hairy 'Merlin' – but it is as Cynon, the British form of his name, that he crops up most frequently in the early Arthurian tales. And no wonder, really, because Cynon son of Clydno was Arthur's uncle.

Towards the end of the twelfth century, some years after Geoffrey of Monmouth released his *History of the Kings of Britain*, a *Life of St Kentigern* appeared. Written by a Cistercian monk based at Furness Abbey in Cumbria, it was a typical product of its time: a sermonising mish-mash of dubious miracles and half-digested history.

According to Jocelin of Furness, St Kentigern's mother was called Thenaw or 'St Thaney'. She was the 'daughter of a certain king, of a most pagan family, in the North land of the Britons'. A fragmentary *Life of St Kentigern* adds that she was impregnated by Owain, a Cumbrian prince who, unable to get close to the object of his affection by any other means, resorted to dressing up as a woman.

Owain was a historical prince of North Britain. He could not have been the father of Cynon (or Kentigern) since he was of entirely the wrong generation. The naming of Owain as the father of Kentigern hints at a kind of desperation. His name was chosen to fill the vacuum created when the original legend was detached from its source.

Geoffrey of Monmouth's bestseller had snatched up the story of Arthur's conception and squirrelled it far away to the south. This left a localised legend without a subject. It was now widely believed that Arthur was conceived in Cornwall, and so a ready-made legend pertaining to his conception in Lothian became available to be rewritten and applied to a Christian saint. That saint happened to be Arthur's uncle, and so the legend was kept in the family. But the legend did not properly belong to Cynon or St Kentigern, and attempts to lend it extra substance – by identifying his father as Owain of North Rheged – only led to more confusion by making a prince of North Britain the cross-dressing father of his own great-uncle.

The muddle extended to the father of the pregnant princess, with some accounts identifying him as King Loth – that is, 'Lludd' or Clydno, the father of Creirwy and Cynon – while others claim that he was Llew, who was involved in the events but in a rather different capacity.

The Christian legend of St Kentigern's birth makes more historical sense if it is seen as a corrupted account of the birth of Cynon's nephew. It was not the mother of Cynon but his sister who fell pregnant thanks to a prince in disguise. The legend goes that Creirwy's father reacted angrily to the news that his daughter was pregnant. He insisted that she marry a swineherd. The princess refused, and so she was taken to the top of a certain hill, placed in a chariot, and driven over the edge.

Miraculously, the chariot floated down to the ground. Nothing daunted, her father then put her into a frail coracle without oars and cast her adrift on the sea. The princess was saved yet again by divine intervention. A helpful school of fish guided her to safety.

Before we follow the pregnant princess on her journey out to sea, we should pause to reflect on the story so far.

Jocelin of Furness wrote his account with one aim in mind – to glorify the saint he knew as Kentigern. His perspective was entirely that of the medieval Church. Even if he had understood the pagan elements in the story, it was customary to portray them in the worst possible light. The result is something between a pantomime and a fairytale.

Take the legend of the cross-dressing prince. This has inspired at least one modern commentator to claim that the father of 'Kentigern' – in fact, the father of Arthur – was a card-carrying transsexual (and quite possibly gay). The real reason why Arthur's father might have been dressed as a woman when he seduced the Princess of Lothian will soon become apparent. But we should note that when the Church borrowed and adapted authentic traditions for its own use it left them prone to delirious modern interpretations. Much the same happened with the legends surrounding the 'Holy Grail'. The trick is not to pile more layers of nonsense onto those already established by monks, but rather to peer through the institutional prejudice to glimpse the truth behind the propaganda.

The pregnant princess was ordered to marry a swineherd. Pigs held a special place in Celtic society, where pork seems to have been served on special occasions, and some might have been reared in exceptional circumstances to provide the very best meat. Even so, pigs and swineherds recur in the early Arthurian sources in ways which suggest that there was more to it than that. One of the ancient tales states that Creirwy's brother was born in a pigsty, while the *Triads of the Island of Britain* have Cynon's son acting as a stand-in swineherd and preventing Arthur from making off with one of the pigs.

Learned bards were thought of as 'salmon', and it seems probable that virginal priestesses were similarly thought of as 'pigs', perhaps because they had the responsibility of handrearing pigs for major feasts. A bard or Druid who acted as the male guardian of a sacred sisterhood would then have been thought of as a 'swineherd'.

When the Princess of Lothian fell pregnant it was assumed that she would marry a 'swineherd', the most obvious choice being her 'sweetheart' Taliesin, then disporting himself as a 'speckled white cock' among the 'hens' of Edinburgh. Torn between two lovers, Creirwy chose to belong to neither. Áedán and Taliesin would have to contend until Doomsday to find out which of them was her true love.

Significantly, pigs were held to blame for the war which had broken out between Gwynedd and Strathclyde, forcing Creirwy to return home to Lothian. This we learn from the Welsh tale of *Math Son of Mathonwy*, which tells us that a wizard named Gwydion stole some magical pigs and brought them to North Wales. The owners of the pigs then attacked Gwynedd. War raged, and while everybody was distracted Gwydion's fellow magician raped a sacred virgin.

The King of Gwynedd demanded a replacement virgin to consecrate his rule, and Gwydion summoned his sister Arianrhod. He organised a simple test to prove her virginal status. Arianrhod failed the test in spectacular fashion: she gave birth to a yellow-haired boy, who was given the name 'Ocean son of Wave'. A kind of afterbirth also fell from her womb. Gwydion picked it up and hid it away, only to discover that it was another boy. But so furious was Arianrhod at the loss of her sacred virginity that she refused to have anything to do with her son, and the boy was raised by his uncle.

Stripped down to its essentials, the *Math Son of Mathonwy* legend casts an interesting light on how Arthur came into the world. The pigs which were smuggled into Gwynedd can be thought of as the priestesses of the cauldron cult whose presence was welcomed by Maelgwyn the Tall. The escalation of the conflict between Strathclyde and Gwynedd left the chief priestess in a parlous position. She escaped, only to be seduced by a lover who deprived her of her virginal status.

The legend does not make it plain, but the maiden who was raped appears to have been known as Arianrhod. In Welsh, her name meant 'Silver Wheel'. This was an apt description of the cauldron, which was round and made of silver. The Welsh also came to think of her as a goddess whose starry court was the constellation of the Northern Crown – *Caer Arianrhod* in Welsh.

Arianrhod can also be interpreted as a Gaelic term rendered phonetically into Welsh. *A' rìghinn rhòid* would have sounded like 'Arianrhod' to British ears, but it translates as 'The Sea-Foam Princess'. Such a designation might remind us of the watery Creiddylad, the 'most splendid maiden' over whom Áedán and Taliesin fought, and brings Arianrhod into line with the Greek goddess of love – Aphrodite – whose name came from *aphros* ('sea-foam').

We shall return to Arianrhod and her tale in due course. For now, we need only note that the legend recalls the outbreak of war in Gwynedd; that this war had something to do with some magical pigs or priestesses; that Gwynedd was attacked by the very land those pigs or priestesses had come from; and that, as a result of the war, a princess lost her virginity.

She lost it in Lothian, and the occasion was the May Day festival. The name given in the Kentigern legend for the princess made pregnant by a cross-dressing prince reveals her Beltane connections. The Church came to think of her as St Thaney, a name which came, via Thanew, from Denw ('den-oo'). The name ultimately derived from the Welsh *tanau* – 'fires'. The Gaelic *teinne* (pronounced 'tenu') also meant 'fire'.

War in Gwynedd had driven the princess back to her Lothian homeland, where she fell pregnant. It was suggested that she should marry her bardic 'sweetheart', Taliesin, but the princess declined the offer. Instead, she was taken to the top of 'the highest mountain, which is named Dunpelder', and there she was placed in a chariot.

Dunpelder, the 'Fort of Spear-Shafts', is also known as Traprain Law. It is a dome-shaped hill which rises 220m above the plain of East Lothian, a few miles east of the Royal Burgh of Haddington. Not only was Dunpelder the site of an impressive hill fort but it was also an important ceremonial centre. It had been used as a place of burial since at least 1500 BC – its phonolitic rock makes a musical sound when struck, which might account for the hill's special status. The great hill fort would appear to have been the main centre of power in Lothian until the Picts invaded in the fifth century AD. With the return of Lothian to British rule, thanks to the efforts of Germanic mercenaries, the power centre shifted westwards to Edinburgh, although Dunpelder probably remained in use for ritual purposes.

One such ritual involved the pregnant princess and a chariot. The chariot – sometimes called the Chariot of Arianrhod – appears on a medieval list of the Thirteen Treasures of Britain, where it is said that 'a man would be quickly transported wherever he wanted to be in it'. With the chariot came another of the Treasures of Britain: the halter of Clydno Eidyn, Lord of Lothian, which 'was fixed to the foot of the owner's bed by a staple' and 'whatever horse one might wish for would be found in the halter'. Both of these treasures ended up in the grave with Arthur.

The chariot was almost certainly some kind of dream-vehicle. It allowed the occupant to go anywhere they wanted to, helped by the halter of Clydno which magically attracted any horse the owner might wish for. Put simply, the chariot was a shamanic instrument. It could carry the dreamer away to the Otherworld. The halter would bridle the dream-horse (a concept which gives us the word 'nightmare') and the chariot would convey its passenger to wherever he or she needed to go to find the answers to their questions.

Jocelin of Furness, putting a Christian spin on the legend, held that the chariot was used as a form of punishment. The princess was driven over the edge of Traprain Law but the chariot floated gently to the ground. Jocelin had misinterpreted the chariot's function. It was not a means of execution; rather, it was the equivalent of a magic carpet which took the pregnant princess on a vision-quest.

She asked the gods what would become of her. Perhaps they told her that the child in her womb was destined to become a hero of international renown.

The princess came down from the musical hill and was taken to Aberlady Bay, a great sandy reserve a few miles north-west of Traprain Law. The Gaelic name for Aberlady – *Obar Lìobhaite* – implies a river-mouth of 'delivery' or 'resignation'.

It was there that the Sea-Foam Princess was delivered to the waves. She was resigned to the sea in a lightweight coracle, accompanied only by her salmon-like bards.

The legends surrounding the birth of Arthur combine two persistent themes, both of which were major elements of the Beltane festivities: fire and disguise.

The spirits were loose that night. People rubbed the ashes from the Beltane fires into their faces to achieve anonymity, allowing the same spirits that had protected them in their fire-leaping exertions to enter into them. The mortals who copulated in the woods were merely the vehicles of the gods and any child conceived that night was a gift from the spirit world.

While everyone was preoccupied with the celebrations, Áedán came to Creirwy, and the fiery Prince of the Forth deflowered the priestess of the fires.

Two locations are mentioned in the legend of the pregnant princess, and together they help us to pinpoint the place of Arthur's conception. They are Dunpelder, otherwise known as Traprain Law, and Aberlady Bay on the shore of the Firth of Forth.

Geoffrey of Monmouth wrongly identified the place where Arthur was conceived (by a king in disguise) as Tintagel in Cornwall. He cannot have plucked this out of thin air. Perhaps Geoffrey had simply misheard, or knew what the place was called and went hunting for somewhere that sounded vaguely similar.

A little to the north of Traprain Law, and east of Aberlady Bay, the ruins of a fifteenth-century castle perch on the edge of steep cliffs. The site is not unlike Tintagel, in that it is a defensive position on a rocky headland, towering above the crashing waves, but whereas Tintagel faces westwards, the haunted ruins on the North Berwick coast look eastwards, across the North Sea. The name of the place is Tantallon.

The castle of Tantallon was built by the Douglas Earls of Angus. In the time of King Henry VIII, the English ambassador wrote of its thick, square walls: 'Temptallon is of such strength as I nede not feare the malice of myne enymeys.' The stronghold was later blasted by Cromwell's artillery. Sir Walter Scott, in his *Marmion* of 1808, described the spot:

His towers, Tantallon vast;
Broad, massive, high and stretching far,
And held impregnable in war.
On a projecting rock they rose,
And round three sides the ocean flows,
A fourth did battle walls enclose,
And double mound and fosse.

The pinkish ruins of the castle are not Arthurian, of course, but the name of the site indicates its significance. Tantallon was the 'Fiery Promontory' (*tân talar*) or the 'Enclosure of the Headland of Fire' (*tân tâl llan*). Its earlier settlement seems to have been specifically associated with beacon fires and the rites of Beltane. It occupied the most easterly point in Lothian and would have been the first place in the kingdom to receive the dawn rays of the Sun when it rose in the morning.

Or very nearly the first. The most prominent feature on the horizon, viewed from the vantage point of Tantallon, is the mighty form of the Bass, which rises sheer out of the sea a mile or so from the East Lothian shore. The Bass is composed of the same volcanic rock which formed the hill of Dunpelder. Now a haven for sea-birds, it was converted to Christianity by a hermit named St Baldred in about AD 600 – a pretty sure sign that it was previously a site of cultic importance. A huge cave cuts through the Bass at sea level, so that the musical rock is effectively hollow, and at its north end stands a formation known as The Pulpit.

The first light of the May Day morn would have struck the Bass as the Sun-god arose from his night spent in the arms of the lunar Anna. Fresh from their woodland pursuits, the people would gather on the headland of Tantallon, looking out across the waves for the signal. The Bass would ring with sound, sending flocks of sea-birds into the air and notifying the folks on the shore that the Sun had returned to the sky.

Sparks would fly as the bonfires were rekindled. Flaming brands were carried from the fires of Tantallon to every clean-swept hearth in the district. The summer had arrived.

And on that May Day morning in the year 558 a child quickened in the belly of the Sea-Foam Princess.

She chose not to marry Taliesin. She climbed the sacred hill to dream her destiny and then set out in a coracle across the Firth of Forth.

Her first port of call was the Isle of May, where the mouth of the Forth estuary opens out into the North Sea.

The island is known as *Eilean Mhàigh* in Gaelic, and perhaps had its own associations with the May Day rituals. Tradition asserts, however, that the isle takes its name from a Scots word meaning 'Maiden'. The rocks of its southern shore delight in being known as Maiden Hair and lie close to the 'Lady's Bed'.

The island stands 50m above the waves, a thin, rugged stretch of hard basalt 5 miles out from the nearest landfall on the coast of Fife. It was a place of safety and seclusion.

A human skeleton was found beneath the altar of the chapel on the Isle of May. A scallop shell had been placed in its mouth. This was the symbol adopted by pilgrims visiting the shrine of St James at Santiago de Compostella in the Galician region of Spain. The Spanish shrine was attached to the seaport of Brigantium (La Coruña), from which waves of migrants departed for the islands of Britain and Ireland. Before its conversion to Christianity the shrine honoured Brigantia, the Venus of the Celtic world. The same goddess had given her name to the Brigantes tribes of North Britain, while in the Hebrides she became Brighid or Bride (pronounced 'breed'), the 'Mary of the Gael'.

Brigantia – like Aphrodite and the Roman Venus – was born of sea-foam and rode to the shore in a scallop shell. In common with other bi-valves, the scallop is redolent of the female genitals and was originally a symbol of the goddess. While the skeleton unearthed on the Isle of May was probably that of a Christian who had been to Santiago de Compostella, this does not preclude the likelihood that the island was formerly a sanctuary dedicated to the Celtic mother-goddess, who was believed to care for women in labour. The island, therefore, made an ideal haven for a pregnant princess.

Having prayed for the safe delivery of her child, Creirwy and her bardic companions took to the sea again. The incoming tide carried them westwards from the Isle of May to the north shore of the Forth estuary. They landed on the coast of Fife, just west of Dumfermline, where they were greeted by one of Creirwy's kinsmen. His name was Serwan. He was a prince of Strathclyde who had settled in the Pictish province of Fib, across the Firth of Forth from Edinburgh. The Latin form of his name was *Servanus*. The Church knows him as St Serf.

Serwan, the son of Cedig, son of Dyfnwal the Old, King of Strathclyde, escorted the princess and her followers north to the great lake of Loch Leven, where Arthur was born.

5

BEAR-GUARDIAN

LOCH LEVEN was bigger then than it is today. Even so, it remains the largest lake in Lowland Scotland. It is roughly triangular in shape. Seven islands rise above its surface. On one of these islands Mary, Queen of Scots, was imprisoned in 1567 after she had given birth to the king who would unite the thrones of England and Scotland. But it was on St Serf's Island, in the south-east corner of the lake, that Arthur first drew breath.

According to the Irish *Book of Ballymote*, St Serf was the son of a Pictish princess. His father had been a prince of Strathclyde and a brother-in-law to Brychan of Manau. Almost certainly, when Brychan joined forces with Gabrán of the Scots and advanced into Perthshire and Angus, Cedig son of Dyfnwal moved north of the Forth to occupy the east coast region of Fife. There, he married a princess of the Picts and fathered a son named Serwan.

Serwan had founded or taken over a religious community based on an island in Loch Leven. At this distance in time it is impossible to be sure about the nature of that community. By the following century, the isle was home to a settlement of *Culdees* or 'Servants of God', which lasted until an Augustinian priory was built on the island in 1150. St Serf's community was probably Christian and his island was, as much as anything, a place of healing.

Creirwy's brother belonged to the island community. The legend of the pregnant princess who made a miraculous journey from Aberlady Bay to Loch Leven, by way of the Isle of May, was later incorporated into the *Life of St Kentigern* by Jocelin of Furness. In Jocelin's account, it was St Kentigern himself who was born on St Serf's Island. But the legend did not properly belong to Kentigern. It had become available, as it were, because Geoffrey of Monmouth had previously misidentified Tintagel in Cornwall as the place of Arthur's conception. Jocelin of Furness then compounded the error by taking a local account of Arthur's birth and applying it to a saint who was in fact Arthur's uncle.

Kentigern was his Gaelic name. To the Britons, he was Cynon son of Clydno. Both names bore witness to his healing abilities. Whether as the 'Great-Hound' Cynon or the 'Hound-Lord' Kentigern, he was linked to a creature which throughout the ancient world was associated with healing. The remains of a Romano-British temple complex at Lydney in Gloucestershire have yielded several statues of dogs, including one with a human face; the temple was dedicated to Mars-Nodens, and the Roman god Mars was represented in his healing aspect as being accompanied by a hound.

The healing goddesses of Mesopotamia were similarly depicted with dogs. The animals were also held sacred to Asklepios, the Greek god of healing, and numerous dogs were kept at his sanctuary at Epidaurus. At the Asklepion healing centre in Turkey the patient would expect to receive a visit from a god whilst dreaming: the god would appear as a dog or a snake, and hounds were trained to lick the afflicted parts of the body to help with the cure. The Greek word for a dog – *kuon* – lurks behind the Hebrew *cohen*, meaning 'priest', and so greatly did the early Church fear such healers that St Paul warned the Christians of Philippi to 'beware of dogs: beware of evil workers.'

Cynon son of Clydno had presumably spent some time in the vicinity of St Serf's Island – long enough to have fathered a son with a Pictish name. It is also probable that he had studied alongside his sister in Wales, returning to the North when the princes of Strathclyde went to war with Rhun of Gwynedd. However, piecing together his history is far from straightforward, for while he was remembered in Welsh tradition as a knight of Arthur's court and one of the handful of survivors of Arthur's last battle, in Scotland he is recalled almost exclusively as a Christian missionary, and only his frequent dealings with the crazy man we know as Merlin hint at any connection with the world of Arthur. There was a process of forgetting at work here; a kind of willful amnesia. The medieval Church was only interested in Kentigern as the first bishop and patron saint of Glasgow, and not as the historical prince named Cynon who was outshone by his illustrious nephew.

All the same, the legends of St Kentigern reveal precisely the sort of pagan underlay that the Church tried so hard to conceal.

The coat of arms of the City of Glasgow features four symbols of Kentigern, which are also grouped together in a simple rhyme:

> There's the tree that never grew,
> There's the bird that never flew,
> There's the fish that never swam,
> There's the bell that never rang.

Each of these symbols has its own story. The legend of the 'tree that never grew', for instance, states that Cynon (Kentigern) was specially favoured by his kinsman

Serwan, who left him in charge of the fire on the island in Loch Leven. Other members of the commune, being jealous of Cynon, deliberately put out the fire. The following dawn, Cynon awoke to find that the fire was dead. He took up a branch of hazel and prayed over it. The branch burst into flame and the hearth-fire was relit.

All domestic fires were extinguished on the eve of Beltane. The hearths were swept clean and in the morning the fires were rekindled using brands from the central bonfires. Symbolically, the old fires represented the dark, wintry half of the year, and the new fires welcomed in the summer months. Cynon was seemingly responsible for reigniting the fire at the Loch Leven sanctuary on May Day morning – no miracle required.

It is significant, though, that Arthur's uncle was associated with the rites of Beltane, since it was those very rituals which had brought his sister Creirwy to St Serf's Island with a child in her belly.

Conceived at Beltane, Arthur would have come into the world on or around 2 February. In our modern calendar this would be 14 February, or Valentine's Day, the festival of true love.

The connection between Valentine – an obscure martyr of the third century – and the feast day of lovers has always proved elusive, mainly becuase there isn't one: it was an accident of history which planted the festival of love on St Valentine's Day.

In the late 1500s much of Catholic Europe adopted the Gregorian calendar. The Protestant authorities in England refused to follow suit, and so the older Julian calendar was retained until the middle of the eighteenth century. By then, Britain was out of step with the rest of Europe to the tune of twelve days. So when the 'New Style' calendar was finally implemented in England, eleven days were lost. Wednesday, 2 September 1752 was immediately followed by Thursday, 14 September.

The change of calendar meant that the dates of the old festivals slipped. The pagan feast of Imbolc, which was traditionally celebrated on or about 2 February, should now fall on 14 February. Imbolc marked the transition from winter to spring – as Beltane celebrated the turn from spring into summer – and honoured the goddess in her maidenly aspect (the Church subsumed the festival into its own calendar, calling it Candlemas or the 'Feast of the Purification of the Virgin'). The quickening of life at the very start of spring gave rise to festivities associated with youthfulness, innocence and purity – the origins of our Valentine traditions.

And so we would be justified in celebrating Arthur's birthday on St Valentine's Day.

The moment of birth was sacred. In Britain, the goddess known as Brigantia, Brighid or Brìde was seen as the protector of women in childbirth. Her equivalent in ancient Egypt had been Hathor, the patron and divine consort of the pharaoh, who presided over the annual flooding of the Nile and the breaking of the amniotic waters. When a noblewoman of ancient Egypt went into labour she was attended by the 'seven Hathors', a group of priests and priestesses who dressed alike in the white linen robes of the goddess cult. Something very similar happened when Creirwy's waters broke. Seven priests and priestesses gathered together in female garb to attend the birth.

The prince who had got the princess pregnant was able to get close to her only by dressing up as a woman. This was no more than a hazy memory of the 'seven Hathors'. Elements of Egyptian tradition had followed the Gaels on their migrations to Ireland and Scotland. Áedán, for all his faults, was a religious man and no doubt insisted on being present when his child was born. He was there in his priestly capacity as one of the seven Hathors.

It is conceivable that Áedán mac Gabráin had worn the same white linen robes when he celebrated Beltane by seducing his beautiful cousin nine months earlier. This would account for the peculiar circumstances in which Arthur was conceived. It would also help to explain the name of Arthur.

There is no record of any man bearing the name Arthur before Arthur son of Áedán. This has not stopped scholars from identifying several alternative candidates for the role of 'King Arthur', nor from arguing that Áedán's son must have been named after an earlier hero whose existence is entirely unproven. In fact, the reason why Arthur son of Áedán has not been more widely recognised as the original Arthur has very little to do with history at all. Artuir mac Áedáin was not a warlord of Southern Britain and therefore – as far as those who insist that Arthur was essentially 'English' are concerned – he could not have been the 'real' Arthur.

Put simply, Arthur could not have been Arthur because he does not conform to a stereotype. The Church meddled with his legends and historians then followed suit. They invented King Arthur – the man-who-never-was.

There was no Arthur in the South. As we shall see, the heroes who followed Arthur into the legends were associates of Arthur son of Áedán. The real Arthur was a hero of the North, and no amount of sophistry or wishful thinking can alter that fact. The name grew in popularity after Artuir mac Áedáin made it famous. How he came by that name in the first place is a story in itself.

The Roman poet Ovid told the story in the second book of his *Metamorphoses*. It starts with a nymph named Kallisto ('Most Beautiful'). She was a virginal huntress who served the Moon-goddess Artemis, or Diana. The name of Artemis was derived from a root-word meaning 'bear' and her followers, including the lovely Kallisto, were known as little 'she-bears'. Like the seven Hathors of Egyptian tradition, the 'she-bears' who served Artemis came to be associated with the 'seven sisters' of the Pleiades star cluster.

Kallisto's extraordinary beauty caught the attention of Zeus, who resolved to sleep with her. But the nymph's devotion to the goddess was such that Zeus could only approach her once he had 'assumed the appearance and the dress' of Artemis. In other words, the mighty Lord of Thunder raped the 'Most Beautiful' priestess while he was wearing women's clothing.

The girl could not disguise what had happened. Artemis angrily 'ordered her to withdraw from her company'. The situation finds its parallel in the Welsh legend of Arianrhod, who reacted with sullen fury to the loss of her virginity. Kallisto gave birth to a boy and named him Arkas. Then Hera, the eternally jealous wife of Zeus, took her revenge by spitefully turning Kallisto into the likeness of a bear.

Arkas had reached the age of 15 and was out hunting one day when he came across his mother, though he did not recognise her because she was in bear-form. Just as he was about to kill her, Zeus intervened and elevated both mother and son to the heavens. Kallisto became the constellation known as Ursa Major – the Great Bear – while her son Arkas, whose name also meant 'bear', joined the neighbouring star-cluster of Boötes, and there he shines as one of the brightest stars in the firmament: the red giant we call Arcturus (*Arktouros* – 'Bear-Guardian').

The name coined for Arthur was surely intended to recall the Greek myth of Kallisto. Seduced by a god who happened to be dressed as a goddess, the Most Beautiful one had given birth to a boy she named 'Bear'. This was the root of the name Arthur.

Properly, he was Arthwr ('arth-oor'), the 'Bear-Man' (Welsh *arth* meaning 'bear', with the suffix *-wr*, denoting a 'person' or 'agent'). The Gaelic version of his name, Artúr or Artuir, would have sounded very much like the Welsh.

His mother was associated with the constellation known as the Northern Crown, which the Welsh thought of as the 'Castle of Arianrhod' (*Caer Arianrhod*). The Northern Crown adjoins Boötes and is considered part of the Ursa Major group. This would appear to indicate that Creirwy was a British version of the little 'she-bear' Kallisto. By naming her son after Arcturus she was also implying that Arthur would have a special part to play as the guardian of Britain. Writing in about 45 BC, the historian Diodorus Siculus had observed that Britain had a cold climate 'since it stretches so far to the north, lying directly under the Great Bear'. As the Bear-Guardian, Arthur might have been expected to watch over the Island of Britain from the vantage point of the stars.

Arcturus reaches its zenith at midnight on or about 30 April, coinciding with the full Moon of Beltane on the very night in 558 when Arthur was conceived.

(The easiest way to find Arthur's star in the northern hemisphere is to locate the seven bright stars of Ursa Major – also known as the Big Dipper or the Plough. Follow the handle of the Plough and keep going until you come to an orange-yellow star which, to the naked eye, seems brighter than any other; that star is Arcturus, the 'Bear-Guardian'.)

It is common in military circles for a person to have more than one name. One only has to look at the credits for the movie *Top Gun* to see that American fighter pilots rejoice in nicknames like 'Viper', 'Goose' and 'Maverick'.

During the First Gulf War of 1991, the commander in charge of the allied forces was variously known as General Schwarzkopf, Stormin' Norman and The Bear. European history throws up many examples of individuals who have borne a sometimes bewildering number of titles.

The Celtic worldview was rather more fluid and flexible than our own and it should come as no surprise that a hero like Arthur would have been known by a variety of pseudonyms.

His mother appeared in a range of guises. Geoffrey of Monmouth referred to her as Ygerna, the 'most beautiful woman in Britain'. As the daughter of Clydno of Edinburgh she was the heron-like Creirwy, but her sweetheart Taliesin knew her as Creiddylad – the 'most splendid maiden in the three islands of Britain'. In the legend relating to her pregnancy she was dubbed Denw or Thenaw ('Fires'), whilst in North Wales she was remembered as the Aphrodite-like Arianrhod. These are some of the names by which she was known by different people and at different times. Each illuminates a different aspect of her story and reflects her various roles as a mortal representative of the goddess: as Creirwy she was the maiden; as Creiddylad she was the sweetheart; as Thenaw she was the mother; and as Arianrhod, the hag.

The traditions of Arthur and his comrades evolved separately in several regions. He was three-parts British – his mother and his paternal grandmother were Britons – and the name by which he is best remembered was a British one. But Arthur's DNA was also Gaelic, and so in some quarters he was known by a name that recalled his Irish roots.

Though the legend of *Math Son of Mathonwy* is mostly confined to the kingdom of Gwynedd in North Wales, there are Gaelic influences at work. The name given to Arthur's mother in the tale – Arianrhod – can be translated via Welsh ('Silver-Wheel') or Gaelic ('The Sea-Foam Princess'). The name given to Arthur in the same story betrays more than a hint of Irishness.

In fact, there are two Arthurs in *Math Son of Mathonwy*. The wizard Gwydion subjects his sister to a virginity test which involves jumping over a stick – a nod to the Beltane fire-leaping ritual. Arianrhod instantly gives birth to a 'fine, chubby, yellow-haired boy' named Dylan Eil Ton ('Ocean son of Wave'). The boy quickly plunges into the sea and takes on its nature. Arthur himself was semi-aquatic: his father was the Prince of the Forth and a Lord of the Isles while his mother was a Lady of Lake who, like the goddess Venus, emerged from the foam of the sea. It is also worth remembering that Creirwy took to the sea when Arthur was in her womb, travelling first to the Isle of May and then to the shore of Fife, where she gave birth to Arthur on an island in a lake.

But Arthur was born of water *and* fire. And so a second child drops from Arianrhod's womb. This 'small form' is hastily wrapped in a velvet scarf and hidden inside a chest by his uncle. The small form turns out to be an infant boy who grows so quickly that by the age of 4 he looks like a child of 8.

His mother disowns him. Sulking over her disgrace – like Kallisto, Arianrhod takes the loss of her virginity badly – she refuses to give her son a name. So her brother plays a trick on her.

The magician creates a ship out of seaweed and sails to Arianrhod's castle on the coast. Posing as shoemakers, Gwydion and the boy lure Arianrhod onto the ship to have her foot measured. At that moment, the boy spies a wren which has landed on the deck. He takes aim and strikes the little bird 'between the sinew and the bone' of its leg.

Arianrhod delightedly exclaims: 'It is with a skilful hand that the fair one strikes!'

Gwydion claps his hands and announces that the boy's mother has unwittingly come up with a name for her son. It is *Lleu Llaw Gyffes* or 'Fair Skilful Hand'.

The inspiration behind the name was Irish. The Irish god Lugh was the bringer of light – a sort of Celtic Apollo – and his titles included 'Boy-Hero' and 'Long-Arm'. It was only fitting that the son of the fiery Áedán and the princess of the Beltane fires should have been given a name that meant 'Light' (*lleu* in Welsh).

However, the Welsh-speaking Britons did not hear *lleu* (pronounced 'day') when the Scots spoke of Lugh. What they heard was *llew* (pronounced 'dew'), which was their word for a 'lion'. Thus, the skilful son of Arianrhod is sometimes styled Lleu or 'Light', and at other times he is Llew.

It was hard to find a lion in Scotland. The country was not exactly teeming with lions, and yet somehow or other the Scots developed a fixation with them. A red lion became the heraldic device of the Scottish kings, at least from the time of William I ('William the Lion') in the twelfth century, and the red lion rampant is still the dominant feature of the arms of the kingdom of Scotland, much as the red dragon represents the nation of Wales.

It is perfectly feasible that the first of the royal lions of Scotland was Arthur, and that the red lion only became the symbol for Scotland because of a misunderstanding. His father had wanted to call him Lugh, but the Britons misheard this as *llew* ('lion'). He was named after a red star – Arcturus – but he was also thought of as the Lion.

He was born on an island in Loch Leven, in the Pictish realm of Fib, which we now call Fife. The Gaelic name for the lake – *Loch Lìobhann* – is difficult to translate: *lìobh* refers to a blood-like slick on a body of water; *lìobhan* means to fawn in a dog-like manner. It could be that the lake was once known as *Loch Lèomhainn* or *Lèoghainn*. This would have sounded more or less the same as *Lìobhann*, although the derivation was different. *Lèomhainn* comes from the Early Irish *léu*, making Loch Leven the 'Lake of the Lion'.

The approximate date of Arthur's birth – 2 February, in the Old Style calendar – can be deduced from the date of his conception at Beltane.

To determine the year of his birth, we need only look to the historical records. For no sooner was he born than the sky fell in.

Maelgwyn the Tall, the 'dragon of the island', had presided over a pagan revival in North Wales. He had welcomed the noble youths of Strathclyde into Gwynedd, where the cult of the cauldron of inspiration flourished on his watch. After his death in about 547, his 'illegitimate' son Rhun became King of Gwynedd. A few years later, his younger son Bruide became King of the Picts.

The Christians of Strathclyde already resented the upsurge in pagan activity, which Maelgwyn had done so much to foster. By the year 553, with Rhun installed as King of Gwynedd and Bruide in overall command of the Picts, the Christians were able to argue that Strathclyde was in danger of being enveloped and over-run by pagans inspired by the sons of Maelgwyn. Prince Elidyr of Strathclyde was stirred into launching an ill-fated attack on Gwynedd, which resulted in his death at Caernarfon. In revenge, the cousins Rhydderch of Dumbarton, Clydno of Edinburgh and Nudd of the Selgovae raided deep into Gwynedd. The war was remembered in the legends of North Wales as having been caused by the presence of magical 'pigs' – or priestesses – in Gwynedd, one of whom was then raped.

In fact, Creirwy daughter of Clydno was smuggled out of Gwynedd and returned to her homeland of Lothian along with the bard she had helped to initiate, her 'sweetheart' Taliesin. Creirwy took up residence in a Castle of Maidens in Edinburgh, where Taliesin acted as an honorary 'swineherd'.

Áedán, meanwhile, had married Domelch, the daughter of Maelgwyn and sister to Bruide of the Picts. The marriage cemented Áedán's position as Prince of the Forth and defender of Manau Gododdin, as well as producing two children: Gartnait, the future King of the Picts, and Muirgein, of lasting memory. What became of Domelch daughter of Maelgwyn is unknown; whether she died or her husband had simply grown tired of her, she was quickly eclipsed in Áedán's eyes by the gorgeous and seemingly unattainable daughter of his Lothian overlord.

The fire and fertility festival of Beltane presented Áedán with the opportunity he required to get close to his beautiful cousin. All accounts agree that he wore some form of disguise – the dazzling white robes of the goddess, perhaps – and that there was a degree of subterfuge, if not outright coercion. Henceforth, the Britons would think of him as *bradog* or 'treacherous'. They knew him as Áedán the Wily.

While he was married to Domelch, Áedán held the balance of power in the North. He was as much a part of Maelgwyn's family as he was related to the lords of Strathclyde. His seduction of Creirwy upset that delicate balance, tipping it irrevocably in Strathclyde's favour. Áedán had betrayed his in-laws by bedding the Princess of Lothian. The child of that union was living proof of Áedán's treachery and a political threat to the sons of Maelgwyn.

A son of Áedán already stood next-in-line for the Pictish throne (as the son of Bruide's sister, Gartnait took precedence in the matrilineal society of the Picts). Now another son had been born to Áedán. Arthur would potentially inherit power throughout central and southern Scotland. The tables had turned dramatically. The sons of Maelgwyn, who till recently had overshadowed the Britons of Strathclyde, were now themselves in danger of being sidelined by the offspring of Áedán mac Gabráin. Arthur's birth had radically altered the political map of North Britain.

The response from the sons of Maelgwyn was swift and savage, and it was the Scots who bore the brunt. The *Annals of Ulster* record the 'flight before Máelchá's son; and the death of Gabrán son of Domangart' for the year 558 – and again, two years later, the 'death of Gabrán son of Domangart' and the 'migration before Máelchú's son i.e. King Bruide'. The *Annals of Tigernach* refer to the same events, giving the mean date of 559 as the year of the death of Gabrán 'King of Alba'.

Bruide son of Maelgwyn swept down from his capital near Inverness, attacking the Scots in Perthshire from the north. At the same time, his half-brother Rhun brought an army up from Gwynedd. Rhun's warriors tore through the Scottish Borders and almost certainly slew Nudd the Generous as they advanced towards the River Forth. The army of Gwynedd camped by the River Forth for a good while as Rhun's soldiers argued over who should have the honour of being the first to cross into Scottish territory. They occupied Manau Gododdin, cutting off any chance of a Scottish retreat to the south.

Surprised in Perthshire by Bruide's lightning attack, the Scots had no option but to flee westwards, back to their original enclave in Argyll. This was the 'migration' before Maelgwyn's son 'i.e. King Bruide'. Áedán was forced back to *Eperpuill* – Aberfoyle, close to the source of the River Forth – as his people ran back to Dalriada. His father, however, was not so lucky.

The Irish *Annals* offer three dates for the death of Gabrán, of which 559 seems the most likely. The *Triads of the Island of Britain* mention the 'faithful war-band' of Gabrán 'at the time of his complete disappearance'. As far as the Britons were concerned, Gabrán the Scorcher had not so much died as mysteriously vanished – just as his more famous grandson would vanish, never to be seen again, some thirty-five years later.

Aided by his half-brother Rhun of Gwynedd, Bruide was able to reclaim much of the Pictish territory in central Scotland that had been annexed by Gabrán in about 525. Bruide's tattooed warriors chased the Scots back to the Coastland of the Gael, but the main target of their attack was Arthur.

Ensconced on their island in Loch Leven, Creirwy and her brother Cynon, along with the infant Arthur, were extremely vulnerable. A hint of the danger they found themselves in was preserved in the legends of St Kentigern.

The second of Kentigern's four symbols, commemorated in the arms of the City of Glasgow, is 'the bird that never flew'. Tradition holds that it was a robin redbreast.

Serwan – St Serf – was inordinately fond of his pet robin and would feed the little fellow with his own hand. But there were some in his island community who, out of jealousy, arranged for the robin to be killed and for Cynon (St Kentigern) to get the blame.

Cynon gently took the little bird in his hands and, by praying over it, restored it to life. The robin never forgot the favour and always sang most sweetly for his saviour, although no explanation is forthcoming for why the resuscitated robin redbreast was the 'bird that never flew'.

Arthur was often associated with redness. He was named after a celestial red giant. He was also associated with various different species of bird, both during his lifetime and afterwards. The Welsh word for a robin – *brongoch* ('red-breast') – has echoes of another name by which Arthur was known, as we shall discover in a later chapter. Perhaps the Christian legend of St Kentigern bringing a dead robin back to life was the equivalent of the Welsh story which had a 'small form' wrapped in a velvet scarf and hidden away inside a chest by his uncle – a 'small form' which grew into a mighty hero named Lleu or Llew.

Surrounded by real and potential enemies, the life of the baby Arthur was imperilled. It fell to his uncle Cynon to save him.

The family left the island in Loch Leven, hurriedly making their way south to the Firth of Forth and the sea-crossing to Edinburgh. Their route took them directly over a steep ridge known locally as the 'sleeping giant'. Hiding in the woods on the flat summit of the ridge, Cynon and his sister watched as Bruide's Pictish spearmen swarmed around the lake, eagerly seeking the child whose birth had unleashed chaos.

The height on which Cynon and Creirwy rested with the babe-in-arms is called Benarty Hill or 'Arthur's Ridge'.

They had barely escaped with their lives. Now Creirwy and Cynon hastened with the infant prince to the safety of their Lothian home, where fresh horrors awaited them.

6

SON OF THE MOTHER

FOR THE people of Britain, 559 – the year of Arthur's birth – would be remembered as a year of blood and tears. For the Scots it had spelled disaster: the death of their king and the loss of the territory he had gained across central Scotland. Before long, the Britons of the North were also reeling. The piecemeal conquest of North Britain had begun.

Arthur and his companions would achieve fame because of the valiant stand they made against the Saxons. The term 'Saxon' was and is used rather loosely. The challenge to the Britons came from various Germanic tribes – Angles, Franks and Jutes, as well as settlers from Saxony – and the word 'Saxon' came to be used generically, and with more than a hint of contempt.

The Welsh still think of the English as *Sais* or 'Saxons'. The Gaelic word for 'England' is *Sasunn*, from which we get the Scots term *Sassenach* – a man of the Lowlands or 'Little Englander'. To the natives, all invaders who originated from the far side of the North Sea were 'Saxons', regardless of whether or not they were truly Saxon. The immigrants, meanwhile, thought of the Britons as *wealasc*, 'foreigners', from which we get the word 'Welsh'.

If Arthur had indeed fought the Saxons his activities would have been confined to the south, and so the myth of the southern Arthur concentrates on his supposed campaign against Saxon enemies. However, the main threat to Arthur's people was posed by migrants from the Angeln peninsula of Schleswig-Holstein. These were the Anglian people who would give their name to England.

There had been a time when the Scots and the Saxons acted in concert. In about 365 the Irish High King married the 'daughter of the King of the Saxon foreigners'. This was closely followed by the 'barbarian conspiracy' of 367, which saw assaults on Roman Britain from all sides. Irish raiders plundered the west coast of Britain, Saxon warships harried the eastern shores, and the Scots and Picts poured down from the north to rampage through the Roman province.

Order was eventually restored, but Roman Britain never fully recovered from the co-ordinated attacks of the 'barbarian conspiracy'.

The departure of the last Roman legion in 409 meant that the Britons were left to their own devices. Of all their enemies, the Picts and the Scots were considered the most troublesome because the northern tribesmen had only to ford the River Forth to enter Britain, whereas the Irish and Germanic raiders had seas to cross. And so, in the middle of the fifth century, the High King of Britain hired Germanic mercenaries to rid the North of the dreaded Scots and Picts.

Back in the third century AD, parts of Friesland in the northern Netherlands had flooded. Waves of refugees crossed the *Mare Frisia* to seek shelter in southeast Britain. They settled in Kent. Some eventually made their way back to their homelands near the mouth of the Rhine, where they merged with the Saxons and Jutes of Germany and Jutland and returned in greater numbers.

It was almost certainly the immigrant community in Kent which gave the 'proud tyrant' Vortigern the idea of employing mercenaries to help deal with his problems in North Britain. The *Kentish Chronicle* recorded the silken words spoken by Hengist, the nominal leader of the settlers, to the hard-pressed British king: 'Take my advice,' he said, 'and you will never fear conquest by any man or any people ... I will invite my son and his cousin, fine warriors, to fight against the Irish [*sic*]. Give them the lands of the North, next to the Wall.'

The offer was a canny one. The Roman army had recruited warriors from the valleys of the Rhine and the Danube to patrol Hadrian's Wall, the most substantial frontier in Roman Britain. Some of these Romanised warriors had remained in North Britain after they were discharged from the army, marrying into the local population and settling in British communities. Hengist knew what he was doing: by rewarding the mercenaries with land in the North, Vortigern would massively increase the strength and numbers of the Germanic settlers who were already there.

The warriors came across the North Sea, packed into forty keels and assured by their soothsayers that they would occupy the country to which they were sailing for 300 years, 'and half of that time, one hundred and fifty years, would plunder and despoil the same'. They took the battle to the Picts and Scots and were grudgingly rewarded with land in the north-east.

The Angles who made up the main body of Germanic settlers in North Britain were typically blue-eyed and flaxen-haired. Pope Gregory the Great famously encountered some of their children in a Roman slave market in 573; when he asked who they were he was told that they were Angles, to which the Pope replied *Non Angli sed Angeli* – 'Not Angles but Angels'.

These 'angels' had come from the former British kingdom of Deywr. They were the enemies of Arthur and his people.

War raged in Southern Britain throughout much of the fifth century, until the Britons fought the Saxons to a standstill at the battle referred to by Gildas as the 'siege of Badon Hill'. In North Britain, meanwhile, the Anglian settlers remained in their east-coast lands. They were held in check by the 'Men of the North' (*Gwyr y Gogledd*), the descendants of the last Romanised *dux Britanniarum* ('Duke of Britain') remembered to this day as Coel Hen, or 'Old King Cole'.

From his military headquarters at York, Coel the Old had defended the whole of the Roman sub-province of *Britannia Secunda* – roughly, from the north of the English Midlands up as far as Hadrian's Wall, and taking in the coastal districts on either side of the Pennine Ridge. The Britons came to think of this region as the Old North, *Yr Hen Ogledd*. Over successive generations the British descendants of Coel divided the territory into a patchwork of petty fiefdoms governed by inter-related princes.

The kingdom of Bryneich abutted Lothian and occupied the east coast of North Britain between the River Tweed and the River Tees. Its last British king was Brân the Old. When he died in 547, the Anglian community in Bryneich proclaimed its own chief king of the territory. Ida became the first 'English' king of the land, which was renamed 'Bernicia'.

Thus, at about the same time as Maelgwyn the Tall was dying of the yellow plague in North Wales, the first British kingdom of the North fell under Anglian domination.

Ida of Bernicia died in 559. His successor Aethelric would command the Germanic warrior-settlers of Bernicia for the next twenty years while the sons of Ida sought to carve out new territories for themselves in the lands of the Britons.

In the same year as Ida died, the region immediately to the south of Bernicia also fell to the Angles. The British kingdom of Deywr stretched along the east coast from the Humber to the Tees; it was renamed 'Deira' when Aelle became its first Anglian king.

The fair-haired settlers now held the whole of the east coast of the Old North and were on their way to establishing the powerful kingdom of Northumbria.

Aelle's first act as the new King of Deira was to lay siege to the British garrison town of York.

Known to the Romans as *Eboracum* and to the Britons as *Caer Ebrog*, York was the key to the Old North. A heavily fortified *civitas* on a major Roman road, it was the former headquarters of the *dux Britanniarum* Old King Coel. The Men of the North simply could not afford to lose such a strategically and symbolically important stronghold.

Successfully defended by its celebrated army of spearmen, York held out against the Angles, although its British chieftain, Eliffer of the Great Host, died in the fighting. He was succeeded by his two sons, Peredur and Gwrgi, who then had the grim task of holding onto this key British asset. Of the sons of Eliffer, one at least – Peredur ('Steel-Spear') – would achieve lasting fame as a comrade of Arthur.

He would be remembered in Welsh legend as 'Peredur Son of Efrog' or Peredur of York, although he is better known today by the name he was given by French romancers of the Middle Ages: 'Sir Perceval'.

Following Arthur's birth, the Picts under Bruide son of Maelgwyn swept the Scots out of Perthshire. Further south, the Angles laid claim to their second kingdom and attacked the British citadel of York. Between Bruide's Picts and the Northumbrian Angles lay the British kingdom of Lothian, the home of Arthur's mother Creirwy and her brother Cynon.

The death of Brân the Old in 547 had allowed the Angles to seize control of Bernicia. The British heir to the throne of that kingdom had been very young at the time. His name was Morgan. Generally dubbed Morgan Mwynfawr – 'Morgan the Wealthy' – he was also known as Morgan Fwlch (perhaps from *balch*, meaning 'proud', or a cognate of the Gaelic *bolg*, 'belly'). The Anglian takeover of his kingdom left Morgan without a throne. He became a prince in exile and an honoured guest at the court of Clydno of Edinburgh.

When Bruide's Pictish spearmen came in search of the baby Arthur in Fife, Creirwy and Cynon fled south from Loch Leven and took ship across the Firth of Forth. But there would be no safety for them in their Lothian homeland: Clydno, their father, was dead.

As told by Jocelin, the twelfth-century monk of Furness Abbey, the legend of St Kentigern describes the persecution of Arthur's uncle by 'a certain tyrant, who was called Morken'. This Morken was 'exceedingly rich and great in the eyes of men' but also a 'vile slave of Mammon' and a 'man of Belial'. The legend states that 'certain sons of Belial, the fruit of vipers of the kindred of the formerly mentioned King Morken' plotted to kill Cynon son of Clydno, who was forced to flee from Lothian and seek sanctuary in Wales.

There can be little doubt as to who this 'King Morken' was – 'persuaded by power, honour and riches to walk in great and wondrous matters above him', he was none other than Morgan the Wealthy. He was a worshipper of the Sun-god Beli Mawr and his Druids or 'vipers' had conspired to kill the children of Clydno at Loch Leven, along with Arthur, the newborn grandson of Clydno of Edinburgh.

Evidently, Morgan had usurped the throne, slaying Clydno in the process, and was taking steps to wipe out Clydno's line.

Jocelin's medieval account gave a hint as to what might have motivated Morgan: a love of money (*Mammon*) and ideas above his station. He had lost his own kingdom to the Northumbrian Angles. The chaos unleashed by the birth of Arthur presented him with the opportunity to seize control of Lothian. Almost certainly, Morgan acted in concert with the Picts to the north and the Angles to the south. In return for power, honour and hard cash, he had staged a coup, exquisitely timed to coincide with the forced migration of the Scots and the Anglian siege of York.

It is hard to imagine a less auspicious start in life for the greatest hero Britain has ever known.

His father's people had been herded back to the Coastland of the Gael and Áedán was marooned at Aberfoyle. Running for shelter, Arthur's mother and uncle had stumbled into the aftermath of an uprising, which saw Morgan the Wealthy snatching the throne of Lothian. The Anglian settlers had launched their bid to conquer North Britain, forcing the British spearmen of York to fight for their very survival. The list of the dead included both grandfathers of Arthur – Gabrán and Clydno – as well as Nudd, the father of the poet Taliesin, and Eliffer of York.

The birth of the dragon had brought fire and blood to the North. There must have been many who cursed him for it.

The Christian legend of St Kentigern indicates that Cynon son of Clydno was hounded from the North by Morgan the Wealthy and fled to the far-off kingdom of Dyfed in south-west Wales (see Map 2). There, he joined the religious community that had gathered around the figure of St David. Cynon's sister and her baby son went with him, finding shelter in the vicinity of St David's settlement.

At the time of the 'barbarian conspiracy' against Roman Britain in 367, south-west Wales had come under attack from Irish warriors of the Déisi tribes of Munster. The Roman authorities decided that the best defence against future raids would be to allow the warriors of the Déisi to settle on the Pembrokeshire coast. The kingdom of Demetia – later known as Dyfed – was therefore formed by Irish tribesmen with ancestral links to the Scots of Dalriada (see Chapter 2).

The peninsula of St David's Head pokes out into the Irish Sea at the edge of southern Wales. A short distance to the north of the cathedral town of St David's stood the 'Red Fort', *Caer Goch*. It was the main base of an influential Irish warrior known to the Britons as Cynyr Ceinfarfog ('Fair-Beard'). *Cynyr* was the Welsh spelling of 'Conor', which was itself a variant form of *Conchrad* or *Cú Chàrainn* ('Hound-Friend').

Conchrad Fair-Beard had connections with the family of Arthur. His first wife had been a daughter of Brychan Brecheiniog, the Irish-born magnate of south-east Wales who was probably the same as the Brychan of Manau who married another of his daughters to Gabrán of the Scots. Conchrad's second wife was reputedly a daughter of Vortimer of Gwent and, therefore, a granddaughter to the 'proud tyrant' Vortigern, the High King of Britain who had hired Germanic mercenaries to do the Britons' dirty work in the North.

Conchrad's Irish connections were as impressive as his British ones. His father, Dauí Tenga Uma, had been King of Connacht, a major province in the north-west of Ireland. And Mugain, the daughter of Conchrad by his second wife Anna, had just married the High King of Ireland, Diarmait mac Cerbaill.

Diarmait son of Cerball came to the throne of Ireland in 559, the same year which saw the birth of Arthur and the death of Gabrán. The Irish *Annals* make note of the fact that Diarmait mac Cerbaill celebrated the 'Feast of Tara' in that very year. Diarmait is thought to have been the last High King of Ireland to have indulged in that pagan ceremony.

The timing was fortuitous. Just as Creirwy and Cynon were escaping from Lothian with the little Scottish prince, Conchrad Fair-Beard became father-in-law to the High King of Ireland and a useful ally to any dispossessed infant of royal Irish blood.

Conchrad also had a son named Cai, whose sister had married King Diarmait of Ireland. When the infant Arthur was settled at the Red Fort on the coast of Dyfed under the guardianship of Conchrad, Cai became Arthur's foster-brother. For the rest of his life, Cai the Tall (or 'the Fair') would be Arthur's faithful companion. He was remembered in the medieval legends as 'Sir Kay'.

Cynon, meanwhile, joined the religious community at St David's Head. Creirwy almost certainly found sanctuary with Non, the daughter of Conchrad Fair-Beard. Her retreat lay just to the south of the St David's settlement, and Non herself was the mother of St David.

Arthur's presence in the locality is commemorated at *Coetan Arthur* ('Arthur's Quoit'), a Neolithic burial chamber on the headland of St David's. A little to the north of the St David's settlement there is a 'Well at the End of Arthur's Land' (*Ffynnon Penarthur*), with its nearby bridge (*Pont Penarthur*), which would suggest that a parcel of land was set aside to provide for the young prince whilst he was being raised with Cai son of Conchrad at the Red Fort.

It was a long way from Lothian, and from Dalriada, but Creirwy, Cynon and Arthur had found homes with the extended family of Conchrad the Irishman. They also enjoyed the protection of the King of Dyfed. His name was Pedr and he too had Irish roots, being the grandson of Vortipor, 'Protector' of Dyfed, and a descendant of the first Déisi settlers in southern Wales.

Pedr's name is the Welsh version of Peter. He would live on in Arthurian legend, appearing as 'Pedrod' in the Welsh tales of the *Mabinogion*. Cai son of Conchrad and Pedr, King of Dyfed, were among the very first warrior-princes to constellate around Arthur. A short while after Arthur arrived in Dyfed, Pedr paid him a great compliment by naming his own son Arthwyr in honour of the northern prince who had come to his kingdom as an infant refugee. To avoid confusion, Arthwyr son of Pedr was remembered in the tales as Bedwyr son of Pedrod, a name which would evolve into 'Sir Bedivere'.

Given the insistence of so many scholars that Arthur must have been a warlord of southern Britain, active in the fifth century, it is a striking fact that the early tales place him in the company of northern princes of the sixth century. One such tale is to be found in the *Mabinogion* collection. It opens with a scene of peaceful domesticity.

Arthur is relaxing in his chamber. His queen and her maidens are at their embroidery, over by the window. Sitting with Arthur are three men – Cynon son of Clydno, Cai son of Cynyr and Owain son of Urien. While Arthur dozes, Cynon describes a strange adventure which once befell him …

Owain, or The Lady of the Fountain preserves the remnants of an authentic tradition. The three men discovered with Arthur at the start of the story belonged to his intimate family circle. All three were men of sixth-century Britain and two of them – Cynon and Owain – were historical princes of the North.

Cynon would go on to enjoy a double life as an Arthurian hero and a Christian saint. Cai would be forever associated with Arthur, both as his foster-brother and his steward or seneschal. Owain was remembered as a great prince, the last hope of his people. The French romancers would call him Yvain, while in Sir Thomas Malory's *Le Morte d'Arthur*, published in 1485, he appears as 'Sir Uwaine le Blanchemains'.

Owain was the son of Arthur's half-sister.

The upheavals of 559 had impacted on Muirgein's marriage plans. When the Picts under Muirgein's uncle, King Bruide, steamrollered through Perthshire they killed her grandfather, Gabrán, and forced Áedán back to Aberfoyle on the edge of the Lennox district. Like the Scots, the 'Lennox Men of Alba' were of Irish descent. They were probably the people known as the Attacotti, a 'warlike tribe', which had joined forces with the Picts and the Scots to raid North Britain as part of the 'barbarian conspiracy' of 367. St Jerome, who had seen warriors of the Attacotti in Gaul during his youth, held them to be little more than promiscuous cannibals.

The Lennox Men were natural allies of the Scots and a proposed marriage between the daughter of Áedán and the son of Masgwid, Lord of Lennox, would have cemented the bonds between the two Irish tribes in western Scotland. But the havoc which erupted in the wake of Arthur's birth threw everything into doubt. Masgwid of Lennox acquired the epithet *cloff* – 'lame' – and the Scots, who had long memories, were unsettled by the prospect of a lame king. At the same time, the Britons were desperate to shore up their border with the Anglian district of Deira. And so Masgwid of Lennox moved south to become a 'judge' over Elmet, a West Yorkshire kingdom centred on modern-day Leeds. He bolstered the British front line against further Anglian incursions and his descendants – including his grandson Gwallog – continued to hold power in Elmet, although they were also identified with the Lennox region around Loch Lomond. Gwallog the Battle-Horseman would emerge in the later legends as 'Sir Galahad'.

Gwallog's father, the son of Masgwid the Lame, would eventually become 'Learned' or 'Literate' – *lleënog*, in the Welsh tongue – but before that he too was known as *gwallog* ('hairy'). His later name would be transmuted by the continental romancers into the legendary 'Sir Lancelot', the father of 'Sir Galahad'. The familiar designation 'of the Lake' simply recalled that Gwallog's homeland of Lennox was dominated by the grand lake of Loch Lomond.

Aged about 12 when her half-brother Arthur was born, Muirgein had perhaps been betrothed to Masgwid's son Gwallog – later Lleënog; later still 'Lancelot of the Lake'. After 559, however, all bets were off. Áedán had fallen back to Aberfoyle, Masgwid was transferred to Elmet, and Lennox became a sub-territory of Dalriada, protected by Áedán mac Gabráin and ruled by the Scots. Suddenly, there was no political advantage to be gleaned from the marriage of Muirgein nic Áedáin to Lleënog son of Masgwid the Lame.

But there was an urgent need to rebuild the shattered alliances of the North. Muirgein would play a significant part in this through her prudent choice of marriage partner.

The tale of her courtship became a Welsh legend. The first stories of the *Mabinogion* collection are known as the 'Four Branches'. Though centuries of oral transmission meant that the names and the locations were altered, the subject matter of these stories was Arthur's immediate family.

The first character to appear in the tales of the *Mabinogion* is referred to as Pwyll, Lord of Dyfed. His name meant 'Discretion' and he was in reality a prince of the North.

When North Britain imploded after the death of Arthur, his legends were disseminated over a wide area by refugees escaping from their Anglian conquerors. The people of North Rheged, a west-coast kingdom roughly contiguous with modern Cumbria, settled mostly in southern Wales and, in particular, in the picturesque Gower Peninsula, which then formed part of the kingdom of Dyfed. They took with them their memories of the lords of their northern homeland. By far the most celebrated of these had been Urien and his son Owain. The Welsh name for the Gower is *Gwyr*, and so, by the Middle Ages, Urien of North Rheged was described as the 'King of Gorre' – even though he had died before his Cumbrian people migrated to the relative safety of Dyfed and the Gower.

Urien is yet another historical contemporary who would accompany Arthur into the legends. Sir Thomas Malory called him 'King Uriens of the land of Gore' and made him husband to 'Morgan le Fay', the name given to Arthur's half-sister Muirgein in the later romances. In fact, Urien was already connected with Arthur's family: his father Cynfarch had married one of the daughters of Brychan of Manau and so Urien and Áedán mac Gabráin were essentially cousins.

The posthumous link forged between Urien and the Gower in South Wales helps to explain why he appears in the First Branch of the *Mabinogion* as a Lord of Dyfed. As the legendary Pwyll, he agrees to spend a year masquerading as Arawn, Lord of Annwn, and holds up his side of the bargain so well that he and Arawn become fast friends. Pwyll is subsequently hailed as both Lord of Dyfed and Lord of Annwn.

As we shall see, Annwn was a specific place – it was part of Áedán mac Gabráin's sea-kingdom. The Pwyll legend points to a fosterage arrangement, in which Pwyll (Urien) and Arawn (Áedán) become brothers and equals. Next, Pwyll is told that if a man of royal blood were to sit on a certain mound he would either receive blows and wounds or see a wonder. Pwyll duly sits on the mound and sees a beautiful woman riding by, wearing a mantle of gold brocade.

Though the mysterious woman appears to be riding slowly on her pale horse, none of Pwyll's men can catch up with her. On the third day, Pwyll himself sets off in pursuit. It is only when he cries out to her to stop that he manages to speak to the woman. She tells him that the purpose of her errand is to see Pwyll, and he instantly proposes marriage. The woman introduces herself as Rhiannon and agrees to marry Pwyll in a year's time.

The name Rhiannon can be arrived at via the Welsh *rhiain* ('maiden') or the Gaelic *rìghinn* ('princess'). The Early Irish *rígan* – meaning 'princess' or 'nymph' – survived in the name of the red-haired goddess of death and battle, the Mórríghan, to whom Muirgein bore more than a passing resemblance.

On the sacred isle of Arthur's burial, Rhiannon was associated with a sisterhood of maidens, the Birds of Rhiannon, whose sweet singing could heal the sick and soothe the troubled soul. Rhiannon – the 'Great Maiden' or 'Little Princess' – was therefore clearly related to Muirgein who, as 'King Arthur's sister, Queen Morgan le Fay', was also associated with a sacred sisterhood based on the island where Arthur was buried.

Back to the legend of Pwyll. A banquet is held to celebrate Pwyll's marriage to Rhiannon. The feast is interrupted by the arrival of a noble youth with a favour to ask. Rashly, Pwyll grants the request before realising that the youth has come to claim Rhiannon. His name is Gwawl son of Clud and he is the man whom Rhiannon was meant to marry against her will.

Since Pwyll can be identified as Urien of North Rheged, who was Áedán's cousin and probably his foster-brother, and Rhiannon can be identified as Áedán's daughter Muirgein, it should in theory be possible to identify Gwawl son of Clud. 'Clud' related to the River Clyde. The British stronghold at Dumbarton was known as Alclud, from the Irish *Ail Cluade*, the 'Rock of the Clyde'. The River Leven, which flows from the southern end of Loch Lomond, empties into the River Clyde at the foot of the Rock of Dumbarton, thereby linking the district of Lennox to the chief river of Strathclyde.

A turf-and-stone rampart constructed in the second century AD by the Roman Emperor Antoninus Pius terminated at Old Kilpatrick on the Clyde, a little to the east of Dumbarton. This was the Antonine Wall, which seems to have been the origin of the name Gwawl son of Clud or 'Wall son of Clyde'. The name Gwawl might also have been a corruption of *gwallog* ('Hairy'). Gwallog's territory of Lennox lay immediately to the north of the Antonine Wall where it meets the Clyde. The original Gwallog acquired 'Learning' and became Lleënog, the forerunner of Sir Lancelot. The romances recall that, spurned by his lover, Lancelot went mad and slept with a woman of Astolat – Alclud, or Dumbarton. It would later be claimed that Lancelot's true love was Arthur's queen, but there may have been an earlier tradition that Lleënog of Lennox was betrothed to Arthur's sister. As a result of the havoc of 559, Muirgein broke off the marriage contract – it could no longer serve its intended purpose – and rejected the 'Hairy' son of the Clyde.

Instead, the Little Princess chose Urien of North Rheged to be her husband.

A Welsh manuscript (Peniarth 147) gives another account of the wedding. This takes the form of Urien's encounter with the Washer at the Ford.

The meeting is said to have taken place at Llanferres on the River Alyn in north-east Wales. The legend states that the hounds of the area used to gather at the Ford of Barking. Nobody dared to investigate the cause of their barking until Urien of North Rheged went to the ford.

He found a woman washing linen in the river. She was the infamous 'Washer at the Ford', a supernatural fairy-woman or *bean-nighe* frequently associated with the Mórríghan. It was considered bad luck to meet her, since the bloodstained clothes she was washing were those of the hero who was doomed to die. The Washer was a harbinger of death. But in a surprising move, Urien seized and ravished her. More surprising still, the woman proclaimed her delight. She told him that she was the 'daughter of the King of Annwn' and that she had been cursed to wash linen at the ford until she conceived a child 'by a Christian man'.

The outcome of this strange meeting was one of the three 'Fair Womb-Burdens of the Island of Britain': 'Owain son of Urien and Morfudd his sister who were carried together in the womb of Modron daughter of Afallach.'

In marrying Urien, Muirgein adopted a new identity: she became Modron, the Matron or 'Mother'. She is only the second 'daughter of Afallach' to appear in our tale, after Gwallwen, the daughter of Avalon who married Maelgwyn of Gwynedd. The 'apple-bearing' Island of Afallach was also known – for reasons which will become clear in due course – as Annwn.

In all, Urien of North Rheged seems to have had three wives. One of them bore an Irish name, Eithne ('enya'). The name meant 'knowledge' or 'fire' and was cognate with Agna ('anya'). Muirgein, as we have seen, was also known as Agna or Anna.

The marriage achieved all that was required of it: it bound Áedán and his family even closer to the British princes of the North, strengthening the ties between Dalriada and Rheged, and it brought forth a young hero. As a consequence, Muirgein was honoured with the title of 'Mother'.

Owain son of Urien would be celebrated by his Cumbrian people as a sort of divine youth – *Mabon ap Modron* or 'Boy son of Mother'. There was something of a cult devoted to the Mabon or *Maponos* in the Cumbrian kingdom. A seventh-century map known as the Ravenna Cosmography identified the Roman fort of Ladyward, near Lockerbie in the Scottish Lowlands, as *Locus Maponi*, the 'Place of Mabon', and an old Welsh poem composed in praise of Owain's military achievements referred to a region of the Lowlands as *Gwlad Mabon*, the 'Land of the Son'.

In the same area we find *Lochmaben* – 'Lake of Mabon' – just north of Urien's capital at Carlisle. Close by lies what was almost certainly the real site of Urien's fateful encounter with the Washer who became the Mother of his son.

The legend recounted in the Peniarth 147 manuscript was designed to present Urien of North Rheged as a 'Christian man'. Annwn might have been another name for Avalon, but the medieval Church preferred to think of it as a pagan hell and so the daughter of its king was cast as an infernal sprite whose evil could only be neutered if she was subdued by a Christian prince. There is in fact no evidence whatever that Urien was a Christian and no reason to believe that he raped his wife at the River Alyn in Wales. The legend has its uses, in that it confirms the marriage of Urien to Muirgein, the 'daughter of Afallach' and 'daughter of the King of Annwn'. But the tale of Urien's meeting with the Washer at the Ford was a blatant attempt by medieval monks to claim a revered pagan prince as one of their own.

Urien met his bride at the 'Ford of Barking' – *Rhyd y Gyfarthfa* in Welsh. It is tempting to suggest that *cyfarthfa* ('barking' or 'battle') was substituted for *cyfarthrach* – 'kinship' or 'intercourse' – not least of all because Urien straightaway had sex with the woman he met at the ford.

Near Gretna, on the north shore of the Solway Firth, stands the ancient tribal meeting place of the Lochmaben Stone. It was once a complete circle of standing stones, but now only one megalith remains on farmland above the mouth of the River Sark. In the Scots dialect, a *sark* is a 'shift' or 'shirt'. The neighbouring river, which flows into the Sark below the Lochmaben Stone, is rather charmingly known as the Kirtle or 'Petticoat'.

The land on which the stone circle stood is called Stormont – from the Gaelic *stair*, meaning 'stepping stones' or a temporary bridge. The stone of the Lake of the Son therefore stands on the mount of the stepping stones above the meeting of two waters both named after types of linen: his Shirt and her Petticoat.

The site was accessible by sea – convenient for Muirgein, who had probably travelled down from Argyll – and was just a short distance from Urien's chief seat at Carlisle.

Surrounded by a gathering of healers or 'hounds', Urien and Muirgein took their marriage vows in pagan fashion by copulating in full view of the assembled throng. Their sexual compatibility was plain for all to see. The consummation of their marriage was no doubt greeted by shouts or 'barks' of acclamation from the crowd.

It is a quaint thought that Urien of North Rheged first coupled with Muirgein 'daughter of Avalon' near Gretna, a border town now famous for conducting hasty marriages.

The marriage yielded two children – Muirgein's fair 'Womb-Burden'. Their daughter Morfydd ('Sea-Treasure') would bedazzle Cynon son of Clydno, so that in time Arthur's uncle would become the lover of Arthur's niece. But it was

Owain, the son of Urien and Muirgein, who would come to be most closely associated with Arthur and would have his own legend in the *Mabinogion* collection of ancient tales: that of *Owain, or The Lady of the Fountain*.

Owain was the last British prince of his Cumbrian people. In the stories that make up the Four Branches of the *Mabinogion* he starts off as the golden-haired boy named Gwri. Kidnapped as a baby, Gwri is raised by one Teyrnon Twrf Lliant ('Great-Lord Sea Thunder'), the 'best man in the world'. This could only mean that little Owain was fostered with his grandfather, Áedán mac Gabráin, the lord of the sea, making Owain a foster-brother, as well as a nephew, to Arthur. When he returned to his parents the golden-haired boy was given a new name: Pryderi, meaning 'Care' or 'Anxiety' – a reflection, perhaps, on the parenting skills of Áedán the Wily. But he remained, in the hearts of his people at least, the Son of the Mother, Owain son of Urien, the beloved prince of the Cymry.

The union of Urien and Muirgein added another historical hero to the Arthurian mix, but as the decade of the 560s dawned things were not looking too good for Arthur's people. The Britons were belatedly responding to the growing menace of their neighbours to the east, the Northumbrian Angles; the Scots were cowering before the might of the resurgent Picts under Áedán's onetime brother-in-law, King Bruide; and the princely son of Áedán was being cared for far away in distant Dyfed.

It would take the arrival of an Irish missionary to repair the battered relations between the Scots and their Pictish counterparts, and bring peace of a kind to the North.

7

DOVE OF THE CHURCH

IN THE remote western reaches of Europe, the gap between native Druidism and the Church of Rome was bridged by Celtic Christianity. Essentially an insular movement, it was eventually forced to conform by adopting the Roman tonsure of St Peter and the centralised method for dating Easter. But while it lasted, the Celtic Church in Britain and Ireland now and then allowed its Druidic roots to show.

The 40-year-old churchman, hunched over a writing desk in a tiny chapel, would claim that 'Christ is my Druid'. He wore his hair in the Druidic tonsure – shaved across the front of the scalp – and his eyelids were stained so that they looked black. He carried a blackthorn staff or *bacall*. His garments were homespun. Perched at his elbow was a crane, a bird long associated with the mysteries of the written word. But he was no Druid. He was an Irish prince who would negotiate a truce between the Picts and the Scots. First, though, he had to go to war against his king.

He had been born in County Donegal on 7 December 521 – a Thursday, his 'lucky' day. A scion of the northern branch of the ruling dynasty of Ireland, he was descended from the celebrated Niall of the Nine Hostages, the man responsible for the kidnap of the teenage St Patrick in Britain. At birth he was given the name Criomhthann ('Fox'). Only at a later date did he become known by his more famous name. The Fox transformed himself into a Dove and became St Columba or *Columchille*, the 'Dove of the Church'.

As a child he was fostered with a priest named Cruithnechán ('Little Pictish One'), who prepared him for his schooling at the monastic college of Moville. Such schools had not sprung up with the advent of Christianity; their origins can be traced back to ancient Egypt. Under the supervision of St Finnian of Moville, the boy worked his way through the Seven Degrees of Wisdom, akin to the seven initiatory degrees of the House of Wisdom in Cairo, until he reached the final level, that of *ollamh*.

An *ollamh* (pronounced 'oh-luv') was a wise man whose learning placed him on a par with the highest in Celtic society. He was allowed to wear the same number of colours in his plaid – six – as a king or a queen. Most importantly, he had mastered the art of letters.

Columba's lifelong love of poetry was further nurtured by his next mentor, a Christian bard named Gemmán, who had the privilege of witnessing the saint's first miracle. A terrified young woman ran to Gemmán for protection against a violent man. Columba stepped forward to offer the girl sanctuary, but the pursuer drove his spear through the girl and she died at Columba's feet. Columba turned to Gemmán and said:

'As soon as the soul of this girl ascends to heaven, so be it that the soul of her killer shall descend to hell.'

The murderer promptly dropped down dead on the spot.

St Columba completed his training under another Finnian – St Finnian of Clonard – whose students at the time included Ciaran, a frequent visitor to the Scottish colony of Dalriada, and Brendan the 'Navigator', who undertook a legendary seven-year journey in search of the Land of Promise. At Clonard, Columba mingled with the very people who would take the Gospel to the Scots before him.

A period of fifteen years followed, during which Columba established a number of Irish monasteries. The first was at his tribal centre of Derry. As he wrote:

> For its quietness and purity,
> For heaven's angels that come and go
> Under every leaf of the oaks,
> I love my beautiful Derry,
> My Derry, my fair oak-grove,
> My dear little cell and dwelling.

The monasteries at Derry ('Place of Oaks'), Durrow ('Plain of Oaks') and elsewhere were founded in the same woodland groves that had served as Druidic temples. This was in line with the strategy proposed by Theodosius, the emperor who had chased the Picts and Scots out of North Britain after the 'barbarian conspiracy' of 367, who recommended that pagan shrines should be adapted for Christian use. Columba was drawn to such groves by an almost Druidic reverence for sacred oaks. Compiling his *Life of Columchille* in 1527, Manus O'Donnell had the saint remark:

> Though I am affrighted truly
> By death and by Hell,
> I am more affrighted, frankly,
> By the sound of an axe in Derry in the west.

There was a practical reason for St Columba's obsession with certain oak trees. As we shall see, it had something to do with the 'angels' that came and went under every leaf, and was integral to the business of writing.

Columba's passion for the written word had grown out of his training as an *ollamh*. It was this love of letters that would land him in serious trouble.

His old friend and tutor St Finnian of Moville had returned from a visit to Rome, bringing with him 'beautiful copies of the sacred books'. Columba could not wait to cast his eye over these volumes and was especially eager to examine St Jerome's translation of the Scriptures. Finnian, however, guarded his books jealously, so Columba took to staying behind in the chapel after evening service, secretly making his own copy of the text.

Manus O'Donnell would later claim that 'at night, while engaged in that transcription, the fingers of [Columba's] right hand were as candles which shone like very bright lamps, whose light filled the entire church'.

St Finnian grew suspicious and sent a messenger to check on the chapel and its contents. The messenger saw that the chapel was suffused with light. He pressed his eye up against a knot-hole in the wooden door and glimpsed Columba copying out the words of St Jerome, his pet crane at his elbow.

It dawned on Columba that somebody was spying on him. He whispered to the bird: 'If God permits it, you have my permission to pluck out the eyes of the youth who came to observe me without my knowledge.'

The crane flew across the chapel, thrust its beak through the peephole and pecked out the eye of Finnian's messenger.

St Finnian first restored the youth's eyesight (blindness was associated with secret knowledge: the youth had evidently seen more than he was meant to). Finnian then demanded Columba's transcript, which Columba refused to hand over. So Finnian brought his case before the High King of Ireland, Diarmait mac Cerbaill, at the royal hall at Tara.

King Diarmait listened to both sides. Then he consulted his advisers and delivered his judgement in accordance with the established law:

'To every cow her calf; to every book its copy.'

Diarmait mac Cerbaill had found in Finnian's favour. Columba was livid.

It is likely that Columba had been spoiling for a fight with Diarmait for some time – at least since the High King had celebrated the Feast of Tara in 559. Diarmait belonged to the southern branch of the Uí Néill; he was also a pagan, and therefore doubly resented by Columba of the northern Uí Néill. Later writers added insult to Columba's injury by replaying the incident of Gemmán and the murdered girl in a slightly different form. Brooding on what he saw as various injustices, Columba made his way back across the mountains to his people in the north. He raised the warriors of the Cenél Conaill and the Cenél nÉogain and, along with the King of Connacht and his army, went to war with King Diarmait.

The forces met at the field of Cúl Dreimhne in the shadow of Ben Bulben, a sacred hill in County Sligo. The encounter came to be known as the Battle of the Books.

As dawn broke, Diarmait marched his warriors three times round a sacred cairn. His Druid, Friochán, then conjured up an *airbhe* or 'Druid-mist' – a sort of supernatural smokescreen. Manipulation of the weather was a Druidic stock-in-trade and magical mists are a familiar feature of Irish lore. The *Annals of the Four Masters* would later refer to the 'Erbhe Druadh' at the Battle of the Books and cite Columba's prayer: 'O God, wilt thou not drive off the fog … which envelops our number?'

Only the night before, St Columba had received a visit from the Archangel Michael, who promised him victory on the morrow but demanded a sacrifice in return. The battle turned into a rout. King Diarmait lost many men – accounts written by churchmen put the number at anything up to 3,000 – while on Columba's side there was only one casualty: 'Mag Laim was his name, for it was he that passed beyond the Erbhe Druadh.'

Columba's illicit copy of the Scriptures was encased in silver and ever after carried into battle at the head of the Cenél Conaill, becoming the reliquary known as the *Cathach* or 'Warrior' Psalter.

When the dust had settled a Synod was held during the annual fair at Teltown in County Meath. Columba was blamed for the massive loss of life at Cúl Dreimhne. As his hagiographer, Adomnán of Iona, put it, Columba was 'excommunicated for some trivial and quite excusable offences by a synod that, as eventually became known, had acted wrongly'. Whether or not leading an armed insurrection against the King of all Ireland was a trivial matter, Columba had to be punished. Arriving late at the hearing, he managed to get his sentence reduced by undertaking to win as many souls for Christ as had perished at the Battle of the Books.

Politics had played a part here: Columba belonged to a powerful faction and Diarmait could not risk an explosion of tribal violence. But Columba was also a firebrand, a noble trouble-maker, and so he was exiled to a remote colony.

Two years after his abortive uprising, Columba and his band of followers set sail from Lough Foyle in a curragh (a buoyant coracle of stout branches wrapped in hides), which Columba christened *Dewy-Red*. A verse entitled *Columba's Farewell to Ireland* – an echo of Deirdre's heartfelt *Farewell to Alba* – captured the saint's distress as he drifted away from his native shores:

How swift is the speed of my coracle,
Its stern towards Derry;
I grieve at my errand over the noble sea,
Travelling to Alba of the ravens,

My foot in my sweet little coracle,
My heart still bleeding.

He was sailing to the Coastland of the Gael and the wild hinterland of the Picts, where the Druidic practice of raven-knowledge was rife.

His first port-of-call was Dunadd, the seat of the Scottish kings on the Kintyre peninsula, where he met with his cousin, Conall son of Comgall.

After the 'complete disappearance' of Gabrán in 559 the throne of Dalriada passed to Conall, the son of Gabrán's elder brother. Conall mac Comgaill belonged to the more pacific line of early Scottish kings stretching back to Fergus Mór and was probably inclined towards Christianity. With Conall as king, the Scots remained subdued in their west-coast enclave, under the thumb of Bruide and his tattooed Picts.

Conall gave Columba permission to establish his monastic headquarters on the Isle of Iona, where Fergus Mór had previously built a church. It would prove to be an epoch-making decision with huge consequences for the future of Scotland.

Columba and his warrior-monks set sail again, ploughing up the coast of Kintyre to the rocky Garvellachs, where Columba's old school-friend St Brendan had founded a settlement. The monks then steered westwards, hugging the southern coast of the Isle of Mull until they caught their first glimpse of the island which would be Columba's home for the rest of his days. One of the brothers cried out '*Sùt i!*' – 'There it is!' – to which Columba replied, 'So be it, and let it be called I.'

The eighth letter of the Gaelic alphabet, *I*, meant 'it' or 'she' and was styled after *iubhar*, the yew-tree. The Isle of Iona was the 'yewy' isle. It now became *Ì Chaluim Chille*, the 'Island of Columba of the Church', or Icolmkill, as Shakespeare would spell it in his tragedy of *Macbeth*.

St Columba uttered a prophetic verse:

I behold Iona:
A blessing on each eye that sees her!
He who does a good for others here
Will find his good redoubled many-fold!

The boat named *Dewy-Red* slipped quietly into a shingly bay at the south end of the island. It was a moonlit night in May, in the year 563.

Manus O'Donnell wrote in the sixteenth century that the landing party was met by two bishops of the isle who:

came to lead Columba by the hand out of it … But God revealed to Colum Cille that they were not true Bishops, whereupon they left the island to him when he told them of their history and true adventures.

This account is somewhat at odds with the traditional tale, which has Columba arriving by chance on a desert isle. As for the two bishops of the island who turned out to be 'not true Bishops', their status was hinted at by the eighth-century *Martyrology of Óengus*, which referred to the 'seven bishops of Hii'. There were no bishops in the Church of St Columba. The seven bishops of Iona must have belonged to a different order altogether.

Columba almost certainly timed his arrival to coincide with the festival of Beltane. Five years had passed since Arthur had been conceived during the Beltane festivities in Lothian. According to tradition, Áedán mac Gabráin had been wearing women's clothing when he seduced his cousin Creirwy, the Scottish prince having joined the Gaelic equivalent of the 'seven Hathors' of ancient Egypt who wore the white linen robes of the goddess cult. The 'seven bishops' of Iona were almost certainly the same as the 'seven Hathors' of the pagan tradition to which Áedán was devoted.

These cross-dressing 'bishops' were offensive to St Columba, whose purpose in coming to Dalriada was to undo the damage that had been done when Áedán fathered Arthur and brought the wrath of the Picts down on his people.

But Columba's resentment went further. He would have known that the child born to Áedán and Creirwy had been fostered with Cai son of Conchrad in Dyfed, and Cai was the brother-in-law of Columba's royal enemy, King Diarmait mac Cerbaill of Ireland.

Columba's mission was to stamp out the age-old paganism practised by Áedán and his family. The saint landed on Iona while the seven priests of Áedán's sect were preoccupied with the Beltane fires, which roared on the west side of the island. The Druids were caught off-guard. Outnumbered, they were forced to vacate the isle. If certain traditions are to be believed, Columba made use of their bonfires to burn their sacred scrolls and manuscripts.

The Dove of the Church was described as an 'island soldier'. His monks were men of war, as an old Irish verse recalls:

Wondrous the warriors who abode in Hi,
Thrice fifty in the monastic rule,
With their boats along the main sea,
Three score men a-rowing.

St Columba had brought a small army with him. Supported by these soldiers of Christ, some of whom were his kinsmen, Columba reminded the pagan priests that their activities had led to the death of their king and the loss of the lands that had been promised to them by St Patrick. They also wore female robes and worshipped a cow-goddess. Columba's aversion to the cult was summarised in a saying attributed to him: '*Far am bi bó bidh bean, 's far am bi bean bidh mallachadh*' –

'Where there is a cow there will be a woman, and where there is a woman there will be witchcraft.' Columba's monastery relied on cattle; it was not the beasts themselves that the saint despised so much as those men and women who venerated the goddess – be she Hathor or Boand or Brighid – in bovine form.

Áedán and his pagan 'bishops' were consequently banished from the isle.

St Columba built his chapel a little to the north of the present-day abbey which stands on the east side of Iona. He created his sacred precinct by digging a symbolic ditch or *vallum*. Crude cells were constructed to house the brethren. The community had to be self-sustaining: the monks fished and farmed, growing corn on the rich, sandy machair of the island's west coast, about a mile from the monastery; workshops provided them with tools and materials.

When his compound was fully established Columba felt ready to undertake his mission to Bruide of the Picts. In the words of an Anglian churchman, the Northumbrian historian known as the Venerable Bede, 'Columba arrived in the ninth year of the reign of the powerful Pictish king, Bruide son of Meilochon; he converted that people to the Faith of Christ by his preaching and example, and received from them the island of Iona on which to found a monastery.' The monastery was in fact already founded when, in 565, Columba set out to meet with Bruide son of Maelgwyn.

His journey took him by sea to Loch Linnhe and then up the Great Glen, passing Loch Lochy and the long, deep lake which took its name from Naoise, the Druid of Nechtán. On the banks of Loch Ness, Columba and his company came across a party of Picts burying a man who had been savaged by the monster of the lake. Columba ordered one of his men to swim across the loch. The lake-monster rose to the surface, its jaws open wide as it raced towards the swimming monk. Columba called out from the shore: 'Go no further. Do not touch the man. Go back at once.' Duly chastened, the monster slipped back into the depths and has remained elusive ever since.

St Columba proceeded north to a thickly forested hill just west of Inverness. Even then, King Bruide's headquarters were 1,000 years old. The hill fort of Craig Phadrig had been reoccupied when Bruide made it his northern capital. Its outer walls rose to a height of 8m, the masonry fused by fire to form solid stone ramparts up to 6.5m thick.

The gates were firmly closed – word of the saint's peremptory dealings with the Nechtán cult at Loch Ness had spread. But Columba had a voice 'so loud and melodious that it could be heard a mile away' and he treated the fortress to a booming rendition of the forty-fourth psalm. The gates opened, and Columba entered Bruide's stronghold.

There followed a contest between Columba and Bruide's Chief Druid, Briochan (from *briogadh* – 'pricked' or 'tattooed'; the name compares with that of Diarmait's

Druid, Friochán). Briochan drew milk from a bull; Columba turned it into wine. The Druid also refused to release an Irish slave-girl so Columba subjected him to a painful seizure, which he cured by means of a pebble of white quartz. The whole affair smacked of Druidic wizardry from start to finish. Naturally, Columba won. 'From that day forth,' wrote Adomnán in his *Life of St Columba*, 'for as long as he lived, the ruler [Bruide] treated the holy and venerable man with great honour as was fitting.'

The Christian accounts are only interested in Columba's conversion of the Picts. They have nothing to say about the real purpose of his diplomatic mission. The birth of Arthur had soured relations between the Scots and their Pictish neighbours. Now, Columba had come to talk peace with King Bruide.

The traditional way of securing a treaty was to offer hostages whose lives would be forfeit if the deal broke down. Columba would also need an interpreter to help him communicate with Bruide. To fulfil both functions – translator and hostage – Columba took with him a noble youth of mixed parentage. He was the half-British, half-Pictish child of Cynon son of Clydno, and he was the cousin of Arthur.

His name was Drust – a name borne by many a King of the Picts. The Scots came up with their own version of the name, adding the familiar suffix to form Drostán. This was rendered in the British tongue as Drystan which, under the influence of French romancers, became the 'Tristan' of the legends.

Dating from the ninth century, the *Book of Deer* contains Latin gospels, samples of Old Irish script and the oldest Gaelic texts in existence. One of these describes the founding of the early abbey at Old Deer in Aberdeenshire.

The story goes that Columba had travelled with St Drostán from the Isle of Iona to Buchan in north-east Scotland, where he was granted the village of Aberdour by 'Bede the Pict'. Columba found a place he preferred at Deer – from the Early Irish *dair*, meaning 'oak' – but Bruide refused to give the site to Columba. Bruide's son then fell ill, and in order to purchase prayers for his son's recovery Bruide granted Columba the land 'from the stone in Tiprat to the stone of the town of Mac-Gartnait'. Columba left St Drostán in charge of the settlement and a monastery was established: it was replaced by a Cistercian abbey in 1213.

The *Aberdeen Breviary*, which dates from 1507, relates that St Drostán was of the royal line of the Scots and St Columba was his uncle. The fourteenth-century Scottish historian John of Fordun stated that Drostán was a great-grandson of Áedán mac Gabráin and his father was a prince of Dyfed in Wales. Other sources suggest that Drostán was the brother of Áedán's mother. In fact, Áedán's mother was a sister of Goleudydd, the mother of Creirwy and Cynon and, therefore, the grandmother of Drostán. Áedán's affair with Creirwy meant that Drostán effectively became his nephew. At the time of Columba's diplomatic mission, the father of Drostán was indeed a prince in Dyfed. Cynon son of Clydno had escaped to

St David's Head in south-west Wales when he was hounded out of Lothian by Morgan the Wealthy. This was imperfectly recalled by Gottfried von Strassburg who, in his romance of *Tristan*, written in about 1200, claimed that Tristan's father had been killed by 'Duke Morgan'.

The legends of 'Sir Tristan' grew up alongside those of Arthur. Tradition maintains that Tristan was a prince of the lost land of Lyonesse. Some have imagined Lyonesse to be a submerged island off the south-west coast of Britain, convincing themselves, as usual, that Arthur and his cronies all haunted the south. But Lyonesse lay nowhere near the Cornish coast. The name was a medieval variant of *Leonais*. British refugees who settled in the Brittany region of north-west France after their Lothian kingdom had fallen to the Angles fondly remembered their homeland as the 'Land of the Lion' – *Leonais* – which became the Lyonesse of romantic fame.

The Tristan of the legends was therefore associated, quite properly, with the 'lost' Lothian kingdom of his grandfather, Clydno of Edinburgh.

For the sake of clarity, we shall henceforth refer to the son of Cynon ap Clydno by his British name – Drystan. He was the son of a Pictish mother and a British father, and his royal blood, Lothian connections and relationship to Áedán the Wily made him useful to St Columba. He accompanied the Dove of the Church to Bruide's northern capital, partly to act as an interpreter and partly as a bargaining counter in Columba's peace negotiations. Drystan remained behind as a hostage when Columba returned to the Isle of Iona. He settled at Old Deer and founded a religious community. His life would have been forfeit had the Scots reneged on the terms of the treaty agreed between Bruide and Columba.

Drystan was eventually joined in Aberdeenshire by another early saint or two, one of them being Fergus, who became his inseparable companion. His familiarity with the north-east region would come in handy many years later when Arthur launched his final military campaign.

Six years had now passed since the birth of Arthur. At last, the Scots could breathe freely again. The dark clouds which had loured over Argyll since the death of Gabrán and the migration before King Bruide were finally dispersed. But peace came with a price-tag. Áedán and his pagan priesthood had lost ground to Columba of the Church. The battle for the soul of Scotland would rage for years to come and it would claim the life of many a hero, including the greatest of them all – the man they called Arthur.

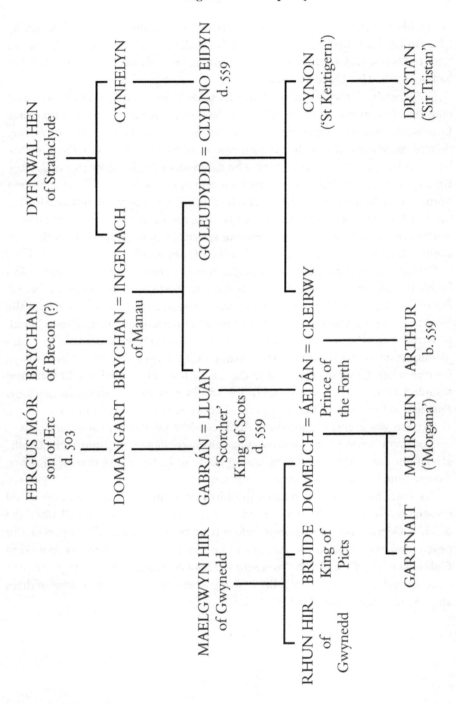

Figure 1 The Descent of Arthur

TWO

DUKE OF BATTLES

'What is certain is this, that Arthur, youth though he was,
was declared King of the Britons. But his natural endowment
was of the noblest: he was fair and beautiful to look on,
of a most chivalrous spirit, and none was more ambitious
of warlike renown.'

John Mair, *History of Greater Britain*, 1521

8

LITTLE-SHOUT

ARTHUR WAS in his seventh year when Columba met with King Bruide. In that same year – 565 – Columba's Irish enemy, King Diarmait, was killed. Diarmait mac Cerbaill died in battle, slain by Áed Dub ('Black Áed') mac Suibne, King of the 'Pictish' Dál nAraidne tribe of Ulster. According to some accounts, Black Áed was Diarmait's foster-son and the High King of Ireland died a ritualistic triple-death: he was burned, drowned and crushed by a falling roof-beam.

The three-fold death was a form of sacrifice reserved for powerful individuals. There was a spate of these killings during Arthur's lifetime and in the aftermath of his death, a fact that can be interpreted in two ways. On the one hand, the triple-deaths of various princes could be seen as an indication that the pagan tradition was alive and well. Equally, such ritualistic violence could point to a way of life that was in crisis. The death of King Diarmait in Ireland spoke not only of the Celtic belief in the inevitability of fate, but also of a society that was at war with itself and clinging to old certainties in the face of a new world order. The pagan gods were being ousted by the worshippers of Christ. Whether the old gods demanded these human sacrifices or the new religion prescribed such deaths as punishment for eminent unbelievers is a moot point.

The death of King Diarmait would have been mourned by Arthur and his intimate circle in south-west Wales. Arthur's adoptive family had been closely related to the Irish High King – his foster-brother Cai was Diarmait's brother-in-law. At the same time, Diarmait's demise was a boon to St Columba in his dealings with Bruide. The High King of Ireland had been killed by the 'Pictish' allies of the Scots and Columba would surely have used this point to illustrate the value of a truce between Bruide's Picts and the Scots of Dalriada. Columba no doubt saw fit to remind Bruide of Diarmait's words: 'Woe to him who contends with the clergy of the churches.'

Diarmait's timely death strengthened St Columba's position and helped him to restore peaceful relations between the Scots and Bruide's Picts. Bruide's half-brother, Rhun the Tall, was presumably satisfied with the arrangement because he allowed Arthur and his family to move north from their exile in Dyfed and set up new homes in Gwynedd.

The Scottish legends of St Kentigern indicate that Arthur's uncle, Cynon son of Clydno, made his way from the settlement at St David's in Dyfed to the old Roman fort of Varis near the coast of North Wales. He was credited with founding a religious community of his own on the River Elwy in Denbighshire. This settlement was then taken over by a British prince whose sister was stepmother to Rhun of Gwynedd. The name of this prince was Asaph, and the monastery became the cathedral town of St Asaph.

The settlement at Llanelwy, which became St Asaph, undoubtedly had connections with St David's community in South Wales: it was named after St Ailbe of Emly, an Irish bishop of Munster who is said to have baptised St David and is commemorated in the hamlet of St Elvis in Dyfed. The likelihood is that an existing community in North Wales was taken over and converted, though not necessarily by Arthur's uncle, and it is interesting to note that the feast day which celebrated St Asaph's deposition fell on 1 May – the pagan festival of Beltane.

St Asaph still honours its Arthurian heritage. The town is twinned with Bégard in Brittany. *Bégard*, a Breton word, means 'Bear'.

Cynon had almost certainly spent time previously in Gwynedd before the war of the 550s. His sister also enjoyed something of a homecoming. Creirwy returned to the long lake of Llyn Tegid where she had initiated the Chief Bard Taliesin some two decades earlier. Her task now was to oversee Arthur's education. Arthur and his foster-brother Cai moved into an old Roman auxiliary fort, which stood near the village of Llanuwchllyn at the southern end of the lake. The place is still known as *Caer Gai* – 'Cai's Fort'.

From about the age of 7 Arthur commenced the Druidic training that would turn him into one of the occasional or 'frivolous' bards of the Island of Britain. He was schooled in the arts of poetry and prophecy under his mother's supervision, and it was during this time that he befriended one of the most intriguing and most misunderstood figures in British tradition: the fellow we would come to know as 'Merlin'.

The character of Merlin is an archetype. Like the original Mentor, who advised the son of Odysseus in Homer's *Odyssey*, he is thought of as a Wise Old Man, ancient and all-knowing. We often imagine him as tall and willowy, with a long white beard and pointy hat, trailing the immature Arthur in his wake and straining, with a greater or lesser degree of patience, to turn the boy into the king he must become. Compared with that familiar image, the real Merlin comes as a bit of a shock. He was neither tall nor much older than Arthur, and his name was not Merlin.

It was the twelfth-century master of confusion Geoffrey of Monmouth who, in his *History of the Kings of Britain*, laid a false trail for future scholars by locating

Arthur's conception at Tintagel in Cornwall. That was bad enough. But where Geoffrey really excelled himself was in mixing up two entirely different individuals to create a sort of hybrid, which he called 'Merlin'.

There are no references to a Merlin in the early sources. The name was a corruption of Myrddin (pronounced 'mer-thin'), which meant something like 'crazy man' or 'fool'. Geoffrey of Monmouth was writing for a largely French-speaking audience that might have detected a faint whiff of *merde* in the name Myrddin, so Geoffrey sanitised it, possibly drawing on the Welsh word for a 'pony' – *merlyn*. By a strange coincidence, the hunting bird known as the merlin is classed as *Falco columbarius*, which would appear to make Merlin the hawkish enemy of Columba, the Dove of the Church.

The Welsh *Triads* or *Trioedd Ynys Prydein* ('*Triads of the Island of Britain*') are a series of mnemonics, preserved in medieval manuscripts, which helped to remind poets and storytellers of the old legends. Most of the *Triads* refer to Arthur and his contemporaries: one, for example, tells us that Arthur was one of the three 'occasional' bards of the Island of Britain, while another lists the 'Three Skilful [or 'Baptismal'] Bards' as:

Myrddin son of Morfryn,
Myrddin Emrys,
and Taliesin.

The Chief Bard Taliesin was also known, at one point, as Myrddin:

Other bards have called me Myrddin,
But soon all kings shall call me Taliesin

So, clearly, the term was not applied exclusively to one person. Anyone who was deemed to be inspired by a form of divine madness might have qualified as a 'myrddin'. But two such crazy men were especially remembered. They were Myrddin son of Morfryn and Myrddin Emrys. Typically, Geoffrey of Monmouth plumped first of all for the wrong one.

He told the story of the Myrddin who was also known as Emrys in his bestselling *Historia Regum Britanniae*. The tale begins with Vortigern, the 'proud tyrant' famous for having secured the support of Germanic mercenaries, an arrangement he sealed by marrying the daughter of the leader of the Saxons of Kent. As more and more foreigners poured into the country the Britons summoned the Saxon chiefs to a conference. Geoffrey of Monmouth stated that this was held at the 'Cloister of Ambrius' – probably Amesbury, near Stonehenge. The Saxons carried concealed weapons into the meeting. At a given signal, they fell upon their hosts. Vortigern survived but was compelled to yield yet more territory to his former allies.

Vortigern's counsellors advised him to build an 'immensely strong tower' as an emergency retreat. A suitable site was found in the mountains of Wales. Geoffrey of Monmouth called it Mount Erith, from *Yr Wyddfa*, the Welsh name for Mount Snowdon. In a parallel account, written 300 years before Geoffrey put pen to paper, a Welsh monk gave the site of the proposed stronghold as Dinas Emrys, the Fortress of Emrys, where a hill was indeed fortified in the post-Roman era, a short distance from Mount Snowdon.

Work on the 'immensely strong tower' did not go smoothly. The foundations repeatedly disappeared. So Vortigern's advisers told him to find a 'lad without a father' whose blood would appease the restless spirits of the hill. Men were sent out in all directions, and in south-east Wales a boy was found who 'never had a father'. The boy's mother, a daughter of the King of Dyfed, confirmed that she had been impregnated by a handsome stranger, a demon who came to her when she was serving in a sacred sisterhood.

The fatherless boy was brought before Vortigern and told of the fate that awaited him. Undaunted, the boy challenged the king's wise men to explain why the foundation stones kept vanishing. When they failed to do so, the lad delivered his own prophecy. Two dragons, he said, were sleeping in an underground pool. The red dragon symbolised the Britons, the white dragon representing the Saxons, and whenever the two were roused from their slumbers they attacked each other savagely. This subterranean struggle was the reason why Vortigern had been unable to build his refuge, and for as long as the red and white dragons were locked in their ceaseless battle the tower would never be finished.

Geoffrey of Monmouth wrote that the fatherless boy was Merlin 'who was also called Ambrosius'. The earlier Welsh account quoted the boy as saying, "'I am called Ambros (in British Embresguletic)'" and, in reply to the king's question, "What is your origin?" remarked, "A Roman consul was my father."'

The legend belongs to the fifth century – 100 years before the time of Arthur – and concerns a Myrddin whom Arthur could not possibly have known.

The lad who 'never had a father' turned out to have been the son of a Roman consul. His name was Ambrosius, or 'Lord Ambrose', as the Britons thought of him. St Gildas, in his *De Excidio et Conquestu Britanniae*, had recalled that the Britons were led to victory at the siege of Badon Hill in about the year 493 by a 'modest man' named Ambrosius Aurelianus, whose parents had belonged to the Romano-British nobility.

Another Ambrosius fought in a battle of 437 at Hampshire, near the south coast of Britain. The indications are that this earlier battle was the result of an uprising in which the Romanised party, with the support of the Church, rebelled against Vortigern, the High King of Britain. Distracted by their internal squabbles, the Britons were easy prey for the Germanic immigrants. The elder Ambrosius appears to have died in about 442 – poisoned, according to some accounts – leaving his son without a father.

As the son of Vortigern's rival, the younger Ambrosius might have made a fitting sacrifice to consecrate the hill on which the 'proud tyrant' wished to build his stronghold. The boy surprised everybody by exhibiting the strange behaviour of a myrddin and prophesying the eventual defeat of the Saxons. He later made good on his promise by rallying the Britons and leading them to a famous victory at Badon Hill, after which – as St Gildas observed – there were several decades of peace, marred only by those all-too familiar 'civil troubles'.

The 'Merlin' of Geoffrey's *History of the Kings of Britain* was, therefore, Ambrosius Aurelianus, the hero of the siege of Badon Hill. The Badon Hill battle is regularly confused with a later Battle of Mount Badon, at which Arthur fought, and Geoffrey only added to the muddle by inventing yet another character called Aurelius Ambrosius, whom he claimed was the brother of 'King Utherpendragon'. Thus, in a febrile attempt to make the pieces fit, Geoffrey wreaked havoc with history.

Geoffrey's first Merlin appeared in his great work of about 1137. He was based on a Romano-British warlord of the fifth century and given a wholly fictitious connection to Arthur's family.

Some years later, Geoffrey of Monmouth discovered the other Myrddin. This might have had something to do with Geoffrey's appointment as Bishop of St Asaph in North Wales. Although there is no evidence that Geoffrey ever visited his See, it is a striking fact that his association with the diocese reputedly founded by Arthur's uncle led to him writing a new version of the Merlin story. It appeared in 1150 and was known as *Vita Merlini*, the 'Life of Merlin'.

Geoffrey's revised account drew heavily on the traditions of the Old North concerning an individual known as Myrddin Wyllt, the 'wild crazy man' whose haunt was the forested region of the southern uplands of Scotland. The *Triads* name Morfryn as the father of this Myrddin, and there was a historical Morfryn who was descended from that venerable Duke of Britain, Old King Coel. Morfryn ('Sea-Hill') was a prince of North Britain. He married a princess of Dyfed – Aldan was her name – and settled in North Wales as a client of Maelgwyn of Gwynedd. Maelgwyn granted Morfryn the cantref of Arllechwedd, just across the River Conwy from Maelgwyn's royal court at Deganwy.

Morfryn was designated *brych*, which implies that he was 'speckled' or tattooed in the Druidic fashion. To some, this gave him a dark and forbidding aspect, and his preference for wearing the hide of a stag only added to his animalistic nature. In Wales, his name was altered slightly, from Morfryn to Morfrân (meaning 'Cormorant'), and he was given the epithet 'Skilful' in recognition of his Druidic abilities. It was he who had surrendered his place in the queue for the cauldron ordeal when Creirwy opted to initiate her cousin Gwyn instead.

In some respects, Geoffrey of Monmouth was right: the genuine 'Merlin' was fathered by a hairy man on a princess of Dyfed. So daunting was Morfrân to look at that he would be one of the few survivors of Arthur's last battle – 'everyone thought he was a devil attending'. He was a powerful presence in North Wales, an accomplished Druid who was associated with Arthur's mother long before Arthur himself was born, and his name is found on a list of the twenty-four horsemen of Arthur's Round Table.

His son would become world-famous, although he would not be known as Merlin until many years after his death. Neither was he known as Myrddin until after he had gone mad. Before then, he was called Menwaedd (pronounced 'menoo-aye-th') or Menw for short.

The *Triads* recall that Menwaedd of Arllechwedd was one of the 'Three Battle-Horsemen of the Island of Britain'. As Menw son of Teirgwaedd he was also one of the three 'Enchanters of the Island of Britain', and one of the 'Three Great Enchantments' was that of 'Uthyr Pendragon (which he taught to Menw son of Teirgwaedd)'. Menw was also named on a medieval list of the twenty-four horsemen of the Court of Arthur: he was one of three 'Enchanter Knights' who could change themselves 'into the form they wished when hard-pressed'. Menw's shape-shifting abilities were on display in the ancient Arthurian tale of *Culhwch and Olwen*, a story in which he turns himself into a bird and weaves a charm of concealment so that Arthur's men can see everyone and nobody can see them. The shortened form of his name – Menw (pronounced 'men-oo') – would appear to derive from the Welsh *mân*, meaning 'puny' or 'small'.

There was a role in Celtic society for those who were short in stature but big in heart. It was that of the *rìogdruth* or 'king's fool'. Such exotic souls are encountered in early Irish literature: they include the musical and prophetic dwarves Fer Fí and Cnú dheireil from the *Book of Leinster* and the *Colloquy of the Ancients*, and Aedh, the king's dwarf who acts as an envoy and go-between in the *Death of Fergus*. In *The Battle of Allen*, a fool named Úa Maigléine is taken prisoner along with his king, and before his execution Úa Maigléine is goaded by his captors into making a 'fool's shout', a 'loud and melodious' noise which was the speciality of the king's fool.

A similar sort of ritualistic bellowing was practiced by poets and prophets in Wales. Writing in the twelfth century, Giraldus Cambrensis – he who conjured up the myth that Glastonbury was the Isle of Avalon – reported that there were certain persons in Wales 'whom you will find nowhere else, called *Awenyddion* or people inspired; when consulted upon any doubtful event, they roar out violently, are rendered beside themselves, and become, as it were, possessed by a spirit.' *Awen* is the Welsh word for 'poetic inspiration'; *awenyddion* simply means 'poets'.

The 'fool's shout' was a means of inducing a trance-like state. Sustained howling would expel oxygen from the lungs, producing semi-consciousness, a feeling of ecstasy and the dissociation necessary for communing with the unseen powers. It is worth noting that St Columba gained entry to King Bruide's hilltop fortress near Inverness by demonstrating his 'loud and melodious' voice – a gift he had no doubt acquired as part of his poetic training. It is also illuminating to discover that the father of the 'puny' Menw was given the nickname Teirgwaedd, meaning 'Triple-Shout' or 'Bright-Shout'. Menw himself was properly known as Menwaedd, the Battle-Horseman of Arllechwedd. Menwaedd translates as 'Little-Shout'.

Even before he lost his wits and became Myrddin Wyllt, the Wildman of the Woods, Menw belonged to a family of inspired shouters. The fourteenth-century *Red Book of Hergest* contains a poem, entitled 'The Discourse of Myrddin and Gwenddydd his Sister', in which Myrddin's twin refers to her 'far-famed' brother as Llallogan or 'Little One of Honour'. The conversation between Myrddin and his sister took place in southern Scotland, where Myrddin was remembered as Lailoken or Laleocen, two variants in the Scots dialect of the Welsh Llallogan. It was as Lailoken that Myrddin appeared in a twelfth-century *Life of St Kentigern*, and in that account Myrddin's sister was identified as Languoreth or Languueth, both being corruptions of the Welsh *glân gwaedd* or 'Pure Shout'.

As the son of a distinguished Druid, Menw was a candidate for initiation into the cauldron cult. The revival of the cult in the 560s, when Creirwy returned to Llyn Tegid, gave Menw the chance to follow in his father's footsteps. He underwent his own cauldron ordeal. His forehead was shaved and emblazoned with the tattoos which announced that he was a 'salmon of wisdom'. He also received a graduation gift from the goddess of the cult. It was a wolf-cub.

Menw and his animal familiar became inseparable. As Myrddin Wyllt he addressed some of his poems to his lupine companion. Geoffrey of Monmouth, in his *Life of Merlin*, would present the crazy man as wearing wolf-skins, a faithful grey wolf by his side.

Just as a young wolf was presented to 'Little-Shout' by the mistress of the cauldron, so a young eagle was gifted to another graduate of the college at Llyn Tegid. The *Triads* refer to the recipient of the eagle as Breat or Brennach, a 'Prince of the North' and an 'Irishman of the North'. It is possible that the name Brennach was related to the Welsh *brenin*, a 'king', or *brân*, a 'raven', both designations being applicable to Arthur. Alternatively, Breat and Brennach might derive from the Gaelic *Breatunn*, a 'Briton' (also *Breatunnach* – 'British'), in which case the 'Irishman of the North' was also a British prince.

Arthur was a British prince and an 'Irishman of the North' whose cauldron initiation would have taken place at around the same time as Menw's. It is perfectly feasible that the young eagle was Arthur's graduation gift and the creature thought best to exemplify his personal qualities. The eagle was associated with far-ranging vision, raptorial speed and high, lonely places; it was also the symbol of imperial power and held sacred to Jupiter or Zeus, the Roman legions having marched behind the eagle standard. There could hardly have been a more fitting animal totem for Arthur son of Áedán.

Early British literature does indeed link Arthur with eagles. The poem *Ymddiddan Arthur a'r Eryr* ('*Song of Arthur and the Eagle*') takes the form of a dialogue between Arthur and his dead nephew, who speaks via the medium of an eagle perched at the top of an oak tree. Rather as Myrddin conversed with his wolf in his poetry, Arthur demands answers to various questions of the eagle and the eagle replies, referring to Arthur as 'bear', 'lion' (or 'light') of the west (or 'gladness') and 'exalted *gwyddfa*'. Dating in its current form from about 1150, the *Song of Arthur and the Eagle* clearly recalls a shamanic relationship in which an eagle acted as Arthur's contact with the spirit world.

In another tale from North Wales, Arthur actually takes on the form of an eagle. This is the story of *Math Son of Mathonwy*, in which Arthur's mother is named Arianrhod ('The Sea-Foam Princess') and Arthur is identified as Llew ('Lion') or Lleu ('Light'). Because his mother refuses to provide him with a bride, the boy's uncle creates one for him out of flowers. The flower-maiden is given the name Blodeuwedd — supposedly from *blodau* ('flowers'), although *blodeunwydd* ('beauty') and *bloeddiwr* ('shouter') might also be considered.

Much of what follows in the tale relates to the death of Arthur. His flower-bride falls in love with another man and conspires to kill her husband. But the hero is protected by powerful magic and can only be slain in exceptional circumstances. Tricked by his wife into revealing precisely what might kill him, Llew is lured into a trap. His enemy strikes him with a specially prepared poisoned spear. Instantly, Llew 'flew up in the form of an eagle and gave a fearful scream. And thenceforth he was seen no more.'

However, he is seen again. His uncle sets out to find him. By following a sow he discovers his nephew in eagle-form, rotting away at the top of an oak tree. This was in the Nantlle Valley — formerly Nantlleu or 'Brook of Lleu' — an area thick with ancient hut-circles, immediately to the west of Snowdon, the tallest mountain in Wales. The eagle is coaxed down from its perch, his uncle restores him to human shape, and Llew takes his revenge on his treacherous wife and her lover.

The transformation of the Arthur character into an eagle takes place in circumstances reminiscent of Arthur's fatal wounding, which would suggest that the eagle was Arthur's soul-animal. But Arthur did not die in North Wales. Rather, he was schooled there. The first of his cauldron initiations almost certainly took place in Gwynedd. By its very nature, the cauldron of rebirth required a symbolic death from which the initiate would be resurrected in a new guise — as Little Gwyn was reborn as Taliesin. The *Math Son of Mathonwy* legend blends Arthur's real death with the ritualistic death of his former self in the cauldron ritual, which is perhaps why the tale states that Llew is never seen again after his eagle-transformation, even though he returns in human form to punish his rival.

Arthur completed his training in the region of Mount Snowdon, probably in the secluded valley of Lleu's Brook. In the *Song of Arthur and the Eagle*, he is referred to as 'exalted *gwyddfa*'. The word *gwyddfa* signifies a 'tomb' or 'monument', and the most exalted of them all is the Welsh mountain known as *Yr Wyddfa*. Its English name is Mount Snowdon. According to legend, the mountain is the tomb of a giant who was killed by Arthur. Welsh folklore also insists that the eagles of Snowdonia – *Eryri* in Welsh – are especially adept at predicting triumph or disaster in peace and war.

In contrast to the popular image, the man we now know as Merlin was not Arthur's aged mentor. If anyone fulfilled that role it was Taliesin – in the words of a medieval Welsh poem, an 'excellent magician' – who belonged to the generation of Arthur's parents. Menw, the little enchanter and battle-horseman who became Myrddin Wyllt, was of an age with Arthur. They were close friends and fellow students. Menw joined Arthur's rapidly expanding band of followers.

The core of that group had clustered around Arthur in south-west Wales. Several of his early associates then travelled north from Dyfed to share in his cauldron training. Pedr, King of Dyfed, appears to have spent some time in Gwynedd: he is commemorated at Llanbedrog in north-west Wales, and in the guise of St Pedrog he was regularly depicted in the company of a stag, which could mean that he became a bosom companion to Menw's father, the stag-like Morfrân.

Pedr's son almost certainly underwent the cauldron initiation in North Wales and was given the name Bedwyr ('Birch-tree Man'). This would evolve into 'Sir Bedivere', but originally it related to the Druidic 'Ogham' alphabet, the letters of which were styled after trees. The graduates of the cauldron school were literate, and it is possible that Arthur, the 'occasional' bard, was also given an Ogham name, the likeliest being Gwern ('Alders'). A thirteenth-century Irish poem refers to the alder as the 'very battle-witch of all the woods, the tree that is hottest in the fight'. Related to the birch, the alder-tree is fond of water and bleeds a red dye when it is cut: like Arthur, who was named after a red giant and destined to wear a red-purple robe, the tree was associated with redness.

Another individual who seems to have passed the cauldron test was a prince of south-east Wales known as Cadog. A nephew to Pedr of Dyfed, Cadog would be closely associated with Arthur, both in the Christian accounts of his life (which presented Arthur in a bad light) and in other sources: he is named, for example, as one of the twenty-four horsemen who fought under Arthur's command. Cadog's initiation resulted in him being awarded the Ogham title of 'Hazels' – *Collen* in Welsh – and it was as St Collen that he arrived in a coracle at his parish of Llangollen, a short distance down the River Dee from the college of Llyn Tegid.

St Collen, we might recall, was said to have banished Taliesin (Gwyn ap Nudd) from the Tor at Glastonbury. Although that almost certainly never happened – not at Glastonbury, at any rate – the legend does reflect a certain ambiguity in Collen's relations with his fellow initiates. St Collen is an elusive character, probably because he was more widely known as St Cadog, but he will prove to have been a key player in Arthur's story. In the *Triads* he is cast as a 'Powerful Swineherd' who guarded the sow which presided over the cauldron cult. This same 'sow' presented Menw and Arthur with their animal spirit-guides and tended to Arthur while he was in eagle-form. The sow was the goddess of the cauldron, represented mortally by Arthur's mother, and in addition to bringing forth a wolf-cub and a young eagle in Snowdonia she gave birth to a kitten. The kitten was thrown into the sea, just as the cauldron initiate was set helplessly adrift in a light coracle.

The kitten was St Cadog's graduation gift, the choice inspired by a pun on Cadog's name. The Welsh word for a 'cat' is *cath*, which is also the Gaelic word for a 'battle'. In Gaelic, meanwhile, a 'cat' is *cat*, which sounded the same as *cad*, the Welsh word for 'battle'. As Cadfael, the original form of his name, St Cadog was the 'Battle-Prince', but his nature was feline: he had the propensity to turn, suddenly and viciously, on his comrades.

Menw was a trained bard, a poet and a prophet, but he was not yet the madman known as Myrddin Wyllt. He first had to leave North Wales and travel to the Borders region of what we now call Scotland.

The southern uplands of Scotland were aptly described by the travel writer H.V. Morton as a 'queer compromise between fairyland and battle-field'. They were the densely forested terrain of the Selgovae or 'Hunters' tribe, whose land formed part of the greater kingdom of Lothian. They had been ruled by a prince of Strathclyde until Nudd, the father of Taliesin, was killed during the strife of 559, when the army of Gwynedd marched up through his territory en route to the River Forth. The realm of the Hunters was then seized by the scion of a rival dynasty.

Gwenddolau son of Ceidio was, like Menw, a descendant of Coel the Old, the warlord who had been appointed 'Duke' of North Britain in the last days of the Roman occupation. After the death of Nudd the Generous in 559, Gwenddolau (pronounced 'gwen-thol-eye') became King of the Selgovae. This had not endeared him to the Britons of Strathclyde, who thought of the Selgovae lands as their own. Gwenddolau was also a confirmed pagan and possibly a devotee of the Persian god Mithra; he would be remembered alongside Urien of North Rheged as one of the 'Bull-Protectors of the Island of Britain'.

Menw son of Morfrân journeyed north to the court of his kinsman, Gwenddolau son of Ceidio. He became Gwenddolau's 'king's fool' – a position of honour. Proudly he wore a thick torque of gold around his neck.

But trouble was brewing.

At the age of 14, Arthur was about to get his first taste of battle.

9

MERLIN WENT MAD

A LIST survives of twelve battles fought and won by Arthur. It is neither detailed nor comprehensive, but it appears to have drawn on an earlier document which might have been written by one of Arthur's companions.

It forms part of the *Historia Brittonum*, a '*History of the Britons*' compiled by a Welsh monk, usually known as Nennius, in the first half of the ninth century. Nennius surrounded himself with a great heap of old sources from which he extracted his material. Like Gildas before him, he described the Roman occupation of Britain, the collapse of Roman rule, Vortigern and the Saxon invasion, the tale of the fatherless boy and the dragons, and the British response to the Saxon menace. 'At that time,' he wrote, 'the Saxons greatly increased in Britain, both in strength and numbers ...'

> ... Then it was that the magnanimous Arthur, with all the kings and military force of Britain, fought against the Saxons. And though there were many more noble than himself, yet he was twelve times chosen their commander, and was as often conqueror.

The term Nennius used was *dux bellorum* – 'Duke of Battles'. He went on: 'The first battle in which he was engaged was at the mouth of the River Glein.' And according to the *Triads of the Island of Britain*, it all started because of a lark's nest.

On the north shore of the Solway Firth, a little to the west of the stone circle where Muirgein and Urien of North Rheged consummated their marriage, the remains of a castle overlook the grassy marshlands of the Solway Merse. The stronghold is triangular in shape, its walls reflected in the water of its defensive moat. The ruins are not Arthurian – they are much too late for that – but an earlier fortress stood a short distance to the south of the picturesque remains of Caerlaverock Castle.

The French poet Robert de Boron would aver that Caerlaverock had once been a 'Castle of Maidens'. The castle became the focus of a dispute between Rhydderch the Generous, King of Strathclyde, and Áedán the Wily, the father of Arthur.

Rhydderch, who had previously joined forces with his cousins Nudd and Clydno in launching a raid against Gwynedd in the 550s, was remembered as a Christian king – a 'defender of the faith' – although his marriage to the 'twin' sister of Menw the enchanter raises questions about his Christian credentials. Nonetheless, Christians like St Columba counted the King of Strathclyde as an ally and were happy to use him as a weapon against the pagans.

The lands of the Selgovae tribe abutted Rhydderch's kingdom. Since the death of Nudd the Generous the territory of the Selgovae had been ruled by Gwenddolau son of Ceidio. Rhydderch was eager to reclaim the region for Strathclyde. He began to move his forces up to the border of Gwenddolau's realm, using Christian settlements as a cover for advancing his troops.

Rhydderch appears to have invited Cynon son of Clydno to found a new Christian community north of the Solway. Cynon left North Wales and established his Episcopal seat at Hoddom Cross, beside the River Annan. He was joined there by his son. After seven years spent as a political hostage in Aberdeenshire, Drystan had been freed from his post at Old Deer. He made his way south to take up residence at Holywood, the site of Scotland's largest stone circle, known as the Twelve Apostles.

Drystan's new home stood above the River Nith, which flows south through the town of Dumfries and into the Solway Firth below the fortress of Caerlaverock. 'Laverock' is an old word for a skylark: the Castle of Maidens was also the 'lark's nest' which would be the cause of Arthur's first battle.

Áedán could see what Rhydderch was up to. The crunch came when Rhydderch attempted to convert the 'Castle of Maidens' into a Christian stronghold, which could then be used as a base for landing troops close to Gwenddolau's border. An eighteenth-century edition of the *Triads* noted that the 'shepherds of Rhydderch and Áedán … fell out for no other cause than a lark's nest'. The word for a 'shepherd' in both Welsh and Gaelic is also the word for a 'pastor'. It was a depressingly familiar situation: Britain was prone to 'civil troubles' whenever Christians and pagans quarrelled with each other.

In response to Rhydderch's moves, Gwenddolau took up residence in a fortress close to his western border. This seems to have been interpreted by the Christian faction as a provocation. The upshot was the Action of Arderydd or, as an entry in the *Welsh Annals* described it: 'The Battle of Arderydd, between the sons of Eliffer, and Gwenddolau son of Ceidio; in which battle Gwenddolau fell; and Merlin went mad.'

The battle was fought in 573, when Arthur was 14 years old.

Arderydd survives as the Cumbrian parish of Arthuret, with its two small wooded hills, the Arthuret Knowes. The Victorian historian William Forbes Skene set out to locate the site of the battle and reported his findings to the Society of

Antiquaries for Scotland in February 1865. Skene was inspired by a passage in John of Fordun's fourteenth-century *Life of St Kentigern*, in which Arthur's uncle, then based at Hoddom Cross, was described as having met a wild and hairy man who had lost his wits after failing to defend his chief in a battle '*quod erat in campo inter Lidel et Carwanalow situato*' – 'which took place in the field between Lidel and Carwanalow'.

'Lidel' was not hard to find. It was the Liddel Water, a river which hugs the Scottish border, flowing south-westwards through Liddesdale to the River Esk, which it joins at a place called Willow Pool, below Liddel Strength, near the Cumbrian village of Carwhinley. W.F. Skene was convinced that 'Arthureth' was a medieval spelling of Arderydd (or 'Arfderydd') and that 'Carwanalow' was the village now known as Carwhinley. The Action of Arderydd would, therefore, have taken place between the lower reaches of the Liddel Water and Carwhinley, immediately to the east of the Solway Firth, more or less on the modern-day border between England and Scotland.

At the Graham Arms hotel in Longtown, Skene learnt that 'Carwinelow was the name of a stream which flowed into the River Esk about 3 miles north of Longtown … and that beyond it was a place called the Roman camp.' He insisted on visiting the site and was taken there by an 'old retired guard'. Heading north out of Longtown, Skene and his guide entered a 'ravine through which the burn of Carwinelow flows'. They crossed over a bridge, rode past the farms of Upper and Lower Moat, and half-a-mile on along the bank of the Liddel they came to the supposed Roman camp, also known as the Moat of Liddel or Liddel Strength. Skene described the setting in his *Notice of the Site of the Battle of Arderydd or Arderyth*:

> It is situated on the top of a high bank overhanging the river. On the north side, the rock goes shear down to the river. On the other side it is defended by pro-digious earthen ramparts, which rise from the field to a height of nearly 30 feet [9m]. The space enclosed by the great rampart measured about 38 yards [35m] from east to west, by about 55 yards [50m] from north to south. There is a small inner citadel measuring 13 yards by 9, and also a well in the enclosure, and on the west side there is second great rampart.

Skene took in the magnificent views from the ancient fortress. The Solway Firth stretched out into the Irish Sea to the west; the prospect to the south was domi-nated by the Arthuret Knowes and the Cumbrian hills beyond, while the vales of Esk and Liddesdale extended away to the north. He also recalled that Myrddin Wyllt – the name taken by Menw after he lost his mind – had referred in a poem to 'the action at Arderydd and Erydon'. Skene suspected that the second of these two sites lay adjacent to the Moat of Liddel:

On the east side of the fort the ground slopes down till it comes to the level of the river at a place called Ridding, not quite half a mile off. Between the fort and Carwhinelow is a field extending to the ridge along Carwhinelow, which is about half a mile off. This is the site indicated by Fordun, viz, the ground between Liddel and Carwhinelow. The old farmer of the Upper Moat, who accompanied us, informed me that the tradition of the country was that a great battle was fought here between the Romans, and the Picts who held the camp, in which the Romans were victorious; that the camp was held by 300 men, who surrendered it, and all were put to the sword and buried in the orchard of the Upper Moat, at a place which he showed me.

The shock of the battle still reverberated in the local memory thirteen centuries after the event. Skene's informant was not entirely right: the battle had not been fought between the Romans and the Picts, but between the Romanised, Christian Britons and the tattooed pagans who resembled the native Picts of the far north.

Skene had discovered the place where Gwenddolau son of Ceidio fell and Merlin went mad. As he wrote: 'I have no doubt that the name of Carwhinelow is a corruption of Caerwenddolew, the caer or city of Gwenddolew, and thus the topography supports the tradition.'

In his eighteenth-century edition of the *Triads*, Robert Vaughn noted that 'upon the first encounter Gwenddolau was slain', along with various others including the 'sons of Morfryn', who were the brothers of Menw or 'Merlin Caledonius', and that 'in the end after great slaughter on both sides, Rhydderch obtained the victory, and Áedán fled the country.'

The *Triads* have more to say about the battle. One of the 'Faithful War-Bands of the Island of Britain' was the 'War-Band of Gwenddolau son of Ceidio at Arderydd, who continued the battle there for a fortnight and a month after their lord was slain.' The phrase 'a fortnight and a month' should not be taken too literally: it simply meant that the unhappy war-band held out for some time before surrendering. There is also mention of the noble 'Retinue of Dreon the Brave at the Dyke of Arderydd'. Since Dreon was a son of Nudd the Generous it is probable that he led the assault on Gwenddolau's fortress on behalf of the princes of Strathclyde.

Two more *Triads* point to what happened and the role played by Menw in the downfall of his pagan lord.

The first of these concerns Corvan, the 'horse of the sons of Eliffer', which 'carried on his back Gwrgi and Peredur and Dunod the Staunch and Cynfelyn the Clumsy to look upon the battle-fog of Gwenddolau at Arderydd'.

Eliffer was the British prince who had died defending York against the Angles in 559. His sons, Peredur and Gwrgi, then became the joint rulers of York. Being

Roman in outlook they took sides with Rhydderch of Strathclyde in attacking Gwenddolau. With them were their cousins, Dunod of the North Pennines and Cynfelyn, who governed the 'Chalk Hill' of Kelso in the Scottish Borders: both would be fondly remembered as 'Pillars of Battle'.

The 'battle-fog of Gwenddolau at Arderydd' to which these notable warriors were drawn was also referred to in a poem composed by Llywarch, Lord of South Rheged and cousin to Muirgein's husband Urien:

> The morning with the dawn of day,
> When Mwg Mawr Drefydd was assaulted,
> The steeds of Mechydd were not trained up.

Mwg Mawr translates as 'Big Smoke', while *Drefydd* relates to Arderydd, or its variant spelling 'Arfderydd'. The word *Arfderydd* seems to have been a British attempt at the Gaelic *Erbhe Druadh* – a 'Druid-mist', such as that which St Columba had countered at the Battle of the Books in Ireland, twelve years before the Action of Arderydd.

The Welsh word for a 'Druid' – *derwydd* – forms the second part of Arderydd or Arfderydd, with the first syllable coming from the Gaelic *airbhe*. The battle took its name not from a place but from the 'Druid-mist' for which it became famous. The Britons were taken aback by this 'Big Smoke', probably because it was an alien tactic. We know from the *Triads* that one of the most remarkable enchantments ever seen in Britain was the 'Enchantment of Uthyr Pendragon (which he taught to Menw son of Teirgwaedd)', and so we can suppose that it was Arthur's father who had instructed Menw in the Irish art of raising a Druid-mist.

Whether it was genuinely supernatural or merely a smokescreen created by burning rowan trees, the 'battle-fog' proved to be disastrous. No sooner had Menw deployed it than Dreon son of Nudd attacked, scaling the ramparts under cover of the mist. In the confusion that followed, Gwenddolau was slain, as were Menw's brethren. To his horror, Menw realised that he had caused the deaths of his lord and his brothers.

Arthur's first battle was fought nearby. Tactically, it was an attempt at preventing reinforcements from reaching the forces besieging Gwenddolau's fortress. It came to be known as *Cad Goddau*, the 'Battle of the Trees' – *Goddau* being Taliesin's name for the forest which sprawled across the upland territory of the Selgovae. Its location can be pinpointed with some accuracy.

If Arderydd was named after the 'Druid-mist', then it is probable that the parish of Arthuret took its name from something else – *Arthwyrd*, perhaps: the 'place of Arthur'. Nennius, the Welsh monk who compiled a list of Arthurian battles, noted that the first engagement took place 'at the mouth of the River Glein'. The Welsh *aber*, a 'river-mouth', can also refer to a junction or confluence of rivers.

The River Lyne is formed by the merger of two rivers a short distance to the east of Gwenddolau's hill fort. The Black Lyne rises at Blacklyne Common in the Kershope Forest, the White Lyne appearing a little further to the east near the old Roman fort at Bewcastle. The two rivers meet at the foot of Haggbeck, and thence the Lyne flows westwards, passing to the south of the Arderydd battlefield, to join the River Esk at Lynefoot, near the modern trunk road heading north into Scotland from Carlisle.

The Celtic place name expert W.J. Watson noticed a 'streamlet placed on Blaeu's map near the head of the Solway', which joins the Solway Firth near Westlinton. Published in 1654, Blaeu's map refers to the River Lyne as 'Leuin'. This was an intermediate stage between the 'Glein' of Nennius and today's 'Lyne' and suggests that the river was once known as *Lleuyn*, which would have sounded like 'gley-in' while preserving Arthur's alternative name ('Lleu'). It was near the confluence of this river – the Glein, Leuin or Lyne – that Arthur fought his first battle.

W.F. Skene noted that one of the poems of Myrddin Wyllt mentioned 'the action at Arderydd and Erydon'. He assumed that the Erydon battle was waged immediately to the east of Gwenddolau's fort. But following the Carwinley Burn through the woods at the foot of the moat, and staying with the stream as it scrawls across the mossy plain in a north-easterly direction, we come to a place called Roddingshead. A short distance away, on the same north-east trajectory, sits the hamlet of Catlowdy.

Catlowdy means 'Battle of Lothian'. The settlement is partway up the western flank of Chamot Hill, on the fringes of the Kershope Forest. The hill peaks at a little over 230m and just behind it, hidden in a fold created by the stream of Bartle's Burn, is a place called Arthur Seat.

The Black Lyne rises to the east of Arthur Seat and flows south to meet up with its sister. The White Lyne winds past Noblestown and Scotstown and then runs alongside an incline called Kays Bank on the way to its confluence with the Black Lyne. A little to the west of Kays Bank is the hamlet of Cays House with its Kayshouseburn. Kays Bank and Cays House lie due south of Arthur Seat, the two Lynes meeting in between.

What is notable about the positions of Arthur Seat and Kays Bank is that they are illustrative of a battle tactic that Arthur would repeatedly employ. Arthur took the high ground and concealed his cavalry above the site of the intended ambush. His foster-brother Cai was stationed beyond the confluence of the River Lyne. Arthur's surprise attack would aim to drive the enemy back towards the river, where Cai the Tall was in place to cut off their retreat.

Arthur's trap was laid in the pass through which an army marching up from York would approach the fort of Gwenddolau. The spearmen of York, under Peredur and Gwrgi, along with the warriors of the North Pennines and Kelso, made their way to 'look upon the battle-fog of Gwenddolau' along this very route. But just as

Menw's deployment of the battle-fog backfired, so Arthur's ambush was spoiled by the hasty actions of one of his kinsmen.

Dinogad son of Cynan White-Shank was a prince of Powys. His mother was said to have been 'of the Scots' and so he was probably related to Arthur. Riding on a horse called Swift Roan, Dinogad overtook the sons of Eliffer, an act for which he would win 'censure and dishonour to this day'. Perhaps Dinogad son of Cynan was impatient to get to the battlefield, or maybe he galloped ahead to give Arthur the signal and, in doing so, betrayed Arthur's position.

The 'steeds of Mechydd were not trained up', wrote Llywarch of South Rheged. It is uncertain whether 'Mechydd' referred to *mechderyn* – 'overlord' – or *mebyd*, meaning 'youth', but what does seem clear is that Arthur's horsemen were flushed out of hiding prematurely. They broke cover, racing down the flank of Chamot Hill, and wheeled round through the dragon's marsh ('Drakemyre') to clash with the sons of Eliffer at Kingfield. And so began the Battle of Lothian, after which Catlowdy was named.

Arthur might have been inexperienced – he was only 14 – but his valour and determination were beyond question. The conflict ranged across the plain as Arthur and his band struggled to hold back the armies of the south and to keep them away from Gwenddolau's fort. But the war-ponies soon wearied and besides, the Battle of Arderydd was already lost.

Besieged in the fortress above the Liddel and haunted by terrifying visions of spectral warriors, Arthur's friend Menw went out of his mind.

Both battles were considered futile. Rather than taking the war to their real enemies the Britons were fighting amongst themselves. It fell in part to the Chief Bard Taliesin to repair some of the damage.

After the flight from Lothian in 559, when his 'sweetheart' took her infant son to Dyfed, Taliesin returned to the land where he had grown up and attached himself to the court of King Brochwael of Powys. Brochwael was dead before long, but Taliesin continued to serve his successor, Cynan White-Shank, and no doubt tutored Cynan's son Dinogad. Sooner or later, Taliesin upped sticks again and made his way to the Carlisle court of Urien and Muirgein; it is possible that Dinogad was fostered there and that Taliesin accompanied him as his bard. Taliesin would devote much of his career to extolling the virtues of Urien of North Rheged and his son Owain.

Taliesin had heard the songs of the minstrels and the murmurings of the warriors. There had been much talk about the 'ascendancy of the Briton'. The identity of this Briton is revealed towards the end of Taliesin's *Cad Goddau* poem:

> Druids versed in letters
> Prophesy that Arthur
> Is the longed-for one of the tribe.

Arthur had proven his mettle at the Battle of the Trees. It became Taliesin's task to persuade the British tribes to unite behind the youthful figurehead. If there were to be any hope for the Britons there could never be another 'futile' battle like Arderydd or Catlowdy. Divisions had to be healed.

Over the following winter Taliesin carried the message around the feasting halls of the North, where he performed his latest masterpiece. He had woven together an account of Arthur's first battle, which sought to raise the skirmish to the level of myth. Skilfully blending humour with deference, Taliesin made sure that every noble warrior was honoured, regardless of which side they had been on. The battle had been waged at the 'top' of Goddau, where the Forest of Celidon began, and in Taliesin's vision it was not men who had fought with each other but the forest itself. The participants were all styled after trees, including Arthur, who appeared as 'Gwern':

> Alders, first in line,
> Attacked without hesitation …

In another account of the battle, Arthur – in one of his guises – is recognised by the sprigs of alder on his shield. The warrior named Bedw in Taliesin's poem might well have been the prince of Dyfed, Arthwyr son of Pedr, who became better known as Bedwyr or 'Sir Bedivere':

> Birches of the great breed
> Was late in arraying himself,
> Not from fatigue,
> But because of his greatness …

It is probable that Pedr of Dyfed was also present at the battle, and is remembered at Pedderhill, just east of Gwenddolau's fort.

Taliesin took care to mention chief after chief, each one in the Druidic form of a tree, and we can imagine the cheers and guffaws that greeted each reference. Delicately, the nature of the battle was transformed from a vicious civil conflict to a coming together of elemental forces around the ascendant one, Arthur son of Áedán, the 'longed-for one of the tribe'.

Menw was distraught. Gwenddolau's men had surrendered, and some had been put to death. He was one of those who had been allowed to escape.

He fled north, into the heart of the forest, still plagued by the spirits who blamed him for Gwenddolau's death.

His salvation lay in finding the source of life itself.

The location of his retreat was revealed by Nikolai Tolstoy in his *Quest for Merlin*. Tolstoy retraced the journey made by one Fergus of Galloway as described in a romance of the thirteenth-century. The original Fergus was closely associated with Drystan and quite possibly fought in the battles of 573 (there is a Fergushill just south of the River Lyne). Certainly, the action of the *Fergus* romance is contemporary with Arthur.

As usual, Cai was characterised as an ill-tempered bully. He set Fergus a challenge, and so Fergus departed from the Moat of Liddel – Gwenddolau's fort – and travelled north until he came to a Black Mountain. This, Tolstoy argued, was the eminence known as Hart Fell, just north of the spa town of Moffat.

Partway up the western side of Hart Fell a chalybeate spring wells up through the ground and streams down a gully of its own making to become the River Annan. Hart Fell was, therefore, the birthplace of a river named after the mother-goddess, Anna or Danu. Two more major rivers rise in the vicinity: the Tweed and the Clyde – Hector Boece wrote in the sixteenth century that the Clyde came 'out of the same mountain within the wood of Calidon, from which rises the Annan'. A mountain which gave birth to so many rivers would have seemed like the centre of the world.

Many years later, Geoffrey of Monmouth pictured Merlin as a recluse living beside a spring 'on the very top of a certain mountain, surrounded on all sides by hazels and dense thorns', from which he could 'watch the whole woodland'. The chalybeate spring – which was 'discovered' again in 1748 and quickly became a tourist attraction – provided him with iron-rich water. Menw became Myrddin Wyllt, the Wildman of the Wood who sought solace at the entrance to the womb of the goddess, the place where life began.

He was not utterly alone. His wolf accompanied him, and for a while he enjoyed the presence of a young priestess, the 'little pig' to whom he addressed his poem *Oianau* ('*Greetings*'). And though he would insist that he was hiding from the soldiers of his enemy, Rhydderch of Strathclyde, his forest abode was anything but secret.

His sister Gwenddydd visited him. She was married to Rhydderch. Myrddin – as he must now be called – moaned:

> The battle of Arderydd and Erydon,
> Gwenddydd – my preparations
> Broke the soul of my lord.

His sister replied:

> I greet the little honoured one,
> Myrddin, wise man and prophet,
> Who would not neglect to greet
> A girlish woman.

They then discussed the future.

Taliesin also met with Myrddin – a summit meeting if ever there was one. Geoffrey of Monmouth made much of the time the two poets spent together in the forest, claiming that a 'new spring had appeared in the woods of Celidon', the waters of which restored Myrddin's sanity. Their conversation was preserved in a poem found in the *Black Book of Carmarthen*. Taliesin did his best to reassure Myrddin that 'the pain of the battle of Arderydd will serve its purpose – the hero is already prepared.' To which Myrddin responded:

> Seven times twenty generous ones
> And fearsome warriors
> Pouring into the Celidon wood.
> This be the song of Myrddin Wyllt.
> Taliesin shall make known my prophecy.

Another visitor was the 'longed-for one of the tribe' himself.

Arthur had been almost as badly affected by his first battle as his traumatised friend. He had wintered nearby, inside his half-sister's territory of North Rheged. Loch Arthur lies some distance to the west of the Arderydd battlefield, just beyond the town of Dumfries. On the north side of the lake is an artificial island or 'crannog'. It is some 30m wide and is connected to the shore by a reedy promontory. The crannog had been constructed about a thousand years earlier: stone boulders were piled onto foundations of alder, birch and oak to form an island which would be reoccupied from time to time up till, and throughout, the Middle Ages.

Trosten Hill rears above the east side of Loch Arthur and shares its name with a small hamlet that nestles between the hilltop and the lake. The name came from Arthur's cousin Drystan – or Drostán, as the Scots knew him. Drystan's main settlement at Holywood was not far away, but through the winter of 573/74 Arthur needed his cousin to be closer at hand.

The longed-for one turned 15 as the battle season of 574 loomed. The time came for Arthur to leave his lake-dwelling. He crossed the River Nith above Caerlaverock and struck eastwards until he came to the Roman road which ran beside the River Annan. He followed the road to the old fort at Bearholm and then made his way along the narrowing valley to the foot of Hart Fell.

Arthur's visit to Myrddin's hideaway became the stuff of legend. When Fergus, in the thirteenth-century romance, found the spot where 'Merlin dwelt many a year' he discovered a lion 'carved from ivory' inside a 'marble chapel'. This was echoed in the tales of Arthur's nephew, Owain son of Urien. Owain, it was said, came one day to a 'huge craggy mound, in the middle of the wood'. To the side of the mound was a grey rock. A serpent dwelt in a cleft in this rock, and beside it was a lion which attacked the serpent whenever it emerged from the cleft. Owain killed the serpent, after which the lion became his friend and guardian. In the French version of the legend, Owain is known as the Knight of the Lion, while the Welsh account is subtitled '*The Lady of the Fountain*'. Arthur – as Llew, the 'lion' – had become firmly associated with the cleft in the mountainside, the mineral-rich fountain that gushed from it, and the Druidic 'serpent' who dwelt in the cleft.

When Arthur came to him, Myrddin was obliged to stop moaning and to console someone else for a change. Arthur felt that he had failed at Catlowdy and so he too blamed himself for Gwendddolau's death.

'For the slaughter of my brothers and Gwenddolau,' Myrddin told him, 'the encounter of Rhydderch and Áedán by the bright Clyde will resound from the northern border to the south.'

He promised Arthur that Rhydderch would get his come-uppance. There would be battle upon battle. Arderydd had been only the beginning. He begged Arthur to cheer up, to stop weeping and to get some rest.

He called him *peiryan faban* – 'commanding youth' or the 'son of the cauldron'.

Rhydderch was worried. He had sent his men out to find Myrddin – not to imprison him, as the crazy man feared, but to offer him shelter. The King of Strathclyde was no fool. He knew that Áedán mac Gabráin would be plotting his revenge.

He sent a messenger to the Isle of Iona to meet secretly with St Columba. Rhydderch was anxious to know whether he would be killed by his enemies. After questioning the messenger about the King of Strathclyde and his people, Columba assured him that Rhydderch would die not at the hands of his enemies but peacefully, at home, on his pillow.

Columba, however, faced a serious problem. In the spring of that year – 574 – a bright comet blazed in the sky. A meteor could herald the death of a king, and perhaps Rhydderch had been persuaded to contact St Columba by the sudden appearance of the comet. The Gaels had a name for this type of heavenly portent: *drèag*.

The dragon-tailed comet was indeed an omen. A king was about to die, and a warlord or 'dragon' would take his place, as predicted by the fiery star.

Somehow or other, St Columba had to find a way of restraining Áedán the Wily and the whole pagan tribe of the *Cenél nGabráin*.

10

STONE OF DESTINY

THE YEAR 574 was a busy one for Arthur. The year before, he had fought his first battle above the confluence of the River Lyne in Cumbria. In the next year he would take part in a series of battles.

Nennius, in his ninth-century list of Arthur's military successes, stated that four consecutive battles were fought above another river, 'by the Britons called Dubglas, in the region Linnuis.' Ptolemaeus, a Roman geographer of the second century AD, had given the name *Linnuis* to the Loch Lomond district that became known as Lennox.

No fewer than four 'Douglas' rivers are to be found in the Lennox region (the Old Irish *dubglass* meant 'dark-grey'). The Douglas Water enters Loch Lomond from the west, above the village of Luss. Another Douglas runs from Loch Sloy into Loch Lomond at Inveruglas, the 'mouth of the *dubglas*'. A second Douglas Water joins Loch Fyne below Inverary and a Douglas Muir lies on the outskirts of Glasgow, between Dumbarton and Milngavie.

Not only are there four Douglas rivers to match the four battles fought by Arthur in the Lennox area, but the whole region is dominated by a three-peaked mountain which looms over the town of Arrochar at the head of Loch Long. The right-hand peak is thought to resemble a shoemaker at work and is known as The Cobbler (Arthur and his uncle pose as shoemakers in the Welsh tale of *Math Son of Mathonwy*), but the proper name for the eminence is *Beinn Artair* – 'Arthur's Mountain'. To the south of its rocky summit, the high ridge known as Arthur's Seat formed a vantage point from which the teenage Duke of Battles could survey the land of Lennox.

One of the battles in this region was also one of the 'Unrestrained Ravagings of the Island of Britain'. It took place when 'Áedán the Wily came to the court of Rhydderch the Generous at Alclud [Dumbarton]'. Such was Áedán's fury that he left 'neither food nor drink nor beast alive'. Myrddin had predicted a sonorous clash between Áedán and Rhyddech by the 'bright Clyde'. Taliesin, too, would refer to a battle 'at the ford of Alclud', where the River Leven, running south from Loch Lomond, emptied into the River Clyde at the foot of the Rock of Dumbarton.

This unrestrained ravaging was a punitive raid. Rhydderch had dragged the Britons into a civil war at Arderydd and Catlowdy. Áedán had little choice but to make an example of Rhydderch. A new coalition was rapidly forming around the youthful commander-in-chief – Arthur son of Áedán – and anyone who fomented division and internecine strife would have to be disciplined, or else Britain was doomed.

There can be little doubt that Arthur was present at the Battle of Alclud. The twin-crested Rock of Dumbarton, where Rhydderch held his court, has its own *Suibhe Artair* – 'Arthur's Seat' – while Castle Hill, across the River Leven from Rhydderch's headquarters, was known, at least as far back as the eleventh century, as *Castello Arturius* – 'Arthur's Castle'.

Another battle had been anticipated by the appearance of the dragon-tailed comet in the sky that spring. Myrddin had also foreseen it: a brutal competition to reach the 'hill of the Irish', which we can assume meant Dunadd, the royal seat of the Scottish kings on the peninsula of Kintyre.

The *Annals of Ulster* record that 574 witnessed the 'Death in the sixteenth year of his reign of Conall son of Comgall who granted the island of Ia [Iona] to Colum Chille.' The *Annals of Tigernach* note that the death of Conall, King of the Scots, was followed by a 'Battle of Delgu in Kintyre', in which the son of Conall fell along with 'many others of the followers of the sons of Gabrán'. Áedán's family was fighting for the throne of Dalriada. *Delgu* suggests a place of thorns (from the Old Irish *delg*), and such a place might have been Ardrishaig, the 'Point of the Briar Headland', near Lochgilphead on the shore of Loch Fyne. This was the eastern approach to the hill fort of Dunadd. Ardrishaig could be reached quickly by boat from Dumbarton, or less quickly overland, via Glenkinglas – where there is a rock called *Agaidh Artair*, 'Face of Arthur' – and across the Douglas Water of Kintyre.

The Celtic place name expert W.J. Watson remarked on the existence of an Arthur's Stream (*Sruth Artair*, recorded in 1573 as 'Struarthour') near Kilmichael Glassary, immediately to the east of Dunadd. As this stream is overlooked by the 224-metre peak of Bad nam Beith ('Birch-Grove') it is likely that the conflict was that to which the poet Taliesin referred as the 'battle of the wood of Beit', fought for the placement of the 'hot spear' – that is, to secure the Scottish throne for Áedán mac Gabráin.

Conall mac Comgaill was dead. With the support of his allies, Áedán had battled his way to the 'hill of the Irish'. Only one thing now stood between Arthur's father and the kingship of the Scots: St Columba, who had let it be known that he favoured another candidate.

The succession of the king was not automatically a matter of birthright. Irish tradition speaks of a ritual known as the *tarbfeis* or 'bull-sleep'. A wise man, chosen by lot, would retire to a spirit-haunted spot, often beside the sea, where he would wrap himself in the skin of a freshly slaughtered bull and pretend to sleep. The local spirits would whisper the name of the chosen king to each other, unaware that the sleeping bull was actually a human eavesdropper. The spirits, then, would name the rightful king.

A memory of this ritual survives in one of the strangest tales of the Welsh *Mabinogion*. The *Dream of Rhonabwy* describes a detailed vision of Arthur and his men, which was dreamt by a man who slept on a 'yellow ox-hide' – 'a main privilege was it to any one who should get upon that hide.' St Columba travelled to the island of Hinba for his version of the bull-sleep. The name of the island was lost in the Middle Ages, when the isles of the west came under Scandinavian rule, but there are clues as to the whereabouts of Hinba. It was not very far from Iona and it boasted an impressive inlet or *muirbolc* – literally, a 'sea-bag'.

The Isle of Staffa rises abruptly out of the sea 6 miles north of the Isle of Iona. Its name is of Norse origin and means 'Island of Staves': Staffa is notable for its hexagonal columns of basalt, which were formed by a volcanic eruption. The same columns make up the Giant's Causeway on the coast of County Antrim, so that Staffa is connected to the north of Ireland by an undersea pavement. This, it was said, had been laid by the legendary warrior Fionn mac Cumhail, and it was Fionn who gave his name to Staffa's most famous feature, the dramatic inlet known as Fingal's Cave (Fingal being the Scottish equivalent of Fionn mac Cumhail). Its Gaelic name is *an Uamh Binn* – the 'harmonious' or 'musical cave'.

And musical it is, like a great organ of stone pipes played by the sea. Felix Mendelssohn was inspired to compose his *Hebridean Overture* by the harmonious cave. John Keats remarked: 'For solemnity and grandeur it far surpasses the finest Cathedrall.' The cave, which faces the island of Columba's church, fulfilled all the requirements for a successful bull-sleep.

Columba had hoped for three uninterrupted nights of solitude on the desert isle, after which he would return to Iona and announce that the chosen king was Áedán's brother, Éoganán. Apart from an entry in the *Annals of Ulster* for 595 – 'Death of Éogan son of Gabrán' – we hear nothing more of Éoganán. The likelihood is that he was a foster-brother to Áedán, perhaps Urien of North Rheged. The names Urien and Éogan were effectively the same, both being related to the yew. St Columba, it would seem, had his eye on a candidate for the throne who, if not exactly Christian, would have been a great deal more pliable than Áedán the Wily. Urien would also have been preoccupied with the affairs of North Britain, leaving Columba free to govern the Scottish kingdom in his stead.

But Columba's peace and quiet on the island of Hinba was rudely shattered. According to his hagiographer, Adomnán of Iona, Columba 'saw one night in an ecstatic vision an angel of the lord sent to him.' The angel brought a 'glass book of the ordination of kings', which named Áedán as the natural successor to his cousin, Conall mac Comgaill.

St Columba refused to take orders from a mere 'angel of the lord'; his heart was set on preventing Áedán from becoming king. The angel took out a whip and struck Columba across the face, leaving a permanent scar. It must have been one heck of an 'ecstatic vision'.

The struggle continued over three successive nights. The angel repeatedly visited Columba, demanding that he observe the constitution and lashing him into compliance. Finally, the saint gave way and returned by boat to Iona, where Áedán was waiting.

The ordination of Áedán mac Gabráin by St Columba is the first recorded instance in the British Isles of a king being anointed by a man of the Church. It would be wrong, though, to assume that Columba had any real choice in the matter. Had Columba not been forced by the 'angel' to ordain Áedán, the stubborn saint would have denounced Arthur's father as an illegitimate ruler and plotted to replace him with a puppet-king, just as he had tried to do with King Diarmait mac Cerbaill in Ireland. Not for nothing was Áedán known as the 'Wily'. He had fought his way to the throne of his father and bent the holy man to his will, ensuring that St Columba himself sanctioned his kingship.

Eleven years earlier, Columba and his warrior-monks had stormed Iona during the Beltane festivities and evicted the seven 'bishops' from the isle. The comet which flared in the sky during that spring of 574 was visible (according to Chinese astronomers) from 4 April to 23 May. It is conceivable that Áedán, taking his cue from the heavenly *drèag*, had contrived to become King of the Scots at the time of the pagan May Day festival (the Moon was full on 21 May that year). If so, it was an insult that Columba would neither forgive nor forget.

The sons and followers of Áedán had gathered for the ceremony. 'As he was performing the ordination,' wrote Adomnán of Iona, St Columba 'also prophesied the future of Áedán's sons and grandsons and great-grandsons, and then he laid his hand on Áedán's head in ordination and blessed him.'

There was much more to the ceremony than that, of course. There was, for example, the matter of the sword and the stone.

The Sword-in-the-Stone legend was popularised by Sir Thomas Malory, whose epic *Le Morte d'Arthur* was published in 1485. Malory set this part of his story in London:

And when matins and the first mass was done, there was seen in the churchyard, against the high altar, a great stone four square, like unto a marble stone; and in the midst thereof was like an anvil of steel a foot high, and therein stuck a fair sword naked by the point, and letters there were written in gold about the sword that said thus:- Whoso pulleth this sword out of this stone and anvil, is rightwise king born of all England.

But there was no such place as England in Arthur's day, and the message of the stone was something else altogether.

Malory's 'great stone four square, like unto a marble stone' compares with the description given by Hector Boece, in regard to Gathelus, the founding-father of the Gaels, of the 'marble chair, or fatal stone like unto a chair', which had travelled with Gathelus from Egypt: 'wherever it was found would be the kingdom of the Scots.' This 'fatal stone' was also known as the Stone of Destiny. By the time Sir Thomas Malory came to write his *Morte d'Arthur*, it had been in London for nigh-on 200 years.

Writing about a century before Malory, John of Fordun highlighted the special provenance of the Stone by quoting the prophecy of Simon Brecc, a descendant of Gathelus, who had raised the Stone from the sea off the coast of Ireland:

Ni fallat fatum, Scoti quocumque locatum
Invenient lapidem, regnasse tenentur ibidem.

If Destiny prove true, then Scots are known
to have been kings wherever men find this Stone.

Jacques Cambray, the author of *Monuments celtiques*, claimed in 1805 to have seen the Stone when it still bore the inscription attributed to Simon Brecc. The Stone had been taken from Scotland by the English king, Edward I, in 1296 as proof that he considered Scotland to be part of his realm. Edward 'Longshanks' removed the Stone from Perthshire and transported it to Westminster Abbey, where every English monarch, from Edward II in 1308 to Elizabeth II in 1953, was crowned upon it. What had once been the Stone which denoted the kingdom of the Scots had become the 'great stone four squre', which legitimised the kings of England.

The Stone of Destiny had been taken to Scone in Perthshire by Kenneth mac Alpin when he established himself as King of Scotland in 842. Previously, it is thought to have rested at Dunstaffnage on the coast of Argyll. What Edward of England commandeered in 1296 was a red sandstone bloc weighing a little over 150kg, crudely chiselled and showing signs of wear and tear (it was Edward, perhaps, who had two iron rings set into the surface of the Stone to make for easier manhandling). This rough stone was probably quarried from the belt of Old Devonian sandstone that stretches across Scotland from Argyll to Tayside – but then, rumours suggest that the Scots tricked Edward I into stealing an irrelevant lump of masonry and kept the real Stone of Destiny safely hidden. These rumours may not have been wholly unfounded.

The original Stone was said to have been marble and was fetched up from the sea. The Isle of Iona has its own rich deposit of Lewisian marble, which lies in a vertical band extending out into the sea from the southern end of the island. The distinctive white calcerous marble is shot through with green veins of serpentine. As late as 1688 it was reported that a great slab of Iona marble served as an altar in the abbey church. Visitors kept hacking bits of it off because it was thought to offer protection against shipwreck.

It would have been in-keeping with Columba's character for him to have laid claim to the true Stone of Destiny, reserving it for his own use and requiring the Scottish kings to find another stone, which they kept at Dunstaffnage, away from the monks of Iona.

The stone from the coronation chair in Westminster Abbey was finally returned to Scotland – under military escort – in 1996, a full seven centuries after it had been seized by King Edward I.

At least one tradition avers that the Stone was the one on which Jacob rested his head at Bethel and dreamt of a stairway to heaven. *Beth-El* ('House of God') shares its linguistic origin with the Greek *Baetylus*, a 'sacred stone' or 'pillar'. The Stone therefore invites comparison with other sacred stones of the Middle East, the most famous being the *Ka'aba* or 'Black Stone' at Mecca, Islam's holiest of holies, which was once thought to house an aspect of Al-Uzza, the Arabian answer to Venus.

In the case of the Stone of Destiny, which was supposedly rescued from Egypt by Gathelus, the resident goddess was the pharaoh's daughter, Scota.

Eventually, the Stone found its way to Argyll, probably with Fergus Mór and his brothers in 498. Andrew of Wyntoun related the Stone's journey to the Isle of Iona in his fifteenth-century *Orygynale Cronykil of Scotland*:

Fergus son of Erc from him then
Did descend line by line
Unto the fifty-fifth generation,
As even man may reckon,
Brought this Stone into Scotland,
First when he came and won that land,
And set it first in Icolmkyll
And Scone thereafter it was brought unto.

Andrew of Wyntoun wrote his '*Original Chronicle*' on the island in Loch Leven where Arthur was born, so we can assume that he had access to an authentic tradition regarding the sacred stone of Scottish kingship.

It was on this very Stone that Áedán was ordained King of the Scots by St Columba in 574.

The saint had returned to Iona, red-eyed and smarting, from his three nights of torment on the island of Hinba. The monks looked doubtful but the warriors of Áedán's retinue were triumphant as they followed the new King of Dalriada along the processional route known as the Street of the Dead.

They approached the enclosure on the east side of the island where St Columba had built his church. Áedán climbed the little rocky hillock of *Tòrr Abb*, the 'Abbot's Mound', so called because it is thought to have been where Columba slept with a stone for his pillow. The knoll, just west of the present-day abbey, is also known as *Dùn nam Manach*, the 'Hill of the Monk', although this might be a corruption of *Dùn nam Manadh* (pronounced 'doon nam man-u'), meaning the hill of the 'omen' or 'destiny'. The fabled Black Stones of Iona stood close to this spot; they were considered 'black' because any oath sworn upon them was especially binding.

Behind the Hill of the Stones, overlooking the Abbot's Mound, stands the Peak of the Raven. The legends suggest that the Stone of Destiny would utter a piercing shriek when the true king placed his foot on it. This was the goddess Scota signifying her approval, and she did so with the voice of a raven. All ears were pricked as Áedán stepped up onto the Stone of Destiny.

The raven screamed, or perhaps a priestess acted as its messenger. Either way, Áedán had the blessing of the Stone. He raised his sword and swung it in an arc over the Stone, promising to uphold the laws and defend the land with the might of his arm.

Sword and Stone were the yin and yang, the masculine and feminine principles of kingship. The Stone was the land, which needed a strong protector; the Sword drew its legitimacy from the land. It was a symbiotic relationship: a sacred marriage.

There is no reference to a sword and a stone in Adomnán's account of Áedán's ordination – nor, for that matter, is there any mention of the Beltane shenanigans, revived around this time, which would have taken place on the far side of the island. But Adomnán was interested only in emphasising St Columba's role in the proceedings.

The saint uttered a barely concealed threat to King Áedán. It was transcribed by Adomnán's predecessor Cumméne the White, seventh Abbot of Iona:

Make no mistake, Áedán, but believe that, until you commit some act of treason against me or my successors, none of your enemies will be able to oppose you. For this reason you must alert your sons, as they must pass on the warning to their sons and grandsons and descendants, so that they do not follow evil counsels ... For whenever it should happen that they do wrong to me or to my kindred in Ireland, the scourge that I have suffered from the angel for your sake will be turned by the hand of God to deliver a heavy punishment on them. Men's hearts will be taken from them; their enemies will draw strength mightily against them.

Figure 2 The Stone of Destiny

Whereas Adomnán would have us believe that the ordination of Áedán was a victory for Columba, the words spoken by the saint to his king reveal the malice in the air. Columba had been outfoxed, but his warning was clear: never again would he allow Áedán or his kindred to oppose his wishes.

Arthur's death warrant was drawn up at that moment. It awaited only a signature.

The saint had already made his choice of successor to Áedán mac Gabráin. When he was asked which of Áedán's sons would follow his father onto the throne – would it be Arthur, or Domangart, or Eochaid Find? – Columba answered plainly:

'None of these three will be king; for they will fall in battles, slain by enemies.'

The Dove of the Church had spoken. Arthur son of Áedán would never be King of the Scots.

Though we think of him as King Arthur, that was not his real title. He was something less and more than a king. The Britons called him *ymerawdwr* – 'emperor'.

The *imperator* title had been conferred on victorious generals in the days of the Roman republic. After Rome became an empire, it was reserved exclusively for the emperor himself.

The 'emperor' designation was part of Rome's legacy in North Britain. Almost certainly, it was applied to those military champions who defended Manau Gododdin – the British redoubt of Stirling on the River Forth. The post-holder wore an imperial red-purple gown of office known in Arthur's day as the 'coat of Padarn Red-Coat', after Paternus, who had succeeded Tacitus as Rome's military governor in the North, and who was in turn succeeded by Aeternus – 'Edern' to the Britons – who gave his name to Edinburgh.

The Red-Coat of Paternus was one of the Thirteen Treasures of Britain that were buried with Arthur. It was the gown of the 'emperor', or *gwledig*, of Manau. But before he could wear it, Arthur first had to secure Manau Gododdin and stamp his authority on the region.

Two battles had already been fought in the Lennox area to the west of Manau – one at Dumbarton, to teach Rhydderch a lesson, and one in Kintyre to put Áedán on the Scottish throne. Geoffrey of Monmouth, whose *History of the Kings of Britain* was written more than 500 years later, knew that Arthur had seen combat in and around Dumbarton and Loch Lomond. His next two battles were also fought in that region.

The strife at Arderydd and Catlowdy the previous year had given the Northumbrian Angles the impression that the Britons were in disarray. The Angles moved to exploit this. Ida, the first Anglian King of Bernicia, had been succeeded by Aethelric in the year of Arthur's birth. The sons of Ida then had to find kingdoms of their own. Theodoric, nicknamed the 'Flame-Bearer', marched his warriors deep into British-held territory in an attempt to seize Lennox. They made for the old Roman fort and 'artificial mound' known as the Cathair, where the Lord of Lennox held his court, near Drymen, at the southern end of Loch Lomond.

Arthur and his men counter-attacked. Taliesin described the scene:

> There was a great battle Saturday morning,
> From sunrise until it grew dark.
> The Flame-Bearer attacked with four armies.
> Rheged and Goddau were arrayed
> As one from Argoed to Arfynydd …

The battle became known as Argoed Llwyfain, the 'Fore-wood of the Elm-water', *Llwyfain* being the Welsh form of *Leamhain*, the Gaelic name for the River Leven. The massed forces of Rheged (the kingdoms of Urien and his cousin Llywarch) and the Gododdin of Lothian combined to overthrow the Anglian intruders. Their battle lines stretched from the Leven, along the Gallangad ('Hill of Battle') Burn and across Craighat Moor, perhaps as far as Killearn on the edge of the Campsie Fells.

Taliesin would sing that Gwallog the Battle-Horseman laid waste to the captured enclosure of his father, Lleënog of Lennox. But the Chief Bard was Urien's poet, and so he portrayed the king and prince of North Rheged as the heroes of the battle:

> The Flame-Bearer with great impetuosity called out:
> 'Will they give hostages? Are they prepared?'

Owain answered: 'Let us rise to battle –
They are not in place, they are not ready.'

Urien rejoined:

> If there be fellowship in kinship,
> Let us raise our banner over the mountain,
> And advance our fame across the border,
> And raise our spears over the heads of men,
> And charge the Flame-Bearer in the midst of his army,
> And slaughter him and his company.

Arthur's fourth battle resulted in the crushing defeat of Theodoric the Flame-Bearer.

Arthur and his army then pushed eastwards to Craigmaddie Muir, above the Douglas Water, north-east of Milngavie and Bearsden, where the last of the *Linnuis* battles took place.

Local tradition maintains that Arthur commanded his forces from a natural rock formation known as the Battle-Crag. A plaque erected at the site notes that the 'Battle of Ardunion' was waged to the north-east of the *Cat Craig* in 'about 570' – 574 to be precise – and that Gwallog of Elmet, Rhydderch of Strathclyde and Urien of North Rheged defeated Hussa, the son of the Anglian King of Bernicia.

The sign also reveals that a standing stone at nearby Ballagan is thought to mark the spot where the Angles made their last stand and was raised in honour of the Britons who died there; when 'the railway was built in the nineteenth century piles of bones were dug up at Dunglass.' On the Gled Knowes above East Ballagan stands Clach Artair ('Arthur's Stone'), while another Arthurstone near Blanefield might indicate a border, standing as it does at Cantywheery, the 'Boundary of the Men of the Forth'.

Arddunion is another of the battles mentioned by the poet Taliesin in connection with Gwallog, the original 'Sir Galahad', and was probably the same as the 'Clyde Moor' battle which the Chief Bard associated with his royal patron, Urien. It was also Arthur's fifth battle. The tradition that he directed the operation from the 'Battle-Crag' would appear to confirm his status as *dux bellorum*, the 'Duke of Battles'.

He was still only 15 years old.

Nennius the monk proffered scant information about Arthur's next engagement: 'The sixth battle was above the river which is called Bassas.' No such river-name survives. We can hazard a guess as to where it was, though, by considering Arthur's strategy. He had helped his father to the Scottish throne and had swept the invading Angles out of Lennox. His next task was to secure the borders of Lothian.

Llywarch of South Rheged (broadly, Cheshire and parts of Lancashire) was already a member of Arthur's coalition. In one of his poems Llywarch would fondly refer to his three sons – Urien, Arawn and Llew – even though he had fathered none of them. The same three individuals are elsewhere described as the sons of Cynfarch, who was Urien's real father. Urien was the cousin of Llywarch. He was also a foster-brother and son-in-law to Áedán mac Gabráin and therefore an uncle as well as a brother-in-law to Arthur.

Áedán goes by the name of Arawn in the First Branch of the *Mabinogion* when, as the 'King of Annwn', he swaps places with Pwyll (Urien). Llew, we already know, was an alternative name for Arthur.

Geoffrey of Monmouth had Arthur restoring three brothers to their former kingdoms after his battles at Dumbarton and Loch Lomond:

> He returned the kingship of the Scots to Auguselus; to Urian, the brother of Auguselus, he gave back the honour of ruling over the men of Moray; and Loth … he restored to the dukedom of Lothian and other nearby territories which formed part of it.

According to Geoffrey, Loth of Lothian was married to Arthur's sister Anna.

Clearly, Geoffrey's 'Urian' was Urien of North Rheged, who was a brother of sorts to both Áedán and Arthur. Under an arrangement brokered by Arthur, the brother of 'Urian' received the kingdom of 'Albany' – that is, Alba, the land of the Scots. The name chosen by Geoffrey of Monmouth for the Scottish king is interesting: Auguselus seems to have been based on Agesilaus, the lame King of Sparta whom the Gaels remembered as the founder of their race. Tysilio, a sixth-century prince of Powys in Wales, indicated that the King of the Scots was actually known as Arawn.

Another version of the name Auguselus, encountered in other accounts, is Angel. This was presumably a corruption of the Gaelic *aingeal* – 'fire' – which points to the 'dear fiery one', Áedán mac Gabráin. Áedán was indeed installed on the Scottish throne after a couple of battles in Dumbarton and thereabouts, while his 'brother' Urien appears to have exercised some jurisdiction over parts of Scotland in the wake of Gwenddolau's death at Arderydd.

This just leaves the third brother – Llew or 'Loth' – who was 'restored to the dukedom of Lothian and other nearby territories which formed part of it'. Geoffrey remarked that the 'British army was put under the command of Loth of Lodensia, with orders that he should keep the enemy at a distance.' In other words, Loth or Llew of Lothian played an identical role to that of Arthur, the commander-in-chief or *dux bellorum*.

Lodensia was another invention of Geoffrey's. There is some evidence that the kingdom of Lothian was known as *Llydaw* and was defended by a figure named *Lleudin Llydaw*, otherwise *Lleudin lluedog* or 'Lleu of the Armies', who was described as being 'of Edinburgh in the North'. An old Welsh poem refers to one 'Llwch of the Striking Hand' defending the border of Edinburgh, the name Llwch deriving from *llewych* – 'light' or 'brightness'. It seems pretty clear that the man responsible for holding Edinburgh and its borders was the 'Light Skilful Hand' (Lleu Llaw Gyffes) of Welsh legend or, as he was also known, Llew, the 'Lion'.

This seems to have been reflected in the medieval names for Lothian: *Loeneis*, in a document of 1158; *Loenes* in 1249, which compare with *Leonais*, the name given to Lothian by British refugees in Brittany. Their *Leonais* – the Lion's land – would evolve into the lost land of 'Lyonesse'.

Perhaps the best indication that it was Arthur who became the Lord of Lothian is to be found in Edinburgh itself. The skyline of Edinburgh is dominated by a volcanic plug which looms over the city. Commonly known as Arthur's Seat, the outcrop is also referred to locally as the Lion's Head. Geoffrey's 'Loth of Lothian' was, of course, Arthur's royal grandfather, Clydno of Edinburgh.

As a young man 'only fifteen years old', Geoffrey of Monmouth remarked, Arthur 'was of outstanding courage and generosity, and his inborn goodness gave him such grace that he was loved by almost all the people.' They loved him because he was successful. He defended the border of Edinburgh 'with orders that he should keep the enemy at a distance'. Herein lies a clue to the location of his sixth battle 'above the river which is called Bassas'.

W.F. Skene, the Victorian antiquary who traced the site of the Battle of Arderydd, disclosed that, 'the name Bass is also applied to a peculiar mound having the appearance of being artificial, which is formed near a river, though really formed by natural causes.' One such Bass stands on the bank of the River Tweed at Dryburgh, on the border of Lothian. It is known as Bass Hill.

A short distance away, due south across the River Tweed, we find an Arthurshiel (*shiel* being a Scots word for a 'hut'). This is immediately to the west of The Street – a major Roman road. The aim of a battle fought in this area would have been to drive the Northumbrian Angles out of Lothian and confine them to their coastal region south of the Tweed.

As for Bass Hill, the Royal Commission on the Ancient and Historical Monuments of Scotland records that the natural mound is topped by an artificial mound in which numerous bodies were buried, many in 'Gaelic sarcophagi of four pieces of thin stone'. It was reported in 1857 that 'Druidical remains' had also been found there. A commemorative Temple of the Muse erected in honour of the poet James Thomson, who composed the lyrics for *Rule, Britannia!*, now crowns Bass Hill.

The area reverberates with Arthurian echoes. Close by stand the three peaks of the Eildon Hills. The northern peak had been fortified back in the Bronze Age, when 40 acres were enclosed by 3 miles of ramparts. In the first century AD the

Roman army built the enormous fort of Trimontium at Newstead, on the south bank of the Tweed, beneath the Eildon Hills. The Roman fort was a staging post on the road heading north; it also kept the Selgovae tribe, whose eastern capital was in the Eildons, in check.

One of the legends that clings to the area concerns a horse-trader named Canonbie Dick. He was crossing Bowden Moor, just west of the Eildons, when he was accosted by a stranger in old-fashioned clothing. The stranger wished to purchase two horses from him and led him through a magical door in the side of a hill and into a vast cavern underneath the Eildon Tree. There, Canonbie Dick saw Arthur and his knights, suspended in timeless slumber and surrounded by weapons and piles of treasure.

In exchange for his horses Canonbie Dick was given the choice of a sword or a horn. Had he chosen well, he would have become 'King of All Britain'. But he first blew the horn before raising the sword. This was the action of a coward.

Arthur and his men are said to be sleeping in many parts of Britain until the time comes when their services are needed. What makes the legend of the Eildon Hills so different is that Arthur and his comrades really did fight in those parts. They forced the Angles back across the River Tweed and east of Dere Street. Bass Hill perhaps became the grave-mound of the warriors who died there.

Arthur had reclaimed the kingdom of his maternal grandfather, Clydno Eidyn. Lothian was now his to defend. For political reasons he could not be seen to be governing Edinburgh all on his own. Various dynasties had a stake in Arthur's coalition – the kindred of Gabrán, the descendants of Old King Coel in North Britain, the princes of Strathclyde – and so some form of power-sharing agreement had to be reached.

Morgan the Wealthy, who had usurped the throne of Lothian in 559, was retained as a subordinate chieftain. Arthur became the military governor of the greater Lothian region, ruling in partnership with his half-sister Muirgein, who also represented the interests of North Rheged.

It became a staple of the legends that Arthur committed incest with his sister and fathered his own nemesis. Geoffrey of Monmouth added to the confusion by stating that 'Loth of Lothian' married Arthur's sister Anna. As we have seen, Muirgein shared her feast day with St Agna (or Agnes), and it is possible that she took the name Anna when she became Queen of Lothian.

But the charges of incest should be approached with caution. At best, they arose out of a misunderstanding; at worst, they were part of a campaign to denigrate the traditional ways of the Britons. Arthur and Muirgein – 'Llew' and 'Anna' – exercised a joint-rule over Lothian, which entailed them entering into a form of sacred marriage: he was the Sword and she was the Stone. Like the royal pairing of brother and sister in ancient Egypt, there was an element of incestuousness in this, although it is unlikely that the ritual marriage of Arthur and Muirgein was anything more than symbolic.

An account of a kingship ritual witnessed in thirteenth-century Ulster does raise some concerns. The newly appointed king was seen to copulate in public with a white mare. The horse was then sacrificed and a broth made from its flesh. The king bathed in the broth and the meat was shared out among the company. This was probably a late and rather decadent version of the Feast of Tara, which Diarmait mac Cerbaill was said to have celebrated on his accession to the throne of Ireland. The white mare stood in for the goddess – a part which would once have been played by a woman – and the meal made from its flesh has the feel of a perverted Eucharist. However, the description of this ceremony was written by none other than Giraldus Cambrensis, whose work on the hoax discovery of Arthur's grave at Glastonbury was such a hotch-potch of misinformation. His account of the kingship ritual in Ulster might likewise have been a blend of observation and propaganda.

The legend that Arthur and his half-sister slept together almost certainly relates to the ceremonial union by means of which they took control of the British kingdom of Lothian.

The *Triads of the Island of Britain* assert that Arthur had three 'Tribal Thrones', one of which was at 'Pen Rhionydd in the North'. *Pen Rhionydd* – 'Peak of the Maidens' or 'Maiden Head' – can be identified as the *castellum puellarum* – 'Castle of Maidens' – which, according to Geoffrey of Monmouth, was situated on Arthur's Seat in Edinburgh. Arthur ruled there with a 'Wealthy Prince' – Morgan the Wealthy – as his Chief Elder and one Cynderyn Garthwys as his Chief Bishop.

Cynderyn Garthwys was his uncle, Cynon son of Clydno, masquerading as 'Kentigern of the Pig-Enclosure'.

11

CAMELOT

THEY MADE a most unlikely pair of travelling companions – Áedán, the pagan King of Dalriada, and St Columba, Abbot of Iona – but in 575 they journeyed together to attend a 'conference of kings' in Ireland. The venue was Druim Cett: probably Daisy Hill, also known as the Mullagh, a few miles from Columba's tribal capital at Derry.

Precisely what took place at Druim Cett is unclear. This is partly because the Christian sources tend to play down Áedán's presence, turning the 'great convention' into little more than the St Columba Show. The two key participants in the conference appear to have been Áedán himself and Áed mac Ainmirech, who was Columba's cousin and the chief of his tribe. One of the outcomes of the talks was an agreement that the war fleet of Dalriada would remain at the service of the Lords of the Uí Néill – Columba's clan – but the Scots would no longer pay tribute to their senior partners in Ireland. In other words, Áedán achieved a measure of independence for his kingdom, freeing his army, if not his navy, from the demands of the Irish.

It was during this same conference that St Columba secured 'protection for poets'.

Columba had a taste for poetry; he was a notable poet in his own right. His poetry was devotional, and there is nothing in his history or manner to suggest that he would willingly have allowed the pagan bards to practice their art freely.

Áed mac Ainmirech, himself a future High King, had commissioned a poem in Columba's honour from Dallán, the chief poet of Ireland. Dallán began to compose his praise-poem at the time of the Druim Cett conference, but Columba stopped him, insisting that the poem would have to wait until he – Columba – was dead. And so, far from using the great convention to secure freedom for poets, the saint actually halted a poet in his tracks.

For a hint of what really happened we must turn to the legends of Arthur. The Welsh tale of *Culhwch and Olwen* provides something of a potted account of Arthur's career, which included a journey to Ireland to seize a marvellous cauldron – the cauldron of Diwrnach the Irishman, who was said to have been the servant of the son of King Áed. Arthur and his companions returned home with the cauldron 'filled with the treasures of Ireland'. In due course it became one of the Thirteen Treasures of Britain.

The cauldron was associated with poetic inspiration. Arthur's capture of the cauldron allowed the bardic tradition to be revived in Britain. This presents a very different version of events from that put forward by the followers of St Columba. The notion that Columba argued in favour of poetic licence at Druim Cett is a little far-fetched. More likely, he was outflanked by Áedán, who insisted that his bards should have the same rights as Columba's monks. Columba's royal cousin could see nothing wrong with this, and so the cauldron cult was reinstated.

Columba showed his sour grapes by ordering Dallán to stop composing his poem. Twice, in as many years, the Dove of the Church had suffered a setback: he had been forced to ordain a king he did not like and now he was required to tolerate the presence of a bardic school on his holy island. He could not allow a poem to be written in his honour when he had just lost another struggle with Áedán mac Gabráin. That was not how he wished to be remembered.

While Áedán was negotiating with Áed mac Ainmirech in Ireland, Arthur almost certainly remained in Britain. His task was to defend the borders of the Gododdin lands, and that meant fighting another battle.

Nennius, in his list of Arthur's victories, called it *Cat Coit Celidon* – the 'Battle of Celidon Wood'.

The Forest of Celidon once spread across much of southern Scotland. It gave Myrddin two of his alternative names: Merlin Silvestris and Merlinus Caledonensis; he was the madman of the Celidon Wood. When he wasn't riding into battle alongside Arthur, or indulging in a little boisterous comedy by interrupting St Kentigern's sermons at Hoddom Cross, Myrddin made his home at the spiritual centre of the forest. Above the stone grotto of the sacred spring on Hart Fell, where Myrddin wrestled with his demons after the Arderydd disaster, a small cairn of stones marks a vantage point, 731m above sea-level. It is known as Arthur's Seat.

Three major rivers – the Annan, the Clyde and the Tweed – all rise close by, the latter near a hill called Crown of Scotland where, many years later, Robert the Bruce would forge an alliance, which resulted in him becoming Scotland's king. This small area appears to have been supremely important, both symbolically and geographically, as it was the key to southern Scotland and the lands of the Gododdin. Arthur's Seat was an ideal place from which to survey the region from on high.

A stream flows down the side of Arthur's Seat to join the Spa Well Burn below Myrddin's spring. The name of this stream is the Auchencat or 'Field of Battle'

Burn. Taliesin, in one of his poems, mentions a battle fought 'by the head of the wood of Cludfein', with Cludfein, or *Clydfain*, meaning 'Clyde Peak'. This would indicate the hill known as Clyde Law which stands 546m high, just north of the spot where the Battlefield Burn meets the River Annan at the foot of Myrddin's mountain.

Taliesin referred to the enemy on this occasion as *peithwyr*. It is feasible that they were the Picts of Galloway, although another possibility arises from the old Welsh word *peithyn*, meaning 'roof-tile'. As far back as the second century AD a Roman geographer had identified a town in Galloway as *Leucopibia*, and this later became the site of a monastery dedicated to St Martin of Tours and known as the White House or *Candida Casa*. The design of the monastery was inspired by Roman architecture, and in addition to its gleaming white walls it probably had something that few of the natives would have seen before: a roof made of clay tiles.

This is speculation – nothing more – but it is conceivable that a band of 'tilers' (*peithynwyr*) had marched up from the *Candida Casa* at Whithorn intent on taking Myrddin's mountain with its sacred spring and challenging Arthur's rule in Lothian. If so, it was a suicide mission. Observed from the high-point of Arthur's Seat, the intruders walked into a typical Arthurian ambush. As they entered the narrow defile below Hart Fell, the signal was given and the *peithwyr* were attacked between the Devil's Beef Tub and the fort of Ericstane.

Áedán was almost certainly with Columba in Northern Ireland at this time. The *peithwyr* war-band defeated by Arthur at the Battle of Celidon Wood might have hoped to take advantage of Áedán's absence. Alternatively, they were sent to their deaths with the aim of provoking a violent response from the Christians of Strathclyde. But if the Men of the Roof-Tiles had indeed struck out from the monastery at Whithorn, we might wonder whether they were acting on information received from someone who knew Áedán's whereabouts and could get a message to the Christian community on the Galloway coast; someone, moreover, who was now engaged in a covert war against King Áedán and his family.

At about the age of 17, Arthur began his campaign to reclaim the territory which had been lost when he was born. His grandfather had annexed much of Perthshire fifty years earlier. With the death of Gabrán in 559, these lands had reverted to the southern Picts.

The start of Arthur's Perthshire campaign can be dated roughly to 576. His first objective would have been to reconquer the Pictish province of Fortriu, which required him to advance north out of Manau Gododdin and take control of the valley of the River Earn.

The river runs eastwards for some 46 miles from Loch Earn. It formed a strategic link between the western kingdom of Dalriada and the mouth of the River Tay on the east coast and came to be known as *Uisge Éireann* – the Irish Water.

The presence of Arthur and his companions can be detected all along its fast-flowing length.

At the eastern end of Loch Earn, where the river is born, stands Ardtrostan – 'Height of Drystan'. Following the river, we pass through the village of Comrie, where the church is dedicated to St Kessog, a name we shall encounter again. Close by, where the river zig-zags suddenly, a hill fort stood on the Hill of Trowan (Welsh *trwyn* – meaning a 'point').

Taliesin made mention of a 'battle near Bre Trwyn' – close to the Hill of Trowan – as well as fighting in the 'Ireland of Eidyn', a reference to the Strathearn region: the Irish Vale which came under the jurisdiction of Edinburgh. Lennoch Wood and the Carse of Lennoch, which adjoins the Carse of Trowan on the north side of the river, might relate to Lleënog of Lennox, the warrior later known as Lancelot.

Further down the river, the chapels at Strageath and Muthill were originally built by St Fergus who, as we shall soon discover, was one of Arthur's knights and an intimate associate of Drystan.

Passing a number of Roman encampments, the River Earn skirts the plain of Auchterarder – 'Uthrardor' in 1305 – which would appear to have been the 'Upland of Arthur'. The church at Auchterarder is dedicated to St Kessog while, in the same parish, a chapel at Aberuthven honours St Cathan, the Scottish name for St Cadog, another of Arthur's knights.

There are at least six references to St Mungo in the topography of Strathearn, including one at Auchterarder. Mungo was the familiar name of St Kentigern – that is, Arthur's uncle, Cynon son of Clydno – who also had a chapel dedicated to him at the top of Gleneagles ('Valley of the Church'), immediately to the south of Auchterarder. Towering over the site of Cynon's chapel is the great bulk of Carlownie Hill, referred to in a thirteenth-century charter as *Kather leuenas*, the 'Lion's Seat'. Due north of Carlownie Hill, looking out across the Ruthven Water towards St Cathan's Chapel, a fort stood above Kay Craig – named after Arthur's foster-brother, Cai. Continuing eastwards along the edge of the Ochil Hills we come to the village of Dunning, the site of a major Roman fort. It was here that, according to legend, St Serf killed a 'dreadful dragon, which devoured both men and cattle and kept the district in continual terror.'

St Serf – also known as Serwan or Servanus – was the patron of the island in Loch Leven where Arthur was born, and the dragon he slew was presumably a champion warrior of the Picts. Serwan was also the dedicatee of the church at Monzievaird, the 'plain of the bards', a little further up the River Earn.

It seems likely that there was a series of running battles in Strathearn as Arthur and his troops pushed eastwards along the valley as far as the mouth of the river, where the Earn joins the Tay. That there was fighting in this region is confirmed by the poet Myrddin Wyllt who, in conversation with his sister, remarked that Rhydderch the Generous, King of Strathclyde, dealt out wounds 'on the blessed day at the ford of the Tay'. But in the Nennius list of Arthur's battles, all these skirmishes were collapsed into one major engagement: 'The eighth battle was at the castle of Guinnion, in which Arthur carried the image of holy Mary, the everlasting virgin, on his shoulders; and the pagans were put to flight on that day.' The eighth battle took place at Abernethy, a Pictish capital which overlooked the mouth of the River Earn.

The village is famous for its Irish-style round tower, one of just two surviving examples in Scotland (the other is at Brechin, the royal burgh named after Arthur's great-grandfather Brychan). The tower shows that Abernethy became a significant religious centre, and although the bishop's seat was eventually moved to Muthil in Strathearn, and then further south to Dunblane, the Christian centre at Abernethy exercised an influence comparable to that of nearby Auchterarder, of which it has been said: 'It is notable that all the great ecclesiastical movements in Scotland should be identified with Auchterarder.' Perhaps this is why Taliesin thought of Strathearn as *Gwenystrad* – the 'Holy Glen'.

The parish church at Abernethy was dedicated to St Brigid of Kildare – the Christian form of the goddess Brighid – by Arthur's half-brother Gartnait after he became King of the Picts in 584. Prior to that, the fledgling monastery at Abernethy appears to have been held sacred to St Ninian, the evangelist associated with the *Candida Casa* settlement at Whithorn on the coast of Galloway.

The problem with St Ninian is that he was largely invented by the eighth-century Anglian churchman known as Bede.

As long ago as 1855 it was suggested that Ninian was in reality St Columba's old tutor, Finnian of Moville. This theory is supported by the fact that Adomnán, in his *Life of St Columba*, made no mention of St Finnian *per se* – instead, he used the names Uinniau and Finnio. These were, respectively, the British and Irish forms of the same name, and it seems probable that Uinniau was the original name for the saint wrongly identified by Bede as 'Ninian'. The *Aberdeen Breviary*, compiled early in the sixteenth century, lists a St Uynninus – almost certainly the same person. The *Perth Psalter*, meanwhile, called him St Vininus; in both cases, he shared his January feast day with St Agned or Agnetis.

If there is one thing that most sources are agreed on it is that Uinniau or St Ninian became the 'Apostle to the Southern Picts', in which capacity a residence at Abernethy would have been only fitting. Since the first part of the name Uinniau (*uuin*, meaning 'white') evolved into the Welsh *gwyn*, the fortress named after Uinniau would have become known as the 'castle of Guinnion'. This, according to Nennius, was the site of Arthur's eighth battle.

The same battle is referred to in a Welsh poem entitled *Pa Gwr* or 'What Man is the Porter?' This poem recounts a conversation between Arthur and the gatekeeper to the Otherworld and offers a précis of Arthur's military career, which included a battle 'in the hall of Awarnach'. It has long been suspected that the 'hall of Awarnach' was at Abernethy, the site of Uinniau's fort, where the Earn joins the Tay.

Tactically, Arthur probably took the high ground of Carlownie Hill to supervise the operation. The southern Picts were forced back from the Ochils and over the plain of Auchterarder to the valley of Strathearn. Arthur's warriors then moved down the river as far as the royal seat at Abernethy, where the Picts were trapped by the confluence of the Earn and the Tay. The fighting was at its thickest around the house of prayer established by the same Uinniau or Finnio with whom Columba had once fallen out over a copy of the Scriptures.

The 'pagans were put to flight on that day', wrote Nennius, 250 years after the event. This overlooks the possibility that two of Arthur's battles of the mid-570s involved Christians loyal to St Columba and his mentor. Nennius justified his statement with a remarkable piece of information: 'Arthur carried the image of holy Mary, the everlasting virgin, on his shoulders' when he fought at the 'castle of Guinnion'. This is pretty much the sole basis for the later claims that Arthur was a Christian.

The Welsh word for the shoulder – *ysgwydd* – is the same as the word for a shield. According to an early British tradition, Arthur's shield was known as *wynebgwrthucher* or 'Face of Evening'. It was this, perhaps, which led Nennius to assume that Arthur bore an image of the 'everlasting virgin' when he went into his eighth battle.

The Western Maidens who worshipped on a western isle were also known as the Daughters of Evening, their goddess being a manifestation of Venus, the Evening Star. To the Gaels, this goddess of love and victories was *Brighid bhòidheach*, the beautiful Brìde, who was the patron deity of the Isles of Brìde (*Eileana Brìde*), otherwise known as the Hebrides. Thanks to a Christian legend, Brìde became the 'Mary of the Gael' and the 'foster-mother of Christ' – like the Madonna, she contrived to remain perpetually virginal.

It is assumed that Uinniau's settlement at Abernethy was dedicated to St Brigid by Arthur's half-brother, Gartnait mac Áedáin, sometime after he acceded to the Pictish throne in the 580s. The likelihood that Arthur sported an image of the beautiful Brighid on his shield when he attacked the house of prayer at Abernethy suggests that the place reverted to the worship of the goddess a decade or so earlier, thanks to Arthur's intervention. That does not explain why Arthur might have chosen to honour the goddess so openly at this point in his career, but the reason might not be too hard to find.

Arthur had got married.

The Britons remembered her as Gwenhwyfar:

Gwenhwyfar, ferch Ogfrân Gawr;
Drwg yn fechan, gwaeth yn fawr.

Guinevere, daughter of Ogfrân the Champion;
trouble when little, worse when big.

She was the 'Great White [Female] Salmon', the 'Great Poison' or the 'Evening-Prayer'. She had a smaller sister, Gwenhwyfach, and together they were the two 'golden-chained daughters of the Island of Britain'. They would also bear the brunt of the blame for the catastrophe that was Arthur's final battle.

One of the *Triads of the Island of Britain* claims that Arthur had 'Three Great Queens':

Gwenhwyfar daughter of Cywryd Gwent,
and Gwenhwyfar daughter of Gwythyr son of Greidiol,
and Gwenhwyfar daughter of Gogfrân the Champion.

In fact, they were all the same person.

The *Triads* also tell us that the 'Three Fair Maidens of the Island of Britain' were Creirwy daughter of Ceridwen, Arianrhod daughter of Dôn and Gwen daughter of Cywryd son of Crydon. The first two, Creirwy and Arianrhod, were alternative names for Arthur's mother, who in both instances was identified as a child of the goddess. The third fair maiden was Arthur's wife, Gwenhwyfar daughter of Cywryd Gwent.

The name Cywryd ('Anger' or 'Fury') also appears in the *Stanzas of the Graves*, a poem which dwells on the burial places of the Arthurian heroes:

The graves wetted by rain –
Men not peevish or severe:
Cerwyd and Cywryd and Caw.

Otherwise, little is known about Cywryd. But his association with the kingdom of Gwent in south-east Wales hints at the real identity of the first father of Gwenhwyfar.

The Welsh kings of Gwent traced their ancestry back to a warrior named Caradog Freichfras ('Strong-Arm'). He seems to have ruled from Caerwent – the old Roman market town of *Venta Silurum* – and to have been close to St Cadog, the Arthurian hero whose kingdom of Glywysyng later merged with that of Gwent.

Caradog Strong-Arm joined the general drift northwards, leaving his South Walian kingdom and settling in the Tegeingl region of Flintshire in North Wales; his friend St Cadog was then based nearby at Llangollen on the River Dee. Three sons of Caradog Strong-Arm are mentioned in Lives of the early saints as having been chieftains in western Gwynedd. Caradog himself appears as the villain in the legend of a Welsh saint – Gwenffrewi, better known as St Winefride – who was associated with a healing well in Flintshire. The story goes that Caradog became so enraged when his beloved Gwenffrewi took holy orders that he struck off her head with his sword. Whatever truth there might have been in this tale has been obscured by ecclesiastical myth-making. There is a very strong chance that Gwenffrewi, whose name relates to *gwenfro* or 'Paradise', was in fact another name for Gwenhwyfar, the daughter of Caradog. The legend states that her brother Owain punished Caradog for his crime, and Owain was indeed the foster-brother of Arthur. For all that, the Gwenffrewi legend does at least locate Caradog in North Wales at about the same time as Arthur was completing his education in that region.

A Welsh manuscript – Peniarth 133 – refers to a 'Gwgon Red-Sword son of the earl of the White Host and King of Tegeingl, son of the King of Manau'. That this Gwgon Red-Sword was close to Arthur is strongly suggested by the *Stanzas of the Graves* poem, in which Gwgon's place of burial is mentioned immediately before that of Arthur. Taking Caradog to have been the 'earl of the White Host and King of Tegeingl', his son Gwgon Red-Sword would have been Gwenhwyfar's brother and therefore Arthur's brother-in-law. The notion that Caradog was also the 'son of the King of Manau' relates to his position as an in-law to Áedán mac Gabráin. It is also worth noting that Crydon – the name given for the father of Cywryd Gwent – was said to have been a son of Cynfarch, King of North Rheged, and among the putative sons of Cynfarch we find Urien, Arawn (Áedán) and Llew (Arthur).

The *Life of St Padarn*, which dates from about 1120, states that Caradog extended the borders of his kingdom into *Letavia*, a Latinised form of the Welsh *Llydaw*. This appears to have been an early name for Lothian (or *Leudonia*, as an early *Life of St Kentigern* called it), but it also occurs in the name of a lake at the foot of Mount Snowdon in Gwynedd. Llyn Llydaw is unusual in being the only lake in Wales to boast a 'crannog', and as these artificial islands are common in Scotland and Ireland it is probable that the lake-dwelling of Llyn Llydaw was home to a Gaelic family, such as that of Arthur. Hence its name: the Lothian Lake.

Caradog extended his influence not only across much of North Wales but into Lothian proper. He achieved this by the simple expedient of marrying a princess of North Britain. The *Triads* recall the surpassing bond of enduring love which Caradog Strong-Arm 'cast upon Tegau Golden-Breast, daughter of Nudd Generous-Hand, King of the North'. (The same triad identifies Caradog as a son of 'Llyr of the Sea' – a comment on his relationship to Áedán of Dalriada.) Caradog married the delightful Tegau, the daughter of Nudd, King of the Selgovae, which meant that he became a brother-in-law to the Chief Bard Taliesin and part of the ruling dynasty of Strathclyde.

Tegau Golden-Breast was one of the three 'Fairest, most Loveable, and most Talked-of Maidens who were in the Island of Britain at that time' – an honour she shared with Muirgein's daughter Morfudd and with Essyllt, the famous lover of Drystan. It is hardly surprising to find that the dazzling Tegau became the mother of Gwenhwyfar, although ironically Tegau was renowned for being one of the most faithful wives in Britain. Whatever personal traits she might have passed on to her daughter, sexual constancy was not one of them. No doubt Gwenhwyfar was as strikingly beautiful as her mother, and as the granddaughter of Nudd the Generous her marriage to Arthur would have helped to legitimise his rule over Lothian and the 'other nearby territories which formed part of it'. It was just history's tragedy that their marriage would not prove to be as chaste as that of her parents.

Tegau Golden-Breast became one of the 'Three Splendid Maidens at Arthur's Court'. Caradog Strong-Arm became one of Arthur's Chief Elders and his 'Pillar of the Cymry'. (*Cymry* – meaning 'compatriots' – was how the Britons thought of themselves.) Mounted on his horse called Host-Splitter, Caradog was one of the Battle-Horsemen of the Island of Britain. He would also be one of the 'Three People who broke their hearts from Bewilderment'.

Arthur's 'Three Great Queens' were all different aspects of Gwenhwyfar or, rather, different aspects of the goddess as they were expressed through the person of Gwenhwyfar. The first was Gwenhwyfar as the goddess in her Maiden form: the daughter of Caradog Strong-Arm and Tegau Golden-Breast, and quite possibly a childhood sweetheart of Arthur's.

The second Gwenhwyfar was the daughter of Gwythyr son of Greidiol – Gwythyr being an early form of Uther. As the daughter-in-law of Áedán mac Gabráin, the son of the Scorcher, Gwenhwyfar manifested the Sacred Bride aspect of the goddess. It so happens that, in her alternative guise of Gwenffrewi (St Winefride), Gwenhwyfar has a church dedicated to her at Gwytherin, a village in North Wales which perhaps took its name from her awe-inspiring father-in-law.

This leaves only the third aspect of the goddess: Gwenhwyfar, the daughter of Gogfrân Gawr or 'Little-Raven the Champion' (*cawr*, meaning a 'giant', is cognate with the Gaelic *cùra*, a 'hero', which seems a more apt interpretation). This Little-Raven the Champion was also remembered in Welsh tradition as *Bendigeid Frân* or 'Brân the Blessed'.

There is much to be said about Brân the Blessed and most of it must wait for a later chapter. In brief, though, he was a son of Llyr, he was crowned 'King of the Island of Britain', and he was primarily associated with a magical cauldron of rebirth. This was the same device as the cauldron of inspiration, and in the poetry of the time we find various references to a blessed youth in connection with the cauldron.

The *Black Book of Carmarthen* contains a poem written in praise of Ceridwen, the cauldron-goddess:

> Vat of paradox, song of Ceridwen, seed of Ogyrwen,
> Varied seed of riches, give speech to the skilful singer.
> Cuhelyn the Wise, pure Briton, of the land of Camlan,
> Skilful his song, bardic grandson of Áedán,
> Completion of Lleu.

A better-known poet than Cuhelyn also sang of this fair youth, Ogyrwen. In his *Cadeir Teyrnon* ('*Chair of the Great-Lord*'), Taliesin praised the 'blessed Arthur' and declared:

> Exalted when wise from the cauldron,
> Ogyrwen thrice-gifted [or 'inspired'].

We know from the *Triads* that Arthur underwent three periods of imprisonment, commensurate with the three 'gifts' of cauldron-inspiration. Elsewhere, in a poem entitled *Song of the Sons of Llyr*, Taliesin sang:

> Superior to the chair is the cauldron of Ceridwen.
> From it comes my tongue's blessed gift,
> Desiring again to praise Ogyrwen.
> Idle poets who praise Ogyrwen, to them
> An abundance of milk and dew and acorns.

Ogyrwen was apparently a 'blessed youth' who was something to do with the cauldron and its inspirational qualities. He compares with the 'blessed raven', Brân, and the heroic champion known as Little-Raven or *Gogfrân Gawr*, the father of Arthur's third great queen.

The 'blessed Arthur' was the prophet of the cauldron. The roots of this role can be traced back to antiquity – indeed, to the ethnic origins of the Gaelic race in the Bronze Age city of Miletus on the coast of Asia Minor. A Milesian legend told of a young goatherd named Branchus, a youth so beautiful that Apollo the Sun-god fell in love with him and bestowed on him the gift of prophecy. Branchus built a temple, which he dedicated to the twins Apollo and Artemis (Diana), at Didyma, a short distance from the city of Miletus along the Sacred Way. This became one of the most important oracles in the classical world, second only to Delphi. Branchus later adopted a son, whom he named Evangelos and who inherited the oracle. Thenceforth, the prophetic gift was passed down from father to son.

The cult of Branchus travelled with the Gaels from the Mediterranean to the islands of the west, where it gave birth to the legend of a beautiful youth, blessed with the gift of prophecy, whose name was 'Raven' (Welsh *brân*, Gaelic *bran*). The same god was invoked by Nostradamus, who saw the future reflected in a bowl of water, and we might suppose that Arthur used a similar technique. He was the fair one of the cauldron and a father to Gwenhwyfar in as much as he was her husband, her emperor and the blessed youth of the cult to which Gwenhwyfar undoubtedly belonged. This gives us the third aspect of Arthur's wife: as the 'daughter' of the Little-Raven, she was the death-dealing Hag who was also the goddess of wisdom.

On paper, it was an excellent match. Gwenhwyfar was a princess, a priestess and an avatar of the goddess Venus (*Gwener* in Welsh) or, as she was known in the Western Isles, the beautiful Bride. A symbolic marriage of convenience to his half-sister Muirgein had enabled Arthur to take on the defence of Lothian, but for him to become the *imperator*, the champion of Britain, something more was required. His marriage to Gwenhwyfar helped him to bind the nobility of the North even closer together, and when he led his warrior-princes in the attack on Abernethy he was more than happy to be wearing his heart on his sleeve.

The wedding ceremony must have been quite an occasion. Gwenhwyfar, we can assume, looked resplendent, tall, pale and thin, in the splendid cloak which belonged to her mother, while Arthur was magnificent in his imperial red-purple robe. Little did he know that the princess he was marrying would become one of the most reviled women in the history of Britain.

The operation in Strathearn was part of a broader campaign to regain control of the Pictish lands which had previously been conquered by Arthur's grandfather, Gabrán. Arthur's next battle, however, was fought closer to home.

The *Annals of Ulster* reveal that the year 577 saw the 'first expedition of the Ulaid to Manau'. One of the principal tribes of Ulster had for some reason decided to invade Arthur's territory in central Scotland. The chief of the Ulaid at that time was Báetán mac Cairill. Medieval genealogists in Ulster would cheerfully describe him as *rí Érenn ocus Alban* – 'King of Ireland and Scotland'.

It is unclear why Báetán mac Cairill should have chosen that moment to attempt the conquest of Manau Gododdin. What is certain is that their first major assault resulted in Arthur's ninth battle which, according to the Nennius list, was waged 'in the City of the Legion'.

The 'City of the Legion' appears in Welsh as *Caerllion* and is often assumed to have been the old Roman fort of Isca, now the town of Caerleon, on the River Usk in south-east Wales. There is no real connection between Arthur and Caerleon-on-Usk, although the parish church there is dedicated to one of Arthur's knights, St Cadog; it should also be noted that Geoffrey of Monmouth dedicated his *History of the Kings of Britain* to a man whose ally had recently seized Caerleon Castle – a coincidence which no doubt added to the myth that Caerleon was the site of Arthur's court. But Caerleon-on-Usk was too far removed from the seat of Arthur's power and the focus of his efforts to have been anything more than a place he might once have visited. His 'City of the Legion' was in the North.

Spanning the pinched waist of Scotland, between the estuaries of the Clyde and the Forth, the turf-and-stone rampart of Antoninus Pius was constructed by the Roman army in the middle of the second century AD and, for a few years, marked the wild frontier of the empire, where Roman legionaries came face-to-face with tattooed Pictish tribesmen.

The Antonine Wall passed to the south of a Pictish roundhouse which stood on a corner of raised tableland above the River Carron. The roundhouse had been commandeered by the future Emperor Vespasian during an earlier attempt to quell the Picts, and around it the 'Valiant and Victorious' XX Legion built a large fortress. Over time, this fortress grew to include ten marching camps and an adjoining enclosure known as the South Camp.

The Romans called their huge fort *Colania*. A short distance away, Vespasian erected a temple in honour of the Emperor Claudius, who had ordered the invasion of Britain. The circular temple, later described as an 'old building in the form of a sugar-loaf, built without lime or mortar', was destroyed in the eighteenth century, but an exact replica can be found among the stables at Penicuik House in Edinburgh. As far back as 1293, the temple was known as *Furnum Arthuri* – 'Arthur's Oven'.

The legions abandoned the *Colania* fortress in about AD 165, withdrawing from the Antonine Wall and retreating to the more imposing wall of Hadrian, many miles to the south. The forts beside the Carron Water were then occupied by the natives, who turned the South Camp into a thriving settlement.

Writing in the sixteenth century, Hector Boece linked the *Colania* fortress with Cruthneus Cameloun or 'Cruithne of Camelon', a (probably mythical) King of the Picts. George Buchanan, another Scottish historian of the sixteenth century, remarked that the Roman wall, 'where it touched the River Carron, had a garrison or fortress which, by its situation and the termination of a number of roads there, had the appearance of a small city, which some of our writers falsely imagine to have been Camulodunum'. Buchanan averred that this 'small city' was more probably 'the city Bede called Guidi' – that is, the city of the Men of the Forth.

Robert Sibbald, in his *Historical Inquiries* of 1707, largely agreed with Buchanan's assessment, although he did wonder whether the 'small city' could have been the remains of '*Camulodunum Brigantium*, which the vulgar call at this day Camelon near Falkirk'. This was an interesting remark. With a disdain for the marvellous that was typical of the Scottish Reformation, George Buchanan had rejected the possibility that the ancient city was 'Camulodunum', but now Sibbald was suggesting that it might in fact have been '*Camulodunum Brigantium*'.

Camulodunum was the 'Fort of Camulos', named after a Celtic god of war akin to the Roman Mars. The name *Camulodunum* was shortened and given a quick respray by the French poet Chrétien de Troyes, who flourished in the latter half of the twelfth century. Writing predominantly for the daughter of Queen Eleanor of England, Chrétien did more than anybody to romanticise the legends of Arthur. He composed lengthy poems about Owain ('Yvain'), Lleënog of Lennox ('Lancelot') and Peredur of York ('Perceval'), and it was in his romance entitled *Lancelot, the Knight of the Cart* that Chrétien wrote: 'Upon a certain Ascension Day King Arthur had come from Caerleon, and had held a very magnificent court at Camelot as was fitting on such a day.'

Chrétien based his vision of Camelot on the Roman city of Camulodunum, now Colchester in Essex. Apart from having been the onetime capital of Roman Britain and the first township to fall victim to Boudica's bloodthirsty revolt of AD 60, Colchester was the site of a *colonia*, a retirement home for Roman army officers. It would not require too much genius to mistake the Roman *colonia* at Colchester for the Roman fort of *Colania* near Falkirk, especially if Robert Sibbald was right and the 'small city' by the River Carron was indeed *Camulodunum Brigantium*: the Camelot of North Britain.

The evidence would appear to support Sibbald's view. When Edward Gibson, Bishop of London, was revising William Camden's *Britannia* in 1695 he remarked of the *Colania* fort that 'There is yet a confused appearance of a little ancient city, where the common people believe there was formerly a road for ships. They call it Camelot.'

William Stukeley, whose *Account of a Roman Temple and other Antiquities near Graham's Dyke in Scotland* focused on the Arthur's Oven temple and the Antonine Wall nearby, reported: 'December 1720. We may still discern the track of the streets, foundations of buildings and subterranean vaults. The country people call it Camelon or Camelot.'

General W. Roy also surveyed the site in the eighteenth century. 'Though this place is probably the Caer-Guidi of Bede,' he wrote, echoing Buchanan's assertion that it was the City of the Men of the Forth, 'yet antiquaries have not been able to determine what was the more ancient name.' Roy continued:

> From its extent and the many vestiges of buildings remaining in it, it certainly hath been one of the most considerable stations belonging to the Romans in North Britain. The town consists of two parts, whereof that towards the south seems to have been the original station, and that on the north a subsequent or additional work.

The massive fortified settlement lay just 1km north of the Antonine Wall on the road leading to the volcanic bulwark of Manau. An anonymous correspondent of 1697 offered more information regarding the paved road that crossed the River Carron by the fort, 'at the end of which stood a great castle, called by the country folks the Maiden Castle, but now little is to be seen of it'.

General Roy's plan, published after his death in 1793, identified an oval mound, measuring some 300m by 150m, a short distance beyond the north-east end of the Roman vallum. This turned out to be a native site – Boece's 'Palace of the Picts'. Photographed from the air in 1949 and then excavated in the 1960s, the mound proved to have supported two circular houses of timber, protected by four ditches and a wooden palisade, dating back to the first or second centuries AD. One of these would have been the roundhouse taken by Vespasian, the other, perhaps, being the Maiden Castle. An account of the excavation of the Camelon forts in 1900 suggests that 'Maden' might be a safer spelling, yielding a 'Mount Maden' – from the Gaelic *Dùn Maidean* or 'Fort of the Sticks', so named after its defensive palisade. Still, the possibility that Arthur's Camelot included a roundhouse devoted to the use of his queen and her maidens cannot be ruled out.

Nennius, the Welsh monk who provided us with a list of Arthur's battles, probably had one of these structures in mind when he wrote that a Roman commander built 'upon the bank of Carron a round house of polished stone, erecting a Triumphal Arch in memorial of a victory'. Perhaps it was this memorial which led to the fort being associated with the Celtic goddess of victories, Brigantia, patron of the tribes of North Britain and the goddess revered in the Hebrides as the beautiful Brìde.

The City of the Legion, where Arthur's ninth battle was fought, was this 'ancient city', known to the locals as Camelon or Camelot. Built by a detachment of the Twentieth Legion on the utmost edge of the empire, it became Arthur's military headquarters, the great base and training ground for his coalition forces.

The remains of Camelot now lie underneath a golf course. The map identifies them as Carmuir or Carmuirs – W.J. Watson interpreted this as the 'Fort of the Wall'. Arthur's presence in the area is attested by the Arthursund or Arthurstone to the north-east of Falkirk and, of course, the Romano-British temple known for many years as Arthur's Oven.

Intent on wresting Manau Gododdin from the Britons and their Scottish allies, the Ulaid of Ulster under Báetán mac Cairill attacked this fort in 577, allowing the 18-year-old Arthur to chalk up the latest in his string of victories.

12

THE ROUND TABLE

ARTHUR WAS not the only hero whose legends were later consigned to the wrong part of Britain. His cousin Drystan would suffer the same fate. Even his homeland of Lyonesse was misplaced. It was the kingdom of Lothian, remembered by British refugees as the Land of the Lion or *Leonais*. But the legends of Tristan came to be associated with Cornwall, and so Lyonesse, it was assumed, must have been a vanished island somewhere off the coast of south-west Britain.

The real Tristan was a prince of the North. In the parish of St Vigeans, near Arbroath, there is a Pictish stone upon which is carved an inscription:

DROSTEN:
IPEUORET
ETTFOR
CUS

This can be interpreted as 'DRYSTAN OF FIFE AND FORTH, AND FERGUS'. The child of Cynon son of Clydno and a Pictish princess, Drystan was a 'man of Fife' (*Fir ibe*) and 'of the Forth' (*Werid* – rendered on the stone as *Uoret*). He spent several years in Aberdeenshire as a guarantor of St Columba's peace deal with King Bruide, after which he moved down to Holywood in Dumfriesshire to be close to his father's settlement at Hoddom Cross. This brought him into the woodland region of Celidon, and according to a Welsh manuscript (Cardiff MS 43) it was to this very forest that Drystan eloped with his lover, Essyllt.

The French poet Béroul composed his romance of *Tristan* in about the year 1200. At one point in the story, the 'Fair Yseut' sends her squire to take a message to Arthur. The squire rides to Caerleon, which we can now identify as the 'City of the Legion' at Camelon, near Falkirk. But Arthur is not there.

The messenger inquired for news of the king and learned that he was at Stirling:

Fair Yseut's squire went along the road which led in that direction. He asked a shepherd who was playing a reed-pipe:

'Where is the king?'

'Sir,' said he, 'he is seated on his throne. You will see the Round Table which turns like the world; his household sits around it.'

'We shall soon be there,' said the messenger.

And soon enough, he discovered Arthur 'on the dais where all the knights were seated.' This was the Round Table of legend.

The Round Table made its literary debut in the *Roman de Brut*, an unreliable verse-history of the kings of Britain written by Robert Wace of Jersey in about 1155. By the close of that century, Béroul had located the Round Table at Stirling.

A little later, in 1478, William of Worcester wrote that 'King Arthur kept the Round Table at Stirling Castle'. A generation on, Sir David Lindsay referred to the rock on which Stirling Castle stands by its old poetic name:

Adew, fair Snawdoun, with thy towris hie,
Thy Chapell-royal, park, and *Tabyll Round* ...

Some sort of Round Table existed at Stirling as late as the sixteenth century, when it was fondly associated with the 1,000-year-old legends: 'in a sport called "Knights of the Round Table", the Institutions of King Arthur were commemorated'.

Béroul described it as a 'dais', a word which derives from the Latin *discus*, a 'dish' or a 'disc'; in Medieval Latin it could also mean a 'table'. There is, in close proximity to Stirling Castle, an object familiarly referred to as the Cup and Saucer. It is a dais which 'turns like the world', in that its shadow, cast by the Sun as it crosses the sky, seems to move with the daily revolution of the earth, offering a rough guide to the time of day. It has been known since time immemorial as the Round Table.

The crag-and-tail outcrop of the Castle Rock looms over a bend in the River Forth. Immediately to the south-west of the rock lies the King's Park, enclosed by William the Lion at about the same time as Béroul was composing his *Tristan* romance. The gardens were landscaped for King Charles I in the first half of the seventeenth century and among the alterations made for that unlucky monarch was the creation of the King's Knot – an octagonal, flat-topped earthwork which rises in a series of terraces around a grassy knoll. The central mound measures nearly 15m across and is much older than the ornamental earthwork which surrounds it. The King's Knot squats in the meadow below Stirling Castle looking rather like a giant push-button, a great green doorbell at the gates of Britain.

The mound around which the King's Knot was raised had long been called the Round Table. When the Battle of Bannockburn was fought nearby in 1314, the English King Edward II (whose father had stolen the Stone of Destiny from

Scotland) rode desperately to Stirling with his followers but was denied shelter by the castle's governor. The poet John Barbour, writing not long after the event, recalled that the king and his men galloped off:

> And besouth the Castle went they thone,
> Rychte by the Round Tabill away.

In the summer of 2011, researchers from Glasgow University, working alongside local historians and members of the Stirling Field and Archaeological Society, conducted geophysical surveys of the King's Knot. The team discovered evidence of a 'circular feature' beneath the surface of the central mound. It was here on this circular 'dais' that the Fair Yseut's messenger found Arthur enthroned and surrounded by his knights. As Béroul intimated, it was not very far from Arthur's headquarters at the City of the Legion: no more than 9 miles of Roman road separated the Round Table at Stirling from the massive fort of Camelon near Falkirk.

Councils of war were held at the Round Table, and special events too, no doubt, such as the wedding of Arthur and Gwenhwyfar. Its importance was more than just strategic, however; the Round Table was a burial mound. Arthur's fellowship of warriors chose to meet there because it was the grave of their mutual ancestor, Brychan of Manau. The *Cognatio de Brachan* recorded Brychan's burial 'in the island which is called Ynysbrachan and which is next to Manau'. The Welsh word *ynys* can refer to an island or a river meadow; the Round Table mound stands on the floodplain of the River Forth, immediately adjacent to the Rock of Manau.

Brychan had shown a previous generation of warrior-princes how to unite as an extended family. His original version of the Round Table, comprising his twenty-four sons and their twenty-four female counterparts, had brought the Scots into alliance with the Britons, allowing Gabrán to annex Perthshire. Arthur revived his great-grandfather's policy. He forged an elite unit of oath-sworn warriors committed to the defence of North Britain. Where better for them to hold their councils than in the field beside the River Forth, at the grave of the mighty Brychan?

Arthur's tenth battle was fought near this spot. Coming after the ninth battle 'in the City of the Legion', the next battle on the list drawn up by Nennius was 'waged on the shore of a river which is called Tribruit'.

The Welsh poem known as *Pa Gwr* – effectively, Arthur's death-song – makes reference to 'the army of Trywrid'. This seems to derive from an old name, recorded in 1165, for the Firth of Forth: *Werid*, from the British word *Gwruid*, meaning 'Men of the Forth'. There were two safe crossing places over the River Forth directly to the west of Stirling. These were the Fords of Frew (Welsh *ffrwd* – a 'stream') and they were the reason why Manau needed a warlord: they were the means of access whereby the Picts could invade North Britain.

It is possible that Trywrid came from the Welsh *drwy* – 'through' – and *Werid*, 'the Forth'. Alternatively, the first syllables of Trywrid and Tribruit could be derived from the word for a 'shore' – *traeth* (Gaelic *tràigh*) – to form a 'shore of the men of the Forth' or a 'shore of conflict', *traeth brwyd*. The area around Stirling was so battle-torn that an early name for the town, *Striveling*, was once thought to mean 'Place of Strife'. The Gaelic name for Stirling – *Sruighlea* – can be interpreted as 'stream of combat' or 'battle-torrent' (*sruth ghliadh*); the Gaelic *sruth* matches the Welsh *ffrwd*, a 'stream'; and those all-important Fords of Frew, which it was Arthur's duty to guard, would have been *drwyffrwd*, 'through the stream', or *trewruid*, 'through the Forth'.

So troubled was the British front line at this point that it required a standing army – the 'army of Trywrid' – to defend those fords, and this was the purpose of the Round Table. At the Battle of the River Forth, Arthur's enemies were almost certainly the Irishmen of Ulster. Led by Báetán mac Cairill, they had crossed the Moyle in 577, intent on seizing Manau Gododdin. They had fought with Arthur at the 'City of the Legion'. Though they lost the battle at Camelon, the Ulaid did not return to Ulster until the following year, giving them plenty of time to launch another assault on Arthur's territory.

Arthur and his men battled with the Ulaid on the bloody shore of the Forth, close by Stirling and the Fords of Frew, and in 578 the warriors of Ulster went back home to Ireland.

Who were the heroes of the Round Table? They were Arthur's *teulu* (pronounced 'tey-li'), his war-band or 'family'. Their twenty-four seats marked the hours on the 'Round Table which turns like the world'.

The Welsh legend of *Math Son of Mathonwy* outlines the circumstances which led to Arthur's birth – a war between Strathclyde and Gwynedd – and reveals that twenty-four 'hostages' helped to bring a resolution to the crisis. The equivalent number of 'damsels' is encountered by Arthur's nephew Owain in his own *Mabinogion* tale.

A Welsh manuscript, transcribed in the fifteenth century, provides a list of the 'ordained' warriors who fought under Arthur's command. Entitled *Pedwar Marchog ar Hugain Llys Arthur* – the '*Four Horsemen and Twenty of the Court of Arthur*' – the manuscript bundles them into groups of three.

The first group consisted of the Golden-Tongued Knights: 'there was neither king nor lord who came to them who did not listen to them, and whatever quest they sought, they wished for and obtained it, either willingly or unwillingly.' Their given names were Gwalchmai, Drudwas and Eliwlod.

Gwalchmai was the original 'Sir Gawain'. His name meant 'Hair of May' (*gwallt Mai*), and though one source refers to him as a son of Llew he is usually presented as the son of Gwyar or Gweir. In fact, Gúaire was an Irish name, and we shall discover who Gúaire son of Áedán was in a later chapter. Gwalchmai would live on in Hebridean lore as 'Sir Uallabh', a variation on the Gaelic *ollamh* or 'wise man'. He was almost certainly a foster-son of Arthur and can be tentatively identified as the long-haired Irish hero known as Mongán who, as the son of Arthur's sister, was a nephew to Arthur, just as Gwalchmai is said to have been. He died fighting in Kintyre in 625.

Drudwas also had an Irish background. He was supposedly the son of Tryffin – presumably the same Tryffin the Bearded who, though an Irishman, ruled the kingdom of Dyfed in south-west Wales at the close of the fifth century. The name Drudwas ('Brave-Servant') could easily have been applied to Cai the Tall, with whom Arthur was fostered in Dyfed: not only was Cai perennially cast as Arthur's seneschal or steward, but he was also the son of a fair-bearded Irish Lord of Dyfed. Cai son of Conchrad, one of the three 'Battle-Diademed Men of the Island of Britain', rode a lively steed called Chestnut Long-Neck and had the misfortune of being killed by his own 'griffon' warriors – the reasons for which will become clear in due course.

Eliwlod son of Madog son of Uther appears in the poem of Arthur's conversation with an eagle. In the poem, the eagle speaks with the voice of Arthur's dead nephew, Eliwlod, giving Christian answers to Arthur's questions. This would suggest that Eliwlod died while Arthur was still alive, and the fact that the name Eliwlod can be translated as 'The Lord Who Seeks a Boar' makes it possible to hazard a guess as to who he was. Known in Scotland as Fergus, he was a close associate and probably a foster-brother of Drystan son of Cynon. Fergus was killed during the pursuit of a notorious boar, after which Drystan's father escorted his body to Glasgow. The name given for Eliwlod's father – Madog – means 'fortunate' or 'seemly' in Welsh, although there were several Irish saints named Maedóc, one of whom was hailed by an eighth-century monk as 'Scotland's diadem'.

These, then, were the Golden-Tongued Knights of Arthur's Court: Gwalchmai (or Mongán, Arthur's nephew and foster-son), Cai (Arthur's foster-brother and bodyguard) and Fergus (Arthur's foster-nephew).

The next three were the Virgin Knights, whom neither giant nor witch nor fiendish being could withstand. They are named as Bors, Peredur and Gwalhafed.

Bors does not appear in the early tales. He was later said to have been a favourite cousin of Sir Lancelot and one of the three knights who succeeded in the quest for the Grail. The names given for his father – Brons or King Ban of Benoic – are corruptions of Brân the Blessed, a British hero associated with the sacred cauldron. It is possible that Brons derives from Brân ('Raven') via the Gaelic *bròn* ('sorrow' or 'lamentation'), although it might also recall the *brongoch* or 'redbreast' which, it was suggested in Chapter 5, was Arthur as an infant. In all probability, Bors was a product of the romantic imagination, and his place at the Round Table was originally taken by Arthur himself.

Peredur Steel-Spear was one of two sons of Eliffer of the Great Host, the British prince who died defending York against the Angles in 559. Peredur later fought against Arthur at the Battle of the Trees in 573, after which he was persuaded to join the Round Table coalition; he stayed the course and perished at Arthur's last battle. His legend, entitled *Peredur Son of York*, is found in the Welsh *Mabinogion*. Continental romancers of the Middle Ages would convert him into the Grail knight called Sir Perceval.

Gwalhafed was similarly altered to 'Sir Galahad', a name first used in the thirteenth-century *Queste del Saint Graal*. His earlier name meant 'Hair of Summer'. The *Triads* list him as one of the 'Pillars of Battle of the Island of Britain', and as Gwenhwyfar's cousin he takes his place alongside Arthur and Gwalchmai in the Welsh tale of *Gereint and Enid*. Taliesin described him admiringly as a 'horse-man in battle' and a 'judge over Elmet'. He was familiarly known as Gwallog ('Hairy'), the son of Lleënog and grandson of Masgwid of Lennox, who took on the defence of the West Yorkshire kingdom of Elmet after the troubles of 559. 'Who has not seen Gwallog has not seen a man,' sang Taliesin.

Gwallog the Battle-Horseman linked Yorkshire, where Peredur ruled in the city of York, with the northern realm of Arthur. All three were intimately associated with the Grail.

The next three knights 'did not flee for fear of sword or arrow'. They were Arthur's Battle Knights – Cadwr, Lancelot and Owain.

Cadwr is introduced as the 'Earl of Cornwall' in the hallucinatory *Dream of Rhonabwy*, a *Mabinogion* tale which drops a number of heavy hints about the death of Arthur. In that story, Cadwr (meaning 'Soldier') is the man 'whose duty it is to arm the King on the days of battle and warfare'. It was our old friend Geoffrey of Monmouth who made him 'Duke of Cornwall' and Arthur's sword-bearer. Geoffrey also claimed that Arthur finally yielded his crown to his cousin Constantine, the son of 'Cador Duke of Cornwall'. Constantine was in fact a churchman who, according to Jocelin's *Life of St Kentigern*, succeeded his father Rhydderch as King of Strathclyde. This would imply that Rhydderch the Generous was the 'Soldier' who armed Arthur on the days of battle. After an inauspicious start, which included going to war against Arthur's father and having his own Dumbarton court ravaged in return, Rhydderch figured out which way the wind was blowing and joined the Round Table alliance. He became Arthur's sword-bearer and donated the sword which was buried with Arthur. Married to Myrddin's 'twin' sister, Rhydderch was also a patron to Cynon (St Kentigern). He rode a horse called Dun-Grey and died in about 614.

Lancelot is another legendary character who did not appear until the Middle Ages: he was first glimpsed, briefly, in *Erec et Enide*, a French romance composed by Chrétien de Troyes in about 1160. The Welsh responded with their own version of the tale, called *Gereint and Enid*, in which Lancelot was given his proper name, Lleënog. He was the 'Learned' or 'Literate' son of Masgwid of Lennox and, therefore, identified with the Loch Lomond region – hence the designation 'Lancelot of the Lake'. His famously illicit love for Arthur's queen was almost certainly a medieval invention, although it is feasible that he had been betrothed to Arthur's sister Muirgein, an arrangement which fell apart when, in 559, Lleënog's kingdom was subsumed into Dalriada. Lleënog instead plumped for 'Elaine of Astolat', the Lady of Shalott; Astolat being a late version of Alclud – the Rock of Dumbarton – it is probable that a noblewoman of Strathclyde was the mother of Lleënog's son Gwallog.

Owain, the son of Muirgein and Urien of North Rheged, was Arthur's nephew and foster-brother. Growing up in the care of Áedán the Wily, 'the best man in the world', led to Owain receiving the nickname 'Worry' or 'Anxiety' – *Pryderi* – and he is known by that name in the first few tales of the *Mabinogion*. He also appears in his own *Mabinogion* legend of *Owain, or The Lady of the Fountain* – the French version is called *Yvain, The Knight with the Lion* – and as Earl Owain in the tale of *Gereint and Enid*. His role in the peculiar *Dream of Rhonabwy* is more ambiguous, for while he and Arthur are playing a board game their war-bands attack each other. Like his father Urien, Owain would be lauded by Taliesin as a 'reaper of enemies', 'praised in song', and to his Cumbrian people he was nothing less than the godlike Son of a divine Mother. He ruled North Rheged for some five years after the death of his father in 590. His warriors were known as 'Ravens' and he rode a horse called Cloven-Hoof.

These were Arthur's three Battle Knights: Rhydderch the Generous, King of Strathclyde; Lleënog of Lennox; and Owain, prince of North Rheged.

The three Enchanter Knights could change themselves into whatever 'form they wished when they were hard-pressed, and therefore no one could overcome them'. Their names were Menw (Myrddin), Drystan and Eiddilig the Dwarf.

Menw or Menwaedd ('Little-Shout') was the son of Morfrân the Speckled and Aldan, a princess of Dyfed. Raised in Gwynedd, he was trained by the cauldron school to be a poet and a 'king's fool'. He briefly served his kinsman Gwenddolau, but his calamitous deployment of a Druid-mist at Arderydd in 573 led to the deaths of his lord and several relatives. Menw then fled into the Forest of Celidon and became Myrddin Wyllt, the Wildman of the Wood. The legends of southern Scotland associate him primarily with Rhydderch the Generous and St Kentigern (Cynon). It was Geoffrey of Monmouth who called him Merlin and granted him everlasting fame.

Like Myrddin, Drystan son of Cynon was based for a while in the Forest of Celidon. The Scots knew him as St Drostán, although his original name – Drust – was Pictish. He travelled with St Columba to negotiate with Bruide of the Picts in 565 and is credited with having established a monastery at Old Deer; his fellow saints Fergus and Maedóc were honoured in the same region. Drystan was also connected with St Vigeans in Angus and the 'church of My-Drust' at Markinch in Fife, very close to the lake where Arthur was born (Drystan, we recall, was 'of Fife and the Forth'). The Britons, however, remembered Drystan as something other than a Christian missionary. He was an enchanter, a shape-shifter, and the lover of Essyllt Fair-Hair, whose name meant 'She Who is Gazed At'. One of the *Triads* names Drystan son of Tallwch ('High-Brow' or 'Pig-Brow') as one of the 'Powerful Swineherds' of Britain who successfully prevented Arthur and his companions from making off with a sacred pig (perhaps Essyllt, a priestess or 'pig' in her own right). His father was similarly associated with swine, being known as 'Kentigern of the Pig-Enclosure', which would suggest that both Cynon and Drystan were guardians of a sisterhood or 'Castle of Maidens', just as father and son alike were remembered as two of Britain's 'Three Lovers'. Drystan was also one of the 'Enemy-Subduers' and one of the 'Battle-Diademed Men of the Island of Britain'. He was the model for the 'Sir Tristan' of medieval romance.

Eiddilig the Dwarf would appear to have been another 'king's fool', diminutive but deadly. In addition to being one of the great enchanters, he joined Drystan and 'Gúaire of Great Valour' in forming the trio of 'Severe Men of the Island of Britain'. He appears as one of Arthur's servants, ironically named Eiddyl the Tall, in the Welsh tale of *Culhwch and Olwen*. A contemporary poem of Arthur's last battle names him as 'Cynddilig of Aeron', *Aeron* being the Welsh version of the Gaelic *Éirin*, meaning 'Ireland'. His proper name was Áed Dibchine mac Senaig and he was a King of Leinster. The epithet Dibchine seemingly meant 'Tiny Dog' (*dub choin*), which would match the 'Hound' element of Cynddilig, while his first name Áed became the first part of Eiddilig. He was probably one of the two 'warhounds' of Ireland mentioned in the poem of Arthur's last battle, which also refers to Áed Dibchine as being 'of the Liffey'. He was succeeded as King of Leinster by Brandub, allegedly the twin or foster-brother of Áedán mac Gabráin.

Arthur's three Enchanter Knights were, therefore, his close friend Menw (Myrddin), his cousin Drystan and the little war-hound of Ireland, Áed Dibchine mac Senaig.

There were three Royal Knights at Arthur's court. No king could refuse them in times of peace 'on account of their beauty and wisdom', while in war 'no warrior could withstand them'. They were Nascien, Medrod and Hoel.

According to later tradition, Nasciens son of Evelake was blinded when he came too close to the Grail. Evelake is a corruption of Afallach, the name of the 'apple-bearing' isle where Arthur was buried. Afallach is also thought to have been a British god analogous to the Irish Nechtán. There was in fact a historical ruler of Strathclyde called Neithon (the Picts knew him as Nechtan). He took the throne of Dumbarton after Constantine had renounced it and he died in about 620.

The father of this Neithon or Nechtan was Gwyddno Tall-Crane, the prince of Strathclyde who presided over the cauldron cult at Llyn Tegid in Gwynedd, and so there is every chance that Neithon was related to Arthur. It is notable that a 'son of Nuithon' and a 'son of Gwyddno' were both present at Arthur's last battle.

Medrod, sometimes referred to as a son of Llew, was the subordinate chieftain and noble warrior who brought the Round Table to its knees. His identity will be revealed very shortly.

In his *History of the Kings of Britain*, Geoffrey of Monmouth had Arthur racing to Dumbarton to relieve his nephew Hoel, who was besieged by Picts and Scots. After a series of battles in Scotland, Arthur and Hoel stood on the banks of Loch Lomond discussing the wonders of the lake and other pools. Hoel's real name was Huail and he shared a father with St Gildas in the form of Caw ('Skilful'), a King of North Britain who was probably the same person as Brychan of Manau, the progenitor of the Round Table family. Clearly, Huail could not have been Arthur's nephew, though they were related. Different traditions exist concerning that relationship: in *Culhwch and Olwen*, Huail son of Caw 'who never submitted to a lord's hand' is Arthur's friend and ally; in the *Life of Gildas*, written by a contemporary of Geoffrey of Monmouth, Huail is an enemy who harasses Arthur from the North. A stone which stands in the market square at Ruthin in North Wales is known as Huail's Stone, and a local legend claims that Arthur and Huail quarrelled over a woman; Huail wounded Arthur in the knee, but Arthur got his revenge by beheading Huail on the stone. It is unclear whether this legend dimly recalls some ritualistic activity or the tragic events surrounding Arthur's downfall.

The three Just Knights of Arthur's court were Blaes, Cadog and Pedrog.

Blaes, the 'master of Merlin', is said to have written up an account of Arthur's battles before retiring to Northumberland. He seems to have become mixed up with a later medieval Welsh storyteller named Bleddri. In reality, he was St Blane (Old Irish *Bláán*), a sixth-century bishop commemorated at Dunblane, just north of Stirling, and in the Strathblane which runs westward from Dunblane to Loch Lomond. Blane was born on the Isle of Bute in the Firth of Clyde and then he and his mother were cast helplessly adrift in a coracle – a familiar story! His death is confidently ascribed to the year 590, and since Arthur and his allies were fighting in Northumberland that year, Blane's retirement would appear to have been rather final.

Originally named Cadfael ('Battle-Prince'), Cadog left his home in south-east Wales and travelled north, becoming involved with the cauldron cult in Gwynedd. He then followed Arthur and the others to Scotland where, as St Catán or Cathan, he came to be associated with Argyll and the Isle of Bute, then part of the kingdom of Dalriada. Tradition states that Áedán mac Gabráin seduced St Catán's sister, who then gave birth to Catán's nephew, the boy known as St Blane.

Late in the eleventh century, Lifris of Llancarfan wrote a *Life* of Cadog which placed the Welsh saint squarely in Arthur's world. Lifris described Cadog's arrival at a 'certain fort, which is on this side of mount Bannog' – almost certainly the 'City of the Legion' at Camelon, just south of the Bannockburn hill. St Cadog began digging the foundations for a monastery and unearthed the collar bone of 'some ancient hero'. This 'revived giant of huge stature' then appeared to St Cadog and disclosed that he was Caw of North Britain: 'Beyond mount Bannog formerly I reigned for many years.' Cadog had exhumed the remains of the father of Gildas and Huail, presumably from the Round Table mound in the field beside the Castle Rock at Stirling (just north of 'mount Bannog'). It is probable that Caw, or Brychan, was also St Cadog's grandfather. The saint transported the remains of the great hero to the site of his new monastery near Dunblane.

Among other things, St Cadog or Catán was said to have become one of the three keepers of the Grail. His name, *Cadwg*, which drew on the Welsh word for 'battle', can also be interpreted as 'keeper'. It is hardly surprising that Geoffrey of Monmouth managed to muddle up Cadog and Cador, the 'Soldier' who can be identified as Rhydderch of Strathclyde. Geoffrey stated that Arthur's queen was brought up in the household of 'Duke Cador', but since St Cadog was a close friend of Gwenhwyfar's father Caradog – they were both chieftains of south-east Wales – the likelihood is that Arthur's wife had been raised as a ward of St Cadog, an eventuality that would prove nothing short of disastrous for Arthur.

Pedrog was another nobleman of South Wales who became a 'saint'. He was known as Pedrog Splintered-Spear, and his skill was such that he survived the slaughter of Arthur's last battle (a Welsh bard of the fifteenth century declared that 'precious Pedrog was renowned with his weapon at the death of Arthur'). Pedrog was, of course, Pedr of Dyfed who, as well as being an uncle of St Cadog, provided shelter for the infant Arthur in 559 and named his own son Arthwyr in honour of his noble guest. In the Welsh tales of the *Mabinogion* he appears as 'Pedrod', the father of 'Bedwyr'. The latter was a constant companion of Cai the Tall and, like Arthur, had probably been fostered with Cai. Pedrog later became a patron saint of Cornwall while his son would evolve into the romantic hero 'Sir Bedivere'.

Arthur's three Just Knights, who dedicated themselves to preserving justice by every law, were Blane 'by earthly law', his uncle Cadog 'by the Law of the Church', and Cadog's uncle Pedrog, 'by the Law of Arms'.

Next were the three Offensive Knights: Morfrân, Sandde and Glewlwyd.

Morfrân the Speckled, also known as Morfryn the Skilful, was the father of Menw or Myrddin. He survived Arthur's last battle thanks to his alarming appearance: 'hair had he upon him like the hair of a stag'. A graduate of the cauldron school and onetime 'brother' to Arthur's mother, Morfrân was one of the 'Slaughter-Blocks of the Island of Britain'. He rode a horse called Pale White Lively-Back.

Sandde Angel-Face also emerged unscathed from the carnage of Arthur's last battle, but in his case it was his beauty that saved him – 'all thought he was a ministering angel.' He was associated with the kingdom of Ceredigion in West Wales, between Pedr's realm of Dyfed and the Meirionydd land of Gwyddno Tall-Crane, and he is said to have been the father of St David. Arthur, along with his mother and her brother, was given shelter at St David's settlement in Dyfed in 559. The mother of St David was also the sister of Arthur's foster-brother, Cai the Tall.

Glewlwyd is remembered as Arthur's gatekeeper and appears as such in the poem *Pa Gwr* or '*What Man is the Porter?*' In this poem, Arthur and Cai posthumously seek entrance to an Otherworldly hall of heroes:

What man is the porter?
Glewlwyd Great-Grasp.
What man is asking?
Arthur and Cai the Fair.
What is the good of your embassy?
In truth, the best there is …

In the tales of the *Mabinogion*, Glewlwyd receives several mentions: he was Arthur's 'chief porter', but only performed this office during one of the great festivals, when the gates to the Otherworld were flung wide open. His 'Valiant-Grey' name and 'Great-Grasp' epithet point to his real identity. He was none other than Caradog Strong-Arm, a prince of south-east Wales who became Arthur's father-in-law, his Chief Officer, Chief Elder and Pillar of the Cymry. His name is found in the poem of Arthur's last battle, the grief and horror of which were too much for him; his world fell apart and his heart broke 'from Bewilderment'.

Morfrân, Sandde and Caradog Strong-Arm were all prominent father-figures at Arthur's court. They were Offensive because it was 'repugnant to anyone to refuse them anything' – Morfrân by reason of his fearsome appearance, Sandde by dint of his angelic looks and Caradog because of his size, strength and ferocity.

Lastly, there were Arthur's three Counsellor Knights.

The first of these was Cynon son of Clydno. Father to Drystan and brother to Creirwy, Cynon was a major presence in Arthur's life. He saved the baby Arthur from Bruide's Pictish spearmen, helped to raise him in Wales, and rode into battle by his side. The Church would insist on remembering Cynon solely as St Kentigern or Mungo, the 'Dear One', quietly forgetting his place in the Arthurian pantheon. One of the few survivors of the final conflict, Cynon was praised by the poet Aneirin as a 'kind-hearted bejeweled lord' and a 'serpent searing and cheerful'.

Arawn son of Cynfarch is next on the list. He appears as the 'Lord of Annwn' in the First Branch of the *Mabinogion*, where he swaps places with Pwyll, Lord of

Dyfed. Pwyll was in fact Urien of North Rheged, and a Welsh poem names Urien and Arawn as brothers of Llew (Arthur). Geoffrey of Monmouth altered Arawn to Auguselus, of which 'Angel' is a variant, arrived at by way of the Gaelic *aingeal*, meaning 'fire'. He was a son of Cynfarch only in so far as Urien was his foster-brother, and he was ideally suited to the role of counsellor to Arthur, for the 'Lord of Annwn' was in reality his father, Áedán mac Gabráin, King of the Scots.

Llywarch, the last of the twenty-four horsemen, was the son of Elidyr the Stout and Handsome, King of South Rheged; Llywarch's cousin Urien ruled the kingdom immediately to the north (they were both descendants of Brychan of Manau). Llywarch took a paternalistic interest in the Round Table warriors – it was he who remembered Urien, Arawn and Llew as his 'sons'. His is a sad tale. After the defeat of Arthur, Llywarch lost his kingdom to the Angles and fled to North Wales, where he settled near the southern end of Llyn Tegid and composed poems lamenting the deaths of his fellow heroes. He became known as Llywarch the Old and died in about 634.

The Counsellor Knights at Arthur's court were therefore his uncle Cynon, his father Áedán and his nominal cousin, Llywarch the Old of South Rheged.

The list of the twenty-four knights is no more than a snapshot. Others must have fought alongside Arthur: one name conspicuous by its absence is that of Urien, King of North Rheged and father of Owain. Even so, it provides us with an insight into Arthur's world and the calibre of the princes who formed his coalition.

Though they came from far and wide – from Leinster and Dalriada and Dyfed, Gwent and Gwynedd, York and Elmet, Lennox and Lothian, Rheged and Strathclyde – they were all bound together by ties of blood, marriage and a common cause.

Some would achieve lasting fame as Arthurian knights: Gwalchmai ('Gawain'), Peredur ('Perceval'), Lleënog and Gwallog ('Lancelot' and 'Galahad'); others would be glorified as saints of the Church – Cynon ('Kentigern'), Pedr ('Pedrog'), Cadog (or Catán) and Blane; among them, too, were the heroes would be come to know as Merlin, Tristan and Uther Pendragon.

They were all contemporaries of Arthur son of Áedán, with whom they each had a personal connection. Never let it be said that we cannot know for sure who Arthur was, or whether he even existed. The list of the four-and-twenty horsemen of his court leaves precious little room for reasonable doubt.

He was Arthur the Emperor, a Scottish prince of British blood, and with his family of warrior-princes he very nearly changed the course of history.

The warfare continued. At about the age of 20 Arthur fought his eleventh battle 'on the mountain which is called Agned'.

There are other editions of the *Historia Brittonum* in which the list of Arthur's victories reads slightly differently and the eleventh battle is located at 'Breguoin' or

'Bregnion'. One manuscript warily backs all comers, calling it *Agned Catbregomion* – the 'Agned Battle of Bregomion'.

Writing 300 years after Nennius, Geoffrey of Monmouth claimed that the mythical King Ebrauc had founded the three northern cities of York, Dumbarton and 'Mount Agned', the latter being the site of a Maidens' Castle. John of Fordun in the fourteenth century explicitly stated that Agned was an old name for Edinburgh. The name compares with Agna or Agnetis – the name of the Celtic 'abbess' who shared her feast day with Arthur's half-sister Muirgein, the 'Anna' of Lothian.

In the *Pa Gwr* poem, Arthur acknowledged that there had been bloodshed at 'Mynydd Eidyn' – the Mountain of Edinburgh. That mountain was the volcanic plug known as Arthur's Seat or the Lion's Head. The Braid Hills rise a short distance to the south-west of Arthur's Seat, their name coming from *bràghaid*, the dative form of the Gaelic *bràigh*, meaning the 'upper part'. The equivalent in Welsh is *brig* – 'top' or 'summit'. This gives us the alternative name for the battle 'on the mountain which is called Agned', and suggests that the conflict ranged over much of the district. It was *Agned Catbregomion* – the 'Edinburgh Battle of the Braid Hills'.

Below the Braid Hills, in the Edinburgh suburb of Fairmilehead, there is a brute of a standing stone, nearly 3m tall and crisscrossed with natural faults which form an X-shape like the Scottish saltire. This megalith is the Caiy Stone, also known as General Kay's Monument. Nearby stood the Cat or 'Battle' Stones – two round cairns which were discovered to contain human skeletons and weapons of iron and bronze (the cairns were removed in the nineteenth century). Other 'battle' stones litter the area, including the Cat Stane which stands on land that now belongs to Edinburgh Airport.

The *Pa Gwr* poem indicates that Arthur contended 'often with dog-heads' near Edinburgh. This can be taken to mean that Germanic warriors launched a series of assaults on Lothian from the Firth of Forth. Some of them would have been Franks from western Germany. Frankish law determined that anyone who dug up or despoiled a buried corpse 'shall be a *varg*': the word meant 'wolf' and is the origin of the term 'vagrant'. The Angles and Saxons had a similar concept. They thought of the 'outlaw' – *utlagh* – as having the head of a wolf. In defending Edinburgh, Arthur would appear to have battled with more than a few of these desperate 'dog-heads'. According to the *Pa Gwr* poem, 'all of Kent' sailed up to the Lothian shore.

The immigrants recognised Arthur as a formidable foe. The headland of Bo'ness juts out into the Firth of Forth to the west of Edinburgh. The place was first labelled on a map of 1335 as *Berwardeston*, an Anglo-Saxon name meaning 'town of the bear-guardian'. This was one of the forts which Arthur fought to defend: it was the 'Fort of Edern', now Carriden, at the eastern end of the Antonine Wall.

Nennius concluded his list of Arthur's victories with one of the most famous, and most problematic, of them all:

The twelfth battle was on Mount Badon in which there fell in one day 960 men from one charge by Arthur; and no one struck them down except Arthur himself, and in all the wars he emerged as victor.

Confusion has long reigned over this battle, mostly because of the saint known as Gildas the Wise. In his scathing open letter to the Kings of Britain, which appeared a decade or two before Arthur's birth, St Gildas referred to a 'siege of Badon Hill' as a watershed victory for the Britons under their warlord Ambrosius Aurelianus. Gildas also remarked that the battle had been fought in the same year as his own birth.

The Badon Hill referred to by St Gildas was probably somewhere near the City of Bath – *Caerfaddon* in Welsh. The 'siege of Badon Hill' was remembered because it had earned the Britons a prolonged period of peace. But any semblance of a truce had broken down in southern Britain by the time Arthur was leading his men to a series of victories in the North.

The 'siege of Badon Hill' had nothing at all to do with Arthur. Sadly, though, the fact that it had been mentioned by Gildas led to the assumption that it must have been the same as the 'Mount Badon' referred to by Nennius as Arthur's twelfth battle, even though the two were entirely unconnected.

It is as if someone had read about the 1781 Siege of Yorktown and immediately jumped to the conclusion that it was the same as the 1862 Battle of Yorktown – a glaring error, but one easily made when the records are not up to scratch.

In the case of Arthur's twelfth battle, the records are almost useless. Apart from St Gildas and Nennius, the only real reference to Badon occurs in the *Welsh Annals*, which note:

518   The Battle of Badon in which Arthur carries the
       Cross of Our Lord Jesus Christ for three days and nights
       on his shoulders and the Britons were victors

This entry is paired with a later one, dated 539: 'The battle of Camlann, in which Arthur and Medrawt fell; and there was plague in Britain and Ireland.' Both entries stand out as being positively verbose in comparison with the entries around them. They were added in at a much later date – at least 300 years after the events – and the best that can be said of them is that they were a misguided attempt at squaring a circle: Arthur fought at a Battle of Mount Badon; St Gildas had mentioned a siege of Badon Hill; *et violà!* By finding a convenient date somewhere between the two the annalists of Wales had invented a battle which never took place.

A more reliable source comes in the form of the *Anales Toledanos*. These Spanish annals state that Arthur's Battle of Camlan took place in 580, which was at least during the real Arthur's lifetime. It so happens that the *Welsh Annals* ascribe the death of Peredur of York to that same year – wrongly, because Peredur perished several years later; but the entries in the Spanish annals and *Welsh Annals* do indicate that a major battle took place in 580.

The *Annals of Ulster* reveal that Arthur's father undertook a naval expedition to the Orkneys in 580 or 581. He did so on behalf of his erstwhile brother-in-law. King Bruide was beginning to show his age, and the next-in-line for the Pictish throne was Áedán's son Gartnait. By quelling a rebellion in the most northerly part of Bruide's realm, Áedán was safeguarding the throne of the Picts for his eldest son.

The same Irish *Annals* indicate that 580 also saw the death of 'Cennaleth, King of Picts'. Galam Cennaleth had been joint-ruler, with Bruide son of Maelgwyn, of the Pictish lands in 552: Galam governed the southern Picts while Bruide controlled the Highland massif. But by 553, Bruide had become the High King of the entire Pictish nation. The outcome of Bruide's elevation was the outbreak of war between his half-brother Rhun of Gwynedd and the princes of Strathclyde, a war which had led to the birth of Arthur.

The death of Galam Cennaleth in 580 should be seen in the context of Áedán's expedition to the Orkneys: both events point to an upheaval among the Picts along the lines of a civil war. This is apparently confirmed by a wildly misdated entry in the *Annals of Tigernach* for the year 752 – 'Battle of Asreth in the land of Circinn between Picts on both sides, and in it Bruide son of Maelchon fell.' The *Annals of Ulster* date Bruide's death more convincingly to 584. Nonetheless, a Battle of Asreth 'between Picts on both sides' does show that the Picts were at war with themselves. Most likely, it was not Bruide but his rival, Galam Cennaleth, who died in the battle.

Áedán mac Gabráin had sailed with his navy to the Orkney Isles, thereby depriving Arthur of a certain amount of military support. This would account for the remark of Nennius that, of the many who fell at the battle on Mount Badon, 'no one struck them down except Arthur himself'. Arthur was fighting without his father's assistance, and possibly without the full Round Table. The battle was fought to preserve the Scottish Highlands for Arthur's half-brother Gartnait and was, therefore, of limited concern to the warrior-princes of North Britain who, like Peredur of York, had other problems to attend to.

The Battle of Asreth was fought 'in the land of Circinn'. Circinn, or Circenn, was a province of the southern Picts, roughly contiguous with Angus and Kincardineshire. The Picts of Circenn were 'crested' (*cìr* – a 'comb'); they cut their hair in Mohican fashion, or perhaps wore headpieces inspired by the crest of a wild boar. They shared this trait with the Orcoi peole of the Orkneys, whose name came from *orc*, a 'young boar'.

King Bruide was being menaced from the north and south by these boar-like Picts. Áedán sailed north to put down the rebellion in the Orkneys.

Meanwhile, Arthur and his heroes were engaged in the hunt for a boar.

We know this from the ancient tale of *Culhwch and Olwen*, which offers a potted, if fabulous, account of Arthur's career. The tale opens with the birth of Arthur's uncle, Cynon son of Clydno, who, because he is born in a sacred enclosure, is given the name Culhwch (pronounced 'kil-hooch') or 'Pig-Run'.

In order to win the hand of the exquisite Olwen, Culhwch enlists the help of Arthur and his warriors. The heroes approach Olwen's father, who sets them a series of daunting tasks, the main challenge being to seize the comb and scissors which are between the ears of a fearsome boar known as Twrch Trwyth. The epic hunt for Twrch Trwyth forms the climax of the tale.

However, there is another boar to be dealt with first. Arthur, we are told, went into the North to hunt the Chief-Boar Ysgithyrwyn ('White-Tusk'). No sooner has this Chief-Boar been dispatched than Menw the enchanter changes himself into a bird so that he can find out whether the comb and scissors are still between the ears of Twrch Trwyth. He tries to snatch one of these items but succeeds only in plucking one of the boar's bristles. The boar rises up angrily, shaking himself, so that 'some of his venom fell upon Menw, and he was never well from that day forward.'

This odd nugget of information allows us to pinpoint the location of Arthur's twelfth battle.

The Chief-Boar 'White-Tusk' was none other than Galam Cennaleth, King of the southern Picts. He was hunted to extinction in 580 at the 'Battle of Asreth in the land of Circinn', which was also Arthur's battle on Mount Badon.

Asreth comes from the Old Irish *israth* – a 'valley'. It was in the Pictish province of Circenn or, as we know it today, Angus. Galam and his crested, boar-like warriors, attempting to attack Bruide's Highland kingdom from the south, walked into a typical Arthurian trap.

The River Isla runs through Glen Isla from its birthplace high up in the Cairngorm Mountains. It coils down through Angus to join the River Tay in Perthshire. Towards the very start of its 46-mile journey the Isla carves a gorge through the southern edge of the Cairngorms where, opposite the crags known as the Duke's Lairs, it is met by the Fergus Burn. Close by stands the farmhouse of Crandart, which took its masonry from the long-vanished Crandart Castle (Crandart seems to hint at *crann-adhair*, the constellation of the Bear). A little further down the valley stands the greystone tower of Forter Castle. One or other of these ancient castles gave its name to the hill which rises above them – the 740m peak known as Badandun Hill.

Badandun is the Gaelic equivalent of Mount Badon. It means something like 'Place of the [Fortified] Hill'. The hill looms over the very spot where Arthur unleashed his cavalry against the Chief-Boar and his spearmen. Galam and the southern Picts were advancing up Glen Isla to invade the realm of King Bruide. Where the valley narrows around Crandart they were caught in a bottle-neck.

Arthur sounded his horn and his mounted warriors streamed down the north-west flank of Badandun Hill, tearing into Galam's startled war-band by the ford across the Fergus Burn. The map marks the place where Fergus – Arthur's nephew Eliwlod, 'The Lord Who Seeks a Boar' – was killed.

In such a confined space the charge would have been devastating. Perhaps 960 casualties was an exaggeration, but it gives an idea of the scale of the carnage. Those who survived the initial impact scattered westwards, fleeing into the hills beyond the Duke's Lairs. Arthur and his horsemen chased them into the adjacent valley of Glenshee and there, in the Valley of Spirits, Galam Cennaleth was cornered and slain.

Glenshee has its own legend of the boar-hunt. For political reasons it became expedient for the Scots to forget all about Arthur, and so the Glenshee legend was grafted onto those Irish prototypes for all things Arthurian, Fionn mac Cumhail and his elite war-band, the *fianna*. But the tale bears such a striking resemblance to the *Culhwch and Olwen* legend that it can be properly attributed to Arthur and his heroes.

The story goes that a large and dangerous boar was terrorising the neighbourhood. King Fingal – the 'Fair Stranger', as the Scots thought of Fionn mac Cumhail – called upon his best warrior, Diarmaid, to exterminate the boar (Fingal was said to have been jealous of Diarmaid, who was having an affair with Fingal's wife). Diarmaid trapped the boar beneath Ben Gulabin in Glenshee and killed it. In the process, he was poisoned by one of the boar's bristles. Local tradition claims that Diarmaid was buried in a grave-mound marked by four large stones, just east of the Spittal of Glenshee.

The legend of Diarmaid and the boar is told of many places – most notably Ben Bulben in Ireland, where King Diarmait mac Cerbaill went to war with St Columba. Among the Scottish descendants of Arthur, the Clan Campbell traces its ancestry back to Diarmaid, taking the boar's head as its family emblem. The success of the Campbell clan can be attributed to its tendency always to side with the winners; by downplaying their Arthurian heritage the Campbells avoided offending the Church – and so Arthur's descendants became the descendants of another, less controversial hero and the legendary boar-hunt of Glenshee was fused with the death of Diarmaid.

The Britons were never so ready to deny Arthur. While the Scots preferred to imagine that it was Fingal's man who was wounded by the boar in Glenshee, the Britons recalled that it was one of Arthur's warriors who fell. The *Culhwch and Olwen* legend argued that it was Menw the enchanter who was poisoned by the boar's bristle and was never the same again. Menw was, of course, traumatised at the earlier Battle of Arderydd, after which he became the madman called Myrddin. But there was one Arthurian warrior who did die as a result of the boar-hunt, and that was Fergus or 'Eliwlod', the foster-brother of Menw's fellow Enchanter Knight, Drystan.

The legends overlap. Arthur went 'into the North' to hunt down the Chief-Boar. He ambushed the Pictish king in the valley of the Isla, in the shadow of Badandun Hill in the land of Circenn, and chased him into the spirit-haunted valley of Glenshee, where the boar was put to death.

The southern Picts were routed. Arthur had saved the kingdom of his kinsman Bruide, preserving the Highlands for his half-brother Gartnait. The decisive victory brought more land under Arthur's control. He was able to impose his authority on two natural thoroughfares running eastwards from Dalriada – Loch Tay and Glen Lyon, the latter being the 'Valley of the Lion', named in Arthur's memory. The whole central plain of Scotland, from Stirling up to the edge of the Cairngorms, now belonged to Arthur the Emperor. He had recaptured the territory once conquered by his grandfather Gabrán, as far east as Blairgowrie and the valley of the River Isla, and he had achieved all this by the age of 21.

But there was sadness, too. According to Jocelin's *Life of St Kentigern*, Cynon son of Clydno was present when Fergus died. Frequently found in the company of Drystan, Fergus was almost certainly Cynon's foster-son. Cynon placed the body in a cart, which was then drawn by two bulls all the way to a place called Cathures on the Molendinar Burn, near the River Clyde. There, Cynon buried Fergus and established a new community. It was said that Cynon called it his 'Beloved Cloister' – *clas cu* in Welsh – but really it was the 'Green Hollow' or *Glaschu*.

Arthur followed his uncle to Glasgow, if only to converse with his 'Golden-Tongued' nephew Fergus, which he did through the medium of his eagle. The Glaswegian suburb of Barrhead is known locally as Arthur's Camp, and there we find an Arthurlie and an Arthurstone. For all we know, Fergus was the first of the Round Table warriors to fall in battle. Arthur could not let him go without the appropriate rites.

The Battle of Mount Badon, fought in 580 in Glen Isla, beneath Badandun Hill, was Arthur's most famous victory. But it marked a shift in the balance of the Round Table.

And an even more dangerous boar was waiting in the wings.

Key to Map 5

1 – Catlowdy	7 – Annandale
2 – Dumbarton	8 – Abernethy
3 – Glassary	9 – Camelon
4 – Lennox	10 – Fords of Frew
5 – Craigmaddie Muir	11 – Braid Hills
6 – Dryburgh	12 – Badandun Hill

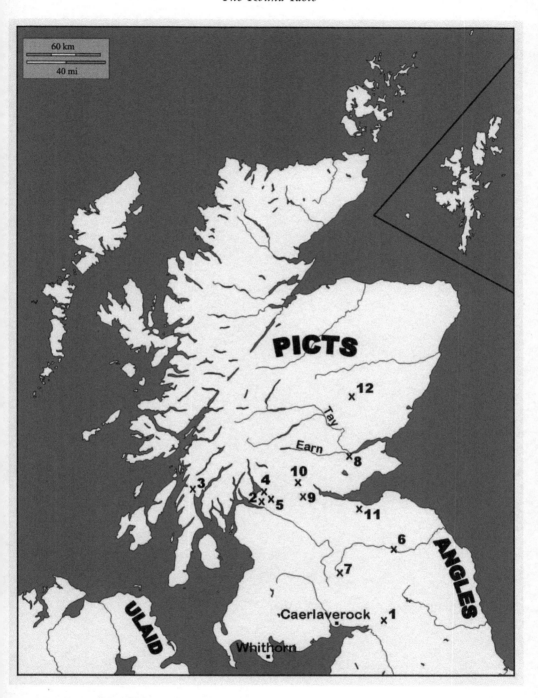

Map 5 Arthur's Battles, 573–580 (after Nennius)

13

MORDRED

THE LIST of Arthur's battles compiled by Nennius in about 830 ends with his triumph at Mount Badon. There is no mention of Arthur's last battle.

It could be that Nennius was only interested in recording Arthur's victories, but there is perhaps a better explanation for his failure to mention the Battle of Camlan. One of Arthur's knights, St Blane, was said to have written up an account of Arthur's battles. Blane's death is ascribed to the year 590, and so any battle which took place after that date would not have made it into Blane's testimony. If Nennius based his list of Arthur's successes on Blane's contemporary report, which has since been lost, then his list would not have included the last of Arthur's battles.

The Irish *Annals* also neglect to mention the Battle of Camlan. They do, however, refer to the death of Báetán mac Cairill, leader of the Ulaid, whose warriors had gone to war with Arthur over Manau in 577. The *Annals of Ulster* announce that Báetán mac Cairill died in 581 and, again, in 587. The *Annals of Tigernach* have Báetán dying in 579, after which Áed Dub mac Suibne became King of the Ulaid of Ulster.

Black Áed was a colourful chieftain of those Irish 'Picts', the Dál nAraidne. In 565 he had killed his foster-father, Diarmait mac Cerbaill. After killing King Diarmait, Áed Dub sought sanctuary on the Hebridean island of Tiree, where a Christian settlement had been established under the aegis of Columba's monastery on Iona. St Columba was horrified to learn that Black Áed had taken holy orders. The saint predicted that Áed Dub would return to his old ways 'like a dog to its vomit … He will be a bloody murderer again and, in the end, killed by a spear, he will fall from wood into water and die by drowning.'

This ritualistic triple-death was no less than Black Áed deserved for having killed the 'King of all Ireland', said Columba, who seems to have forgotten that he too had gone to war against Diarmait mac Cerbaill.

The Irish annalists failed to agree on the date of Áed Dub's death. The *Annals of Ulster* ascribe it to 585 and 588, while the *Annals of Tigernach* offer 583 and 586.

The sequence of events is rather murky, to say the least, but they went something like this:

Báetán mac Cairill led the 'first expedition' of the Ulaid to Manau Gododdin in 577. They lost a battle or two against Arthur and returned to Ireland in 578. Báetán did not abandon his plans to seize Manau, though, and a second expedition of the Ulaid must have occurred at some stage. Báetán mac Cairill died sometime between 579 and 588 – a date of around 582 seeming most likely – and there was indeed another Battle of Manau fought during this period.

The second entry in the *Annals of Ulster* for the year 582 reads: 'The battle of Manu, in which Áedán son of Gabrán son of Domangart was the victor'; and in 583: 'The battle of Manu *won* by Áedán.' The *Annals of Tigernach* record a *Cath Manand* or 'Battle of Manau, in which the victor was Áedán mac Gabráin' in 579; although, to be on the safe side, the *Tigernach* annalist entered the 'Battle of Manau' again for the following year.

As we have seen, the Spanish *Anales Toledanos* give the year 580 as the date of Arthur's Battle of Camlan. A more accurate date would be 582 or thereabouts, when Áedán won the Battle of Manau against Báetán mac Cairill's warriors of Ulster. There is every chance that this was indeed a 'Battle of Camlan' and that Arthur survived it – he would live on for another twelve years.

The 'first expedition' of the Ulaid to Manau resulted in the ninth battle of Arthur, at the 'City of the Legion'. This was the great fortress of Manau Gododdin. Built by a detachment of the XX *Valeria Victrix* Legion a short distance to the north of the Antonine Wall, it was the *Colania* garrison which came to be known as Camelot. It is probable that the Ulaid warriors attacked Arthur's headquarters again when they made their second expedition to Manau. This time, they were repelled by Arthur and his father, Áedán mac Gabráin.

The site of Arthur's military headquarters is now called Camelon. The place name has two syllables – 'came-lon'. In the Scots dialect, it is *Kemlin*, while in Gaelic it is known as *Camlan*.

'After Manau,' sang the poet Taliesin, 'many turned for home, departing from the heaped-up slaughter.' The Irishmen of Báetán mac Cairill had finally been defeated. And yet, only a year or two later, 'the Gael abandoned Manau'. Why on earth would the Scots have relinquished control of Stirling and its environs? More to the point, why had Arthur abandoned his post?

The answer hinges on the ritualistic death of Black Áed mac Suibne, King of the Dál nAraidne, which can now be dated to about 584. Áed Dub had replaced Báetán mac Cairill as King of Ulster. Black Áed's successor promptly took control of Stirling and Manau Gododdin. He was able to do so because he was Arthur's brother-in-law.

His name was Fiachna mac Báetáin (no relation to Báetán mac Cairill). He was a chieftain of the 'Pictish' Dál nAraidne and became King of Ulster after the death of Black Áed mac Suibne.

Precisely when Fiachna mac Báetáin married Áedán's daughter is unknown, but it is possible that the arrangement was planned as far back as 575, when the 'great convention' of Druim Cett was held on the very border of the tribal lands of the Dál nAraidne. The Dál nAraidne had long been allies of the Scots of Dalriada, and at some point in time between 575 and 584 that alliance was strengthened by the marriage of Fiachna mac Báetáin to Muirgein, daughter of Áedán mac Gabráin.

Muirgein's latest marriage was remembered in the traditions of Wales, as preserved in the tales of the *Mabinogion*. In the Four Branches of the *Mabinogion*, Muirgein appears as the little princess, Rhiannon, who first married Pwyll, Lord of Dyfed (Urien of North Rheged) and gave birth to Pryderi (Owain). Later, with her son's approval, she entered into a marriage with Manawydan, whose Scottish equivalent was Manannán son of Lir. Both the Irish Manannán and the British Manawydan were sons of 'Llyr of the Hosts', the same lord of the isles who, in addition to being one of the 'Battle-Horsemen of the Island of Britain', was Arthur's father, Áedán the Wily.

Fiachna mac Báetáin became the 'dear one of Manau' – Manannán – only after he had replaced Arthur as the protector of Manau Gododdin in 584. The *Pa Gwr* poem which reflected on Arthur's military career recalled Fiachna's appointment as the commander of the forces of the North:

Manawydan son of Llyr,
Wonderful profound the counsel
That brought Manawyd
To the army of Trywrid.

The union of Fiachna and Muirgein produced two sons. In an attempt to resolve ideological differences in the kingdom of the Scots, the boys were raised by different foster-fathers.

One of the boys was named Laisrén or Laserian ('Light' – a theme which ran in the family). Laisrén was born in Ireland but grew up in Scotland, where he joined the monastic community on Iona and lived for a while as a hermit on Holy Island, off the coast of Arran in the Firth of Clyde. He would eventually become the first bishop and patron saint of Leighlin, an Irish diocese joined with the sanctuary of Brighid at Kildare. Some sources make Laisrén a rather youthful 'confessor' to St Columba, who seems to have adopted him. Known familiarly as 'My Laisrén' or *Mo-Lais*, he would be honoured as St Molaise. He died in about 639.

If Laisrén became a man of God, his brother was thought of as the son of a god. According to an ancient Irish text, Fiachna mac Báetáin was the 'sole king' of his Ulster province:

He had a friend in Scotland, to wit, Áedán, the son of Gabrán. A message went from him to Áedán. A message went from Áedán asking him to come to his aid. He was in warfare against the Saxons. A terrible warrior ['*h-uathmar*'] was brought by them to accomplish the death of Áedán in the battle. Then Fiachna went across, leaving his queen at home.

While Fiachna was fighting in Britain alongside his father-in-law, a noble-looking stranger arrived at Muirgein's fort and told her that her husband was in grave danger. The danger could be averted, however, if Muirgein consented to sleep with the stranger. She duly spent the night with him. In the morning, as the stranger set out to join Áedán and Fiachna on the far-off battlefield, he paused on the threshold and announced:

> I go home,
> The pale, pure morning draws near;
> Manannán son of Lir
> Is the name of him who came to thee.

The child born from Muirgein's one night stand with the sea-god of the Hebrides was given the name Mongán – 'Little Long-Haired One'. The boy enjoyed a sort of dual paternity, being sometimes known as Mongán son of Fiachna mac Báetáin and sometimes as Mongán son of Manannán mac Lir (Fiachna and Manannán being two aspects of the same person). It was widely accepted that Mongán was the reincarnation of the legendary hero Fionn mac Cumhail, and he met his death in Kintyre thirty years after the death of Arthur.

The eighth-century *Voyage of Bran* rather charmingly named the mother of Mongán as Cáintigerna or 'Beautiful Lady'. It is possible that this had some bearing on Geoffrey of Monmouth's decision to call Arthur's mother Ygerna – a corruption of *tigerna* ('lady') – and that his famous account of Arthur's conception was influenced by the curious tale of Mongán's parentage. Mongán was, of course, Arthur's nephew. He had allegedly been conceived when his father was away fighting, although in fact his father seems to have been in disguise, having taken on the persona of Manannán. If nothing else, the legend suggests that royal husbands adopting some form of disguise in order to engender heroes was common practice in Arthur's extended family; perhaps Mongán was another Beltane baby, born – like Arthur – during the 'blackthorn winter' of early February. He was known to the Britons as Gwalchmai ('Hair of May') and became Arthur's nephew and foster-son, the model for the 'Sir Gawain' of the romances.

The marriage of Fiachna and Muirgein was successful in its own terms: two sons, one raised by Arthur, the other by Columba of the Church. But it was also a political alliance. This was recognised by the new name adopted by Muirgein. She was now known as 'Maithgemma of Monad' – from *maith geamhna*, 'good pledge', although the name might also hint at Muirgein having been a little 'bear-cub' or *math-gamhna*. The designation 'of Monad' is especially revealing.

There are references in Irish literature to a place called Dùn Monaidh. In the eleventh-century poem of the *Birth of Áedán mac Gabráin*, Muirgein's grandfather Gabrán is referred to as the 'King of Monad of the market'. The Druidic sons of Uisnech who had accompanied Deirdre of the Sorrows were described during their time in Scotland as being 'from Dùn Monaidh' while the *Book of the Lays of Fionn*, which recounted the exploits of that Arthurian doppelgänger Fionn mac Cumhail, told of the taking of Dùn Monaidh. Other Irish heroes who visited Dùn Monaidh included Cú Chullain, the poster-boy of the epic *Cattle-Raid of Cooley*, who came to Dùn Monaidh while searching for his wife in Alba, and Conall, King of Ulster, who solicited support for his rebellion against the King of Ireland from the inhabitants of Dùn Monaidh.

The Gaelic word *monadh* is cognate with the Welsh *mynydd*, both signifying a 'moor' or a 'mountain'. *Dùn* generally meant a 'hill fort'. Evidently, the 'Hill fort of the Heath' was an important place in early Scottish history. Professor William J. Watson, in his *History of the Celtic Place-names of Scotland*, noted that the fort of Dùn Monaidh was often referred to as *baile rígh Albain*, the 'homestead of the King of Alba'. Various sites have been proposed, including Dunadd and Dunstaffnage, both seats of the Scottish kings, but the probability is that Dùn Monaidh was to be found on the Isle of Iona. It was perhaps the hill of Dùn Í, the highest peak on the island, or, more likely, one of the fortresses on the west coast of the isle: *Dùn-Bhuirg*, the Hill of the Fortification, or *Dùn Mhanannáin*, the Fort of Manannán, which stand at the edge of Sliabh Meadhonach, the 'high moorland' of Iona.

By styling herself 'of Monad', Muirgein was advertising the fact that she and her husband had taken up residence on the sacred isle of the Scots. The island of Columba's church was also to be known as the home of the 'dear one of Manau', Manannán mac Lir. What is more, both Fiachna and Muirgein were associated with a sacred sisterhood of nine maidens based on the Isle of Iona. This set-up would provide ample material for the later legends but it was guaranteed to infuriate St Columba, who liked to think of the little isle as belonging exclusively to him and his monks.

As a conciliatory gesture, Fiachna and Muirgein surrendered one of their sons – Laisrén – to be brought up in Columba's Christian settlement, the other being raised by Arthur. The same equitable arrangement applied to the use of the Isle of Iona: the saint and his brethren were required to share the island with Muirgein and her maidens (sometimes referred to as Manannán's magical pigs). In the grand scheme of things, the marriage of the King of Ulster to the queen of Lothian brought Áedán's family a big step closer to the destiny predicted by St Patrick. The descendants of Fergus Mór were indeed becoming the kings over Ulster and Alba.

Fiachna's elevation to the lordship of Manau Gododdin coincided with the death in 584 of Bruide of the Picts. Bruide's successor was Gartnait son of Áedán, so that Áedán's family now controlled practically the whole of Alba, from the Lowlands to the Orkneys.

There was only one snag. St Patrick had prophesied that the Scottish kings would reign supreme over the north of Ireland and the Pictish realms, and this was fast becoming a reality. But it had been brought about by Arthur's military genius, Áedán's politicking and Muirgein's marriages. These were not quite the terms that St Columba would have wanted. St Patrick's prophecy was coming true, but it was the pagan kindred of Áedán who had brought it to fruition.

After years of war, Arthur was finally able to step down. His half-brother Gartnait was the new King of the Picts and his Irish brother-in-law had taken charge of Manau. By the age of 25, Arthur had pacified the North. He could now enter a period of semi-retirement.

The Clann Arthur traces its pedigree back to Arthur son of Áedán. Arthur's clansmen rose to prominence in the Argyll and Cowal heartlands of the original Scots. They supported those medieval fighters for Scottish independence – William Wallace and Robert the Bruce – but fell from grace in 1427, when King James I of Scotland had Iain MacArthur executed for opposing his plans for more centralised government.

The MacArthurs were renowned for the antiquity of their line:

> There is none older, save the hills,
> The Devil and MacArthur.

In the genealogy of the clan, Arthur's father is identified as Iobhair, a name related to Uther by way of *iubhar*, the 'yew' (see Chapter 16), and the son of Arthur is called Smerbe or Smervie Mór (perhaps from *smior* – a 'hero' or the 'best').

The *Triads* cite one Llachau son of Arthur as one of the 'Fearless Men' and one of the 'Well-Endowed Men of the Island of Britain'. The word *llachau* properly means 'lashes' or 'slashes', although it might be a variant of *llachar*, 'flashing' or 'glittering'.

Another possibility is that Llachau recalled the element of 'stone' (Old Irish *art*) which was present in the name of Arthur. The Gaelic word for a stone is *clach*, the equivalent in Welsh being *llech* (plural *llechau*). The term for 'emery' – a coarse stone used for polishing metal – is *clach-smior* in Gaelic, with *smior* ultimately deriving from the Greek *smeris*, 'polishing powder'. It is nice to think that Arthur might have trained up his son to keep his armour bright by scouring it with sand and stone, so that the Scots nicknamed him Clach-Smior, the 'polishing stone' or the hero who glittered, which became shortened to 'Smerbe' or Smervie the Great. The Britons retained the *clach* part but called him Llachau: the stone that flashes, the sword that slashes.

Llachau is given an unhappy fate in the early sources, which suggest that he was killed by Arthur's foster-brother Cai. Another son of Arthur – perhaps the same one – was named Duran (from the Welsh *dur*, 'steel', or the Early Irish *dúr*, meaning 'hard'). An old Welsh poem records the three-line verse or *englyn* sung by Arthur over the death of his son:

Sandde ['Angel-Face'] drive the raven
From the face of Duran;
Dear the love of the mother who raised him.

It is impossible to tell how many natural sons Arthur had, and there is a tradition that he and Gwenhwyfar were incapable of having children. At least one of Arthur's sons – Gwalchmai – was actually his sister's son, whom Arthur raised as a foster-parent. But whether he had offspring of his own to raise or not, there was time, in the second half of the 580s, for Arthur to relax and bring up children at his home on the shores of Loch Fyne.

The original seat of the Clann Arthur was at Strachur, a beautiful little bay on the east side of Loch Fyne. In Gaelic, Strachur is *Srath Chura*, the 'glen of the heron' or 'the guardian', and takes its name from the River Cur which empties into the sea-loch at Strachur. The settlement was once named after Arthur's nephew St Molaise, who no doubt spent some time there.

An old legend states that a man in a grey cowl first came to Strachur and slept at the base of an alder tree before deciding to make his home there. The legend is echoed in the old Gaelic saying, '*MacArtair Strath Churra o bhun an stoc fheàrna*' – 'MacArthur of Strachur from the root of the alder' – and recalls the connection, previously noted, between Arthur and alders.

Arthur's new home faced westwards, looking across the clear water to the Crag of the Eagle. The Campbells, a cadet branch of the Clann Arthur, would inherit the ancient lands of Dalriada, becoming the Dukes of Argyll and establishing their chief seat at Inverary, on the opposite shore of Loch Fyne from Arthur's homestead. Although the Campbells eventually occupied and dominated much of the territory which had once been ruled by Arthur, they were careful not to offend the Church, choosing instead to trace their ancestry back to Diarmaid, the legendary Irish warrior who was fatally injured while hunting a monstrous boar.

There are references in old Scottish manuscripts to a 'powerful Lion of Loch Fyne' (*Leomhan lonn Locha Fíne*) and 'The chief-hero of Loch Fyne' (*A cheannlaoch Locha Fíne*) – both have an unmistakeably Arthurian ring about them. The Gaelic name *Loch Fìne* means the lake of the 'vine' or the 'family'. With its ready access to the sea, Strachur stood at the entrance to a pass through the ridge of Drumalban which separated Dalriada from Lennox and Strathclyde. It was an ideal spot from which Arthur could defend the eastern approaches to his father's kingdom while rearing a new generation of heroes.

Life at Strachur might have been pleasant enough, but the hot, dry summer of 589 presaged another season of war. Whatever happiness Arthur had known was about to be brought to a shattering end.

Far away to the south, the Britons were in trouble. War had returned to southern Britain and in 577 – the year which saw Arthur battling with Báetáin mac Cairill and his Ulstermen in Manau – the Saxons won a crucial victory at the Battle of Dyrham. The immigrants had hacked their way along the Thames Valley and through to the Severn Sea.

In the North, things were very different. Arthur's efforts in central and southern Scotland had brought order to the northern frontier, allowing the Men of the North to concentrate their fire on the Northumbrian Angles.

There had been changes in the Anglian leadership. Edwin, King of Deira, had been ousted by his northern neighbours, the Angles of Bernicia, after the death of his father Aelle in 588. Edwin was now in exile in Gwynedd – presumably, he got on well with the native Britons. The same could not be said of Hussa. He had fought against Arthur in 574 at the Battle of Craigmaddie Moor; he now governed the Anglian kingdom of Bernicia. Hussa banished Edwin in an attempt to unite the Anglian territories of Bernicia and Deira, but the move came too late. By the year 590, the Angles of Northumbria had been driven back to the edge of the sea.

The combined forces of Elmet, Rheged, Lothian and Strathclyde had the Anglian warriors pinned down on the tidal island known to the Britons as Ynys Medcaut. Today, we call it Lindisfarne. A little further down the coast an Irish army was besieging the Anglian stronghold of Bamburgh. Just one more push, and the Angles would have been wiped out in North Britain.

It is worth taking a moment to consider the implications of this, for they are truly momentous. Had the Angles of Northumbria been destroyed there would never have been a place called *Engla land*.

The first known use of the word 'England' dates from 897, 300 years after the death of Arthur. The country could not have come into being had there been no Land of the Angles for it to be based upon.

In 590, the whole course of British history was about to be changed. The Men of the North were poised to reclaim their lost lands on the east coast. This would have left the Saxons in southern Britain vulnerable to a British counter-attack. The entire island could then have been restored to its Celtic natives and the language spoken from Lothian down to London would have been Welsh.

Arthur had shown the Britons how to operate in unison against all invaders, be they Picts, Irishmen or Angles. At Lindisfarne in 590, all that hard work was about to pay off. The North would be free again. Arthur's legend was assured.

Lindisfarne was and is a holy island, a steep hill rising out of the North Sea flats on the shoulder of Britain. A few miles to the south, a basaltic outcrop bursts through the coastal sands to form the base for a mighty fortress. The Britons knew it as Din Guayrdi, although it was soon to be renamed by Hussa's successor, Aethelfrith, in honour of his wife, becoming first Bebbanburgh and finally Bamburgh. It had probably been the capital of the lost British kingdom of Bryneich, just as it would serve as the chief seat of the Anglian kings of Bernicia.

Bamburgh would live on in Arthurian lore. Sir Thomas Malory, author of *Le Morte d'Arthur*, considered it to have been the castle he called Joyous Garde. It was to this castle that Sir Lancelot took Guinevere after he had rescued her from Arthur's jealous rage; when Lancelot was expelled from Arthur's court at Carlisle, the castle became known as Dolorous Garde. The Lancelot tradition, it should be said, grew in part out of the English folktale of the Laidley Worm – a dragon or serpent-woman associated with Bamburgh – which also involved a character called Childe Wynd or Kempe Owyne, otherwise known as Arthur's nephew, Owain son of Urien.

The original 'Sir Lancelot' – Lleënog of Lennox – was almost certainly present at the siege of Bamburgh, as was Arthur's Irish brother-in-law, Fiachna mac Báetáin. The legend of Muirgein's seduction by Manannán mac Lir seems to date from this time: Áedán had summoned his son-in-law to help him fight against a 'terrible warrior', *h-uathmar*, which might have been a corruption of Hussa. Fiachna duly brought his host to *Dùn nGuaire I Saxanaib* and took his place alongside Áedán and his Irish allies.

The legends suggest that the Irish contingent stormed the bastion of Bamburgh. The romantic tradition has Lancelot going to war against the King of Northumberland at the request of Queen Guinevere. Lancelot is said to have attacked the fortress, gaining access by way of a cavern underneath the castle's chapel; he slew a monster and released an enchanted maiden who had been encased in copper. Surrounding the castle were the gravestones of many a British warrior, but these then disappeared and the castle became known as Joyous Garde – Lancelot learned that it was his fate to be buried there. Such was the tale told in the *Lancelot-Grail* or *Vulgate* cycle of about 1215. The *Prose Lancelot* claims that the hero had to penetrate the castle's defences by nightfall and then occupy the fort for forty days, which he failed to do. Behind all this fancy mythologising we might detect a temporary victory for the Irish forces at Bamburgh.

There were casualties, of course. One of them would appear to have been St Blane. He was Arthur's kinsman, the nephew of St Cadog, and one of the Round Table knights. His legend states that he 'retired' to Northumbria and died in 590 – the year of the Bamburgh siege.

So where was Arthur? It is inconceivable that he would have been absent from what should have been the Britons' finest hour. The question, then, is whether he would have been fighting alongside the Irish forces at Bamburgh or with the Men of the North at Lindisfarne – or was he in fact overseeing the entire operation?

One clue is provided by the map. Just inland from Lindisfarne stands the oddly misplaced Bamburgh Hill, above a hamlet called Blawearie (the 'plain' or 'battle-field' of the Men of the Forth). Immediately to the south is a hill known as Barty's Law. As usual, Arthur had taken the high ground. He was holding his cavalry in reserve, hidden among the woods on the edge of the Kyloe Hills, ready to deal with any Anglian warriors who managed to break through the British lines. The chances are that he was also co-ordinating both armies in their joint operation against the last Anglian strongholds.

The Britons were staring victory in the face.

Then things suddenly took a spectacular turn. One of the three 'Unfortunate Assassinations' was committed by one of the 'Savage Men of the Island of Britain'. The victim was one of Britain's three 'Battle-Leaders'.

In short, a 'foreigner' named Llofan Severing-Hand murdered Urien, King of North Rheged.

The site of the assassination was Aber Lleu – the mouth of the 'Lleu' or 'Low'. It is generally thought to have been Ross Low, a stream that runs into the North Sea at Budle Bay, between Lindisfarne and Bamburgh.

Llywarch of South Rheged had the grim task of rescuing his cousin's head and smuggling it away to safety. In Llywarch's words:

A head I carry on my arm
From necessity out of Bryneich;
Once a hero, now a great bier's burden.

Undermined by treachery, the British coalition collapsed in disarray.

Of such reversals history is made. Under Arthur's command, the Round Table warriors had defeated all comers. They had pacified the North and then took the battle to the encroaching Angles, driving the immigrants back to the sea. The hopes of Britain hung on the final defeat of the Angles. The opportunity would never arise again.

How could it all go so wrong? To make sense of the calamity we need to go back a few years.

The kingdom of Bryneich had fallen to the Angles, who renamed it Bernicia, in 547. The heir to the throne of Bryneich, a young chieftain named Morgan, became a prince in exile at the Lothian court of Clydno Eidyn.

Twelve years later, shortly after Arthur's birth, the Angles laid claim to the adjacent British province of Deywr, which they called Deira. At the same time, Bruide's Picts swept down from the Highlands to drive the Scots out of Perthshire and Morgan seized the throne of Lothian. He had been motivated, according to the legends surrounding Cynon son of Clydno, by a love of power and money.

Morgan was usually known as *mwynfawr* – 'wealthy'. He was a pagan who had some bardic or Druidic attributes, and so the Britons thought of him as 'able' or 'skilful'. The word they used was *medrod*.

Under continental influence, the 'able' Medrod was transformed into 'Sir Mordred'.

When Arthur took upon himself the defence of Lothian, roundabout the year 575, Morgan was relegated once again to the status of a subordinate prince. He became a servant of Arthur and his half-sister and co-regent, Muirgein. Known in Lothian as Llew and Anna, Arthur and Muirgein came to be thought of as the incestuous siblings whose sinful coupling led to the births of Mordred and Gawain. In neither instance was this quite true: Morgan (or Medrod) was Arthur's son only in so far as Arthur was his royal master; Mongán (or Gwalchmai) was the son of Muirgein who was raised by Arthur as his foster-son.

The leopard had not changed his spots. Morgan was obsessed with the loss of his Bryneich kingdom. He had sought to compensate for that loss by usurping the throne of Lothian in 559, only to lose control of Lothian to Arthur. By 590, the Britons were on the brink of retaking Bryneich from the Angles, but Morgan must have suspected that he would not be allowed to govern the land he was born to rule. Arthur no doubt had other plans.

Cupidity and ambition prompted Morgan to betray his own people. It was he who commissioned the assassination of Urien. He had acted in concert with the Angles before. Now, as the Northumbrian Angles were facing extinction, they made Morgan an offer he couldn't refuse.

The traditions hold that Arthur left 'Medrod' in charge of his kingdom when he set out on a military expedition to Rome and that 'Medrod' rebelled against him in his absence. Rome is clearly a misnomer – although references to Rome's unreasonable demands for tribute do at least give an indication as to who Arthur's real enemy was. But, as the legends suggest, Arthur had left his kingdom in Morgan's hands while he sought to crush the Angles on the coast of North Britain.

Morgan grasped his chance. The Royal Knight became a Red Ravager.

The *Triads* speak of three 'Unrestrained Ravagings of the Island of Britain'. The first of these occurred when Áedán the Wily attacked Rhydderch's court at Dumbarton in 574. The others involved Arthur and 'Medrod'. When Morgan came to Arthur's court he 'dragged Gwenhwyfar from her royal chair, and then he struck a blow upon her'. Arthur responded by visiting the third unrestrained ravaging on Morgan's court. But Morgan had vanished, taking Arthur's queen with him.

The abduction of Gwenhwyfar is a staple of the legends. A happier version of the story has Lancelot rescuing Queen Guinevere and whisking her away to his castle of Joyous Garde. But that was a later tradition. The Lancelot legend was fabricated merely as a sugar coating for a very bitter pill.

The medieval troubadours were not alone in reinventing history to make a better story. The Church also made use of the material, investing it with its own idea of a happy ending.

Caradoc of Llancarfan was a contemporary, and probably a friend, of Geoffrey of Monmouth, the churchman whose *History of the Kings of Britain* ignited the European craze for all things Arthurian. In his twelfth-century *Life of Gildas*, Caradoc of Llancarfan introduced the legend of Arthur's deadly rivalry with Huail son of Caw, the brother of St Gildas, and promoted the myth that Glastonbury in Somerset was the 'glassy city, which took its name from *glass*', thereby paving the way for the spurious claim that Glastonbury was Avalon. Caradoc also seems to have been responsible for the legend that St Gildas ended his days near Glastonbury, and in order to beef up the saint's profile Caradoc dragged Arthur into his story.

It is unlikely that Gildas the Wise ever met Arthur. All the same, in his *Vita Gildae*, Caradoc of Llancarfan allowed the saint to help in resolving a crisis involving Arthur. Caradoc had St Gildas arriving at Glastonbury when a certain Melwas was king in the 'Summer Country'. At the time, Arthur was besieging the famous Tor because Melwas had:

> violated and carried off Gwenhwyfar, taking her to Glastonbury … owing to the invulnerable position's protection due to thicketed fortifications of reeds, rivers and marshes. The rebellious king had searched for his queen throughout the course of one year and at last heard that she resided there. Whereupon he roused the armies of the whole of Cornwall and Devon and war was prepared between the enemies. When he heard this, the abbot of Glastonbury, attended by the clergy and Gildas the Wise, stepped-in between the contending armies and peacefully advised his king, Melwas, to restore the ravaged lady. And so, she who was to be restored was restored in peace and good will. When these things had been done, the two kings gave to the abbot the gift of many domains.

Compared with this improbable yarn, the romantic myth of Gwenhwyfar's abduction by her lover Lancelot is a model of historical accuracy. There is no evidence that an abbey existed at Glastonbury in Arthur's day and no firm grounds for believing that Arthur ever went there. The issue of Gwenhwyfar's abduction was not settled peacefully. And, as we shall see, far from helping to defuse the situation, the clergy worked actively to exacerbate it.

Only one aspect of Caradoc's fable is worthy of scrutiny – the name given for the king who abducted Gwenhwyfar. Caradoc called him Melwas. The name was formed by the conjunction of two seemingly contradictory elements: *mael* ('lord' or 'prince') and *gwas* ('man-servant'). Melwas, then, was a princely retainer, a royal underling. This was precisely the status held by Morgan the Wealthy in Arthur's Lothian. He was a born king who was obliged to serve as a client or 'lord-servant' of Arthur the Emperor.

He was also the third and worst of the 'Dishonoured Men' of Britain, because his perfidy led to the 'strife of Camlan'.

Urien's assassination put an end to the British dream. The failure to destroy the Angles in 590 was catastrophic for the Britons, who would never get another chance to finish off the English. Morgan's outrage demanded urgent action. Arthur and his father raced north to quell the rebellion.

Arthur's court had been devastated. The *Triads* insist that Morgan 'left neither food nor drink in the court that he did not consume'. Morgan had been acting as Arthur's regent in the North; literally holding the fort while Arthur and the others drove the Angles back into the sea. He had 'dragged Gwenhwyfar from her royal chair', abusing her physically and sexually, in an attempt to declare himself King of the North. But with Arthur's war-band hurriedly returning from the Anglian lands, Morgan must have panicked. He destroyed what he could and fled.

The *Annals of Ulster* relate a victory for Áedán mac Gabráin at a 'battle of Leithreid' in 590, with the *Annals of Tigernach* favouring 588 for the 'battle of Leithrigh'. The Welsh *lleithder* implies 'moisture' or 'dampness'; *lleithig* can mean a 'couch' or a 'throne'. The Gaelic *leith* suggests a 'side' or 'share', while *rèidh* might signify a 'plain', 'slope' or 'ridge', and *rìgh* is a 'king'. The Battle of Leithreid or Leithrigh could, therefore, have witnessed the ravaging of the king's share or the damp slope.

Craig Leith overlooks the town of Alva on the plain of the River Devon in Clackmannanshire, north of the Firth of Forth. To one side of this 'Leith Ridge' stood the Pictish hill fort of Dumyat; on the other, just north of the town of Dollar, stands Castle Campbell, watered by the twin brooks known as Burn of Care and Burn of Sorrow, the latter running down from King's Seat Hill. Conceivably, this was the damp place where Morgan held his throne – the 'share' which had been allotted to him by Arthur the Emperor above the water-meadows of the 'black' Devon.

What makes this specific location so intriguing is that it was probably the original Dolorous Garde of the romances. Before it became Castle Campbell, late in the fifteenth century, it was known as Castle Gloom, after the Gaelic *doilleir* – 'dark' or 'dull' – from which the name of the Dollar Glen is derived. It was but a short step from *doilleir* to the Welsh *dolurus*, 'grievous', and thence to the castle of Dolorous Garde, the unhappy place of Gwenhwyfar's confinement.

The original Castle Gloom stood in the greater district of Manau Gododdin. The proximity of the Pictish hill fort of Dumyat suggests that Morgan had acquired allies among the southern Picts, who had reason to hate Arthur since he had killed their lord ten years earlier at the Battle of Badandun Hill. With a renegade army of Pictish spearmen under his command it would have been an easy thing for Morgan to swoop down on Arthur's Camelon camp and snatch Gwenhwyfar from its Maiden Castle. Morgan then retreated to the safety of his own stronghold in the Dollar Glen, hoping that the Pictish warriors of Dumyat would safeguard him against Arthur's fury.

Arthur and his father attacked Morgan's fortress. Though the victory was attributed to Áedán, for Arthur it was a solid defeat. Morgan had escaped across the Ochil Hills to the north, protected by a rearguard of Pictish spears.

Morgan the Wealthy had brought down the British alliance in its hour of triumph. He had betrayed Arthur and, worse, kidnapped and raped his queen, the soul of the land, the power behind the throne. As Arthur and Áedán descended on Morgan's fort, the traitor got away, disappearing with Gwenhwyfar into the northern realms of the Picts.

14

THE LAST BATTLE

GWENHWYFAR WAS held to blame for her violation. The *Triads* remember her as having been more faithless that the 'Three Faithless Wives of the Island of Britain' because 'she shamed a better man than any'.

She might not have been entirely innocent. For all that Arthur was an outstanding warlord he does not seem to have sought kingship, being content to let others rule. Morgan, meanwhile, never stopped seeking a kingdom to replace the one he had lost in his youth to the Angles, and ambition can be a compelling quality. There is also the question of children. Although several individuals were identified as sons of Arthur, some of those at least were foster-children. Uncertainty surrounds Arthur's capacity for fathering children; perhaps his own experiences as an infant had scarred him.

Morgan, who was several years older than Gwenhwyfar, was not lacking in vigour. Together, the dishonoured man and the faithless wife would establish a family: the Clann Morgainn, as it was called in the medieval *Book of Deer*. This was Morgan's dynasty in north-east Scotland.

Through his treachery, Morgan became a king of sorts. The *Book of Deer* classified the leader of the Morgan clan as a *tóisech* – a lord who collected rents but did not have the status of a High King. Still chafing at the loss of their lord, Galam Cennaleth, the southern Picts accepted Morgan as their new 'Chief-Boar'. The Britons came to think of him as Twrch Trwyth: 'Essence of Boar' or 'Boar's Piss'. The Welsh *twrch* is the same as the Gaelic *torc*, the genitive and plural of which is *tuirc* (small wonder that the medieval romancers imagined that Arthur and his heroes enjoyed the odd crusade against the Turks!). Morgan became the man who had once been a king but was turned into a boar for his sins. The desperate hunt for this king-turned-boar would form the climax of Arthur's career.

The epicentre of the Morgan clan was the Hill of Tillymorgan, above the valley of Strathbogie in Aberdeenshire. The hill was fortified with ditches and pallisaded ramparts. Gwenhwyfar quite possibly preferred the relative comfort of the old Glenmailen Roman camps nearby at Ythan Wells.

Arthur's anguish was phenomenal. He became a Red Ravager, more ruthless even than Morgan the Wealthy: 'For a year neither grass nor plants used to spring up where one of the three would walk; but where Arthur went, not for seven years.' As if in sympathy with his bitter mood the skies darkened in 591 and 592, according to the *Annals of Ulster* (there was an eclipse of the Sun on 19 March 592, close enough to the old New Year to be attributable to both years). The omens, it seemed, were not good.

One strange aspect of Arthur's predicament is the fact that his half-brother Gartnait was King of the Picts. Gartnait had succeeded his uncle Bruide to the throne in 584. Now Morgan and Gwenhwyfar had taken refuge in Gartnait's kingdom. Theoretically, it was in Gartnait's power to hand the fugitives over to Arthur. That he did not do so requires an explanation.

The Picts had long been divided into two tribal federations. The northern Picts occupied the mountains and glens of the Highlands while their southern cousins, who had been ruled by Galam Cennaleth up until the Battle of Badandun Hill, held the lower-lying areas to the south and east of the Highland massif. It is conceivable that Gartnait, though nominally King of the Picts, had little or no control over the southern Picts, and especially those who had flocked to their new 'Boar', Morgan the Wealthy.

At the same time there seems to have been a breakdown in the relationship between Áedán and his eldest son. The only evidence for this is an Irish story found in the fourteenth-century *Yellow Book of Lecan*. The *Scéla Cano meic Gartnáin* tells of an outbreak of savage rivalry between Áedán and Gartnait, and we shall return to it in a few chapters' time, for at the centre of the dispute was a cauldron of silver and gold. For now, the story allows us to speculate that Gartnait had become a pawn in a greater power struggle. He was taking his orders from someone who claimed to be a higher authority than Áedán mac Gabráin, the King of the Scots.

Had Gartnait been amenable to the pleas of his father and his half-brother he would surely have allowed Arthur to march through the Highlands to attack Morgan's stronghold from the west. This would have been the swiftest and most straightforward option. But Gartnait was unyielding. No doubt he had been promised much in return for obstructing Arthur's plans.

A different strategy was called for, and the one that emerged was audacious in the extreme. Prevented from assaulting Morgan's position from the land, Arthur would have to invade Aberdeenshire from the sea.

But Áedán's renowned navy was marooned on the wrong side of the country. A new battle fleet had to be created. To oversee the construction of this flotilla, Arthur called upon the services of one of the three 'Seafarers of the Island of Britain'. His name was Gereint son of Erbin and he came all the way from distant Cornwall. Gereint's reward for bringing his maritime experience to the enterprise was to be given his own tale – *Gereint and Enid* – which stands alongside those of Owain and Peredur in the *Mabinogion* collection.

It all took time, and even when the ships had been built and men gathered from as far afield as Gwynedd and Galloway, there was a year spent feasting and training and bonding in the halls of Lothian. The cauldron was pressed into service, to enforce a new battle-oath and to convince the warriors of their invulnerability. The warriors of the cauldron imbibed a sweet mead, described as 'pale', 'clear', 'white' and 'blue'. At least one poet of the time would blame this mead for the disaster that followed, claiming that it turned to 'poison' in their bellies.

At last, four years after the calamity at Lindisfarne, Arthur 'rushed like an eagle to the estuary'. With Gereint as his admiral of the fleet and Drystan to act as guide and navigator, the warships of the Gododdin set sail, ploughing the Firth of Forth out into the North Sea. Men and horses rode the waves as the battle fleet turned north.

The entries in the *Annals of Tigernach* for the year 594 cite battles of 'Ratha in Druadh' and 'Áird Sendoim' and the deaths of the sons of Áedán ('Bran & Domangart & Eochaid Fínd & Artur') in a Battle of Circenn.

A little more laconically, the *Annals of Ulster* refer to a 'battle of Ráith in Druad', a 'battle of Ard Sendaim' and the 'slaying of Áedán's sons i.e. Bran and Domangart', all in the year 596.

There are reasons to believe that the *Tigernach* annalist got the date right; 594 was the year in which Arthur's fleet set sail, and all hope was lost.

The ships made their way up the Pictish coast, almost as far as Peterhead, the 'Land of the Headland'. Arthur and his warriors landed just south of this promontory, driving their ships onto the shore at a 2-mile stretch of sand called Cruden Bay.

Memories of a violent seaborne assault hover around this charming, eastward-facing beach. The ruins of Slains Castle, perched on the northern spur of the bay, inspired Bram Stoker to write the scene in *Dracula* where a bloodthirsty hellhound leaps ashore from a ghost-ship. Some believe that the name of the bay recalls a 'Slaughter of Danes', although it is more likely that Cruden derives from *cruaidh* – 'hard' or 'painful', as in *cruaidh-theinn*, 'severe affliction'. On the southern wing of the bay there is a Cave Arthur, where he perhaps gave thanks to the sea; to the north, there are the rocky Step and Busks of Arthur Fowlie (from *foghlais*, a little stream). At the head of the dunes of Cruden Bay we find an Ardendraught or 'rising ground of the enchantment', *draucht* also being a Scots word for an 'artful scheme'; maybe the Picts deployed a ghost-fence or some other trick. Clearly, something momentous happened at this long sweep of sand, and what that might have been is suggested by the immediate proximity of Longhaven, beneath Stirling Hill between Cruden Bay and Peterhead. In Welsh, Longhaven would appear as *Llongborth* or 'Harbour'.

'In Llongborth I saw Arthur,' sang the poet Taliesin:

And brave men who hewed with steel,
The Emperor, leader of our endeavour.

'Steel' is also *cruaidh* in Gaelic, giving rise to a potential 'Bay of Steel', a place of armour, weaponry and anchors.

Taliesin's song speaks of grain-fed horses, 'long their legs, with the pace of a stag', charging ashore to become 'white with foam' and 'jaded and gory from battle'. There were 'biers beyond all number', 'men in terror, bloody heads', a 'great driving force' and a 'terrible torrent'. Morgan's Pictish allies were well-prepared. They had watched the impressive fleet as it came up from the Forth, and 'before they were overpowered, they committed slaughter'. The sand of Cruden Bay was reddened and littered with bodies.

This was the Battle of Áird Sendoim (*sendo-s* being an emphatic form of the definite article: the fighting took place at The Headland), but the Britons remembered it as the Battle of Llongborth. It was waged on the 'coast of Mordei' – that is, Moray – and we are told that 'Arthur subdued the Mordei that owed him homage'. He had beaten the southern Picts into submission at Badandun Hill; now, fourteen years later, he had terrorised them yet again. But there were losses on Arthur's side, too. 'In Llongborth Gereint was slain,' mourned Taliesin.

Gereint son of Erbin, the 'enemy of tyranny', had brought Arthur and his task-force this far, but he fell at Cruden Bay. Another poem of Arthur's last campaign honoured Gereint's contribution:

Gereint from the south gave a shout,
Lightning white the gleam on his shield;
Lord of the spear, liberal lord,
Sound of the sea, praise of the sea,
The way of the sea was the way of Gereint:
A generous lord you were.

The Pictish defenders crumbled before the overwhelming force of Arthur's amphibious landing. Drystan had spent several years of his life in this region: he knew the lie of the land. Steadily, the fighting moved inland as Arthur sought to break through to Morgan's hill.

Following the Water of Cruden, Arthur's strike-force came to Hatton, with its Arthurseat. More Pictish spearmen were advancing eastwards from Tillymorgan, along the River Ythan. Arthur's army marched forward to meet them near Arthrath. The dragon banner flew at Drakemyre, beneath the hill of Fortrie; a bard shouted the challenge at Auchnavaird, and battle commenced at Auchnagatt, along the Catto Burn and Catcraig.

Arthur's advance was unstoppable; he had waited four years to exact his revenge. Sooner or later he reached Morgan's fort, visiting upon it one of the 'Unrestrained Ravagings of the Island of Britain' and destroying everything in sight. This, we can assume, was the Battle of 'Ráith in Druad', the 'Fortress in Druid-land', *ràth* being an Early Irish term for a fortified residence surrounded by an earthen rampart. Typically, though, Morgan had escaped.

Fearing that his rival had fled westwards into the Highlands, Arthur continued into the mountainous realm of his half-brother. At the head of Glen Livet, on the eastern edge of the Highland massif, we find yet another Arthur's Seat (the site was recorded as 'Suiarthour' in 1638; today it is just 'Suie'). It is a measure of how unreliable, and perhaps even hostile, Gartnait had become. Arthur was forced to take up position just inside the realm of the northern Picts, both to cut off Morgan's escape into the Highlands and to prevent Gartnait's spearmen from joining Morgan's rebel army.

Morgan must have known this day would come. On the face of it, his options were limited.

Arthur had come at him from the east, but had quickly moved to block any retreat to the west and the refuge of Gartnait's Highland glens. Heading north would have trapped Morgan between Arthur's army and the sea. That left only one direction for Morgan to take.

Morgan spotted his opportunity. So many warriors of the Gododdin had joined Arthur on his mission that Lothian and Manau must have seemed undefended. What is more, Arthur's lengthy and elaborate preparations for the invasion could not have gone unnoticed. Morgan, too, had laid his plans.

Even then, an Anglian army was sailing up from the coast of Northumbria. If Morgan could outrun Arthur and join his Pictish spearmen up with his Anglian allies, he could take possession of Manau Gododdin.

The famous boar-hunt had begun. The Welsh legend of *Culhwch and Olwen* tells of how Arthur gathered his warriors from far and wide and sailed for 'Ireland', where he first fought with that 'Essence of Boar', Twrch Trwyth, and his seven young pigs. An attempt to parlay proved fruitless. Twrch Trwyth then made his way towards Arthur's land, with Arthur and his heroes in hot pursuit. A series of vicious skirmishes took place as the mighty boar headed in the direction of Mynydd Amanw, the 'mountain of Manau'. The conflict continued as Twrch raced towards Llwch Tawy (Loch Tay). Arthur summoned the help of Devon and Cornwall – or at least Gereint son of Erbin, prince of that southern peninsula – before finally cornering the king-turned-boar at a river. This, essentially, is what happened: Arthur landed on the coast; Morgan made a break for Manau and the Castle Rock at Stirling; Arthur chased him down through Aberdeenshire and across the 'Cold Ridge' of the Grampians.

The breast-shaped hill of Bennachie is where Arthur left his mark at Arthur's Cairn (*Arthouriscairne*, as it was recorded in 1595) and surveyed the prospect to the south. His scouts had reported sightings of an Anglian war-fleet coming to the aid of the treacherous Morgan.

Arthur tore down to the coast, pausing perhaps at Arthurhouse between Fordoun and Inverbervie, but he was too late to stop the Anglian warriors from landing.

Things had taken a dreadful turn. Arthur was now tracking two armies – Morgan's Picts and his Anglian reinforcements – as they sought to mount an invasion of Manau Gododdin.

He followed them south into Angus where, between Letham and Cairnconan Hill, another Arthur's Seat occupies the hill of Dumbarrow. Morgan took the higher position of Dunnichen Hill nearby. In the *New Statistical Account of Scotland*, compiled in 1845, the Reverend James Hendrick observed that a 'confused tradition prevails of a great battle having been fought on the East Mains of Dunnichen, between Lothus King of Picts, or his son Mordred, and Arthur King of the Britons, in which that hero of romance was slain.' This 'confused tradition' was not quite as far-fetched as it seemed to the Reverend Hendrick. Arthur and 'Medrod' did indeed pass by on the way to their fateful encounter.

The opposing forces turned westwards, moving into the long vale of Strathmore. Arthur manoeuvred his war-band to keep south of Morgan, blocking a sudden sally towards Manau. Keeping pace with each other, the rivals advanced towards Gowrie.

Arthur's battle-weary warriors marched through Foffarty to Scotstoun Hill and down to the Mains of Fullarton. Across the Dean Water, Morgan led his forces to the River Ericht (from the Old Irish *airecht*, a 'gathering'). Crossing the river just north of Blairgowrie, he came to the Morganstone. He must have realised by now that he could not outflank Arthur, and so he decided to stand and fight, the Morganstone marking the vantage point from which he directed his forces. The River Ericht flowed away from his position, past the fortress of Rattray, to Pictfield and Aberbothrie, where it formed a crooked T-junction with the River Isla.

Aberbothrie, with its East and West Cairns, preserves the old Roman name for the Forth – *Boderia*. The River Forth is a fair distance away to the south, but the Ericht and its confluence (*aber*) with the Isla almost certainly represented a boundary, the geographical limit of the region controlled by the Men of the Forth. This was territory which had once been controlled by Arthur's grandfather, who gave his name to Blairgowrie. A little further up the River Isla stands Badandun Hill, where Arthur had ambushed the 'Chief-Boar' of the southern Picts in 580. It is probable that the area to the west of the Isla had, since Arthur's defeat of Galam Cennaleth, been counted as part of Manau Gododdin and that the River Isla had become the 'New Forth'.

Morgan's rebel army had reached the edge of the territory of Manau – a poem of the time states that Morgan 'with confidence cursed the country of Manwyd'.

Here was the line which Arthur could not let them cross. Arthur found his own high ground, facing the junction of the two rivers, on the ridge which came to be known as Arthurbank. Before it was destroyed in the 1790s there stood, at the east end of the Arthurbank ridge, an Arthurstone.

Between them, the Morganstone and the Arthurstone delineate the field of battle. A poem of the time mentions another standing-stone:

A stone on open ground in the region of Lleu's land,
  The boundary of the Gododdin's border.

This would have been the large cup-and-ring marked stone which stands just east of Arthurbank. It is known as Macbeth's Stone, a local tradition claiming that the Scottish king made his last stand there. The legend appears to have been wrongly applied to Macbeth, for it was Arthur who drew up his troops along the south bank of the River Isla in the Pictish province of Circenn.

It was one of the most important battles in British history. A conflict of this magnitude would surely have been commemorated in verse. Indeed, two versions of an early poem exist: in their separate but overlapping ways, both present vivid glimpses of the battle and the men who fought and died there.

The relevance of this poem has been overlooked. Part of the reason for this is the widespread belief that Arthur's last battle was fought at a place called Camlan. As we have seen, *Camlan* is the Gaelic name for Arthur's military headquarters – the old Roman fortress at Camelon near Falkirk. It could be that 'Camlan', in the context of Arthur's last battle, is a corruption of *Camhan* ('cavan'), a hollow plain, and that it now appears on the map as Camno. Between the Arthurstone at the eastern foot of Arthurbank and the 'Macbeth Stone' south-west of the village of Meigle lie the Mains of Camno, and it was on this stretch of farmland that Arthur fought his last battle.

The battle commemorated in the poem known as *Y Gododdin* ('*The Gododdin*') has been repeatedly ascribed to a different region altogether. The poem makes several references to 'Catraeth', which happens to be the Welsh name for the Roman fort of Cataractonum in North Yorkshire, around which grew the town of Catterick. Generations of scholars have therefore assumed that, sometime roundabout the year 600, the Gododdin warriors of Lothian mounted a disastrous raid into England and were wiped out at the Roman fort in Catterick. But that assumption is wrong.

The poem was composed by Aneirin, the bardic son of the King of the North Pennines, Dunod the Staunch, who had fought at Arderydd and Catlowdy in 573. A contemporary of those other poets, Taliesin, Myrddin and Llywarch, Aneirin was present at Arthur's last battle. He later composed his marvellous elegy in the time-honoured manner of the bards: lying inside an earthen chamber with heavy chains around his legs until the verses were fully formed in his head. It is believed that *Y Gododdin* was first sung at Edinburgh shortly after the catastrophic battle.

Taliesin – who gets an appreciative nod in Aneirin's poem – had previously referred to Catreath in his own song of the *Battle of Gwen Ystrad* (probably the military operation in Strathearn):

> The men of Catraeth arose by appointment
> Around a victorious battle-lord and cattle-raider,
> Urien, the restless chieftain ...

The same 'men of Catraeth' now stood with Arthur on the bank of the River Isla, preparing to do battle with Morgan's horde. They were the warriors of the 'battle-shore' (*cad traeth*), or perhaps of the 'Hard Land', a district to the west of Lothian, comprising much of Manau Gododdin, which was known in Latin as *Calatria* or *Calateria*. In other words, they were the defenders of that notorious place of strife, the River Forth near Stirling.

(Another possibility was raised by William Stewart who, in his *Buik of the Chroniclis of Scotland*, which dates from 1535, accused Arthur and his comrades of having betrayed their 'aith' or oath. A 'battle-oath' would have been something like *cad-rhaith* in Welsh, and those who swore it might have been the 'Men of Cadrhaith'. A similar concept is conveyed by the term *cadwraeth* – *cadwriaeth* in an older spelling – which implies a solemn obligation to hold, keep or preserve something. The 'men of Catraeth' would have been oath-sworn to defend Manau Gododdin: they were the 'army of Trywrid'.)

The warriors who fought beside Arthur in that last campaign had gone to another shore of battle in 594, sailing up the Pictish coast with their weapons and horses to storm the beach at Cruden Bay – a 'battle-shore' if ever there was one. Aneirin, in his *Y Gododdin* poem, treated the entire campaign as one long battle, granting an honorary verse to Gereint son of Erbin, who died in the first assault. According to Aneirin, some 300 (or 363) 'golden-torqued' warriors had gone to the battle-shore as the war-band of 'Mynyddog Mwynfawr', the wealthy lord of the mountain and Chieftain of Edinburgh. The poet estimated that when these 300 tired and ragged men reached the River Ericht, they faced an enemy numbering 10,000.

Only the shorter of the two surviving versions of *Y Gododdin* mentions Arthur by his familiar name. Because scholars have for so many years been unreasonably keen to deny any association between Arthur and North Britain, the reference to Arthur in the poem has been passed off as an allusion to an unidentified Arthur of the south. The plain truth is that Aneirin's *Y Gododdin* not only presents one of the very first references to Arthur in British literature, but it does so in the context of a campaign involving the forces of Edinburgh, Lothian and Manau. Even those parts of the poem that were interpolated at a later date are Arthur-related: one small section of *Y Gododdin* commemorates a different conflict – the Battle of Strathcarron in 642 – and the death of Domnall the Speckled, King of Dalriada; Domnall the Speckled was a nephew of Arthur.

That the name 'Arthur' occurs only in one of the extant versions of the poem is immaterial. He is present throughout in one guise or another, often as 'Mynyddog', the rich prince of the Edinburgh mount known today as Arthur's Seat.

The poem names others who fought at the battle: Cynon son of Clydno receives much praise, as does Owain son of Urien; a man named Cadfannan ('Warrior-of-Manau') was probably Fiachna mac Báetáin, and another Irishman, 'Cynddilig of Aeron', was almost certainly the diminutive war-hound of Leinster, Áed Dibchine. Caradog Strong-Arm was present, as was Peredur of York with his steel weapons and his son Gwgon the Hero. Áedán mac Gabráin was there, and we can be sure that Menw (Myrddin) and his father Morfrân were among the throng, as were Sandde Angel-Face and Taliesin and many, many more.

Some had hastened north to strengthen Arthur's lines around the 'border of Ban Carw' – recalled today at East and West Banchory, where the River Isla forms a shape like a stag's horns, a short distance from Arthur's position. To the north, where the River Ericht cuts through a narrow glen, Morgan watched from the side of the Morganston Burn.

What followed would decide the fate of Britain.

First, there was talking. In front of Arthur's position, between Arthurbank and the River Isla, is a place called Cronan, which might recall the blighted attempts to negotiate. *Cron*, an Old Irish word, implies blame, harm and accusation; *crònan* signifies a murmuring, or a dirge.

Feelings were running too high; there was too much at stake, too much rancour in the air, for the talks to go smoothly.

The *Triads* state that, after the 'futile' battles of Arderydd and Goddau (Catlowdy) in 573, the 'third and worst' was Arthur's last battle, 'which was brought about because of a quarrel between Gwenhwyfar and Gwenhwyfach'. This places the blame squarely at the feet of those two 'golden-chained' women, Gwenhwyfar and her smaller sister-in-law, Muirgein, suggesting that it was their inability to see eye to eye that led to the carnage.

Another source paints a very different picture. One of the most subversive and revealing accounts of the build-up to the battle is given in the *Mabinogion* tale of the *Dream of Rhonabwy*, in which the title character sleeps on a yellow ox-hide and receives a detailed vision of Arthur and his men eternally poised on the brink of conflict. All the familiar heroes are there, their names recurring from the list of Arthur's Round Table horsemen and the *Y Gododdin* poem. Rhonabwy's guide and interpreter in the strange world of the dream introduces himself as Iddog son of Mynyo, though he admits that he is better known by his nickname, *Cordd Prydein*, the 'Churn of Britain':

> ... I was one of the messengers between Arthur and Medrod his nephew, at the battle of Camlan; and I was then a reckless youth, and through my desire for battle, I kindled strife between them, and stirred up wrath, when I was sent by Arthur the Emperor to reason with Medrod, and to show him, that he was his foster-father and his uncle, and to seek for peace, lest the sons of the Kings of the Island of Britain, and of the nobles, should be slain. And whereas Arthur charged me with the fairest sayings he could think of, I uttered unto Medrod the harshest I could devise. And I am therefore called Iddog Cordd Prydain, for from this did the battle of Camlan ensue. And three nights before the end of the battle of Camlan I left them, and went to Llech Las in North Britain to do penance. And there I remained doing penance seven years, and after that I gained pardon.

The unknown author of the *Dream of Rhonabwy* ended his bizarre account with the statement that no one, 'neither bard nor gifted seer', could possibly understand the dream without a book to explain the many telling details which had been woven into the tale. As we shall see, though, even without a codebreaker the story yields much, dropping hefty hints as to who or what sparked the battle.

The Battle of Camlan is not recreated in Rhonabwy's dream; instead, Arthur and his nephew Owain play a tense board game while their respective warriors attack each other furiously. The enchanted atmosphere of the tale is heavy with the threat of civil war and a pervasive aura of treachery.

Much of what the *Dream of Rhonabwy* has to tell us must be considered in a later chapter. For now, it is worth noting that a tradition existed of an *agent provocateur*, a trusted individual who stirred up the already heightened emotions in order to make sure that the battle went ahead. He was identified as the 'Churn of Britain', although *cordd* can also mean a 'tribe' or 'host', so that Iddog son of Mynyo was perhaps of the 'family of Britain'. And after just seven years of penance, he was pardoned for the role he had played in procuring the death of Arthur.

Far away on the Isle of Iona, St Columba suddenly said to his servant, 'Strike the bell':

> Summoned by this sound, the brethren quickly ran to the church, the saint going on ahead of them. He knelt down before them and spoke:
> 'Let us now pray fervently to the Lord for this people and for King Áedán, for even now they are going into battle.'

In his *Life of St Columba*, written a century after Columba's death, Adomnán of Iona noted that King Áedán and his sons went into battle against the Miathi.

The Miathi were the Pictish tribesmen who had been previously identified as *Maeatae* by Dio Cassius in the 220s: they lived 'very near the wall which divides the island [of Britain] in half'. Their presence in the vicinity of the Antonine Wall, which ran clean through Manau Gododdin, effectively separating the Britons from the Picts, is attested in two place names: Myot Hill to the west of Stirling and Dumyat to the east. They were a tribe of southern Picts, those perennial enemies of Arthur, and they had adopted Morgan the Wealthy as their honorary chieftain.

There is no mention in Adomnán's account of the Anglian presence at Arthur's last battle. But then, by the time Adomnán was writing his *Vita Sancti Columbae* the Christian community on Iona had developed strong links with the Anglian kings of Northumbria. It would have been impolitic for Adomnán to record the fact that the Angles had fought alongside the Pictish Miathi against Arthur.

Geoffrey of Monmouth indicated that another element had been drawn into the fray. In his *History of the Kings of Britain*, Geoffrey remarked that, in addition to living adulterously with Arthur's queen, the self-serving 'Mordred' had agreed to hand over the lands of Bernicia and Deira to the Northumbrian Angles, thereby undermining everything that Arthur and his comrades had been fighting for. Geoffrey's Mordred brought 'Scots, Picts and Irish' into his rebel alliance, along with 'anyone else whom he knew to be filled with hatred' for Arthur. In all, Geoffrey reckoned, 'the insurgents were about eighty thousand in number, some of them pagans and some Christians.' There had then taken place a desperate battle, at the end of which Arthur's men occupied the seashore, followed by a cross-country pursuit and the final confrontation by a river.

Everyone who hated Arthur was ranged against him: renegade Scots and Irish, vengeful Picts and the dreaded Angles, pagan and Christian united in their eagerness to crush the Duke of Battles.

Sir Thomas Malory, author of the fifteenth-century epic *Le Morte d'Arthur*, believed that the battle was started by a snake:

> And when the knight felt himself stung, he looked down and saw an adder, and then he drew his sword to slay the adder, and thought of none other harm. And when the host on both parties saw that sword drawn, they blew beams, trumpets, and horns, and shouted grimly. And so both hosts dressed them together. And King Arthur took his horse, and said: Alas this unhappy day! and so rode to his party. And Sir Mordred did likewise. And never was there seen a more dolefuller battle in no Christian land …

The notion that a snake was the cause of the battle is an interesting one if we remember that Druids were also known as 'Adders' (*Naddred*). However, the same story is told of another battle fought in Arthur's world. When the Campbells confronted the MacDougalls at Kilmaronaig, near the mouth of Loch Etive in Argyll, their negotiations were interrupted by the sudden appearance of a snake. Swords were drawn to kill the creature and this was mistaken as a signal for battle to commence. Of course, the legend might have been borrowed from Malory's magnum opus and tacked on to an obscure battle involving Arthur's descendants; equally, though, Malory might have tuned into a Scottish tradition when composing his very English epic.

Either way, the talks broke down, and so the two sides went to war.

The confrontation lasted a week – in Aneirin's words:

Tuesday they put on their black gear.
Wednesday they sharpened their spears.
Thursday it was certain, they said.
Friday, hateful lamentation.
Saturday, lively their mutual action.
Sunday, their red blades hostile.
Monday, till the chief's pale thigh ran with blood.
The Gododdin spoke truly after their toil:
When they returned to Madog's tent
Of a hundred, but one man returned.

Aneirin's poem, combined with the topography of the area, allows for a partial reconstruction of the battle. The Morganstone, north of Blairgowrie, stands approximately 7 miles north-west of Arthur's position, the fort of Rattray lying roughly midway between them. Morgan's forces extended eastwards for several miles (the *Y Gododdin* poem refers to one very important place name, which we shall look at shortly). Arthur's smaller army was lined up along the River Isla. The odds against him were enormous.

Morgan knew Arthur's tactics, having fought alongside him on many occasions as one of the Round Table horsemen. He certainly knew well enough not to blunder into a textbook Arthurian ambush. The fighting was very much out in the open. Still, Arthur decided that his best option was to attack on two fronts, adapting his ambush strategy to suit the circumstances.

The *Triads* recall that Arthur made a fatal error when he divided his army into three. Initially, though, the gambit might have worked.

The Anglian warriors of Northumbria were probably ranged along Morgan's right flank, with his Pictish supporters on the left. Arthur chose to attack both wings of Morgan's army. Drystan, with his superior knowledge of the southern Picts, was delegated to lead the charge against the Miathi spearmen at Pictillum, east of the River Ericht. Peredur of York, who knew better than most the fighting skills of the Angles, led his detachment through Princeland and Bennathie, west of the Ericht. The plan, such as it was, would have been for Drystan and Peredur to attack Morgan's force from both sides at once, driving the centre of Morgan's army down the plain of the Ericht to where Arthur was standing.

It was a bold – maybe a desperate – manoeuvre. Its success would have relied much on the enemy's fear of Arthur and his champions. Its failure was down to something that Arthur had not anticipated.

Aneirin left us snapshots of Arthur in action:

Hero beneath the double shield,
Speckled his brow and his spring like a willow.
There was fire and tumult on the battle-mount,
There were swift spears and sunshine,
There was food for ravens, the raven's profit.
And before the promise was broken,
And dew fell on the eagle of gentle gait,
And the black wave spread over the hill's breast,
The world's bards judged men of valour.
Hindered were his words, his advice,
Rejected, the meeting of princes with men.
And before he was buried under the hill
Of The Horse, the wise earth of his coffin,
Awash with his blood was his armour,
Victorious son of the fierce Wolfish one.

Peredur and his son Gwgon (or his brother Gwrgi) came to grief at Rattray. Their war-band lost its nerve, turned 'faithless' and melted away. The sons of York perished at the moated fort.

Rattray is invariably twinned with the township of Blairgowrie on the opposite bank of the Ericht. Blairgowrie means the '[Battle]field of Gabrán's land', while Rattray in Gaelic is *Raitear* – perhaps 'Fort of the Quarter'; the current name of the village appears to be an anglicised version of *ràth-tràigh* or 'Fort of the Shore', the fortress having stood on the floodplain of the Ericht. The Britons chose to remember it as the Bloody Fort, *Caer Greu*. The *Triads* tell us that Peredur and his brother, or his son, had an appointment to meet with Eda Great-Knee, a name inspired by Ida, first Anglian King of Bernicia. Abandoned by his war-band, the famous Peredur Steel-Spear was killed by his Anglian enemies.

While Peredur was dying at Rattray, Drystan was hacking his way through the Pictish spears a little further to the east. Arthur remained on the lush plain of Camno, ready to receive the onrush of Morgan's warriors as they came down the Ericht towards him. What he was not prepared for was a surprise attack from the rear.

'From Din Dywydd they attacked', groaned the poet Aneirin, as if unable to believe what he had seen. A 'raucous pilgrim army' had come up from the south, catching Arthur unawares.

Arthur's attention had been fixed on the river in front of him and the high land beyond. One third of his army had attacked Morgan's rabble from the west, another third attacking from the east, in order to drive the rebels in Arthur's direction. But a 'tempest of pilgrims' had come up from behind, and Arthur had only a third of his total force to protect him.

Chaos descended in an instant.

Safe on the island of his church, Columba was keeping track of the battle.

'After a short while,' wrote Adomnán of Iona, 'he went outside and, looking up at the sky, said: 'Now the barbarians are turned in flight and victory is granted to Áedán, though it is not a happy one.' 'From Áedán's army,' Adomnán wrote, 'three hundred and three were killed, as the saint had also prophesied.'

The number given by Adomnán 100 years later is eerily similar to the reckoning made by Aneirin in his poem of the battle: roughly 300 dead, or almost everybody who had fought on Arthur's side.

St Columba must have been receiving messages from the hilltops: he looked up to the sky before telling his monks that King Áedán had won the battle. The southern Picts had been routed. Arthur's daring strategy nearly succeeded; if only all his enemies had been in front of him.

Adomnán's version of events suffers from his urge to present Columba as omniscient. He was quick to link the outcome of the battle with Columba's prophecy concerning Áedán's sons. The saint had announced that at least three sons of Áedán would 'fall in battles, slain by enemies'. Adomnán gladly revealed that the saint's words had now come true: 'Artuir and Eochaid Find were killed soon afterwards in the battle with the Miathi.'

Columba, of course, had been right all along.

The Battle of Camlan – *Cad Gamlan* – would enter the Welsh language as a byword for confusion. From the moment the 'raucous pilgrim army' entered the conflict, attacking Arthur from the rear on the plain of Camno, there was nothing but horror, bewilderment and ghastly slaughter.

More than two centuries after the battle in Angus, Nennius described a 'wonder' of Scotland. This was a 'valley in Angus, in which shouting is heard every Monday night; Glend Ailbe is its name, and it is not known who makes this noise.'

The valley was named after St Ailbe, a sixth-century Irish bishop and patron saint of wolves. He was renowned for having baptised St David, the patron saint of Wales, and dedications to Ailbe of Emly seem to have followed Arthur and his circle from Wales up to Scotland.

But there is no Glen Ailbe in Scotland anymore. The Celtic place name expert W.J. Watson surmised that the 'Glend Ailbe' of Nennius might now be Glen Isla, the valley in which Arthur's last battle was fought. Designated *Glenylif* in 1233, Glen Isla was mentioned earlier as the edge of a province that stretched from the River Tay to a place called 'Hilef'. This, again, was the exact site of Arthur's last battle.

'Hilef' survives today in the town of Alyth and the prominent Hill of Alyth, north-east of Blairgowrie. Robin Smith, in *The Making of Scotland*, interprets Alyth as 'The Strength' (*A Lith*), although the Gaelic name for the hill simply suggests something noble, high or stately (*Àilt*). It was a place of supreme importance to the southern Picts whose former king, Galam, had borne the epithet *Cennaleth* or 'Chief of Alyth'.

Aneirin referred to the Hill of Alyth as the Alledd (pronounced 'ad-eth'):

Again the battle-shout about the Alledd,
The battle-horses and bloodied armour,
Until they shook with the passion of the great battle …

According to Aneirin's eye-witness account, the battle came to an end on a Monday, when 'the chief's pale thigh ran with blood'. And according to Nennius, more than 200 years later, mysterious shouting was heard every Monday in the valley in Angus which ran from Alyth to the River Tay.

Arthur was attacked south of Alyth. He fought his way across the plain of Camno to the eastern end of Arthurbank. A standing stone, named in his honour, once stood on the spot where he received his fatal wound.

A description of those final moments can be found in the *Vera historia de morte Arthuri* ('*True Story of the Death of Arthur*'), which dates from about 1200. The anonymous account has Arthur leaning on his shield, exhausted and gravely injured. Dropping to his knees, he orders his men to disarm him so that his own weapons do not add to his injuries. A handsome youth then approaches on horseback. In his right hand he carries a shaft of elm: 'The shaft was stiff, not twisted or knotted, and was sharper than any such because it had been tempered in water and fire and finally dipped in adder's venom.'

The young man rides up to Arthur and hurls the elm shaft at him. Straightaway, Arthur knows that his death is assured. Blood runs down his pale thigh. The battle is over.

'There is despair and anguish among those gathered around and lamentation for the safety of the Britons,' wrote the author of the *Vera historia de morte Arthuri*.

Cai the Tall was last seen racing south to take revenge on the friend who had betrayed Arthur.

Gwenhwyfar was held prisoner near Alyth, awaiting her fate.

Arthur was carried from the field … and vanished into the legends.

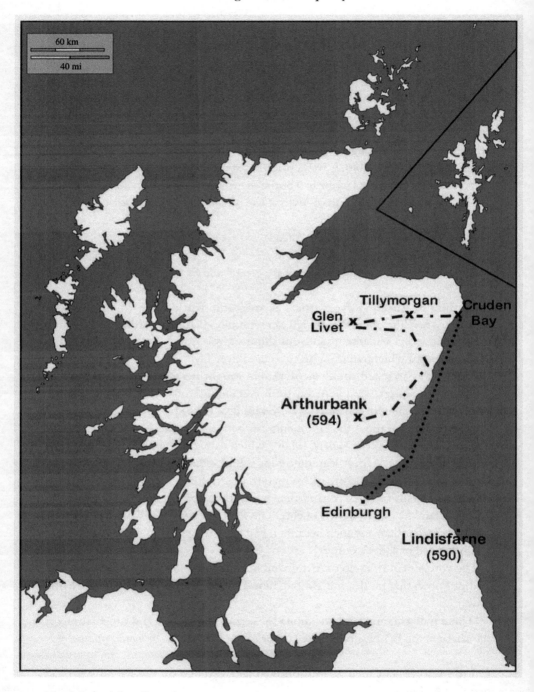

Map 6 Arthur's Last Campaign

THREE

TWILIGHT OF THE GODS

'Yet some men say in many parts of England
that King Arthur is not dead …
and men say that he shall come again …
I will not say it shall be so, but rather I will say:
here in this world he changed his life.'

Sir Thomas Malory, *Le Morte d'Arthur*, 1485

15

THE MAIMED KING

IT IS unclear how many sons of Áedán mac Gabráin died during Arthur's final campaign. The *Annals of Tigernach* name four: 'Bran & Domangart & Eochaid Fínd & Artur.' The *Annals of Ulster* name just two: Bran and Domangart. Adomnán, writing his *Life of St Columba* about a century after the events, explained that 'Artuir and Eochaid Find' were killed in the 'battle with the Miathi' and that Domangart 'fell slaughtered in battle in England'. All three records ultimately derive from the same place – the monastery of St Columba on the Isle of Iona – and so their inability to agree about who actually died is somewhat perplexing.

Most intriguing are the references to a son of Áedán named Bran. Adomnán made no mention of him at all in his *Life of St Columba*. The *Annals of Ulster*, however, aver that it was Bran and Domangart, not Arthur and Eochaid Find, who died at the battle in Strathmore.

If the Irish were uncertain as to whether or not Bran even existed, the Britons had little doubt that *Bendigeidfrân* – 'Brân the Blessed' – was a great hero. His legend, as told in the *Mabinogion* collection of traditional tales, throws a fascinating light on the cause and the outcome of the last battle.

The story is set largely in North Wales, although the events took place further to the north. Brân son of Llyr ('Raven son of Sea') was crowned 'King of the Island of Britain'. He was sitting on a rock overlooking the sea one day with his brother Manawydan beside him. Manawydan son of Llyr was the same as the Irish Manannán mac Lir; he can be identified as Arthur's brother-in-law, Fiachna mac Báetáin, the 'dear one of Manau'.

The brothers spied thirteen ships bringing an Irish king, Matholwch, who wished to draw the Island of the Mighty closer to Ireland and sought the hand in marriage of Brân's sister, Brânwen ('White-Raven'). Brânwen daughter of Llyr was described as one of the 'chief ladies' of the Island of Britain and the 'fairest damsel in the world'.

Brân consented to the match, but one of his brothers 'on his mother's side' reacted with rage and mutilated the horses of King Matholwch. By way of reparation, Brân presented the Irish king with a marvellous cauldron, 'the property of which is, that if one of thy men be slain today, and be cast therein, tomorrow he will be as well as ever he was at the best, except that he will not regain his speech'. Once again, the cauldron was at the heart of the issue.

Brânwen and Matholwch were duly married and had a son, whom they named Gwern. But the insult of the injured horses still smarted with Matholwch's followers, and the Irish king began to mistreat his bride. Unable to communicate with her brother, Brânwen trained up a speckled starling (*druid* in Gaelic) to carry a message to Brân in Britain. As soon as Brân learned that his sister was being abused he set sail for Ireland. His fleet was so large that the Irish mistook the masts for a forest in the ocean.

Brân and his warriors were greeted with the news that Matholwch had granted his kingdom to Gwern, his son by Brânwen. Brân the Blessed and his company were lured into a hall on the promise of peace talks, unaware that the Irish king had secreted armed warriors inside the hall, hidden inside leather sacks. Recognising the trap for what it was, Brân's troublesome brother threw the boy Gwern headlong into the fire. A cry was heard: 'Dogs of Gwern, beware of Pierced Thighs!' And the battle commenced.

The Irish had the advantage of the cauldron, so that their fallen warriors could be restored to life. Disaster loomed for the Britons, until Brân's brother climbed inside the cauldron and stretched himself out, shattering the precious vessel and bursting his own heart in the process. Unable to resuscitate their dead, the Irish were eventually defeated.

But Brân the Blessed had sustained a fatal injury: he had been wounded in the foot by a poisoned spear. Only seven of his men remained alive. He ordered them to cut off his head and 'bear it to the White Mount in London, and bury it there, with the face towards France.'

Brân's sister died of a broken heart. Back in Britain, Brân's companions discovered to their horror that a usurper had stolen the kingdom. Caradog, a 'son of Brân', had been left in charge, but he was overwhelmed with grief when he and his fellow guardians were attacked and could not see who was wielding the sword against them.

The ragged band of survivors tarried for seven years at Harddlech (from *Arth-llech* – 'Arthur-stone') and for a further eighty years in a spacious hall overlooking the ocean, where they were entertained by Brân's talkative head and became known as the Assembly of the Noble Head. Finally, they opened a door in the hall which had previously been closed to them and made their way to London, where they buried Brân's head in the White Mount.

The *Triads* make an explicit connection between Brân and Arthur. One of the 'Fortunate Concealments of the Island of Britain' was:

> The Head of Brân the Blessed, son of Llyr, which was concealed in the White Hill in London, with its face towards France. And as long as it was in the position in which it was put there, no Saxon oppression would ever come to this island.

But Arthur, in a fit of hubris, 'disclosed the Head of Brân the Blessed from the White Hill, because it did not seem right to him that this Island should be defended by the strength of anyone, but by his own.' It was Arthur's fault, then, that Britain was overrun by Germanic immigrants. Those Anglo-Saxon settlers were later conquered by William, the bastard Duke of Normandy, who built a White Tower on the White Hill in London, and around it grew the Royal Palace and Fortress commonly known as the Tower of London. A tradition which dates back at least as far as the reign of King Charles II maintains that the tower is guarded by six resident ravens – each one a reminder that Brân's name meant 'Raven'.

It is doubtful in the extreme that Arthur ever visited London. The notion that Brân's head was buried there and Arthur later dug it up again is a late invention: no trace of this legend predates the destruction of the old London Bridge by fire, just as Geoffrey of Monmouth was putting the finishing touches to his *History of the Kings of Britain*.

Work began on a new stone bridge across the River Thames forty years later. It took thirty-three years to build and when it was completed in 1209, it was one of the wonders of the world. A popular children's rhyme recalled the difficulties encountered in its construction and its superiority over its timber predecessors. The same rhyme also contained a dark hint of human sacrifice:

> What has this poor prisoner done,
> Prisoner done, prisoner done?
> Off to prison she must go –
> My fair lady.

There were precedents for the use of children as foundation sacrifices. A child's skeleton was unearthed from the foundations of the Bridge Gate at Bremen in Germany when it was excavated in the nineteenth century. The remains of children were also discovered in the foundations of buildings at Gezer and Megiddo in ancient Israel. The Biblical *Book of Kings* observed that the reconstruction of Jericho would require the sacrifice of two children.

Closer to Arthur in time and space, the legend of Vortigern's tower and the proposed sacrifice of a 'fatherless boy' – which gave Geoffrey of Monmouth his Merlin story – reflected a traditional practice. Nennius, the monk who compiled a list of Arthur's battles, also noted that Vortigern's son, Vortimer, had asked to be buried 'upon the rock where the Saxons first landed', arguing that if his wish was honoured the hated Saxons would 'never remain in this island'. But Vortimer's last request was sadly ignored.

The failure of the Britons to deploy Vortimer's corpse as a palladium, guarding the Island of Britain against foreign intrusion, had by the fifteenth century evolved into the legend of Brân's head and its unfortunate disclosure by Arthur. Vague and guilty memories of child sacrifice during the building of London Bridge probably bolstered the legend; it is possible that a child or two had also been buried when the curtain walls and towers were added to the White Tower of London at the same time.

There was no burial of the head of Brân the Blessed in London, and no exhumation of that head by Arthur. But there were lingering rumours of a foundation sacrifice which did take place in Arthur's world and which might have influenced the later stories.

Very little is known about him, but in many ways Oran is the true patron saint of the isle of Columba's church. The royal burial ground of Iona surrounds St Oran's chapel, the *Teampull Odhráin*, which is one of the oldest ecclesiastical buildings still in use in Scotland. Sixty kings of Scotland, Ireland, Norway and France are said to lie buried in *Reilig Odhráin* – Oran's Cemetery – on Iona.

The earliest surviving account of the legend of St Oran belongs to twelfth-century Ireland. Having arrived on the Isle of Iona, St Columba turned to his followers and said: 'It would benefit us if our roots were put down into the ground here. Someone among you should go down into the soil of the island to consecrate it.'

Other versions of the legend have St Columba dreaming that a terrible famine 'would never cease unless he buried a man alive', or that mischievous spirits disrupted the saint's attempts to build his church and so a propitiatory sacrifice was called for.

Only one man stepped forward as a volunteer. His name was Odhrán or Dòbhran, and he was said to have been St Columba's brother.

The Dove of the Church told him: 'I shall give you the kingdom of God, and I shall give you this, that no one who makes a request at my tomb or resting-place will be granted it unless he first seek it of you.'

A version of the legend recorded in 1698 states that St Oran was prematurely buried in an upright position and his tomb reopened after twenty-four hours. A later account from 1771 drew heavily on local traditions:

> Three days afterward Columba opened the grave to see what might be the fate
> of his friend. Oran opened his swimming eyes and said:

Chan eil an t-Eug 'na annas,
'S chan eil Ifrinn mar a dùbhrar;
Cha tèid math am mugh',
'S cha bhi olc gun dìoladh.

Oran's words were translated by Alexander Carmichael in his *Carmina Gadelica* thus:

Nor is heaven as it is alleged,
Nor is hell as it is asserted,
Nor is the good eternally happy,
Nor is the bad eternally unhappy.

St Columba was riled. He 'called out in a great hurry':

Ùir, ùir air sùil Odhráin,
Mun labhair e tuille còmhradh!

Earth, earth on Oran's eye,
lest he blab anymore!

The message that Oran brought back from the Otherworld contradicted St Columba's teachings. Even so, the shadowy Oran became the tutelary spirit of the royal graveyard on the island of Iona.

There is some degree of overlap between the British legends of Brân the Blessed and the accounts of St Columba's burial of St Oran: just as Brân's head continued to chatter after it was severed from his body, so St Oran 'blabbed' after his death. Both Brân and Oran were supposedly buried as protective sacrifices and subsequently disinterred. On balance, it would seem that Brân the Blessed and the obscure St Oran were one and the same. *Òran*, which in modern Gaelic means 'song', derives from the earlier *amhran* – a 'song' or 'poem' (*ambrán* in Middle Irish). British ears might well have mistaken *amhran* or *ambrán* for 'The Raven', which was the precise meaning of the name of Brân.

Unsurprisingly, Adomnán of Iona did not include the story of Oran's sacrifice among the many miracles he attributed to Columba. His *Life of St Columba* does, however, feature a very odd episode which has more than a hint of sacrifice about it.

The story is found in the first part of Adomnán's hagiography, which deals with the Columba's prophetic abilities, and appears under the heading: 'The saint's prophecy about a layman called Gúaire son of Áedán.'

According to Adomnán, Gúaire mac Áedáin was 'the most powerful man in the whole of Dalriada at that time'. He enquired of St Columba one day how he would die. The saint told him: 'Neither in battle nor at sea will you die. But a companion of your journey, whom you do not suspect, will be the cause of your death.'

It was a sinister pronouncement. Gúaire questioned him further. 'Perhaps,' he said, 'one of my entourage of friends is thinking of killing me, or my wife is plotting my death through sorcery for love of a younger man?'

Columba told Gúaire, 'That is not how it will come about.'

'Why will you not let me know about my killer now?' asked Gúaire.

Columba said, 'The reason I do not wish to speak plainly and reveal which of your companions will cause your death is to save you from troubling yourself every time you are reminded of the fact, until the day comes when you discover the truth of this matter for yourself.'

Some time later, St Columba's prediction came true. Adomnán tells us that Gúaire son of Áedán was sitting under an upturned boat one day, scraping away at the jagged point of a wooden spear, when he heard a commotion. An argument had started, and Gúaire quickly rose to his feet to intervene, carelessly dropping his knife, which cut his knee badly.

All at once Gúaire realised that the knife was the 'companion of his journey' of whom he had suspected nothing. The wound failed to heal and eventually Gúaire son of Áedán, the most powerful layman in the kingdom of the Scots, died from his self-inflicted injury.

Many commentators have remarked on the peculiar nature of this tale. In his analysis of 'The Strange Death of Gúaire mac Áedáin', Jean-Michel Picard of University College, Dublin, drew attention to the similarities between the story of Gúaire and the legends of the Fisher King. Gúaire was sitting under a fishing boat and whittling away at what would appear to have been a fishing spear when he was hurt. There are countless examples of gods and kings who suffered wounds to their feet, knees or thighs, and studies in mythology and linguistics have concluded that all such injuries are essentially sexual – it is the victim's reproductive capabilities that are destroyed. The wound really occurs to the genitals, and the harm done to the king's virility is reflected in his realm, which becomes the infertile Waste Land.

In Arthurian tradition, the Fisher King has been wounded through both thighs. He can find relief from his constant agony only when sitting in a boat, fishing. His emasculation casts a devastating blight over the kingdom, although this state of affairs can be reversed if – and only if – the right questions are asked.

Brân the Blessed was also wounded through both thighs, although it was the wound to his foot that would prove fatal. The poisoned spear which struck Brân in the foot compares with the knife which cut Gúaire's knee: both wounds refused to heal and both occurred to parts of the body which are recognised as euphemisms for the sexual organs. And there are other references to poisoned spears and thigh-wounds in the early Arthurian literature.

We know from Aneirin's *Y Gododdin* poem of Arthur's defeat that the battle came to an end when 'the chief's pale thigh ran with blood'. The *True Story of the Death of Arthur*, which appeared in about 1200, describes the spear with which Arthur was fatally wounded as a sharpened elm shaft 'dipped in adder's venom'. A poisoned spear also ends the life of Arthur's alter ego, Llew Skilful Hand, in the Welsh tale of *Math Son of Mathonwy*.

Apart from the account of his strange death in Adomnán's *Life of St Columba* there is no record of Áedán having had a son named Gúaire – which seems odd if, as Adomnán claimed, Gúaire was the strongest, most valiant man in the whole of Dalriada. There are, though, many references in the British sources to a hero with a remarkably similar name.

The *Triads* tell us that one of the 'Three Enemy-Subduers of the Island of Britain' was 'Gweir of Great Valour' (the other two were Arthur's grandfather Gabrán and his cousin Drystan). The same 'Gweir of Great Valour' also appears in the legend of *Gereint and Enid*, the eponymous hero of which died during the beach landing at the start of Arthur's final campaign.

The 'Three Exalted Prisoners of the Island of Britain' were Llyr Half-Speech, Mabon son of Modron and Gwair son of Geirioedd (*geirioedd* or 'Strange-Speech' is synonymous with Llyr's epithet 'Half-Speech', a reminder that the Britons found Áedán's Irish tongue confusing; Mabon or 'Son son of Mother' was Arthur's nephew and foster-brother, Owain). Alongside Drystan and Eiddilig the Dwarf, Gwair of Great Valour was also one of the 'Three Severe Men of the Island of Britain'. Returning to Aneirin's *Y Gododdin* poem, we find that a person named Gweir was present at Arthur's last battle:

> And before Gweir the Tall was buried and under 'Dywarch'
> He earned mead-horns, the prime son of Mighty-Horse.

Most famously, Gweir was named as the father of Gwalchmai, the Arthurian hero who became the 'Sir Gawain' of the romances.

The various spellings of Gweir, Gwair and Gwyar were all attempts at converting the Irish name Gúaire into the language of the Britons. The proper meaning of *gúaire* is 'hair of the head', although the Clan MacQuarrie argues that the name signified 'proud' or 'noble' (which could be true: the words Caesar, Kaiser and Czar all stem from a root meaning 'long-haired'). Some of those same descendants of Gúaire took the names *MacKcurra* or *MacKwra*, suggesting that *gúaire* was cognate with *cùra*, a 'protector' or 'guardian' (also *curaidh*, a 'hero' or 'champion' – Welsh *cawr*). Arthur, we may remember, set up home at Strachur, in the 'valley of the guardian'.

Though he was celebrated in the British traditions of Arthur, Gúaire was of Irish stock and was famous for his long hair. He was the father of the equally hirsute Gwalchmai ('Hair of May'), who was also said to have been the son of Arthur's sister and, therefore, a nephew to Arthur. One of Arthur's nephews – the son of his half-sister Muirgein – was Mongán, the 'dear long-haired one', who could well have been the youth known to the Britons as Gwalchmai. Mongán was semi-divine: his paternity was shared between Fiachna mac Báetáin and the sea-god Manannán mac Lir, and he came to be thought of as the reincarnation of that legendary Irish hero, Fionn mac Cumhail. In all likelihood, Arthur was Mongán's foster-father.

The conclusion that Gweir of Great Valour, or Gweir the Tall, was also Gúaire son of Áedán, the most powerful layman in Dalriada, is irresistible. There is no mention of a Gúaire son of Áedán in the Irish *Annals*, although there are the references to a Bran son of Áedán who died at the same time as Arthur. The British legend of Brân the Blessed concerns a 'King of the Island of Britain' whose death had much in common with the death of Gúaire. Furthermore, the posthumous adventures of Brân's talking head are echoed in the legend of Columba's sacrifice of Oran on the Isle of Iona. It has already been noted that Brân and Oran were probably the same person, and though Adomnán of Iona studiously avoided mentioning Bran or Oran he did relate the story of the strange death of Gúaire and St Columba's foreknowledge of the fatal injury.

As all these different names dance before our eyes we might begin to see them coalescing into one figure: the most valiant man in the kingdom of Dalriada in those days. It should come as no surprise to find that just to the west of Arthur's grave, beyond a broad sweep of beach on the edge of the Atlantic, stands a rock known as *Carraig 'ic Gúaire* – the Rock of the Son of Gúaire – whilst immediately to the south of his burial mound lies the 'Gully of Bran's Lad' and a short distance to the east is *Cnoc Odhráin* – Oran's Hill.

St Columba had previously told King Áedán that three of his sons would 'fall in battles, slain by enemies'. Ever eager to confirm the accuracy of the saint's predictions, Adomnán later explained that 'Artuir and Eochaid Find were killed soon afterwards in the battle with the Miathi [southern Picts]'. But by giving his account of the strange death of Gúaire son of Áedán – who is mentioned nowhere else in the Irish sources – Adomnán indicated that things were not so straightforward.

Gúaire had pressed St Columba into revealing more about his fate.

Columba said that Gúaire would not die in battle or at sea, but that an unsuspected companion would be the cause of his death.

Gúaire's response still sends a chill down the spine: 'Perhaps one of my entourage of friends is thinking of killing me, or my wife is plotting my death through sorcery for love of a younger man?'

The final conflict came about because Arthur's wife absconded with another man, but that was not the end of the treachery. As we shall soon discover, Arthur was also betrayed by one of his entourage of friends.

Put into context, the conversation between Gúaire and St Columba is extremely revealing. It suggests that the 'most powerful' son of Áedán had an inkling that someone was plotting against him. More to the point, it indicates that St Columba had some knowledge of the plot. When first questioned, he confidently predicted that the son of Áedán would be killed by a long-term companion, but he quickly clammed up when Gúaire probed further.

According to Adomnán's account, Gúaire's death was caused by his own clumsiness. He was sitting under an upturned boat, scraping away at a barbed wooden spear, when he got up to investigate a fracas which had broken out nearby, dropping his knife and cutting his knee. So let us ask the question: if St Columba really had known that the most powerful man in the kingdom would cause his own death in this inept manner, why could he not have warned him to be more careful? Why the extraordinary reticence, the refusal to speak plainly about the matter? And why did Adomnán bother to include the story in his *Life of St Columba*, when the prophecy was so intentionally vague and the saint clearly avoided doing anything to protect the most valiant man in the kingdom?

Adomnán stated that Gúaire had been sitting under a boat when the tragedy struck. Traditionally, Arthur's ship was named *Prydwen* ('Fair-Form'); Geoffrey of Monmouth, however, believed that it was Arthur's shield that was called Prydwen. If Gúaire had been sheltering under an upturned shield, rather than a boat, then it would appear that he had surrendered, or at least called a truce, when he was fatally wounded.

The anonymous *True Story of the Death of Arthur* suggests that this might have been the case. After the battle, an exhausted Arthur leant on his shield. He dropped to the ground and asked his friends to remove his armour. It was as he lay prone with only his shield for protection that a youth approached on horseback and thrust a poisoned elm shaft into him.

Brân the Blessed was wounded in much the same way. Ambushed by hidden warriors, Brân received a poisoned spear-wound to his foot during a desperate battle, not with the southern Picts but with the followers of an Irish king.

Brân son of Llyr shared with Gúaire son of Áedán the quality of being *caled* – 'hard' or 'severe'. His name meant 'Raven', and there is a longstanding tradition in Cornwall that Arthur was reincarnated as a raven after his death. As *Gogfrân Gawr* or 'Little-Raven the Champion', he was deemed to have been one of Gwenhwyfar's three father-figures. Brân was 'crowned King of the Island of Britain'; Gúaire was the 'most powerful man in the whole of Dalriada'. Brân's sister Brânwen was also associated with ravens, as was Arthur's sister Muirgein, who is often compared with the raven-goddess known as the Mórrígan.

Muirgein's marriage to Fiachna mac Báetáin, Lord of the Dál nAraidne of Ulster, placed Arthur in the role of brother-in-law to his successor as defender of Manau Gododdin. Fiachna became Manannán, the 'dear one of Manau'. A Fort of

Manannán (*Dùn Mhanannáin*) stands less than a mile to the north of Arthur's grave. The Britons remembered Fiachna as Manawydan son of Llyr, and it was with his brother Manawydan that Brân was sitting on a rock overlooking the sea when they first saw the ships of Matholwch, King of Ireland, approaching the Island of the Mighty.

The name Matholwch derives from a word meaning 'Prayer' or 'Worship'. The arrival of the Irish king who wanted to draw the Island of the Mighty closer to Ireland replicated St Columba's landing on the Isle of Iona in 563. Columba was the scion of one of the ruling dynasties of Ireland, and the violence which attended his forceful occupation of Iona is recalled in the mutilation of King Matholwch's horses by one of Brân's brothers 'on his mother's side'.

St Columba and his warrior-monks drove the Druidic priesthood – the 'seven bishops of Hii' – off the island. With the accession in 574 of Áedán mac Gabráin as King of the Scots, however, Columba was obliged to share the island with a sacred sisterhood led by Áedán's daughter, Muirgein. This is glossed in the legend of Brân the Blessed as a marriage between Matholwch of Ireland and Brân's sister Brânwen. The product of this figurative marriage was a son born of two cultures. There was indeed a son born to the pagans Muirgein and Fiachna who became a 'confessor' to St Columba: his name was Laisrén ('Light'), but he is better remembered as St Molaise.

It is inconceivable that Columba's monks would have happily shared the Isle of Iona with Muirgein's priestesses and Áedán's Druids. The legend of Brân the Blessed recalls that Matholwch and his men began to abuse and mistreat Brân's sister, and in Adomnán's *Life of St Columba* we find a bizarre little story, which similarly points towards friction between the adherents of the rival faiths.

It occurred on the thirtieth anniversary of the saint's arrival on Iona – that is, during the pagan festival of Beltane in the year 593. Columba drew the attention of his followers to a band of 'angels sent from the throne on high to lead my soul from this body'. But, as he told his companions:

> … now they are delayed suddenly, and wait standing on a rock across our island Sound. It is as if they wished to come near me to call me from the body, but as they are not allowed to approach any closer they will soon hurry back to the heights of heaven.

St Columba had many meetings with 'angels' and it is difficult to see why on this occasion they should have been unable to cross a narrow stretch of sea-water. They were presumably of a kind with the 'angel' which visited St Columba on his desert isle and bullied him into ordaining Áedán as King of Dalriada, and with the 'angels' who rushed to Columba's assistance when he was attacked by pirates in one of the wilder parts of the Isle of Iona: in neither instance did the sea present much of an obstacle to them.

The rock that these 'angels' were standing on, across the Sound of Iona from Columba's monastery, was the Island of the Women, *Eilean nam Ban*, to which all females were reputedly banished by the Christian community. It is possible that they were hurling curses across the sea, though it is equally feasible that they were simply celebrating Beltane and that Columba chose to interpret their rituals as a threat to his very existence. He had spent thirty years of his life based on Iona and yet, in all that time, he had failed to extinguish the fires of paganism. The island was not yet entirely his own.

A little over a year after Columba watched the 'angels' performing their rites, Arthur was dead. The death that had been predicted for Gúaire son of Áedán had come about.

The legend of Brân the Blessed suggests that it was the harassment suffered by Muirgein and her sacred maidens at the hands of Columba's monks which led to the final battle. Like Arthur, Brân set sail with a great fleet; like Arthur, he was lured into a trap, surrounded by unseen enemies; and like Arthur, Brân was wounded by a poisoned spear. The number of survivors, both of Brân's last battle and of Arthur's, was seven.

Gúaire son of Áedán was wounded in the knee, Brân the Blessed in the foot, both injuries being comparable with the grievous injury to the genitals which afflicted the Fisher King of Arthurian legend.

Before we consider the precise nature of that wound there is another character from the early literature who is worthy of note. The ancient Welsh tale of *Culhwch and Olwen* presents a truncated account of Arthur's career. Along with his fellow heroes, Arthur comes to the aid of his kinsman Culhwch in tackling a series of impossible challenges. These include the seizure of the cauldron of inspiration from the 'servant of the son of King Áed of Ireland' and the hunting of the two Chief-Boars, Galam Cennaleth of the southern Picts and Morgan the Wealthy. The heroes are set those tasks by a 'Chief-Champion' called Yspaddaden, whose name meant 'Castrated'.

The tale of *Culhwch and Olwen* ends when the heroes return to the 'Castrated Chief-Champion' and shave him, removing his beard, skin and flesh. Goreu son of Constantine then seizes the Chief-Champion by the 'hair of his head' and decapitates him.

According to the *Triads*, Goreu son of Constantine was Arthur's cousin. Geoffrey of Monmouth would claim that Arthur, with his last breath, nominated Constantine as his successor. The beheading of the Castrated Chief-Champion by Arthur's close relatives mirrors the decapitation of Brân the Blessed by his surviving companions. The chief had been emasculated, wounded in the 'knee' or the 'foot' by a poisoned spear, and his life was ended by those who were closest to him.

It was inside the 'hidden retreat' of the Fisher King that the Grail procession was witnessed. Among the objects carried in that procession was a lance from which dripped three streams of blood. At the sight of this Bleeding Lance those present began wailing and lamenting. If the right questions were asked about the lance and its associated treasures, the wounded king would be healed.

We can start that healing process by determining what kind of weapon might have caused Arthur's fatal injury.

There are numerous clues. Adomnán tells us that Gúaire was whittling away at a barbed wooden spear when he dropped his knife and gashed his knee. The 'Castrated' Chief-Champion, Yspaddaden, was wounded (in the kneecap) by a poisoned spear, as was Brân the Blessed (in the foot). Another Welsh legend has Llew Skilful Hand struck in the side by a poisoned javelin 'so that the shaft started out, but the head of the dart remained in': this special spear had taken a year to make, partly because it could only be worked on 'during the sacrifice on Sundays'. The *Vera Historia de morte Arthuri* disclosed that Arthur was pierced by an elm shaft which was 'sharper than any such because it had been tempered in water and fire and finally dipped in adder's venom'.

The Welsh word for 'elm' – *llwyfen* or *llwyfanen* – is not a million miles from *llwyfenau*, the Welsh word for the loins. This raises the possibility that the anonymous author of the *True Story of the Death of Arthur* misinterpreted the word for 'loins', or perhaps that he found the concept of a 'loin-spear' too gruesome to countenance.

Irish tradition speaks of a weapon known as the *Gáe Bulg*. The legendary hero of Ulster, Cú Chullain, was trained in its usage on the Isle of Skye:

> The *Gáe Bulg* had to be made ready for use on a stream and cast from the fork of the toes. It entered a man's body with a single wound, like a javelin, then opened into thirty barbs. Only by cutting away the flesh could it be taken from that man's body.

In other accounts, the spear had seven heads, each with seven barbs. It was considered a weapon of last resort. Cradled between the toes, the spear was kicked upwards into the victim's groin, where it splintered, sending its tiny hooks coursing through the body. The name *Gáe Bulg* can be translated as 'Death Spear', 'Barbed Spear' or 'Belly-Spear'.

The climactic battle was done when the loin-spear was driven up into Arthur's underbelly and the 'chief's pale thigh ran with blood'. The wound was ghastly. The spear first took Arthur's manhood before it took his life.

A simple spear was insufficient for the task. The intention was to castrate Arthur, and the reason for this is simple.

Arthur was 'Little-Raven the Champion', otherwise known as Brân the Blessed. The cult of Brân can be traced all the way back to the Bronze Age city of Miletus, the original home of the Milesian Gaels, on the Ionian coast of modern-day

Turkey. There, the Sun-god Apollo fell in love with a beautiful youth named Branchus and granted him the gift of prophecy. Branchus then adopted a son, whom he named Evangelos ('Good News Messenger') and who inherited the prophetic gift from his father. The oracle was thenceforth handed down from father to son.

The term 'Father' had a particular application to Áedán mac Gabráin: it formed the basis of his title 'Uther'. It was also the seventh and highest initiatory grade in Mithraism, a warrior cult from which Christianity borrowed much of its mythology. Two of the lower grades were 'Raven' and 'Lion', which were also alternative names for Arthur. Whether or not Áedán and Arthur were devotees of the Mithraic mysteries, they clearly upheld the tradition of prophetic verse ('raven-knowledge') which went back to the Milesian Branchus. In the Welsh tradition, the prophetic youth was remembered as Brân ('Raven'); in the Irish tradition, the name evolved into Oran ('Song').

St Columba had expressed his misgivings at travelling to 'Alba of the ravens' when he first left Ireland in 563. Thirty years later, he still had not vanquished the raven cult. It was when he saw the Beltane festivities being celebrated on the thirtieth anniversary of his arrival that he resolved to destroy the pagan cult of Brân. The specialised spear required for the task would take a year to fashion, the preparations for its deployment being made during Sunday services. The loin-spear was designed to mutilate Arthur's genitals before its poison killed him, for that was the way of the sacred isle.

It was how one god overthrew another.

16

NAVEL OF THE SEA

THE *TRIADS of the Island of Britain* indicate where Arthur was buried. After 'Medrod' had united the 'Saxons, the Picts and the Scots' in rebellion, Arthur 'succeeded by violence' in landing on the coast:

> And then there took place the Battle of Camlan between Arthur and Medrod, and was himself wounded to death. And from that he died, and was buried in a hall on the Island of Afallach.

The *Triads* also note that the first of the 'Perpetual Harmonies of the Island of Britain' was to be heard on this island, where '2,400 religious men' prayed to God 'ceaselessly and forever'. Clearly, the Island of Afallach had become home to a prominent Christian community.

The word 'Afallach' derives from the Gaelic *abhall* (pronounced 'av-ull'), an 'apple-tree' or 'orchard' (compare the Gaulish *avallo* – an 'apple'), and relates to the term *ubhalach*. The Island of Afallach was the 'apple-bearing' isle.

Writing in about 1150, Geoffrey of Monmouth provided a description of the island:

> The Island of Apples gets its name 'The Fortunate Island' from the fact that it produces all manner of plants spontaneously. It needs no farmers to till the fields … It produces crops in abundance and grapes without help; and apple trees spring up from the short grass in its woods … and men live a hundred years or more. That is the place where nine sisters exercise a kindly rule over those who come to them from our lands. The one who is first among them has greater skill in healing, as her beauty surpasses that of her sisters. Her name is Morgen …

She was of course Muirgein, Arthur's half-sister, who was herself identified as a 'daughter of Afallach'.

Geoffrey's description of the Island of Apples was lifted almost word for word from an earlier account written by Isidore of Seville, which stated:

> The name of the Isles of the Fortunate signifies that they bear all good things, as if happy and blessed in the abundance of their fruits … Pagan error and the songs of the secular poets have held that these islands be Paradise because of the fecundity of the soil. Situated in the Ocean to the left of Mauretania [Libya], very near the west, they are separated by the sea flowing between them.

St Isidore was deemed to have been 'the last scholar of the ancient world'. He was an exact contemporary of Arthur.

Isidore's account was far from being the earliest reference to the Isles of the Fortunate. The same isles had been mentioned several times by Plutarch, a Greek historian and Roman citizen of the first and second centuries AD. Plutarch's *Life* of Quintus Sertorius – a Roman statesman who flourished 100 years before the birth of Christ – relayed what Sertorius had learnt about the 'fortunate isles' from Spanish mariners. 'The islands are said to be two in number, separated by a very narrow strait, and lie 10,000 furlongs [roughly 1,250 miles] from Africa. They are called the Isles of the Blessed.'

Plutarch added that the islands abounded in 'fruit and birds of every kind' and were a few days' sea-journey from Spain:

> Moreover an air that is salubrious, owing to the climate and the moderate changes in the seasons, prevails on the islands … the south and west winds which envelop the islands sometimes bring in their train soft and intermittent showers, but for the most part cool them with moist breezes and gently nourish the soil. Therefore a firm belief has made its way, even to the barbarians, that here are the Elysian Fields and the abode of the Blessed of which Homer sang.

Homer was not the only poet of the ancient world to have sung of those blessed isles. Pindar, a Greek poet of the fifth century BC, thought of them as a single island:

> And those that have three times kept to their oaths,
> Keeping their souls clean and pure,
> Never letting their hearts be defiled by the taint
> Of evil and injustice …
> They are led by Zeus to the end –
> To the palace of Kronos,
> Where soothing breezes off the Ocean
> Breathe over the Isle of the Blessed.

The Greek poet Hesiod, who lived at least 100 years before Pindar, also referred to the Isles of the Blessed in the Western Ocean.

By the twelfth century AD, the Isle of the Blessed had come to be thought of as the 'Island of Apples' – whence Avalon, from the Welsh *afallen*, an 'apple-tree'. The connection with apples was picked up on by Giraldus Cambrensis, who fostered the myth that Glastonbury in Somerset was once known as '*Inis Avallon*, that is *insula pomifera*, "The Island of Apples"' on the grounds that the apple 'was once abundant in that place'.

But Giraldus was thinking of the wrong kind of apple.

The apple has received quite a bad press over the years. Most infamously, it is said to have been the forbidden fruit of the tree in the midst of the Garden of Eden. Eating this fruit, the serpent had argued, would make Adam and Eve 'as gods, knowing good and evil'. Nowhere in the *Book of Genesis* is the apple specifically mentioned, and the assumption that the cause of mankind's fall was an apple is usually put down to a linguistic coincidence, the Latin words for 'apple' and 'evil' being more or less the same.

The ancient Greeks also knew that apples could lead to trouble. Ovid told the story of Atalanta, a virginal huntress devoted to the service of Diana (Artemis), who avoided marriage by challenging her suitors to a foot race, which she invariably won. The goddess Artemis presented one of these suitors – Hippomenes, the 'fourth in descent from the lord of the sea' – with three golden apples from the 'gleaming tree' with 'golden tinkling branches' which grew in 'the best part of the island of Cyprus'. Hippomenes raced against Atalanta, prudently dropping the golden apples one by one. The nymph stopped to pick up the apples and lost her foot race. The lovers then desecrated a temple by consummating their marriage in the sacred precinct and were promptly turned into lions.

It was an apple that started the Trojan War. The gods of Olympus held a wedding banquet but neglected to invite Eris, the goddess of Discord. Eris came to the feast and rolled a golden apple into the banqueting hall. The apple was inscribed with the word *Kallisti* – 'For the Most Beautiful'. Three goddesses clashed over who deserved the prize and the outcome of their contest was ten years of bloody conflict at the city of Troy.

Yet another Greek myth concerned the theft of the golden apples of immortality from the Garden of the Hesperides. A branch of golden apples had been the gift of Gaia, goddess of the Earth, to Hera on the occasion of her marriage to Zeus. The branch was planted on an island in the west, where a sisterhood known as the Western Maidens, Sunset Goddesses or Daughters of Evening protected the tree and its precious fruit. But the singing maidens were not averse to helping themselves to the golden apples, and so a sleepless, many-headed dragon was set to guard the tree.

The semi-divine hero Herakles (Hercules) was tasked with stealing the golden apples from the isle of the nymphs. He discovered the whereabouts of the island by wrestling the shape-shifting Old Man of the Sea into submission, and then tricked Atlas – supposedly the father of the Western Maidens – into fetching the apples for him. The goddess Athena later restored the stolen apples to their proper place in the garden in the west.

A similar theft occurs in Irish legend. Cian was the father of Lugh, the Celtic Apollo. When Cian was killed by Lugh's mortal enemies, the three sons of Tuirenn, Lugh punished the brothers by setting them a series of daunting challenges. The first of these was to collect three golden apples from the Garden in the East of the World:

> ... and no other apples will do but these, for they are the most beautiful and have the most virtue in them of the apples of the whole world ... they are of the colour of burned gold, and they are the size of the head of a child a month old, and there is the taste of honey on them, and they do not leave the pain of wounds or the vexation of sickness on anyone that eats them, and they do not lessen by being eaten for ever.

The only assistance Lugh would allow the sons of Tuirenn was the loan of the boat of the sea-god Manannán mac Lir. The brothers sailed to the garden of the golden apples, only to find that 'the king's champion and the fighting men of the country are always guarding it, and the king himself is chief over them'. Still, the sons of Tuirenn managed to steal the apples by turning themselves into hawks.

As we now know, Manannán mac Lir was Arthur's brother-in-law, also known as Fiachna mac Báetáin. The Irish legend brings us much closer to Arthur and his world – and, indeed, to the Island of Apples or Avalon, for the palace of Manannán was to be found at Emhain Abhlach, the 'apple-bearing' place.

The Wildman of the Woods, Myrddin Wyllt, hid from his enemies in an apple-tree after the Battle of Arderydd:

> Sweet apple-tree growing in the glade,
> The wandering one hidden from Rhydderch the royal,
> Trampled its base by the searching host.

An apple-tree is hardly an effective hiding-place. Strangely, though, Myrddin's example was to find its echo many years later, during another civil war.

The future King Charles II led a Scottish army to defeat at the Battle of Worcester in 1651, after which the prince was obliged to hide from his Parliamentary pursuers in a tree. When the English monarchy was restored in 1660, the tree became famous – many inns were named 'The Royal Oak' – and Charles II was depicted as a sort of Green Man or Lord of the Greenwood, his dark features peeping out through the leaves of an oak in a manner reminiscent of Myrddin Wyllt. The age-old festivities of May Day, which had been proscribed by the Parliamentary regime, were revived on the birthday of King Charles, 29 May, when the populace commemorated their king's escape by wearing oak leaves. The date became known as Oak-Apple Day.

A tale told by Geoffrey of Monmouth seems to confirm that the tree in which Myrddin hid was not an apple but an oak. Myrddin was out hunting one day when he and his companions came to a spot underneath an oak tree 'whose branches spread high into the air'. The oak stood beside a spring and fragrant apples lay in the soft grass around it. The men began to eat these apples. Soon 'they were out of their minds, bit and scratched each other like dogs, screamed, foamed at the mouth and rolled demented on the ground'. Myrddin realised that the madness-inducing apples had been left there for him by a spurned lover.

What kind of apples could start wars, confer immortality, make men 'as gods' and drive them out of their minds?

The answer is a very particular kind of apple.

The gall wasp is a tiny creature of the Cynipidae family. The adult female lays her eggs individually in the developing leaf buds of an oak tree. Chemical secretions cause the leaf tissue to mutate, forming a bulb around the egg. These bulbs are usually between 2cm and 5cm in diameter and provide sustenance for the wasp larvae that hatch inside them. Brown, yellow or pinkish-red in colour, they hang from the branches like golden apples.

The Welsh word for an 'apple' – *afal* – is also the word for an oak apple or gall.

The word 'Druid' is thought to derive from a Proto-Indo-European root meaning 'Oak-Knower'. The Roman author Pliny explained the Druids' obsession with the oak: 'Anything growing on these trees they regard as sent from heaven and a sign that the tree has been chosen by the gods'.

One such parasitic growth, much prized by the Druids, was the mistletoe, an ancient 'cure-all' and fertility drug. If the white globules of the mistletoe appeared like the 'silver apples of the moon', the 'golden apples of the sun' were the oak galls which also had their medicinal uses. Oak apples are the most naturally astringent vegetable products around. They have been used in the treatment of ailments ranging from cuts and burns to cancer. The tannins of the oak apple, when combined with charcoal and magnesium oxide, made a 'universal antidote' to poisoning.

Gall wasps have a notable tendency to hover around dead bodies. Those primitive societies in which corpses were flensed – laid out in the open to be stripped of their flesh by natural processes – might well have regarded the larvae as the reincarnated spirits of the dead, reborn inside the oak galls. The larva of the gall wasp consumes the spongy interior of its 'apple' until all that remains is a golden ball of paper-thin tissue housing a 'worm' or 'fly' – the pupated wasp – which makes a 'tinkling' sound when shaken. This might account for the 'golden tinkling branches' of the 'gleaming tree' from which Artemis took the golden apples and gave them to Hippomenes. An Irish king once heard such sweet tinkling music from a branch of these apples that all care and sorrow were instantly forgotten; the king traded his wife and children for the magical branch and was only reunited with his loved ones after he had visited Manannán mac Lir at his palace of Emhain Abhlach in the Land of Promise.

It was one thing to notice that the gall wasp was attracted to dead bodies and that its young grew up in the gilded cages of the galls, thereby forming a link between the spirits of the dead and the tinkling music of the golden apples. It was another thing altogether to associate the golden apples with a catastrophic loss of innocence and the fall of mankind. And yet it was very much the case that the oak apple drove a wedge between the gods and men and, at the same time, plunged the human race into history. For better or worse, the golden apples made us what we are today.

In his groundbreaking study, *The Origins of Consciousness in the Breakdown of the Bicameral Mind*, Julian Jaynes advanced the theory that in the beginning the gods spoke to us directly by means of statues, burning bushes and disembodied voices. This was the period in mankind's development when, as Thales of Miletus observed, 'all things are full of gods'. Jaynes reasoned that some form of crisis overtook humanity during the second millennium BC. In short, the gods stopped talking. A more scientific way of putting it would be that the left hemisphere of the brain began to dominate, so that the image-forming right hemisphere could only make itself heard in dreams, poetry and psychotic episodes. The cause of that epoch-making crisis can be traced to the golden apples.

History starts with the written record. The earliest inks were mostly carbon-based and created by burning materials to make soot. But then a remarkable discovery was made. Oak apples, when crushed, yield a substance called gallo-tannic acid. This could be added to 'green vitriol' or ferrous sulphate (the magic inherent in this material was expressed in an alchemical rubric: *Visita Interiora Terrae Rectificando Invenies Occultum Lapidem* – 'Visit the interior of the Earth and by purifying you will find the Secret Stone'; the first letters of the Latin maxim spell the word VITRIOL). The resulting solution could then be fermented and added to a binder, such as gum arabic, to create a lasting purple-black ink.

The beauty of iron-gall ink was that it flowed smoothly and was almost impossible to erase. By the middle of the seventh century BC, iron-gall ink was in common use. Copies of the Torah were made using the indelible ink, and the same substance was used to write the Dead Sea Scrolls. It became the principal means of preserving written records and remained so right up until the nineteenth century; it gave us the works of Shakespeare, the King James Bible and the American Declaration of Independence, along with countless other documents. But the development of writing was not all good news. With it came the rise of bureaucracy, the codifying of laws and an analytical, pernickety mindset. We became trapped in the world of left-brain logic and pedantry, losing touch with the connectedness we had previously known. The words of the gods were frozen in ink and pinned down on the page like so many dead butterflies in a display case. Unable to hear the gods any more, we began to bicker and quarrel over sacred texts.

Immortality was assured, for we could now preserve the deeds of heroes for all time, but that brought with it an awareness of mortality and the birth of self-consciousness. We became as gods, knowing (or at least able to argue about) good and evil, and we have been struggling to make sense of our place in the universe ever since.

The fall from prehistory into history, from a world full of gods into one ruled by the laws of men, began with the golden apples which grew on the tree in the midst of the garden. That tree was the World-Tree, the centre of the universe. Eve herself was originally a tree-goddess, her name ('Ever Living One') being related to *Ivo*, the yew, and it is likely that the God of the Old Testament, YHWH, was once a tree-god, as was Zeus or *IOVE*, to whom the oak was sacred.

According to Julius Caesar, who declared that the Druidic system of learning originated in Britain, the Druids had a secret alphabet of their own, but in their private and public records they used Greek letters. St Columba also studied Greek grammar in his continuance of the tradition of the *ollamh*. The Druids, however, preferred to commit most of their wisdom to memory, thereby avoiding the kind of arguments which arise over the interpretation and relative values of texts. By way of contrast, St Columba's faith was based almost entirely on the written word. His was a religion of The Book.

The spread of Christianity relied on its transmission of the Word, which required endless copying of the Scriptures. As Columba himself proved at the Battle of the Books, this could be a divisive practice.

Columba's reverence for oak trees was quintessentially Druidic. He praised the 'heaven's angels that come and go under every leaf' of the oaks at Derry, and what else could these 'angels' have been but the little gall wasps, which laid their eggs under the leaves and provided St Columba with the ink he needed to make his books? On the Isle of Iona he planted his church next to the Hill of the Oak and established a busy scriptorium. Calves were bred for their skins (the best vellum came from unborn calves) and golden apples were crushed for their gallotannic acid. Thanks to the oak galls of the 'apple-bearing' isle, Iona became the 'cradle of Christianity in the North' and a veritable factory of sacred texts, one of which – the *Book of Kells*, also known as the *Book of Columba* – survives as Ireland's finest national treasure.

The year 563 was Iona's Year Zero. The guidebooks give the impression that before St Columba came to the island there was nothing there, and it was the Dove of the Church who turned the little low-lying isle into 'Alba's holiest of holies', as Alec and Euphemia Ritchie put it in *Iona Past and Present*. One of the island's most fervent Victorian admirers called Iona the 'Mecca of the Gael' and the 'Metropolis of Dreams'. The poet Kenneth MacLeod rejoiced in the 'Grail-lit Isle', 'Iona of my heart, my grail'. To Columba, it was *I mo chridhe, I mo ghràidh* – 'Iona my heart, Iona my love' – while, more recently, the novelist Isabel Colegate made reference to 'the outposts and lonely places of the world, the faint torch of truth, the wide white light of the island of Iona'.

It is a small island, 3 miles long and a mile or so wide, floating like a leaf on the sea off the south-west tip of the Isle of Mull, approximately 1,250 miles from the coast of Africa and 'very near the west'. The southern part of Iona is predominantly moorland, purple-grey with rock and heather, while the north end is dominated by Dùn Í, the green and rocky Hill of Iona. Between the two high-points, the island is saddle-backed and green with exceptional fertility, skirted by rocks and dazzling white sands which turn the sea turquoise. The bedrock is Lewisian gneiss, the very first rock to solidify on the Earth's surface: rock so ancient that it preserves no fossil records. Predating life itself, the Isle of Iona is simply one of the oldest places on the planet.

Iona was the island of the apple-tree – *afallen* – or rather the golden-apple-bearing oak. As Geoffrey of Monmouth recalled it had once been ruled by nine sacred sisters whose leader was 'Morgen':

> It was there we took Arthur after the Battle of Camlan ... Morgen received us with due honour. She put the king in her chamber on a golden bed, uncovered his wound with her noble hand and looked long at it. At length she said he could be cured if only he stayed with her a long while and accepted her treatment. We therefore happily committed the king to her care and spread our sails to favourable winds on our return journey.

Islands inhabited primarily or entirely by women were a feature of the Celtic world, but nowhere are they more frequently encountered than in the *immrama* or 'voyage' sagas of Irish tradition. The *Voyage of Bran* is one of the oldest surviving examples. Its hero was out walking in Ireland one day when he heard music of such beauty that he was lulled into a pleasant sleep. On waking, he found a silver branch lying beside him. He took the branch back to his stronghold, where a beautiful woman 'in strange raiment' sang to him:

> A branch from the apple-tree of Emhain
> I bring like those one knows ...
> There is a distant isle
> Around which sea-horses glisten ...

Full fifty quatrains are devoted to extolling the island's wonders:

An ancient tree there is with blossoms,
On which birds call the canonical Hours;
In harmony it is their habit
To call together every hour.

Though they were supplanted by the '2,400 religious men' whose hourly praises gave rise to the first of the 'Perpetual Harmonies' of Britain, the sweet-singing birds of the isle were remembered in the legend of Brân the Blessed as the 'Birds of Rhiannon' whose song charmed Brân's companions as they laid his head to rest in a 'spacious hall' overlooking the sea – the same hall as that in which Arthur was buried on the Island of Afallach.

Without grief, without sorrow, without death,
Without any sickness, without debility,
That is the sign of Emhain:
Uncommon is an equal marvel.

Bran was determined to visit the marvellous isle and set sail from Ireland. He met Manannán mac Lir riding the waves. Manannán treated Bran to another exposition of the wonders of the isle, which was also Manannán's home. Bran and his crew then found the island. The chief of the island's women threw out a ball of sticky thread and pulled the mariners to the shore. They were royally entertained for many years and lost all track of time.

The *Voyage of Bran* would influence the later *Voyage of St Brendan*, which recounted the seven-year journey undertaken by Columba's old school-friend in search of the Land of Promise. The *Voyage of St Brendan* was little more than an attempt to paint a Christian gloss over an older tradition. In reality, the Land of Promise, *Tir Tairngire*, was not that difficult to find: an old Irish poem tells of a meeting between St Columba and Arthur's nephew, Mongán son of Manannán, and remarks that Columba came 'from the flock-rich Land of Promise', which would seem to acknowledge that the island of Columba's church was *Tir Tairngire*.

The *Voyage of St Brendan* in turn influenced the *Voyage of Máel Dúin*, the hero of which discovered the Island of Women when he sailed north from Ireland:

The green-backed wave brought them over the calm sea to an island with a mound and a fortress full of folk.
Beautiful maidens dwelt therein, as they could see; the bath they tended was filled with the brightest water.

Their noble mother came on a swift horse to greet the travellers; after their bath, the ringlet-haired, open-handed woman set all in readiness and said:

'All who dwell here will not die; rest unbounded, clothes of soft and gentle weave will be your portion ...'

The *immrama* stories tend to agree that the island could prove difficult to leave. The leader of the beautiful maidens used her sticky thread to make sure that the travellers could not get away; when Máel Dúin and his companions finally escaped, 'sorrowfully, the female host wept for those adrift on the endless wave'.

The palace of Manannán mac Lir in the Land of Promise was known as *Emhain Abhlach* ('yu-an av-lach'). *Emhain* pertained to the yew-tree, the 'firm, strong god' of the Druids, although there is evidence to suggest that the Irish *eo* – 'yew' – could refer to any large sacred tree, including the 'apple-bearing' oak of Iona.

Eo was one of the early names for Iona, and was still in use in the ninth century AD when a German monk wrote:

On the Pictish coast is an isle of the sea,
Floating amidst the waves, Eo is its name,
Where rests the body of the Lord's saint, Columba.

Adomnán of Iona thought of the island as 'yewy'. He called it the 'Iouan isle', *Ioua insula*, which was simply a Latinised version of *Emhain*, or *Evonium*, as Hector Boece called it: the seat of forty Scottish kings. The significance of *Ioua* perhaps lies in its similarity to *Iehoua* – 'Jehovah' in Medieval Latin. Similarly, the transition from *Ioua* to *Iona* might have had something to do with the fact that in Hebrew a 'dove' is *Yonah*, the Latin equivalent being *Columba*.

Columba himself insisted that the island should be known as *I*, the Gaelic letter which was styled after *iubhar*, the 'yew'. The Isle of Iona was associated first and foremost with a sacred tree or trees, and this is implicit in the name of *Emhain Abhlach*: the 'Yew-place of Apples'. Astonishingly, the island was still being referred to as *Emhain Abhlach* as late as the thirteenth century.

Raghnall son of Somerled was the Norse King of the Isles and Lord of Argyll until his death in 1229. He built a Benedictine monastery on Iona in 1203 – the Deed of Confirmation still exists in the Vatican – but the monastery was torn down by the clergy of Northern Ireland. All the same, Raghnall's monastery was destined to be the medieval successor to Columba's primitive church, and Raghnall's sister also founded an attractive nunnery on the isle. A Gaelic poem written in praise of Raghnall son of Somerled highlights a possible source of division between the King of the Isles and the churchmen of Ulster:

Emhain Abhlach of the yews,
Bright the colour of the crests of its trees –
Fresh place of the dark blackthorn
Where the poet's offspring, Lugh, was raised …

The intrusion of women onto the isle was bad enough, but worse was Raghnall's insistence on remembering what the monks wanted everyone to forget: that the isle of Columba's church was also *Emhain Abhlach*, the place of the sacred apple-bearing trees. The thirteenth-century poem exalted 'Emhain of the fragrant apples' and the 'bright apple-trees', which grew in the 'fruitful place' of its sacred burial mound.

More than 600 years had gone by since the death of St Columba and still there were those who associated Iona primarily with its sacred trees and, implicitly, with the family of Arthur. This was anathema to the Church. By celebrating the fact that Iona was the 'Island of Afallach' or *Emhain Abhlach*, the praise-poem for Raghnall reminds us that the island was also the home of Manannán mac Lir; it was the blessed isle ruled by Muirgein and her nine beautiful maidens and the last resting place of the greatest hero Britain has ever known.

Deirdre of the Sorrows (see Chapter 2) had another name for her 'island in the sea':

Beloved is Draigen,
Dear the white sand beneath its waves …

It was the isle of the *draigen* – 'blackthorn' – or, as Raghnall's praise-poem phrased it, the 'fresh place of the dark blackthorn'. A map of Iona published by Alec and Euphemia Ritchie in the 1920s reveals the existence of a Garden of Thorns on the south-east flank of Dùn Í, just below the Ascent of the Rose (*Bruthach an Ròis*). The blackthorn is a member of the Rose family, and one of its earliest uses was as a hedge protecting orchards from grazing animals.

A quaint tradition states that the beautiful Brigid grew up on the south-east flank of Dùn Í, and it was from there that the 'Mary of the Gael' was transported by angels to Bethlehem to serve as midwife and foster-mother to the Christ-child. St Brigid was once a powerful goddess in her own right: celebrated throughout the Celtic world as Brigantia, she was honoured in the Hebrides as Brìde ('breed'). Her shrine at Kildare in Ireland was protected by an impenetrable hedge of thorns, and her sanctuary on Iona appears to have been similarly hidden within a thorny enclosure and surrounded by roses or 'may' which bloomed during the blackthorn winter of early spring, around the time of Brìde's Imbolc festival.

Deirdre's name for the island offers an explanation for the title by which Arthur's father is generally known. Uther Pendragon is an anglicised form of *Iothair pen*

Draigen. The first part is made up of *eo* (*iubhar* – 'yew') and *athir* (*athair* – 'father'). It is the same as the name of the Roman god Jupiter: it meant 'Yew-Father'.

Fittingly, Áedán had played the Jupiter role in the conception of Arthur. In order to approach the most beautiful Creirwy he had 'assumed the appearance and the dress' of the goddess, just as Zeus (the Greek name for Jupiter) had in the myth of Kallisto and Arkas/Arcturus. Áedán was remembered in the *Mabinogion* tradition as the Zeus-like Great-Lord Sea Thunder, 'the best man in the world'. He was the lord of the sea and the champion of the sacred island – that is, he was *pen Draigen*, the chief of the blackthorn isle.

The notion that the blessed isle was guarded by a many-headed 'dragon' goes back at least as far as the legend of Herakles (Hercules) and his theft of the golden apples. In the Irish legend of the sons of Tuirenn the garden is protected by the 'king's champions and fighting men', the 'king himself being chief among them'. The many-headed dragon of the garden might have been the blackthorn – the sap of which served as a binder in the production of ink while the fruits, known as sloes, appeared like so many eyes watching over the golden-apple tree and its mysteries – but it was also the king's champion or 'dragon of the island'.

Far from having been an insignificant place before Columba arrived and made it his home, Iona had long been held sacred by Deirdre and her Druids and by others before them.

Plutarch, the Greek essayist of the first century AD, described the islands off the coast of Britain 'in the general direction of the sunset': 'The natives have a story that in one of these, Kronos has been confined by Zeus, but that he, having a son for a gaoler, is left sovereign lord of these Islands, and of the sea, which is called the Gulf of Kronos.'

Kronos was one of the descendants of Gaia, the Earth, and Ouranos, the Sky. He had overthrown his father and was himself overthrown by his son Zeus, who imprisoned him in an island of remarkable beauty, where Kronos slept inside a cave, resting on a rock which looked like gold.

Several hundred years before Plutarch, the poet Pindar had disclosed that the pure and worthy were conveyed by Zeus to the 'palace of Kronos':

> Where soothing breezes off the Ocean
> Breathe over the Isle of the Blessed.

The tradition that Kronos, the father of Zeus, was imprisoned in a western isle off the British coast was of great antiquity. Plutarch noted that Kronos rested 'with Briareus keeping guard over him as he sleeps, for as they [the natives] put it, sleep is the bond forged for Kronos.' Like Arthur, Kronos was not dead but merely hibernating, guarded by the 100-headed Briareus, much as the sacred tree of the apple-isle was safeguarded by the blackthorn or briar-rose.

Kronos was the chief god of the Golden Age. He was later conflated with Chronos, the personification of Time, but his original role was that of a god of vegetation and the harvest; his symbol was the sickle. He bears comparison with the Egyptian Osiris, another fertility god who became a Lord of the Dead. His closest parallel in British mythology was Hu Gadarn ('The Mighty'), who came from the East and introduced the arts of agriculture to the Honey Isle, which then became known as the Island of Hu (pronounced 'hee') or the 'Island of the Mighty'. Among the early names for Iona were *Hii* and *Ie*, which would strongly suggest that it was also the Island of Hu, where an eternal vigil was kept over the slumbering god of the harvest.

Plutarch referred to the place where Kronos was imprisoned as the 'isle Ogygian'. Strabo the geographer noted that this island lay in the North Atlantic; he also observed that Homer had called it 'the island of Ogygia, where is the Navel of the sea'.

The ancient Greeks held that the *omphalos* or 'navel' of the world was located at Delphi, where the celebrated oracle was based. Homer's *Umbilicus maris* would have been the marine equivalent of Delphi and nothing less than the spiritual centre of the Western ocean.

Perhaps the extreme age of Iona's rocky foundations meant that the island was thought of as the birthplace of the oceanic world. What is beyond doubt is that Iona possessed precisely what one would expect to find at the World-Navel or *omphalos* – a World-Tree. This majestic growth connected the physical plane with the upper and lower realms of the sky and the earth (as the son of the Earth and the Sky, Kronos was himself a sort of World-Tree). The World-Tree stood at the centre of the world like a cosmic peg; it was the tree which grew in the 'best part of the island of Cyprus', the tree found in the midst of the Garden of Eden. Christians venerate the World-Tree in the form of the 'Holy Rood', the Cross on which Christ was crucified. Other cultures imagined their gods as hanging from the World-Tree, sacrificing themselves to themselves and acting as a bridge between this world and the next. The importance of the Isle of Iona in this context is that it was the isle of the sacred tree. It was *Emhain Abhlach*, the 'apple-bearing' island, which was also the 'yewy' isle, *Ioua insula*, or *eo*, the 'yew'.

As with the Greek Delphi, Iona was once the home of a prophetess and her attendant priestesses. The Greeks thought of these Western Maidens as the daughters of Hesperius, the Evening Star: they were the nymphs of the 'Hesperides'. When the Greeks discovered that the Morning Star and the Evening Star were one and the same they dedicated the bright planet to their love-goddess Aphrodite, whom the Romans called Venus. The Venus of the Celtic world was Brigantia, who was known in the Western Isles as Brighid or Bride – a verse in the *Carmina Gadelica* refers to the Hebrides as *Eileana Bride*, the Islands of Bride, whose inhabitants were *Aois-Bhrighde*, Bride's People. The folk of the Hebrides were under the special patronage of the Evening Star – as was Arthur when he named his shield 'Face of Evening' – and so they had something in common with the Daughters of Evening who sang so beautifully in the Garden of the Hesperides while they tended the tree that bore the golden apples of the immortalising ink.

The Sunset Goddesses also sang for Kronos, the god of the dead who slept among the roots of the World-Tree on the island, which lay 'in the general direction of the sunset'. Kronos had supplanted his father, Ouranos the Sky-god, by castrating him. Zeus had in turn displaced Kronos by castrating him with his own sickle. Osiris was also deprived of his reproductive organs when his brother rebelled against him. And with the castration of Arthur, another Golden Age came to a violent end. But that was unavoidable if the 'Navel of the sea' was to be dedicated exclusively to Columba of the Church.

There was no place for women on the island of Columba's church. From that point on monks, not maidens, would sing kings to their rest on the isle of the blessed. All females were banished to the smaller, less hospitable *Eilean nam Ban*, the Island of the Women. They were gone, but not forgotten.

A strange remark was overheard on Iona in the nineteenth century:

Thiodhlaic mi mo naoi nighnean mar sheachdnar an Cill mo Neachdáin ann an Í.

I buried my nine daughters as seven in the Chapel of my Nechtán on Iona.

The Hebridean memory is long and deep – who can tell what tragic circumstances lay behind that statement, or when it was first uttered?

It is true that a Chapel of my Nechtán once stood at the foot of Dùn Í, beneath the Garden of Thorns. This was where Deirdre of the Sorrows sang to the Sun with her Nechtán-worshipping Druids, where the flame-like Brighid blossomed in her loveliness and the nymphs of the Hesperides and the nine sisters of Avalon, like the muses of old, kept up their perpetual harmonies. With the death of Arthur, the maidens lost their foothold on Iona. They have never regained it. Could it be that the memory of nine daughters buried in seven graves in the Chapel of my Nechtán is all that remains of the nine maidens who once ruled the blessed isle?

Not quite. Their sweet singing is heard no more. But their heritage, like that of Iona as a whole, was not entirely lost.

A short Gaelic phrase, collected by Alexander Carmichael and published in 1881, says it all:

I nam ban bòidheach.

Iona of the beautiful women.

17

TREASURES OF BRITAIN

THE ISLE of Iona became the subject of an intense ideological tug-of-war between Britain and Ireland. This impacted on the legends and myths of both cultures, so that on the one hand Iona was conflated with Ireland and, on the other, the Island of The Mighty was mistaken for Britain. It is a measure of the sacred status of Iona that two nations were so eager to call it their own.

Homer referred to the 'island of Ogygia, where is the Navel of the sea'. The name came from Ogyges, a legendary Flood-survivor. His equivalent in Irish lore was Fintan, who married the granddaughter of Noah and alone survived the deluge by turning himself into a salmon and becoming the first of the Druidic 'salmon of wisdom'.

Ogyges was also said to have founded the cult of the Mysteries at Eleusis, near Athens. As the survivor of an ancient culture he was able to pass on his wisdom to a select few by way of his Mysteries. The adjective *Ogygian* meant 'primal', 'from the dawn of time' – a fair description of Iona's primeval geology – and if the Navel of the sea was the Isle of Iona, then its association with Ogyges might have implied a connection with the Mysteries.

To put it another way: if the 'apple-bearing' isle was also the *omphalos* or 'navel' of the Atlantic, associated with the wisdom of a culture which predated the Biblical Flood, then it is likely that the island was also the home of a Mystery cult comparable with that which Ogyges had established in Greece.

The term 'mystery' originally carried the meaning of hidden secrets and religious experience. The Mystery cults of the ancient world practiced initiation ceremonies which involved a symbolic descent and return from Death's kingdom. The pattern of the initiatory journey is deeply imprinted on the human psyche: it forms the structural basis for most of the stories we tell. But the Mystery schools were not about the vicarious thrills of somebody else's journey. Their initiates were expected to experience the process of death-and-rebirth for themselves.

The legends of the Holy Grail hint strongly at some form of Mystery cult. What that might have involved has been obscured over the years by differing accounts of what the Grail actually was. But one thing can be said for certain – it was not the cup of the Last Supper.

The French poet Robert de Boron first claimed that the Grail was Christ's chalice in his *Joseph d'Arimathie*, otherwise known as *Le Roman de l'estoire dou Graal*, which he wrote in about the year 1200. Christ's blood was allegedly collected in the chalice when his body was brought down from the Cross. The cup then found its way into Britain and the 'Vales of Avalon' in the west.

Robert de Boron's story appeared very shortly after the monks of Glastonbury announced that they had found the grave of Arthur. The man who oversaw the Glastonbury dig, Henri de Sully, had previously been in charge of the abbey of Fécamp in Normandy, where a quantity of Christ's blood was held as a holy relic. The notion that the cup containing Christ's blood was brought to Glastonbury by none other than Christ's uncle is as unfounded as the claim that Arthur was buried there: both legends were manufactured for the purpose of boosting the finances of Glastonbury Abbey; they were a brilliant marketing scam.

But one falsehood generally leads to another. The lack of any real substance to the myth of the *San Greal* or 'Holy Grail' created a vacuum, into which stepped the conspiracy theorists with their tales of the 'Royal Blood' or *Sang Real*. The argument goes that the Church has kept an explosive secret hushed up for centuries, that this secret concerns the bloodline of Jesus Christ, and that the 'Holy Grail' was an occult symbol for that bloodline. All that can be said about this theory is that the Church has only itself to blame. By hijacking the Grail legends in the first place, the medieval Church created the very conditions in which such wild theories could prosper.

The earliest literary appearance of the Grail came in *Le Conte du Graal*, an incomplete masterpiece composed by the French poet Chrétien de Troyes in the 1180s. The tale starts with Perceval the Welshman, who was correctly identified in the Welsh version of the legend as Peredur of York, one of Arthur's twenty-four horsemen. Perceval meets three knights in the forest – the Welsh account names them as Gwalchmai, Gweir and Owain – and resolves to become a knight himself.

His adventures bring him to the 'hidden retreat' of the Fisher King. There, Perceval is presented with a sword which 'could not be broken except in one singularly perilous circumstance known only to him who had forged it'. He then sits down to dinner with the Fisher King and witnesses a strange procession involving a white lance which drips blood from its tip, a shining grail of gold and precious stones and a silver carving platter.

There is no mention of a 'grail' in the Welsh version of the tale, where the procession involves a spear running with three streams of blood and a large platter carrying a man's head, which is also covered in blood.

Perceval neglects to question the meaning of this strange procession and wakes in the morning to find the mansion deserted. He is later criticised by a damsel for his failure to ask the question. In Wolfram von Eschenbach's extraordinary *Parzifal* (early 1200s) the damsel is called Cundrie 'La Surziere' and is seen wearing a hood embroidered with turtle-doves – the dove being the perennial symbol of the Grail. Wolfram also suggested that the Grail was not a cup but a heavenly stone known as *lapsit exillis,* which bore more than a passing resemblance to Scotland's royal Stone of Destiny (see Chapter 10).

Later accounts brought in more crusading. In the *Quest of the Holy Grail,* the Saracen leader Evalach is converted to Christianity. Evalach is clearly a corruption of Afallach and so stands as a signpost pointing, like the dove and the Stone, to the island of Arthur's burial. The author of the *Quest* also identified the Grail Castle as 'Corbenic'. And with that, we now turn to a list of the grave-goods that were buried with Arthur, including those which formed part of the mystical procession witnessed inside the 'hidden retreat' of the Fisher King.

They were known as the Thirteen Treasures of the Island of Britain. Welsh tradition asserts that they were gathered together by Myrddin, who disappeared with them into a 'Glass House, and they remain there for ever'.

A manuscript of the fifteenth or sixteenth century lists the Thirteen Treasures or *Tri Thlws ar Ddeg Ynys Prydain.* Earlier lists survive, but without the accompanying comments.

First, there was *Dyrnwyn,* the white-handled sword of Rhydderch, of which it was said that 'when drawn by a noble man it would burst into flames from its hilt to its tip ... Everyone who asked for it would receive it; but because of its peculiarity, everyone used to reject it. And for that reason he was called Rhydderch the Generous.'

Arthur's own sword had failed him during his last battle. The Grail legends continually harp on the issue of a sword destined to break when it was most needed. Chrétien de Troyes disclosed that the jinxed sword could only be repaired at 'the lake beyond Cotouatre' – that is, *Scottewatre* or the River Forth.

The sword which accompanied Arthur into his grave was donated by his near-neighbour and kinsman, Rhydderch of Strathclyde. Geoffrey of Monmouth thought of him as 'Duke Cador' (from *cadwr* – 'soldier') and he appears in this guise in the revelatory *Dream of Rhonabwy,* in which it is his 'duty to arm the King on the days of battle and warfare'. This implies that Rhydderch had the honour of being Arthur's sword-bearer. The description of Rhydderch's sword matches that of Arthur's as given in the tale of Rhonabwy's dream:

And the similitude of two serpents was upon the sword in gold. And when the sword was drawn from its scabbard, it seemed as if two flames of fire burst forth from the jaws of the serpents, and then, so wonderful was the sword, that it was hard for anyone to look at it.

This was the weapon which Arthur took with him into the Otherworld. Taliesin, in his poem of Arthur's burial, called it Rhydderch's 'sword of lightning slaughter'.

With the sword came another of the treasures: *Hogalen Tudwal Tudklyd* or the 'whetstone of Tudwal Tudglyd; if a brave man sharpened his sword on it, it would draw the life-blood from any man it wounded, but if a coward sharpened his blade on it, his opponent would be unaffected.'

Tudwal of the Clyde was the father of Rhydderch the Generous.

The second treasure on the list was the 'hamper of Gwyddno Tall-Crane', *Mwys Gwyddno Garanhir,* 'food for one man would be put into it, and food for one hundred would be found inside it when it was next opened.'

Like his cousin Rhydderch, Gwyddno was a prince of Strathclyde. He had settled in North Wales, where he became involved with the cauldron cult at Llyn Tegid. It was Gwyddno who sent his son Elffin down to the weir on the River Dovey with instructions to bring back 100 pounds worth of salmon; instead, Elffin found only a Dovey coracle containing an initiated bard, whom he named Taliesin.

The 'hamper' of Gwyddno was possibly the wicker coracle of the cauldron ritual. One man was put into it, but a man equal to 100 pounds worth of salmon was found inside it when it was next opened.

It can be surmised that the coracle of Gwyddno was also the boat in which the Fisher King went night-fishing in order to ease his constant pain. Its cultic relevance will become apparent very shortly.

Third on the list of treasures was *Korn Brân Galed o'r Gogledd,* the 'horn of Brân the Severe from the North': 'whatever drink one might wish for would be found in it.'

The quality of being 'hard' or 'severe' was shared by three Arthurian heroes: Drystan, Eiddilig (Áed Dibchine) and 'Gwair of Great Valour'. Both Gúaire and Brân were considered 'severe', which is hardly surprising since they were the same person.

A medieval Welsh poet had this to say about Brân:

> Brân the Hard they called him,
> Descended from the tribe of the Men of the North;
> Taliesin, that excellent magician,
> Made him better than the three Generous ones.

The *Triads* confirm that Arthur was indeed 'more generous' than the 'Three Generous Men' of the Island of Britain.

Notes written in the margins of a Welsh manuscript indicate that the Horn of Brân was a key treasure. Myrddin had first to acquire Brân's drinking horn before he could obtain the other treasures. He then placed these treasures inside the 'Glass House' or the castle known as 'Corbenic' (from *cor benoît* – 'blessed horn') where the Grail was also held.

The same Welsh marginalia state that the Horn of Brân was the horn which Hercules had torn from the head of the centaur. Another Greek legend claimed that it was Zeus who ripped the horn from the head of his nanny goat. In both instances, the horn became the cornucopia or 'horn of plenty' which, like the horn of Brân the Blessed, was a symbol of abundance.

The horn had other properties. Robert Biket, in his twelfth-century *Lai du Cor*, suggested that the horn would dispense its contents over any man whose wife had been unfaithful; Arthur, of course, ended up drenched. Otherwise, the horn was specifically associated with Arthur's family: his nephew and foster-son Gwalchmai was remembered in the Hebrides as Sir Uallabh O'Còrn or 'Sir Wiseman son of Horn'.

The fourth treasure was *Kar Morgan Mwynfawr*, the 'chariot of Morgan the Wealthy'. Also known as the Chariot of Arianrhod, it was rumoured that 'a man would be quickly transported to wherever he wanted to be in it'.

An accompanying treasure – the fifth on the list – was the 'halter of Clydno Eidyn', *Kebystr Clyddno Eiddyn*, which was 'fixed to the foot of the owner's bed by a staple' and 'whatever horse one might wish for was found in the halter'.

There was nothing unusual about the burial of a chariot with an important Celtic individual. In Arthur's case, the halter had belonged to his grandfather while the chariot was the one in which his mother undertook her vision-quest on the summit of Traprain Law when she was pregnant, just a few months before Morgan the Wealthy usurped her father's kingdom.

Both items came from Lothian. They were the chariot and halter which Arthur took with him into the Otherworld, allowing him to go wherever he wanted to and to bridle any horse he might wish for.

The sixth treasure was the knife of Llawfrodedd the Horseman 'which could carve for twenty-four men to eat at a table'.

Arthur, it would seem, was expected to reconvene his Round Table war-band in the afterlife and would need a special knife to carve their choice cuts of meat.

Llawfrodedd the Bearded appears among Arthur's retinue in the *Mabinogion* tales of *Culhwch and Olwen* and *The Dream of Rhonabwy*; he was also the owner of one of the 'Three Prominent Cows of the Island of Britain'. His name meant 'Sadness' or 'Melancholy' (*llawfrydedd*), which would suggest that he was probably better known as Arthur's Counsellor Knight, Llywarch the Old.

Llywarch's kingdom of South Rheged fell after the disaster that was Arthur's last battle. He was driven into exile in North Wales, where he lived near Llyn Tegid until his death in about 643. Llywarch's melancholy poetry reveals that he thought of the Round Table warriors as his sons and mourned their deaths bitterly.

The parish of Llanidloes, south of Llyn Tegid, takes its name from a seventh-century churchman whose father was said to have been a son of a red-bearded knight called Llawfrodedd. This at least places Llawfrodedd the Horseman in the right time-frame and geographical region to have been the last known survivor of Arthur's Round Table.

The seventh item on the list of treasures was *Pair Dyrnwch Gawr*, the 'cauldron of Diwrnach the Champion', which 'would not boil the meat of a coward but would quickly boil the food of a brave man'.

This was the most important treasure of them all. Taliesin called it the Cauldron of Five-Trees.

Traditionally, five magical trees protected Ireland: they were an oak, a yew and three ash-trees.

In many cultures, including that of the Norsemen who ruled the Hebrides in the Middle Ages, the World-Tree was an ash, of the genus *Fraxinus*. It was the tree of spears; its tough but flexible wood being excellent for making weapons. A sprig of ash could bring about prophetic dreams, while snakes were repelled by its bark and leaves. Best of all, the ash secretes a sugary substance which, when fermented, becomes what the Norsemen called the Mead of Inspiration: who-ever drank it became a poet or a scholar. This mead was the cauldron's 'liquor of science and inspiration'.

The ancient Greeks believed that Zeus created the first men from the ash tree and that the sugary extract, which they called *méli* ('honey'), was fed to the infant Zeus by nymphs known as Meliae. These nymphs had been born of the blood of Ouranos, the Sky, when he was castrated by his son Kronos; they were also thought of as the daughters of Oceanus, the god of the Atlantic Ocean.

The Gaelic word for the ash-tree is *uinnse* ('oo-in-shu'). The Druidic Ogham alphabet drew the letter 'n' from *nuin* ('noon'), which also meant 'ash'. The Irish equivalent of the Scottish *nuin* is *nion*, from the Old Irish *nin*, which referred to the letter 'n' and to the Ogham alphabet in general. The ash was the tree of letters.

The Old Irish *nin* was also related to the Welsh *nen* ('Heaven', 'roof-beam' or 'lord') and perhaps to the Early Irish *nóin*, 'evening'. The Irish *nion* could also mean a 'wave' or 'branching' – that is, having boughs – and from *nion* came *Nionon*, 'Heaven'.

It was the ash-tree which provided Taliesin with one of his names for Iona. Annwn ('an-noon') has long been thought of as a Celtic realm of the dead, which in many ways it was, but it derived from the Gaelic *A' Nuin* – 'The Ash'. The alternative spelling of Annwn, *Annwfn*, could be arrived at via the Gaelic *nèamh*,

'Heaven', the firmament or 'region of bliss', which itself comes from the Old Irish *nem*, the Welsh *nef* and the Old Celtic *nemos*, a 'woodland grove' or 'sanctuary'. Taliesin's Annwn was the same as his Honey Isle, and the Cauldron of Five-Trees was the property of the 'Lord of Annwn' who guarded the World-Tree on the Isle of Iona.

The cauldron was – and is – a remarkable artifact (an Appendix to this book explains where it can be seen today). It was made up of several silver plates, richly decorated and chased with gilt, which were held together by metal bands but could easily be dismantled, hence the tendency of the cauldron to fall apart immediately after use. Its base plate had once been the decorative part of a horse's bridle, and so the cauldron was often referred to as a 'horse', its function being akin to that of the shaman's 'horse' or drum, which gave him access to the other worlds. In Aneirin's *Y Gododdin* poem, 'Gweir the Tall' is described as the 'prime son of Mighty-Horse', thereby reminding us that Arthur, as *peiryan faban*, was the 'son of the cauldron'.

There are indications that when Columba's monks stormed the Isle of Iona in 563, the cauldron was prudently hidden in a lake. Matholwch, the Columba character in the tale of *Brânwen Daughter of Llyr*, told Brân the Blessed that he had seen a large man dragging the magnificent vessel out of the Lake of the Cauldron. This lake still exists, although it is now known as the 'Lake of the Pot of Iona' – *Loch Poit na h-Í*. The silent, reedy, tooth-shaped pool lies about a mile inland from the Iona Ferry terminal on the Isle of Mull and is reputedly the haunt of a supernatural *each-uisge* or 'water-horse'.

By securing protection for his poets at the Druim Cett conference in 575, Áedán was able to reinstate the cauldron cult. Thereafter, the vessel became a source of friction between the Druidic priests and the monks of Columba. Among the legends of Manannán mac Lir, who shared the island of Columba's church, are those concerning a golden cup of truth which would break if three lies were spoken over it, but would piece itself back together if three truths were uttered. St Columba allegedly borrowed the golden cup and broke it; he then had to return it to Manannán to be repaired.

The cauldron also proved to be a bone of contention between Áedán and his eldest son. The fourteenth-century *Yellow Book of Lecan* contains the 'Story of Cano son of Gartnán', in which Áedán bitterly contests the kingship of Scotland with 'Gartnán son of Áed son of Gabrán'. Gartnán was in reality Muirgein's brother, Gartnait mac Áedáin, who became King of the Picts in 584.

The story goes that Gartnait had been living happily on an island until the birth of his son upset Áedán's political game-plan. Gartnait arranged for his son to be fostered and then hid a vat of gold and silver, killing the four men who concealed it so that only he and his son knew of its whereabouts. Áedán invaded the island and massacred its inhabitants; Cano sought shelter with relatives in Ireland and

Áedán discovered the precious vat: 'Now they say that Satan came to Áedán and told him where the vat was, so that it was taken by him to his own store-room, and there was not a penny of it lacking.'

It is possible to read too much into the *Scéla Cano meic Gartnáin*, and historically the story is unreliable, but it does seem to reflect a troubled state of affairs revolving around Áedán's family, a royal island and a 'vat of gold and silver'.

The same vat features prominently in the Welsh tales of the *Mabinogion*. In *Owain, or The Lady of the Fountain*, Arthur's nephew first hears about the mysterious cauldron from Cynon son of Clydno and sets out to face the challenge. Owain visits a castle of twenty-four maidens and then comes to a green tree beside a fountain, where a silver bowl rests on a marble slab. By casting water onto the slab Owain conjures up a violent tempest, at which point his cauldron adventure begins in earnest.

Owain also found the bowl when he was out hunting with his stepfather in *Manawydan Son of Llyr*. Inside a magical fortress, Owain discovered:

[a] fountain with marble work around it, and on the margin of the fountain a golden bowl upon a marble slab, and chains hanging from the air, to which he saw no end ... And he was greatly pleased with the beauty of the gold, and the rich workmanship of the bowl, and he went up to the bowl and laid hold of it. And when he had taken hold of it his hands stuck to the bowl, and his feet to the slab on which the bowl was placed, and all joyousness forsook him, so that he could not utter a word.

Speechlessness was associated with the cauldron, for those who had experienced its mysteries were forbidden to talk about them.

Owain's mother set out to find her son. She too entered the strange fortress and became stuck fast to the bowl. Straightaway, darkness fell, thunder roared and the fortress vanished with mother and son both trapped inside it.

A holy bishop later confessed that he had arranged the enchantment as a punishment for Owain's mother, Muirgein.

The primeval 'island of Ogygia', Homer's 'Navel of the sea', is best remembered as the isle on which Odysseus was kept prisoner for seven years by the sea-nymph Calypso.

Returning from the Trojan War, the wily Odysseus had visited the underworld, where he spoke with the shade of Achilles and learnt that those who were not prepared for death lived on as 'mindless disembodied ghosts' in Hades.

Later, after his crew was lost in a shipwreck, Odysseus was washed up on Calypso's island, which was also the *omphalos* or belly button of the ocean. Calypso's name meant 'concealment', and the time Odysseus spent in her cave amounted to a period of expiation, a seven-year penance for the bloodshed at Troy, and a profound induction into the Mysteries. Odysseus was one of the earliest heroes to discover how difficult it could be to leave the Island of Women, but his years on the island, when he acted as guardian of the World-Tree and Lord of the Dead, ensured that he was absolute for death and, therefore, free to live.

Hundreds of years later, the Mystery school on Iona was still producing warrior-poets. It empowered Arthur and helped him gain his famous victories, but Columba and his monks considered the warriors 'disorderly' and took steps to remove them from the isle.

The cauldron cult also accounts for the many tales of adulterous love which weave through the Arthurian romances. Creirwy became Taliesin's 'sweetheart' through their mutual initiation; Drystan's legendary love for Essyllt was also probably a cauldron coupling – a daughter of Culfanawyd or the 'Sty of Manawyd', Essyllt was one of Manannán's magical pigs, which is as much as to say that she was one of the nine beautiful maidens of the sacred isle.

A legend attached to St Kentigern tells of a queen who fell in love with a soldier and gave him a precious ring. Her jealous husband took the ring from the soldier's finger and flung it into the River Clyde; he then demanded that his wife show him the ring. In desperation, the queen turned to St Kentigern, who already knew about the affair. Kentigern went fishing and caught a salmon. The missing ring was found inside the fish.

This legend has a lengthy pedigree (it can be traced back to ancient Greece in the fifth century BC), but the fact that the ring was recovered from a 'salmon' suggests that the queen's lover was really a cauldron initiate.

What follows is an attempt to reconstruct something of the cauldron ritual, based largely on the Arthurian legends and the Mystery schools of the ancient world.

The initiate was chosen by lot. A bannock of pot-parched corn was toasted on a griddle, with one edge being deliberately scorched. The bannock was then broken up and shared. Whoever received the charred portion was the chosen one.

A soul-partner was also selected to be the initiate's sweetheart, nurse and chief mourner.

The initiate knelt or sat on a marble slab. On Iona, this would have been the sacred Stone of Destiny, or something like it. His soul-partner gave him a draught from the cauldron in a drinking-horn; both of them had to be careful not to spill a drop, for the woman was playing the part of the goddess of the cauldron (an old Gaelic proverb recalls that *Chuir Brìghd' a làmh sa bhobhla* – 'Brìde put her hand into the bowl') and any clumsiness on her part would imply that both she and her cauldron-partner were unworthy.

Taliesin listed a number of ingredients present in the liquor, including wheat and honey, herbs and berries, cresses, sea-foam, wort and vervain. There were probably hallucinogenic substances in the 'sweet mead' too. Peering into the cauldron, the initiate would see images of gods and animals swimming around his own reflection.

He then suffered a form of sacrificial 'three-fold' death. Almost certainly he received a stunning blow to the head and was stabbed in the thigh. Taliesin referred to ritual thigh-piercing in his poetry ('Let the thigh be pierced in blood'; 'To my knife a multitude of thighs have submitted') and the folklorist Lewis Spence noted similiarities in the ancient Mexican practice of blood-sacrifice through the piercing of the thighs and the maxim quoted by Nietzsche: '*increscent animi, virescit volnere virtus*' – 'the spirit grows, strength is restored by wounding.'

Arthur underwent the ordeal more than once, and so his alter ego Brân the Blessed was known as 'Pierced Thighs'. As Llew Skilful Hand, he was capable of striking the leg of a Druidic 'wren' precisely 'between the sinew and the bone'.

The third form of symbolic death might have involved a snake-bite. The initiatory snake-bite originated with Gathelus, the progenitor of the Gaels, who was bitten in the neck while in Egypt. One of the Grail stories concerns Arthur's father-in-law, Caradog Strong-Arm, who had a snake attached to his arm by his parents; the snake nearly drained his life away (fortunately, the golden oak-apples formed the basis of a 'universal antidote' to poison). It is worth noting that one of the plates which made up the cauldron depicts a cross-legged figure holding a snake. The injection of venom would have stimulated the body's immune system while inducing breathing difficulties, vomiting, paralysis, convulsions and delirium – all symptoms of the shamanic trance – along with skin pallor, pins and needles and partial or complete loss of vision (blindess was frequently associated with the Grail). The snake was valued by the Druids, who were sometimes known as 'adders', and was one of the creatures deemed sacred to the goddess: at Brìde's spring festival of Imbolc it was said that 'the serpent shall come from the mound'.

The initiate was then imprisoned in a 'coffin' or 'chest' or laid on a 'Bed of Marvels'. Like Lazarus, he was entombed, and his soul-partner wept for him. His body was held down by chains – partly to protect him from harming himself – while he drifted in and out of consciousness, surrounded by the mouldering relics of the ancestors. His soul was thought to be making its journey to the Otherworld.

After three days and nights the initiate was 'rescued' from his enclosed tomb and placed inside a wicker coracle, covered with a leather canopy. This was then set adrift on the sea. As an old Welsh poem has it, 'The conduct of the water will decide thy merit.'

Wherever he landed, the initiate would be released from the wicker-and-leather womb and reborn, Venus-like, from the waves. His memory was restored by a drink from the Well of Memory. On Iona, this spring was *Tobar na h-Aoise*, which can be found on the north peak of the island's highest hill; usually translated as 'Fountain of Youth', *Tobar na h-Aoise* is better rendered as the 'Well of Antiquity' or the 'Spring of Naoise', after the Druidic lover of Deirdre who was also associated with the Well of Life on the hill at the sacred centre – or navel – of Ireland.

The graduate was presented with a new name to mark the death of his old life and the start of his new one. His forehead might have been tattooed with salmon-like speckles, for he was now a 'salmon of wisdom', but he was forbidden to speak of his ordeal.

Only the bravest responded to the cauldron's challenge. It was a consummation devoutly to be wished, though a wise man would fear its terrors. It was thus a blessed curse, a fearsome desire, and its paradoxical nature was summed up by a neat juxtaposition. The Gaelic word *grathail* captured the 'terrible', 'fearful' aspect of the Mysteries, while *sannt* (Early Irish *sant*) conveyed the sense of 'lust' or 'desire', the compelling urge to undergo the trial.

This, then, was the 'terrible desire' – *sannt grathail* (pronounced 'saunt gra-hal') – which passed into European folklore as *sant graal*, the 'Holy Grail'.

The next item on the list of the Treasures of Britain was Arthur's robe of office. It was *Pais Badarn Beisrydd*, the 'coat of Padarn Red-Coat': 'if a noble man put it on, it would fit, but it would not fit one base-born.'

Padarn Beisrudd ap Tegid – Paternus Red-Coat son of Tacitus – was, according to tradition, the Romano-British official who commanded the frontier warriors of the Votadini (later, the Gododdin) during the latter days of the Roman occupation of Britain. His son Aeternus (Edern) was the father of Cunedda of Manau, who founded the kingdom of Gwynedd in North Wales. From Cunedda, the imperial red-purple robe would have passed down to the subsequent defenders of Manau, including Brychan and Áedán, until it came to Arthur, who relinquished control of Manau Gododdin to his brother-in-law Fiachna mac Báetáin in 584.

In one of his poems, Taliesin praised the 'blessed Arthur', admiring his 'swift devastations', his 'sovereign leadership' and his 'red-purple robe'. The red Roman robe of Paternus went into the grave with Arthur as if to indicate that the line had been severed: the glorious defenders of Manau belonged to the past.

Two more items on the list were the 'crock and dish of Rhygenydd the Cleric' (*Gren a desgyl Rhygenydd Ysgolhaig*): 'whatever food might be wished for would be found in them.'

The treasures were expected to fulfil their magical functions in the afterlife where, in the feasting hall of the heroes, Arthur would be served with whatever sweetmeats he desired.

Ysgolhaig translates as 'scholar', with the archaic meaning of 'cleric'. The name Rhygenydd appears to relate to the corn crake (*rhygen yr yd*). A poem attributed to the Irish hero Fionn mac Cumhail honoured the corn crake for singing 'from eve till morn, deep in corn, a strenuous bard!' The shy bird was also featured in the illuminated *Book of Kells* or *Book of Columba*, where it was shown intertwined with a heron.

The man who donated his crockery must have been one of Arthur's learned and literate companions – perhaps Cynon, the clerical 'St Kentigern', whose sister was the heron-like Creirwy.

The next treasure was the magnificent *Gwyddbwyll Gwenddolau ap Ceidio* – the 'play-board of Gwenddolau son of Ceidio: if the pieces were set, they would play by themselves. The board was of gold and the men of silver.'

Gwyddbwyll (pronounced 'gwith-boo-ud') was a board game similar to the Irish *fidchell* or 'wood-sense'. One player positioned his King at the centre of the board and arranged four Princes or Defenders around the King. The other player had eight Raiders, which he placed at regular intervals around the edge of the board. As the enemy Raiders closed in, the King had to escape to the edge of the board, helped and protected by his Defenders.

The game seems to have had a magical application and was particularly appropriate for a king who was outnumbered and surrounded. In *The Dream of Rhonabwy*, Arthur and his nephew Owain play games of *gwyddbwyll* beside a river while their respective warriors attack each other in what appears to have been an endless repetition of Arthur's final 'futile' conflict.

The divinatory aspect of the game is also on show in the tale of *Peredur Son of York*, an early version of the Perceval myth, in which the *gwyddbwyll* is known as the Chessboard of the Empress. The original Peredur of York fought against Arthur when the stronghold of Gwenddolau was attacked in 573, but soon joined Arthur's Round Table after that first 'futile' battle. The *gwyddbwyll* board of Gwenddolau was one of the spoils of the Battle of Arderydd and was associated with Peredur, the joint-King of York, before it went into the grave with Arthur.

The last treasure to be listed is an odd one. It was said of *Llen Arthur yng Ngernyw* – the 'mantle of Arthur in Cernyw' – that 'whoever wore it was invisible, though he could see everybody.'

Cernyw (pronounced 'kern-yoo') was a place in south-east Wales, once ruled by one of Arthur's Just Knights, St Cadog. It is also the Welsh name for Cornwall – an unfortunate coincidence which has done much to frustrate Arthurian scholarship. Geoffrey of Monmouth for one became obsessed with Cornwall, locating Arthur's birth and last battle there, even though it is highly unlikely that Arthur ever set foot in south-west Britain.

In fact, *Cernyw* was simply the 'Cairn of the Sacred Trees'. It derives from the Welsh *carn* (Gaelic *càrn* – a 'heap of stones raised over the tomb of a hero') and *yw* (meaning 'yews'). Cernyw, then, was the burial mound on the 'yewy' isle in which

Arthur and his comrades suffered the ritual imprisonment of the cauldron ordeal, and in which Arthur was laid to rest with the Treasures of Britain.

The cloak of invisibility which Arthur wore at the moment of his burial was not a material item. If any cloak went into the grave with him it was probably the brocade mantle of his mother-in-law, Tegau Golden-Breast. Like Arthur's drinking-horn, this cloak had the ability to measure a woman's faithfulness, giving Arthur a fighting chance of finding a more steadfast partner in the Otherworld.

Another treasure that is sometimes mentioned is the Stone and Ring of Eluned. This appears in the tale of *Owain, or The Lady of the Fountain*, in which Owain is inspired to face the cauldron challenge by Cynon son of Clydno and eventually becomes the guardian of a sacred spring. He receives help from a maiden named Luned (Chrétien de Troyes described her as a 'winsome brunette, prudent, clever and polite') who gives him a ring set with a precious stone. When the ring is turned so that the stone faces in towards the palm, the wearer becomes invisible.

We shall discover shortly how the stone and ring worked, rendering Arthur invisible as he was placed in his grave.

The greatest hero Britain has ever known was laid to rest in a 'hidden retreat' under the Cairn of the Yews on the apple-bearing isle which was also the Navel of the sea and the site of the World-Tree or 'Annwn'.

His friend Myrddin gathered together the Treasures of Britain and deposited them inside the 'Glass House' with Arthur. They were surrendered by Arthur's friends and family so that Arthur would not go into the Otherworld empty-handed and all his needs would be catered for.

The treasures were handed over because their owners no longer had need of them. They knew that the death of the Bear-Guardian, Arthur the Emperor, meant nothing less than the death of Britain.

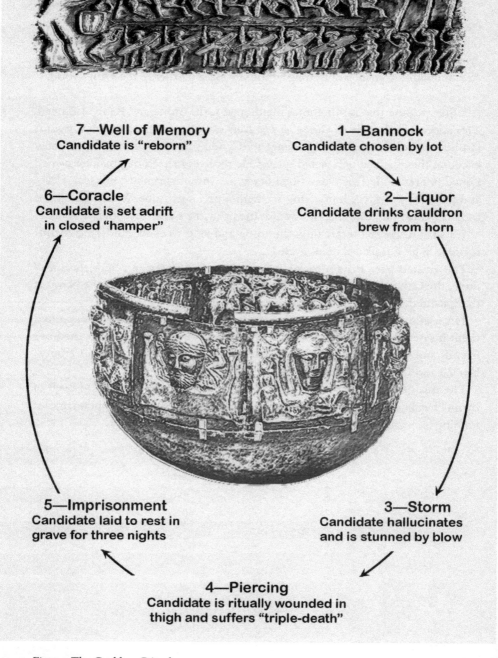

7—Well of Memory
Candidate is "reborn"

1—Bannock
Candidate chosen by lot

6—Coracle
Candidate is set adrift
in closed "hamper"

2—Liquor
Candidate drinks cauldron
brew from horn

5—Imprisonment
Candidate laid to rest in
grave for three nights

3—Storm
Candidate hallucinates
and is stunned by blow

4—Piercing
Candidate is ritually wounded in
thigh and suffers "triple-death"

Figure 3 The Cauldron Ritual

18

THE JOURNEY OF ARTHUR

THE GRAIL procession takes place inside the burial mound. Those who are fortunate enough to witness it are able to heal the wounded king if they will only ask the right questions about what they see – a head on a platter, a golden gleaming bowl, a lance dripping with three streams of blood.

The king cries out for justice. It was not just Arthur who was betrayed, but a whole nation. Every time the legends of Arthur and his people are retold from the point-of-view of their enemies his wounds bleed afresh.

If the king is to be healed we must be brave enough to confront the truth and tell it like it was.

St Columba was an old man. On the thirtieth anniversary of his arrival on Iona he had watched the pagans in their white linen robes celebrating Beltane and he had sworn to be rid of them. All that was needed was the right opportunity.

It came a year later. Arthur sailed with his fleet from the Firth of Forth and fought his way onto the beach at Cruden Bay. Messages flew back and forth. Anglian warships set out from Northumbria as Arthur chased Morgan and his Pictish spearmen down into Angus. The final conflict loomed.

The opposing forces lined up in vale of Strathmore. Morgan's army of Picts and Angles was ranged along the valley, from the Hill of Alyth to the River Ericht and beyond. Arthur's warriors faced them across the River Isla. The fate of Britain hung in the balance.

Arthur sent one of his trusted Round Table partners with a message for Morgan. The man chosen for this delicate task was Gwenhwyfar's foster-father. But Arthur's message of conciliation never arrived. It was twisted into a provocation.

This was the version of events revealed in *The Dream of Rhonabwy* by Iddog son of Mynyo, who would be forever remembered as the 'Churn of Britain':

... through my desire for battle, I kindled strife between them, and stirred up wrath, when I was sent by Arthur the Emperor to reason with Medrod ... and to seek for peace, lest the sons of the Kings of the Island of Britain, and of the nobles, should be slain. And whereas Arthur charged me with the fairest sayings he could think of, I uttered unto Medrod the harshest I could devise. And therefore I am called Iddog Cordd Prydain, for from this did the battle of Camlan ensue.

The first act of treachery, then, was to ensure that the bloodshed was not averted. With the inevitability of grand tragedy, the great battle began.

Iddog then made himself scarce: 'And three nights before the end of the battle of Camlan I left them, and went to the Llech Las in North Britain to do penance. And there I remained doing penance seven years, and after that I gained pardon.'

Arthur, meanwhile, had divided his force into three to attack both flanks of Morgan's army. The fighting continued through the Saturday and Sunday.

And then, disaster struck.

Aneirin, who witnessed the horror, gave vent to the shock he had felt:

> A stone on open ground in the region of Lleu's land,
> The boundary of the Gododdin's border.
> To battle! To battle! Blow the horn! Blow the horn!
> A tempest of pilgrims, a raucous pilgrim army ...
> From Din Dywydd they attacked ...

They had come up from the rear and hacked into Arthur's guard near the stone which stands 3.5m tall on the hollow plain of Camno.

To understand what happened we need to establish two things: the identity of Iddog son of Mynyo, the 'Churn of Britain', and the location of the fort of Din Dywydd, from which the pilgrim army marched to launch its surprise attack on Arthur's position.

According to Adomnán of Iona, the monastery of St Columba had a daughter house on the Scottish mainland. Adomnán called it *cella Diuni* – the 'chapel of Dúin'. Columba had foreknowledge of the death of one of his monks, a man named Cailtan, who was the *praepositus* or 'prior' of the chapel of Dúin. The chapel, Adomnán informs us, was named after Cailtan's brother.

The name Cailtan can be derived from the Gaelic *calltuinn* – 'hazel' – which in Welsh was Coll or Collen.

St Collen was the hermit who was also said to have banished the 'King of Annwn', Gwyn ap Nudd, from the Tor at Glastonbury. Elements of that legend were invented by the monks of Glastonbury in a last-ditch attempt to save their abbey from ruin. Nevertheless, the memory of ideological conflict between Collen and the Chief Bard of Britain is not without substance.

Adomnán gave the location of *cella Diuni* as being 'by the lake of the River Awe' in Argyll. The River Awe empties into Loch Etive near Taynuilt. Almost directly opposite the mouth of the River Awe stand the remains of the priory of Ardchattan.

The priory was founded in 1230, and there is little evidence that a major monastic settlement existed there much earlier. All the same, the priory of Ardchattan 'by the lake of the River Awe' might offer a clue as to the site of the real *cella Diuni*.

Ardchattan, the 'Height of Cattan', took its name from a sixth-century saint known as Catán or Cathan, who was much associated with the kingdom of Dalriada. Arthur's father Áedán was suspected of having impregnated Catán's sister, who then gave birth to St Blane or Bláán. One of Arthur's Round Table warriors, St Blane was styled 'triumphant Bláán of the Britons'. He apparently lost his life fighting against the Northumbrian Angles in 590.

Catán is the Gaelic form of Cadog, a name borne by another of Arthur's knights. A quick study of the medieval accounts of St Cadog's life points us to the probable location of the chapel of Dúin – the mainland offshoot of Columba's monastery on Iona.

St Cadog's ancestral roots lay in the North: his great-grandmother was said to have been a daughter of Cunedda of Manau. Cadog's father was a King of Gwent in South Wales whose brother, Pedr of Dyfed, was yet another Arthurian warrior-prince. According to the *Life of St Cadog* written by Lifris of Llancarfan in the eleventh century, Arthur, Cai and Bedwyr got involved in helping Cadog's father to elope with Cadog's mother. The tale is wildly inaccurate, and characterises Arthur as a would-be rapist, but it is built on a core of fact. Arthur spent his earliest years in the vicinity of St David's in Dyfed; his foster-brother Cai was related to St David. Bedwyr, as the son of Pedr of Dyfed, was St Cadog's cousin, and it seems highly probable that Cadog was involved with the settlement at St David's, where he would have encountered Arthur, Cai and Bedwyr.

Two more Arthurian knights had connections with St David's in the south-west of Wales. Cynon son of Clydno was said to have studied there after he had escaped from Morgan's murderous fury in Lothian, and Sandde Angel-Face is thought to have been the father of St David. It could be argued that the nucleus of Arthur's Round Table was the fraternity which had first gathered at St David's: a close-knit group of interrelated princes. One of these was St Cadog, who apparently resented the fact that St David was proclaimed Archbishop of Wales – a case of wounded pride, perhaps, or the grievance of a brother who has been passed over in favour of his younger sibling.

First known as Cadfael ('Battle-Prince'), Cadog was principally associated with South Wales: he established a monastery at Llancarfan in the Vale of Glamorgan; a church and hospital were dedicated to him at Caerleon-on-Usk. He is also said to have befriended St Gildas and to have rubbed shoulders with both Maelgwyn and Rhun of Gwynedd. Like his friend Caradog Strong-Arm, King of Gwent and future father-in-law of Arthur, Cadog joined those princes who made their way into North Wales in the 560s, when Arthur settled in Gwynedd. The signs are that Cadog was inducted into the cauldron cult in North Wales. Taking the Druidic name of Collen, he fetched up in a coracle at his new base at Llangollen on the River Dee, just south of the Tegeingl region then governed by Caradog Strong-Arm. An old stone cross stands at Llangollen: known as Gwenhwyfar's Cross – *Croes Gwenhwyfar* – it reminds us that Arthur's queen was raised in Cadog's household.

The *Life of St Cadog* also has the saint visiting the court of 'a certain king, Rhydderch by name'. Forgetting that Rhydderch was supposed to be Christian, Cadog forced the King of Strathclyde to humble himself. His adventures in the North continued with his arrival 'at a certain fort, which is on this side of mount Bannog, which is said to be situated in the middle of Scotland'. St Cadog started digging the foundations for a monastery and unearthed the remains of his grandfather Brychan of Manau, or Caw of North Britain, as he was also known. The owner of the bones appeared as a spectre to St Cadog and announced that 'beyond mount Bannog [he had] formerly reigned for many years'.

It was suggested earlier that Brychan's remains were laid to rest in the Round Table mound in the field below Stirling Castle. St Cadog gathered up the bones of his ancestor and carried them to the site of his new monastery, where 'the kings of the Scottish folk presented him with twenty-four homesteads' – one for each member of the Round Table alliance.

Cadog's new monastery lay a little to the north of Stirling and just to the west of Dunblane, where his nephew St Blane is commemorated. Back in the first century AD, the Romans had built a sizeable fortress on a tapering spit of land where the Ardoch Burn joins the River Teith on its way to the River Forth. The town which grew up around this busy camp became known simply as *An Dùn* – 'The Fort'. It was the gateway to the Highlands.

The River Teith, which runs immediately to the west of The Fort at Doune, probably took its name from *taith* – a 'message' or a 'pilgrimage'. A mile or two upriver from Doune, the Annat Burn flows down into the Teith, creating a waterfall along the way which is known as the Cauldron Linn. 'Annat' signifies a mother-church (*annaid*), and where the Annat Burn meets the River Teith there stands a natural mound on which can be seen the ruins of the old parish church of Kilmadock.

Kilmadock – the 'Chapel of My Aedóc' – was dedicated to 'Docus the Briton'. In Ireland, this Docus was known as Mádoc the pilgrim. Docus is simply a shortened form of Cadog. The parish church of Doune was named in honour of St Cadog or 'Docus the Briton'. The Irish form of his name, Aedóc, would have sounded to Welsh ears like *Iddog*.

He was, according to the *Triads of the Island of Britain*, one of the three knights who became the keepers of the Holy Grail.

The Welsh tales of the *Mabinogion* give more than one account of what took place.

One of the more mysterious characters in Welsh myth is Dylan Eil Ton ('Ocean son of Wave'). Presumably he existed, because Taliesin composed an elegy to him ('Wave of Ireland, and wave of Manau, and wave of the North, and wave of Britain'), and yet all that we know of him from the legend of *Math Son of Mathonwy* is that he was some sort of twin brother to Llew the lion, that his element was the sea, and that he was struck a fatal blow by his uncle Gofannon, the god of smith-craft.

If the rumours were true, and Arthur's father did get Cadog's sister pregnant, then St Cadog would have been a *de facto* uncle to Arthur. Furthermore, there are hints in various sources that Arthur's sword was engineered to fail him at a critical moment, and in circumstances known only to the man who had forged it. Chrétien de Troyes would remark that the sword could only be 'rehammered, retempered and repaired' at the lake beyond the River Forth. This lake was Loch Venachar (once *Loch-bannochquhar*), from which emerges *Eas Gobhain*, the 'Cascade of the Smith' – one of two waters which join near Callander to form the River Teith, which then runs past the Chapel of My Aedóc and the fort of Doune.

Taliesin's *Death-Song of Dylan* indicates that the youth known as Ocean son of Wave was violently pierced by a poisoned weapon. The same fate befell his supposed twin brother, Llew Skilful Hand. In *Math Son of Mathonwy*, the death of Llew is described in some detail.

He had married a woman made of flowers, but she fell in love with another man – the 'Bright Crowned One', Gronw Pebyr, Lord of Penllyn. Llew's life was charmed, so his treacherous wife inveigled him into explaining how he might be killed. Llew told her that the spear which could kill him would take a whole year to make and could only be worked on during the Sunday mass. He would also have to be standing on the rim of a cauldron by the side of a river.

The spear was prepared. Llew's rival staged his ambush on a 'Hill of Battle'. As Llew emerged from his cauldron-bath, close by a stone which stood in the ground, the Lord of Penllyn hurled the poisoned spear. It struck Llew in the side, 'so that the shaft started out, but the head of the dart remained in'.

Penllyn lies in the Vale of Glamorgan, a short distance from St Cadog's first monastery at Llancarfan. There is no record of St Cadog having been a metal-worker, but images of the saint tend to show him holding a spear. And as we have seen, St Cadog had a close relationship with Arthur's queen.

The name given for Cadog in *The Dream of Rhonabwy* is Iddog, a variant form of Aedóc – as in 'My Aedóc', to whom the chapel at Doune is dedicated. In Rhonabwy's vision of Arthur and his friends, Iddog identifies himself as a 'son of Mynyo'. Really, this was *Mynyw*, the Welsh name for the settlement of St David's in Dyfed.

The familiar Dewi means 'David' in Welsh, although the older form of the name is Dewydd. The pilgrim army which attacked Arthur by the River Isla had come up from Din Dywydd, the 'Fort of David'. Latinised as *cella Diuni*, the daughter house of Columba's monastery had been dedicated to St David, probably at around the time of the saint's death in about 589. Adomnán noted that the offshoot of Columba's monastery was named after the brother of Cailtan. As Cailtan was the Gaelic form of the name Collen, which Cadog adopted after his cauldron initiation, then he was indeed a 'son of Mynyw' and one of St David's brethren.

Cadog was delegated to carry messages between Arthur and Morgan the Wealthy because of his paternal relationship with Gwenhwyfar. Unbeknownst to Arthur, Cadog was under instructions not to sue for peace. He altered Arthur's conciliatory messages so that the climactic battle became unavoidable.

As soon as the fighting started on the Friday, Cadog left the field. As his namesake, Iddog son of Mynyo, put it in *The Dream of Rhonabwy*, he 'went to the Llech Las in North Britain to do penance. And there I remained doing penance seven years, and after that I gained pardon.'

The Llech Las or *llech glas* was the Grey Stone. It was a natural landmark, an erratic boulder deposited by glacial action on a hill beside the River Teith, a mile downriver from the Roman fort at Doune. It is said that St Cadog spent seven years of his life at the Hermit's Croft near the ruined church of Kilmadock, and this appears to echo the tradition that Iddog did penance for seven years at the Grey Stone.

It also helps to explain the legend of St Collen's battle with Taliesin on the summit of Glastonbury Tor. Glastonbury was a misidentification of the town of the Grey – *glas* – Stone, where Cadog betrayed his pagan friends.

It was no more than 40 miles from the scene of Arthur's last stand to the monastery established by St Cadog near Doune and named after his brother in Christ, St David. While Arthur and his companions were fighting for Britain's survival that fateful weekend, Cadog was back at *cella Diuni*, briefing his warrior-monks.

In his *Life of St Cadog*, Lifris of Llancarfan told a strange story. It concerned a 'certain very brave leader of the British (or Britons), called Ligessog, the son of Eliman, also surnamed Llaw hir, that is, "Long Hand"'. This Ligessog 'slew three soldiers of Arthur, the most illustrious King of Britannia' and then fled to St Cadog for protection. After seven years, Arthur arrived 'with a very great force of soldiers'. Cadog offered to put the matter before a distinguished panel of judges – including St David – and it was agreed that Arthur should receive compensation for the lives of his soldiers. St Cadog then tricked Arthur over the reparation. When Arthur, Cai and Bedwyr discovered this, Arthur sought the saint's forgiveness for having been so unreasonable.

The Christian legends of St Cadog frequently brought him into contact with Arthur and his heroes but sought to portray the saint as an independent operator.

This was at a time when the Church was using Arthur as a convenient foil to be trumped by any old saint who might happen to be passing. A separate tradition recalls that Cadog was one of Arthur's twenty-four knights, and so it seems odd that he should have sheltered a 'very brave leader' of the Britons who had killed three of Arthur's men. What is more, Ligessog was given sanctuary for seven years, just as Iddog son of Mynyo supposedly did seven years of penance for having caused Arthur's final battle.

The implication is clear: Cadog knowingly harboured one of Arthur's enemies. Ligessog Long-Hand was no ordinary chieftain. He would appear to have been a special sort of warrior – a lone fighter or champion (*llawr*). His name was derived from *cess*, a word meaning 'spear'.

He was better known as St Kessog and was widely regarded as the patron saint of Scotland before that honour was conferred on St Andrew in the tenth century. Not to be confused – as he often is – with the Irish-born Cessán, a 'son of the King of Alba and chaplain to Patrick', St Kessog was based at the 'dark village' of Luss by the side of Loch Lomond. He also had churches dedicated to him in Strathearn and at Blanefield in Glasgow. St Kessog's Fair was held at Callander, beside the Cascade of the Smith, a short distance up the River Teith from St Cadog's church near Doune.

The designation 'son of Eliman' points to St Kessog having been the murderous Ligessog. *Eliman* means 'The Liman' – a corruption of *Laomainn*, the Gaelic name for Loch Lomond.

This was the man who had been chosen to assassinate Arthur: a warrior who fought alone; a soldier of Christ who knew Arthur; a killer whom the early Church would revere as a patron saint of Scotland.

The pilgrims celebrated mass on the Sunday. Their confessions were heard, and absolution granted. Then they set off, marching up the valley of the Allen Water and along the Roman road from Braco to Perth. At Kettins, south of Coupar Angus, they could rest and finalise their plan of action.

St Columba had predicted that Arthur's death would be brought about by a companion of whom he suspected nothing. The Dove of the Church had now arranged for the emperor to be surrounded by enemies he thought of as his friends.

They attacked on the Monday. There was panic on the plain of Camno as the pilgrim army descended.

Arthur had divided his army into three. Two of those divisions were fighting with Morgan's allies on the far side of the River Isla. Only a third of Arthur's force was on hand to protect him.

Caradog Strong-Arm fought desperately to defend his son-in-law. The full horror of what was happening must have dawned on him very quickly. Lifris of Llancarfan, in his *Life* of St Cadog, referred to Caradog as 'Pendiuin': he was the chief or keeper of the fort of St David at Doune, as well as being Cadog's friend and probably his foster-brother. The legend of Brân the Blessed – treacherously ambushed by an Irish chieftain – tells of how Caradog and his fellow defenders of Britain were assailed by a traitor who concealed himself with a Veil of Illusion, so that his sword seemed to strike at them out of a dark mist (a play on words: 'darkness' and 'fog' can both be expressed in Welsh as *caddug*). Caradog's life was spared because the rebel was his kinsman, but he was left a broken man.

Arthur fought his way across the plain of Camno to the ridge of Arthurbank – the 'Hill of Battle', by the side of a river – but his sword was damaged and his strength was spent. He sank to his knees at the spot where the Arthurstone stood. He might have been accustomed to fighting naked, in the Celtic manner. Now he covered himself with his shield.

The sound of raised voices caught his attention. He staggered to his feet as a young warrior approached, the barbed spear primed and poised between his toes.

The loin-spear found its mark, and the chief's pale thigh ran with blood.

Cai the Tall was last seen heading off in pursuit of a cat-like creature.

This we know from the final lines of the poem *Pa Gwr* or '*What Man is the Porter?*' The poem starts with Arthur and Cai hailing the gatekeeper to the Otherworldly hall of heroes. It is a death-song, in which Arthur recounts the brave deeds and triumphs that he and his warriors achieved in their lifetimes.

Cai, we discover, confronted a dangerous cat:

> His wonderful shield went
> Against *cath palug*.
> When darkness hid him,
> Who pierced *cath palug*?
> Nine score angry
> And quick ones were its meat.
> Nine score princes …

And there the poem ends, mid-sentence.

Fortunately, the *Triads of the Island of Britain* have something to tell us about *cath palug*. The story takes us back to North Wales at about the time that Arthur completed his education and underwent the first of his cauldron initiations. The chief priestess who gave Menw his wolf-cub and presented Arthur with a young eagle at his graduation also brought forth a kitten. It was thrown into the sea – cast adrift in a coracle – but it swam ashore and was raised by the sons of Palug.

The cat grew up to become one of the three 'Great Oppressions of the Island of Britain'. It slew 180 of Arthur's warriors before Cai started out with what remained of Arthur's war-band to destroy it. Arthur and his men had been wrong-footed. They had assumed that the cat was *ballog* – 'speckled', as Druids were – but they were mistaken. It was, in fact, *balog* – a 'priest'.

The memory of the dangerous cat-priest lingered in parts of Scotland. Many hundreds of years later children in Galloway played a game which involved passing a burning stick from hand to hand and chanting 'About wi' that! About wi' that! Keep alive the priest-cat!' Sooner or later the stick would get too hot to be handled and the child who put out the flame was given a forfeit. The original 'priest-cat' was *cath palug*, the 'speckled' friend who turned against Arthur and his men.

He was the priest known as Catán or Cathan. (The Clan Chattan, whose name derives from Catán, still think of themselves as the Clan of the Cats.) The word for a 'cat' in Gaelic is *cat* – in Welsh, it is *cath*; both are strikingly similar to the words for a 'battle' (Gaelic *cath*, Welsh *cad*), which was the real origin of the cat-priest's name. He was, of course, St Cadog – sometimes 'Cattwg' – the Battle-Prince. They had thought he was speckled which, as Collen, he probably was. But he was also a priest, and he betrayed Arthur.

We can only guess at what motivated Cadog to double-cross his friend. Arthur's wars had cost him dearly: he had lost his nephew, Blane, in 590 and probably a son, Fergus or 'Eliwlod son of Madog', ten years earlier. He could have been jealous: maybe it was Arthur's decision to place Caradog 'Pendiuin' in charge of The Fort, rather than Cadog himself, that proved to be the final straw. The Gwenhwyfar connection is also intriguing: perhaps Cadog felt Arthur had failed his foster-daughter. But, all in all, it seems likely that Cadog had been talked into doing what he did with the promise of a glorious red martyrdom. He would become St Maedóc, 'Scotland's diadem'.

Cadog unleashed his pilgrim army against Arthur. They slaughtered dozens of Arthur's men. But Cadog had remained at *cella Diuni* while his warrior-monks were doing their worst, and there he received a message.

Adomnán of Iona stated that the message had come from St Columba, who was keeping abreast of things. Columba knew that Cadog's death was imminent. According to Adomnán, St Columba urged the prior to return quickly to Iona.

Lifris of Llancarfan told a slightly different story. In his *Vita Cadoci*, he would claim that St Cadog had been translated to 'the Beneventan monastery', where the saint assumed the guise of *Sophias* ('Wisdom'). It was there that St Cadog was advised of his approaching fate:

> … For tomorrow a certain cruel king will ravage this monastery, and, whilst thou will be celebrating the divine mysteries of the mass, a certain soldier, leaving his confederates, will enter the monastery, and piercing thee with the point of a spear will cruelly slay thee over the altar.

The very next day St Cadog had begun to sing mass when 'the aforesaid tyrant, having collected his army, wasted the suburbs contiguous to the town, and some of the troops came into the monastery to plunder.' One of the horsemen drove his spear into St Cadog. A church was raised over Cadog's remains 'which no Briton is permitted to enter'.

Why should no Briton have been permitted to enter the church of Cadog, or Docus the Briton, unless it was because no Briton could be trusted not to defile the shrine of the man who had stabbed Arthur in the back?

The 'Beneventan monastery' to which Cadog was translated, and in which he was killed, is alleged to have been the Italian commune of Benevento. Understandably, the Church took great pains to distance the culprits from their deeds, and so Cadog was miraculously spirited away from his homeland and smoothly transformed into somebody else. But the monastery where St Cadog died was not really so far away. It stood near the town or market-place (*venta*) of the 'tapering land' (from Old Irish *benn* – a 'horn'). This was the town which had been identified by a Roman geographer of the second century AD as *Bannatia*. It was the Roman fort built on the horn of land where the Ardoch Burn joins the River Teith – the town we now call Doune. Quite possibly, it was also the township where St Patrick was born: *Benna Venta Berniae*. In Aneirin's *Y Gododdin*, it was 'Madog's tent', and by the time the remnants of Arthur's noble war-band got there barely one in a hundred of them was left alive.

Cai the Tall hacked his way through to the chapel where Cadog was praying and speared the treacherous cat-priest in front of the altar. Then Cai was in turn killed by three of Owain's Raven warriors.

The monastery had been dedicated to Cadog's spiritual brother, St David. After Cadog was martyred a church was erected in his honour – the chapel of My Aedóc at Kilmadock – but no Briton was allowed inside it.

Arthur was still breathing. Ahead of him lay a journey of such torment and anguish that it was remembered for centuries. An old Gaelic curse puts it succinctly: '*Siubhal Artair ort!*' (pronounced 'shoo-ul art-air orrt'); 'The journey of Arthur upon thee!' The word *siubhal* implies a 'crossing', both in the sense of travel and dying.

His wound was hideous. Muirgein perhaps took a long look at her half-brother's mutilated body and finally decided that the barbs could be cut away from his flesh and his life saved, but such an operation could not be carried out in the field. Arthur would need the very best of care, and for that he had to be transported to the Isle of Iona – a long and painful journey.

A stretcher was improvised to carry his pallid body down to the River Isla. He was gently laid down in a lightweight boat. As the daylight faded, the boat caught the current and the wounded emperor was swept along the curling river to its junction with the Tay.

Drifting in and out of consciousness, Arthur found moments of relief from his agony as the boat turned north and was paddled upriver. The warm July night closed around the wounded king as the little boat floated, mile after mile, through the shadows of Strath Tay. Heading westwards, the boat passed the Point of Lyon and slipped through the gorge of Taymouth. Perhaps a speedier craft was waiting at Kenmore, ready to ferry Arthur from one end of Loch Tay to the other.

The party encountered a problem at the western end of the loch – how to carry Arthur over the whitewater course of the Falls of Dochart. It is possible that the group rested at *Tir Artair* – Arthur's Land – on the north shore of Loch Tay until a solution had been found. The Fingal Stone which stands at Killin points to the presence of a hero whose dreadful journey was about to take him through the 'Valley of Anguish', Glen Dochart, to Loch Iubhair, where a local legend holds that a great Irish warrior died while trying to jump from one island to another.

Most of the distance to Loch Fyne could have been covered by water. In the meantime, messengers raced ahead to summon Arthur's ship from its mooring in the bay of Strachur, ready to receive the body of the prince.

It is said that a ghost-ship haunts Loch Fyne. The ancient galley is associated with Arthur's descendants, the Campbells, whose ancestral seat is at Inverary, across the placid water from Strachur. The phantom vessel appears on Loch Fyne whenever the death of a senior clansman is nigh and then strikes a direct course to the west. Three crewmen are said to be visible on its deck. The last reported sighting was in 1913.

According to Geoffrey of Monmouth, three men crewed the ship which carried Arthur to the Island of Apples: they were Myrddin, Taliesin and Manannán, whose home was on the apple-bearing isle.

Unconstrained by material laws, the ghostly galley of Loch Fyne has been seen to travel overland towards the sunset. The route taken by Arthur and his shipmates was longer. His galley had to sail south into the Kilbrannan Sound and round the Mull of Kintyre before it could set a course for the sacred isle. Those extra sea-miles were costly.

At last, they reached the Atlantic and sailed up past the islands of Islay and Colonsay, then across the open sea to the Isle of Mull, beyond which lay Iona. But the light in Arthur's eyes was dimming. The splinters remained inside him, and the venom burned.

He knew that he was dead but he still had one last trick up his sleeve. Timing, though, was everything.

St Columba had told him that he would die neither in battle nor at sea. An excrutiating journey of several days had brought him from the battlefield to the coast of Mull, but he could go no further. His ship changed course and made for the sheltered harbour of Carsaig. Arthur and his attendants were deposited on the stony beach. The ship turned about and sailed away.

Arthur was carried up a steep valley into the hinterland of Mull. The party trudged past *Cnoc Bhràgad*, the 'Hill of the Neck' (or 'Pledge'), and into the wooded hills of Brolass.

A long peninsula probes westwards out to sea from the main body of the Isle of Mull. The Isle of Iona lies just off its tip. The Brolass hills stand at the opposite end of this tongue of land, known as the Ross of Mull, and marked the eastern extent of Gaelic territory: the nearby settlement of Pennyghael ('Head of the Gael') stood on the border between the realm of the Scots and that of the Picts, who occupied the rest of the island of Mull.

High up in the hills between Carsaig and Pennyghael runs a brook called *Allt Mhic-artair* – the 'Stream of the Sons of Arthur'. It trickles down through the trees, past the Brook of the Friend (or the 'Elegy') and the Glen of the Sergeant's Pasture, to enter the sea at the Shore of the Bee. Where the stream rises on the side of the Craggy Mountain stands a 'Spirit-hill of the Stream of the Sons of Arthur' – *Sithean Allt Mhic-artair*. It was here, or very near this mound, that Arthur gazed for the last time towards the west.

A single swordstroke sliced his head from his shoulders.

His body was buried above Pennyghael, on the boundary of his people's territory. It is unclear what Brolass means, but it could be derived from *bruig glass* – a green or grey 'grave-mound'; a 'spirit-hill' or *sithean*. Of the Sons of Arthur who laid his body to rest in its mound above the stream, some were no doubt sacrificed to form his honour-guard. They died to protect the body of their lord, both in this world and the next.

The remainder of the solemn party waited in the hills until they saw the ship returning to fetch them. They made their way down to the shore of Loch Scridain and the small inlet called *Port na Birlinne*, the 'Bay of the Galley', where they boarded the ship once more.

As the evening passed into a moonless night, the barge moved silently towards the open sea along Loch Scridain. Up until the end of the eighteenth century, the sea-loch was more commonly known as Loch Leffan or Leven. Arthur's life had begun on a Lake of the Lion. Now his journey was ending on another Lake of the Lion as his head was carried to its final destination on the Isle of the Blessed.

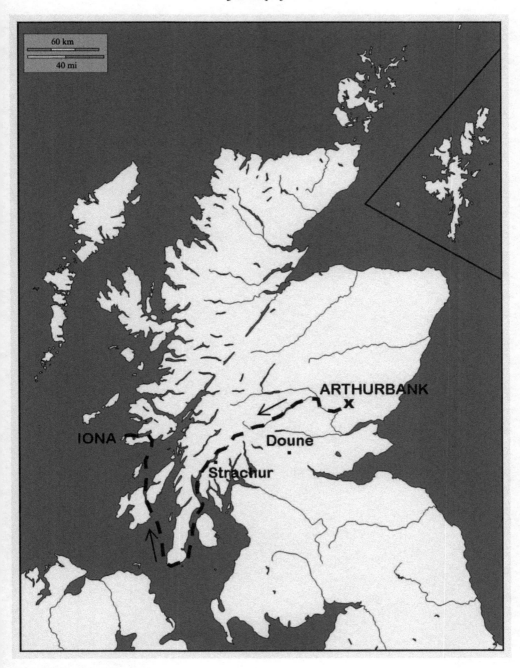

Map 7 Arthur's Final Journey

19

HOUSE OF THE SPIRITS

SAINT COLUMBA had not been the only one to foresee the final battle. Myrddin, too, had seen it coming – as he wrote in his poem *Afallen*:

> I predict a battle in Pictland
> To deal with the fierce twisted simpleton.
> Seven ships will cross a wide lake,
> And seven hundred cross the sea to conquer.
> By the means of the old-dog, for the many who come,
> Except seven, death afterwards brings sadness.

The theme of the seven survivors recurs in Arthurian literature. The head of Brân the Blessed was accompanied to its grave by the seven survivors of Brân's battle against the Irish king and his hidden warriors. These seven were the men whom Brân had commanded to cut off his head and bury it in the White Hill.

The Celts thought of the head as the seat of the soul. Arthur's head was buried at six in the morning of Friday 23 July 594.

There was a new Moon that night. Under cover of darkness, the ship carrying the precious head ghosted its way along Loch Scridain. Putting in at *Port Gart an Fhithich* – the 'Gloomy Bay of the Raven' – a small party disembarked and stole across the moorland of south-west Mull. Their aim was to reach the silent waters of Loch Poit na h-Í, a natural place for votive deposits. But St Columba had almost certainly stationed one of his relatives, St Ernán, at the head of that lake, so the party crept to a smaller pool, just east of the Lake of the Pot of Iona. This was the pool known as *Loch an Dreaghain*, the 'Lake of the Dragon' (or 'Champion'), and into its dark waters was cast Arthur's crooked sword.

The first light of dawn was showing as the men crossed the rough ground to the shore where, at the 'Point of the Son of Áed' (*Rubha Mhic-aoidh*), they were picked up once more by the ship. The boat slipped round the north end of the Island of the Women and across the Sound of Iona, through the Strait of Misery, and on to the western side of the blessed isle.

By then, they had been spotted. St Columba was in the habit of wading into the sea to say his morning prayers. When the ship appeared, he acted swiftly. According to Adomnán of Iona, the saint called his monks together and addressed them, 'making his point with great emphasis': 'Today I shall go to the machair on the west coast of our island, and I wish to go alone. No one therefore is to follow me.'

The term *machair* is used in western Scotland, as *links* is in the east, to describe the fertile, sandy land above a beach. Columba's monks grew much of their food on the machair. By announcing that no one was to follow him, St Columba was withholding his monks from their daily labour in the fields.

Fortunately – in so far as it allowed Adomnán to tell the tale – one of the monks disobeyed his ageing master. Taking a different route, the wayward monk tracked St Columba to the west coast and mounted a little low hill. From this vantage point he watched as Columba climbed a green knoll and stood praying with his arms outstretched.

'Strange to tell – look!' gasped Adomnán, 100 years later. 'For holy angels, the citizens of the heavenly kingdom, were flying down with incredible speed, dressed in white robes, and gathering around the holy man as he prayed.'

We have encountered these angels before – they were the same 'angels' who, only a year or so earlier, had been unable to cross the 1-mile-wide sea to reach Iona. As ever, they behaved rather strangely: 'After they had conversed a little with St Columba, the heavenly crowd – as though they could feel that they were being spied on – quickly returned to the heights of heaven.'

Columba flew back to his monastery in a rage, demanding to know which of his monks had followed him. The monk begged for forgiveness. St Columba took him to one side and, 'laying stern threats on him', made him promise never to divulge 'the least part of this secret concerning his angelic vision so long as the saint should live.'

Adomnán added a curious coda to his account of Columba's 'conference' with the angels on the mound: 'One should take note of this story, and think carefully about the nature and extent of the sweet visits by angels that no one could know about but which were, without doubt, very frequent …' The 'angels', Adomnán averred, often came to St Columba 'as he stayed awake on winter nights' or 'prayed in isolated places while others rested'. No reason is given for the saint's determination to keep these visits secret.

After Columba's death three years later, the disobedient monk opened up about what he had seen. And so, wrote Adomnán, the 'knoll where St Columba conferred with the angels confirms by its very name what took place there, for it is called Cnoc nan Aingel, that is, the angels' knoll.'

On some maps of Iona the hill is still known as the Hill of the Angels, or *Cnoc nan Aingeal*. Only *aingeal* does not mean 'angels'. It can signify a single angel, but it is better translated as 'light' or 'fire'. An eighteenth-century manuscript explained it properly: 'One of the highest and most centrical [mounds] in Icolmkill is called Cnoc-nan-Ainneal, i.e. the Hill of the Fires.'

The mound stands at the end of the road, looking out across the machair to the ocean beyond. Travelling westwards, in the general direction of the sunset, there is no more land until one reaches the east coast of America.

There is only one metalled road on Iona. It runs south from the main village and the ferry terminal, hugging the eastern shore as far as Sligineach, where it turns sharply to cross the spine of the island. Passing the central Hill of Odhrán on the right and the Hill of the Plain (*Cnoc na Mona*) on the left, the road comes to a sudden end at a gate which opens onto the machair. The last farmstead on the left is called Sithean. The large green mound rises above the driveway to the croft, a few metres before the road's end. The alternative name for the knoll, *an Sìthean Mór* (pronounced 'un shian mor'), means the 'Big Spirit-Mound'.

The tradition of the isle is that this 'small green hill' once hosted a 'Druidic temple of twelve stones, each with a human body buried beneath it'. The Welsh traveller Thomas Pennant reported in 1772 that the mound was surmounted by a stone circle. Previously, in 1760, the island had been visited by Richard Pococke, Protestant Bishop of Ossary and Meath in Ireland, who told Pennant that on the eve of St Michael's Day (29 September) the islanders brought their horses to this hill, on which stood a cairn and a circle of stones, and led their horses thrice round the mound in a sunwise direction.

The dragon-slaying Archangel Michael was the Christian equivalent of Beli Mawr, in whose honour the fires of Beltane were lit on the threshold of summer. It was for this reason that the mound was known as the Hill of the Fires. As Taliesin the poet proclaimed, it was also the 'Victorious Beli' who defended the 'Honey Isle', and so we can assume that the great Spirit-Mound of Sithean was held sacred to the god of the Sun.

All traces of the cairn and stone circle are long gone: they were removed, along with many other sacred stones on the island, during the eighteenth century. But there are still those who claim to have heard 'sweet music' emanating from the Hill of the Fires. This should come as no surprise for, as Lady Gregory noted in her *Gods and Fighting Men*, 'a house of peace is the hill of the Sìdhe of Emhain' – the hill of the ancestral spirits on the Isle of Iona. The thirteenth-century poem written in praise of Raghnall, King of the Isles, also observed that the '*sídh* of Emhain' is a 'fruitful place':

Fine the region of the man of the mound
Who has drunk the fruit of the honey:

To go to the fair *sídh* of the mound
Is to go to the smooth fort of mead.

It was to the 'smooth fort of mead' that Arthur's burial party was heading.

Piloted by Fiachna mac Báetáin – or Manannán mac Lir, as he is more romanti-
cally known – the funeral barge sailed down the west side of the island. It passed
the Fort of Manannán and the Port of the Dead Man. The ragged shoreline thrust
out into the sea, the Island of the Harp shielding the pristine, crescent beach of
Port Bàn, immediately to the south of which stands the Rock of the Son of Gúaire.

The boat grounded on the soft white sand. The funeral party continued on
foot. They crossed the greensward of the machair above the Bay at the Back of
the Ocean, *Camus Cùl an t-Saimh* (the Gaelic name for the long beach actually
suggests a 'Bay at the Back of the Champion', since the *Carmina Gadelica* indicates
that *samh* could refer to a 'god' or a 'giant'). Dressed in their ceremonial white
robes, the party approached the Big Spirit-Mound.

St Columba was also racing to get there, as fast as a 72-year-old could.

Taliesin left us an account of the burial. It takes the form of his poem *Preiddeu
Annwn* – the '*Treasures of Annwn*':

> I praise the ruler, bright-chief, lord of the land,
> Whose rule is extended beyond the world's shore.
> Gúaire's prison was prepared in Caer Sidi,
> After the manner of Pwyll and Pryderi;
> No one before him went into it.
> By the heavy grey chain the faithful servant was fettered,
> And before the treasures of Annwn roughly it held him,
> And with rapture he continues his poetic song.
> Thrice the fullness of Prydwen went into it:
> Except for seven, no one rose from Caer Sidi.

Caer Sidi was the 'Fort of the Sìdhe', the sacred burial mound and house of the
spirits in which the cauldron's warrior-poets had undergone their ritual imprisonment, and where Arthur was now laid to rest. Others had been there before
him, including such initiates as Pwyll (Urien) and Pryderi (Owain) – but Arthur's
head was the first of the burials that day.

The Chief Bard continued:

> I will not cease my earnest, honourable song
> In Caer Pedryfan, the quarter of the all-powerful,
> In praise of the cauldron of lofty utterance.

By the breath of nine maidens it is warmed:
It is the cauldron of the Lord of Annwn, whosoever desires it;
A band about the rim, around the edge,
It will not boil the meat of a coward, it will not avail him.
The sword of lightning slaughter departed from Rhydderch
And was deposited in the hand of the man of the Leven,
And before the door of the entrance to hell lamps burned.
And when we went with Arthur, famous toil,
Except seven, no one rose from the Mound of Mead-Drunkenness.

Arthur was not buried alone. The 'man of the Leven' – probably Lleënog of Lennox: 'Lancelot of the Lake' – was interred with him, privileged to be clutching the sword which Arthur could no longer hold, and the 'faithful servant' Cai was almost certainly buried alongside his foster-brother.

So many had set out with Arthur on his last mission – 700, according to Myrddin; three times the capacity of Arthur's ship, said Taliesin – but so few had made it home alive.

I will not cease my earnest song of the lord-protector
In Caer Pedryfan, island of the staunch door.
Mid-day and jet-black darkness mingled,
Bright wine the liquor for the retinue.
Thrice the fullness of Prydwen we went on the sea:
Except for seven, no one rose from the Mound of the Overlord.

Adomnán, in his careful account of the proceedings, intimated that St Columba went alone to the mound, observed only by an inquisitive monk. Taliesin suggests otherwise. There were several monks of Iona watching, and their 'bishop' inter-vened in the ceremony:

Not lower am I than the book-learned leader
Who saw nothing of Arthur's valour beyond the Glass Fort.
Thrice twenty missionaries watched on the wall;
A miserable tryst, the speech of their overseer.
Thrice the fullness of Prydwen went with Arthur:
Except for seven, no one rose from the Mound of Riches.

St Columba was horrified. He had been poised to demonstrate his command of the cosmos. The burial of Arthur's head had stolen his thunder. He marched at the head of his warrior-monks to the Hill of the Fires to confront the few who had survived his treachery.

Taliesin remembered the moment with bitterness. Three years later, when Columba died, the Chief Bard mockingly referred to the Dove of the Church as *Ercwlf*, the Welsh name for Hercules. Wielding his blackthorn staff like the club of the famous Greek hero, St Columba had (like Hercules) stolen the precious golden apples from the nymphs of the sacred garden.

> Overturned was the Moon,
> Like night in the day,
> When came the famously free
> Ercwlf, chief of baptism.
> Ercwlf said
> Death was not grievous.
> Our shield against the Picts –
> By him it was broken.
> Ercwlf the conjurer
> Made the Moon come out.
> Four columns of equal length,
> Red-stained the gold among them;
> Ercwlf's columns
> Would not venture a threat,
> A threat they would not dare …

As the Chief Bard noted elsewhere, in his *Treasures of Annwn*, daylight and darkness mingled at the moment of Arthur's burial. The Moon was 'overturned', like 'night in the day'.

The anonymous *True Story of the Death of Arthur* would claim that Arthur's body was left outside a chapel dedicated to the Virgin while his funeral service took place, the entrance to the chapel being too narrow to admit his body. Suddenly a storm blew up, a mist descended – and when the air cleared Arthur's body was nowhere to be seen.

Among the Treasures of Britain there was supposedly a cloak which rendered Arthur invisible at the 'Cairn of the Sacred Trees'. There was also a ring and stone which could make the wearer invisible. This was the Ring and Stone of Eluned, the goddess of the Moon. When the ring was turned, the Moon stone obscured the Sun, leaving a bright corona but cloaking the land in darkness.

The total eclipse took place at a minute or two before six on the morning of 23 July in the year 594. The *Annals of Ulster* recorded it as *Defecto solis.i.mane tenebrosum* – 'Eclipse of the sun, i.e. a dark morning' (as an expert has remarked, this was 'the first genuine eclipse record from the British Isles'). The eclipse so unnerved Columba's monks that they refused to take up arms against Arthur's burial party.

Naturally, St Columba insisted that it was he who had made 'the Moon come out' and nothing whatever to do with pagan magic or the cosmic tragedy of Arthur's death. But the saint was flustered, and with good reason: Arthur had succeeded in replicating the circumstances surrounding Christ's crucifixion, which had similarly taken place on a Friday, and during a solar eclipse; 'And it was about the sixth hour, and there was a darkness all over the earth until the ninth hour. And the sun was darkened, and the veil of the temple was rent in the midst.'

Christ had been nailed to the World-Tree at Golgotha. Arthur's head was buried at Annwn, where the World-Tree stood at the Navel of the sea. The burial of Arthur's head at the very moment of the total eclipse, when 'Mid-day and jet-black darkness mingled', must have shaken St Columba to the core. He had conquered the blessed isle for Christ; now his arch-enemy had upstaged him. A greater magic than Columba's was at work. No wonder the saint marched up to the burial mound with his monks arrayed in four columns, hoping to intimidate the burial party.

Taliesin had dubbed Columba *Ercwlf* – 'Hercules' – in his poem entitled *Mawrnat Erof*, the 'Death-Song of Erof', but it is unclear what 'Erof' signified. Perhaps the Chief Bard was playing on the word *eurof*, a 'goldsmith'. The warrior-monks who marched behind their overseer to the Hill of the Fires had 'red-stained gold' among them, which might have been Taliesin's way of hinting that Columba had received a payment of gold from the Northumbrian Angles in return for betraying Arthur. There were, after all, 'Englishmen' living amongst the monastic community on Iona: one of them was Columba's baker.

Another possibility is that *erof* was Taliesin's attempt at the Irish word *erbhe* or *airbhe*, a 'mist'. St Columba had countered a Druid-mist at the Battle of the Books in Ireland. The eclipse that occurred when Arthur was buried also had the cloak-like properties of a sea-mist.

Such was Taliesin's contempt for the Dove of the Church that he marked Columba's death with another poem, intimating that 'Erof' went so far as to enter the burial mound when Arthur's head was being laid to rest:

Erof the cruel came.
Huge gladness,
Huge sadness,
Was the doing of Erof the cruel.
He betrayed Jesus,
Though he believed.
The earth quaking,
And the Moon imprisoned [or 'ashamed'],
And a shaking of the world,
And baptism shivering.

A huge step,
Erof the cruel he made,
Going in scolding
In the midst of the sad company,
Even to the bottom of hell.

The possibility that St Columba ventured into Arthur's burial mound is also entertained in an old Irish poem. The *Conversation of Columba and the Youth at the Cairn of the Plain of Iona* comes with the caveat that, according to some, the youth was Arthur's nephew, Mongán son of Fiachna.

Columba said, 'Where have you come from, youth?' The youth replied:

I have come from strange lands, and from familiar lands, to learn from you the spot on which true knowledge was born, and the spot on which ignorance will be buried.

St Columba questioned the youth further but did not like what he was hearing. Finally, he cried out 'Enough!' and, with a glance at his followers, he went aside with the youth to ask him 'about the heavenly and earthly mysteries'. The monks watched from a distance as Columba and the youth conferred in private.

As soon as their conversation was over, the youth vanished. The monks plied the saint with questions about his talk with the youth, but Columba was tight-lipped. It was better, he said, 'for mortals not to be informed of it.'

It is a common mistranslation. Many scholars have argued that the *Stanzas of the Graves* refer to Arthur's grave as the 'world's wonder', as if to say that it could never be located. The word used in the poem is *anoeth* – something 'strange' and 'wonderful'. There can be little doubt that Arthur's chambered tomb was a place of wonders. It was one of the most sacred places in Britain: *Caer Oeth and Anoeth*, the 'Strange and Wonderful Fort', in which Arthur had previously been imprisoned as part of the cauldron ritual.

The poem *Englynion y Beddau* ('*Stanzas of the Graves*') also reveals that there was a 'family of Oeth and Anoeth' – 'naked was their vassal and their servant; their burial-place can be sought in Gwanas'. There were other 'long graves' in 'the upper part of Gwanas', although these seem to have been neglected: the poem remarks of those who were buried there that no one knows 'what is their plaint, what is their message'.

It may be that Gwanas drew on *guaineas*, a Gaelic word meaning 'liveliness', for the Isle of the Blessed was the youthful Land of the Ever-Living. But *gwanas* was also an old Welsh word, the meanings of which included 'peg', 'clasp', 'stay' and 'abode'. As such, it summarised the exact nature of the World-Navel, which was both a 'peg' holding the three worlds together and the 'abode' of the blessed dead.

Those who were buried in the 'upper part' of the Navel of the sea were probably interred at *Cladh na Meirghe*, the Burial-place of the Banner, on the high ground above the main village on Iona.

Traditionally, *Cladh na Meirghe* was where unbaptised children were buried. It was deemed to be halfway between the the machair and the church of St Columba. The monks would pass the Burial-place of the Banner as they made their way back to the monastery from the cornfields on the west side of the island.

Towards the end of Columba's life, the monks began to experience a 'wonderful and strange' sensation as they passed *Cladh na Meirghe*. They became aware of a 'wonderful fragrance' and a pleasant sense of heat, and a 'strange, incomprehensible joy' filled their hearts. Columba, it was said, had sent his spirit out to meet them, but their elation might have had something to do with the fact that they were passing the graves of Arthur's men, those warriors of the cauldron whom the monks had considered 'disorderly'.

The Burial-place of the Banner would have been a mass grave. The more privileged were laid to rest in the 'Big Spirit-Mound' (*an Sìthean Mór*) or, as Columba and his monks preferred to call it, the Hill of the Angels.

Taliesin, in his *Treasures of Annwn*, gave it a raft of descriptive titles: it was the 'Fort of the Spirits' (*Caer Sidi*), the 'Fort of the Quarter' (*Caer Pedryfan*), the 'Fort of Mead-Drunkenness' (*Caer Medwyd*), the 'Fort of the Overlord' or 'Excess' (*Caer Rigor*), the 'Fort of Riches' (*Caer Golud*), the 'Fort of Manannán' (*Caer Vandwy*), the 'Fort of Singing' or 'Honour', or 'Fort of the Steep Sides' (*Caer Ochren*), in addition to which he called it *Caer Wydyr* – the 'Glass Fort' or 'Fort of Science'. It was the 'Glass House' into which Myrddin took the Thirteen Treasures of the Island of Britain, 'and they remain there for ever'.

The mound was also known as the 'Bright Fort', *Caer Gloyw*, although this led to confusion, *Caerloyw* being the Welsh name for the city of Gloucester. In the Welsh legends it appears as the Mound of Sacrifice, from which Pwyll (Urien) got his first glimpse of the lovely Rhiannon, and the shining fortress in which Pryderi and his mother Rhiannon (Owain and Muirgein) became stuck fast to a golden bowl.

How long the chambered burial mound had been in use is anybody's guess. Experiments conducted in other burial chambers in Scotland by an archaeologist and an acoustician revealed that chanting and drumming inside these mounds could produce strange effects, ranging from giddiness (*guaineas* in Gaelic) to altered states of consciousness and feelings of ecstasy. They were more than just burial mounds – they were the cathedrals of their day. But the Big Spirit-Mound on Iona had an additional role as the sacred site of the Beltane fires. It is conceivable that, over the years, the fires which had burned at the grassy knoll had caused the stone surfaces inside the tomb to melt and fuse. This would have given the interior walls a glassy appearance. In the light of oil-lamps or flaming torches, the polished walls would have shone like gold.

Arthur's head was left inside the chambered cairn 'under the protection of the sea'. It was the sacred mound in which the Golden Age god of abundance slept on a rock which looked like gold. The noble head of Arthur rested on a mantle of gold brocade and the treasures of Britain – the flashing sword and the whetstone, the cauldron and the drinking-horn, the chariot and halter, the carving knife, the crock and dish, the hamper, the Red-Coat and the marvellous *gwyddbwyll* game – were arranged around it.

Many theories have been advanced to account for the name of Iona. In 1792, the Reverend Dugal Campbell translated the name as *I-thonn*, the 'Island of Waves'. In about 1850 it was argued that Iona derives from *Ì shona*, the 'Fortunate Isle' or 'Isle of the Blessed'. Popular tradition holds that it was once the 'Druids' Isle' (*Innis Dhruidhnean*) though 'Island of Starlings' (*druidean*) might be more apposite, pointing towards a potential *Ì Eòin* or 'Island of Birds'.

Another eighteenth-century theory held that Iona – *Ì Eòin* – was the 'Isle of St John'. It may be no coincidence that Arthur's severed head, like that of John the Baptist, ended up on a bloody platter.

But of all the suggestions put forward, one in particular recalls the fact that Arthur the Bear-Guardian was buried in a mound on the island. In his remarkable guide to *The Scottish Islands*, the architect and seafarer Hamish Haswell-Smith proposed that the name of Iona derived from the Norse *Hiöe*. He translated this as the 'Island of the Den of the Brown Bear'.

Adomnán of Iona told another intriguing tale about the Big Spirit-Mound. It 'happened about seventeen years ago', he said, which would date the events to about the year 680.

A severe drought had baked the fields dry. The monastery's food supply was threatened. After some debate, the monks came up with a plan. They paraded through the pastures, carrying St Columba's tunic and some of the books which he had copied with his own hand. The monks shook the tunic three times over the furrows and then stood on top of the Hill of the Angels, 'where from time to time the citizens of heaven used to be seen coming down to converse with the saint', and there the monks read aloud from Columba's books.

It was an unashamed attempt to invoke an older magic. And it worked. That same day ('wonderful to tell', wrote Adomnán), the sky that had been cloudless throughout March and April was suddenly filled with clouds rising up from the sea, and 'heavy rain fell night and day'.

The monks seem to have remembered that, when all else failed, mists could be raised and the weather manipulated from the sacred burial mound of *Sìthean Mór*.

But Arthur's head was not allowed to rest in its mound. Two legends point to the likelihood that his head was moved.

First, there was the Head of Brân the Blessed. It was carried by the seven survivors – the Assembly of the Noble Head – from Arthurstone to a 'spacious hall' at a 'fair and regal spot overlooking the sea', which was also the 'hall on the Island of Afallach' in which Arthur was buried. Two doors to the hall were open, but the third was closed. After eighty years of feasting and entertainment the third door was opened and the assembly set out with Brân's head to bury it in the White Mount.

The burial of Brân's head was one of the Fortunate Concealments. But Arthur dug up the head of Brân the Blessed 'because it did not seem right to him that this Island should be defended by the strength of anyone, but by his own'. This would have been quite a feat, for Arthur was himself the blessed 'Raven' Brân – how could he possibly have disinterred his own head?

There is also the strange legend of Odhrán, the 'brother' of St Columba who was prematurely buried on Iona and then dug up again. No two accounts agree as to why St Columba felt the need to bury Odhrán – to avert a famine; to secure the foundations of his church; or simply because it would be a good thing to consecrate the ground – but all are in accord over what happened when Columba returned to the grave. Odhrán 'opened his swimming eyes' and delivered a report on life in the hereafter which offended the saint's beliefs. 'Earth, earth on Oran's eye, lest he blab anymore!'

The legend compares with the poem of St Columba's conversation with the vanishing youth at the cairn: again, the saint was told things 'about the heavenly and earthly mysteries' which appalled him.

We now know that it was St Columba who plotted against Arthur, who conspired with one of the friends in Arthur's entourage and arranged his death so that the Isle of Iona would belong exclusively to the Church. Thanks to Taliesin's eyewitness statements, we also know that Columba took the 'huge step' of forcing his way inside Arthur's burial mound, 'even to the bottom of hell'. We know, too, that the survivors of Arthur's doomed mission were 'entertained' by his talking head, and can take it that any posthumous utterances spoken by Arthur would have upset his Christian adversary.

St Columba reputedly told his victim, 'I shall give you the kingdom of God, and I shall give you this, that no one who makes a request at my tomb or resting-place will be granted it unless he first seek it of you.'

And therein lies the clue.

The monks were building a stone wall around the fertile fields of the machair. St Columba had only days left to live. He was taken across the Plain of Iona in a cart and helped up onto the Big Spirit-Mound so that he could speak to his followers. 'Today,' he told them, 'is the last time you will see my face here at the machair.'

Columba then turned to face the east and raised his hands.

'From this hour, from this instant, all poisons of snakes shall have no power to harm either men or cattle in the lands of this island for as long as the people who dwell here keep Christ's commandments.'

Adomnán confirmed, 100 years later, that 'even to the present day, the venom of vipers' three-forked tongues has been unable to harm man or beast.'

There are no venomous snakes native to the island. St Columba was really announcing that he had finally rid the blessed isle of those Druidic 'adders' with their 'three-forked tongues'.

Just a day or two later, the saint received a visit from another 'angel'. He saw it hovering inside his chapel during mass, and that midnight the Dove of the Church was found dying in front of the altar.

What had he done to convince himself and his monks that they would never again be bothered by 'serpents'?

Odhrán, it is assumed, was buried at the entrance to Columba's sacred precinct. One comes to the chapel of St Oran, where dozens of kings and lords of the isles were buried, before one reaches St Columba's abbey. But the road to the abbey starts much further back. Known in medieval times as the Street of the Dead – *Sràid nam Marbh* – it ran all the way from the shore near the modern jetty where the Iona ferry lands many a visitor to the island.

Royal corpses were brought to a bright, sandy bay on the east side of the isle and laid on a low mound above the dunes. The road running south from the village passes the island's war memorial and then cuts clean through this unobtrusive mound. It is said that the remains of kings and lords were paraded three times around the mound before they were carried along the Street of the Dead to the abbey complex.

The old road to Columba's church starts at this strange little mound, which is known as *An Ealadh*. Strictly speaking, it means 'The Tomb'. A Gaelic dictionary adds that the *ealadh* was specifically 'the place in Iona where the dead were placed on landing'.

But there is another meaning of *ealadh*, which is 'learning' or 'skill', especially in the sense of poetry or a 'song' (*ealaidh*). It is also the case that, in modern Gaelic, *òran* means 'song': it derives from the Middle Irish *ambrán*, and therefore links Odhrán with that prophetic songsmith, Brân. The alternative spelling – *amhran* – could be rendered into Welsh as 'Arawn', one of the names given to Arthur's father.

No king was buried on Iona without first being placed on The Tomb of *An Ealadh*, with its connotations of skilful song and knowledge. By placing Arthur's head at this spot, the aged saint made sure that it guarded the processional route to his monastery ('no one who makes a request at my tomb or resting-place will be granted it unless he first seek it of you'). More than that, it functioned as a 'Keep Out!' sign. The Celts were so superstitious about heads that few pagans would have dared to pass one without magical protection. What could possess more magic than the head of Arthur? Like the head of Brân the Blessed, which was held to have safeguarded Britain from 'Saxon oppression', the head of Arthur was deployed to prevent the bards and Druidic 'adders' from returning to the island of Columba's church.

The beautiful beach above which Arthur's head was reburied in The Tomb is known as Martyr's Bay. The name supposedly commemorates the massacre of sixty-eight monks by Viking marauders in 806. The Gaelic name for the bay – *Port nam Mairtir* – does, however, suggest another possibility. The bay might have been named after the presiding genius whose lifeless eyes gazed out over its silvery sands, hence *Port na M'Artair* – the 'Bay of My Arthur'.

For hundreds of years, lords and heroes were brought to the Isle of Iona and their bodies rested on the little low mound at the head of the bay. They were then conveyed to the royal burial ground of *Reilig Odhráin* 'because it was the most honourable and ancient place that was in Scotland in their days', as the Dean of the Isles, Donald Monro, wrote in 1549.

Their remains were ferried to the blessed isle by oarsmen rowing to the rhythm of the Iona Boat Song:

> *Iomair o, 'illean mhara,*
> *'Illean o horo eile*
> Heave-ho, isle of the sea ...

> Isle of the deep, in deep sleep dreaming,
> Sails to thee a king a-sleeping,
> With thy saints, into thy keeping.

> *Iomair o, 'illean mhara,*
> *'Illean o horo eile* ...

Figure 4 Arthur's Grave

20

THE LIGHTS GO OUT

THE STORY of Arthur is the story of the Old North and the efforts of the Britons to preserve their lands and freedom. That they failed to do so was down to treachery and betrayal. Within a few years of Arthur's death it was all over for the Men of the North.

In this chapter we shall take a brief look at what became of Arthur's circle – those who had survived the horror of his last battle.

The tale of *Culhwch and Olwen* telescopes Arthur's career into a series of superhuman challenges. After the king-turned-boar Twrch Trwyth has been chased into a river and his treasures seized (though the boar escapes), and before the Castrated Chief-Champion is beheaded, there is one final task to be accomplished. The heroes are required to fetch the blood of the Black witch, the daughter of the White witch, from the Head of the Valley of Grief 'on the confines of hell'. Arthur sets out once more 'towards the North' and comes to the witch's cave. Taliesin and Áedán are there to advise him. There is a vicious struggle. Arthur finally strikes at the witch with his dagger and cuts her in two. 'And Caw of North Britain took the blood of the witch and kept it.'

Following the battle on the banks of the River Isla, Gwenhwyfar was taken captive. Tradition states that she was held in the timber-laced Iron Age fortress on Barry Hill, overlooking Alyth and the field of battle, where her fate was decided.

The legends of St Kentigern claim that Myrddin laughed out loud when the queen of 'King Meldred' tried to deny her adulterous nature. There was no room for mercy. Willing accomplice or hapless victim, Gwenhwyfar had helped to destroy Arthur. So she was destroyed.

As like as not, she was taken down to the Burn of Quiech below the hill. This, it was suggested earlier (Chapter 3), was 'Bealach Gabráin', the pass in which Muirgein had been born nearly fifty years earlier. Appropriately, then, it was here that Gwenhwyfar's smaller sister struck a blow upon her.

An alternative account of what happened can be found in the Welsh legend of Gwenffrewi ('St Winefride'). The legend states that Caradog, a nobleman of North Wales, lusted after the lovely Gwenffrewi. She announced her intention of becoming a nun, and in his rage Caradog cut off her head. A healing spring burst from the ground where her head fell. The woman's head was reattached to its body by another saint and the sacred spring at Holywell in Flintshire was dedicated to St Winefride.

Undoubtedly, the well existed long before the legend was concocted. It formed part of the sub-kingdom of Tegeingl, which was ruled by Gwenhwyfar's father, Caradog Strong-Arm. Woefully misplaced, the legend of the woman beheaded by Caradog when she insisted on becoming a nun would appear to recall the punishment meted out to Arthur's queen.

A mile or two south of Alyth, and just east of the spot where Arthur was wounded, sits the village of Meigle. The old village school is now a museum housing more than thirty carved stones of Pictish design. Many of them came from the churchyard at Meigle. The most famous and impressive of the stones – *Meigle 2* – stands 2.5m tall and is known as the Vanora Stone.

Hector Boece told the story early in the sixteenth century: 'Guanora', Queen of Britain and wife of King Arthur, commenced an affair with the 'Pictish' King Mordred while Arthur was absent on a military campaign. Arthur caught wind of this and confronted Mordred at the Battle of Camlan. 'Guanora' or 'Vanora' ('White Wave') is the Scottish version of Gwenhwyfar, arrived at via the Latin *Wenebara*. Her burial mound is said to be in Meigle churchyard and according to Boece, 'every woman, except nuns, abhors to stamp on that sepulchre'.

The Vanora Stone once stood at the gateway to Meigle church. The church occupies the site of an earlier shrine established in about 606 by the monks of Iona. The rear of the stone depicts mounted warriors and mythical beasts while its central panel shows a figure in an ankle-length gown being savaged by wild animals. Some have interpreted this as an image of Daniel in the lions' den. Others insist that it represents the execution of Gwenhwyfar.

Putting all these traditions together, a picture emerges. Arthur's men had to collect the blood of Gwenhwyfar – the Black witch, whose mother was the White witch, Tegau Golden-Breast. She was hunted down at the Head of the Valley of Grief, where ghostly cries of alarm and distress could still be heard many years later, on the border of the hellish lands of the Picts, where stood the Hill of Alyth and the fortified 'Ridge of the King': Barry Hill.

According to the *Culhwch and Olwen* legend, she was cut in two by Arthur's knife and her blood collected by 'Caw of North Britain'. The *Triads* recall that it was Gwenhwyfar's sister who struck her a terrible blow, while the Gwenffrewi myth asserts that it was Caradog who beheaded her, a spring miraculously appearing at the spot where her head hit the ground.

The blood of the Black witch was needed so that the Castrated Chief-Champion could be shaved. Dreadful as it sounds, it would appear that Gwenhwyfar was bled to death by her father or her sister-in-law and her blood collected in the cauldron. Whether it was hoped that this might help save Arthur's life or there was some other magical intent, we may never know. But the platter on which Arthur's head rested in the grave was quite possibly soaked in the blood of his wife.

The deed was done beside the Water of Quiech (or *Quaich*, a two-handled drinking cup or bowl) at the site of the Dovecote Well. The bloodless body was then carried south along the Isla to Meigle, where it was dumped in the boggy meadow which gave the village its name.

Her body was cut in two. The same could be said of her reputation, which suffered further as the result of a papal decree. The village of Meigle was referred to in the legend of St Andrew as 'Migdele'. This forges a tenuous but irresistible link between Gwenhwyfar and another fallen woman, the Galilean Mary of Magdala (Hebrew *Migdal* – a 'tower'). It so happens that just three years before the death of Arthur, Pope Gregory the Great declared that the Magdalene had been an adulterous sinner and a prostitute. At *Mygghil* or *Migdele* in Perthshire, the Church found a British answer to Mary Magdalene and Gwenhwyfar was cast as the archetypal Scarlet Woman.

The monks of Columba's church raised a shrine to her at Meigle, perhaps in memory of the role she had played in her husband's downfall. Elsewhere, she was transmuted into that obscure paragon of chastity, St Winefride. The reality is that Gwenhwyfar was neither a whore nor a nun. Had it not been for the obsession of the early Church with categorising women as either colourless virgins or incorrigible harlots, she might have been remembered for what she was: a princess, a priestess, a queen and, for a while at least, the beloved wife of Arthur the Emperor.

Pedr of Dyfed and Drystan son of Cynon put a great distance between themselves and the tragic events in the North. They sailed for Cornwall, in the far south-west of Britain, presumably to carry the news of Prince Gereint's death at Cruden Bay to his father Erbin.

They landed near Padstow on the north coast of Cornwall. Padstow was once *Pedroc-stowe*, the 'holy place of Pedrog'. It stands on the bank of the River Camel, where Geoffrey of Monmouth imagined that Arthur's last battle was fought, and close to Tintagel Head, where Geoffrey presumed that Arthur had been conceived.

St Pedrog is named in a seventeenth-century Welsh manuscript as one of the seven survivors of Arthur's last battle, but he did not live for much longer. The latest date for his death, as given in *The Lives of the British Saints*, is 594 – the year of the battle itself.

Pedr or Pedrog received the interesting epithet 'Splintered-Spear', which suggests that Arthur's long-term companion took the barbed spear which had inflicted Arthur's death-wound with him to Cornwall, where it became an object of awe and veneration. A monastery was raised at Padstow in Pedr's honour. His relics were later transferred downriver to Bodmin.

Drystan, meanwhile, stayed in Cornwall, guarding Pedr's remains and spreading the legends of his cousin Arthur in the region. His efforts ensured that the tales of Arthur quickly took root in Cornish soil. Close to the River Fowey, south of Bodmin, stands a tall stone which not so long ago loomed over a crossroads a short distance from its present position. The front of the long stone bears a late sixth-century inscription: DRVSTANVS HIC IACET CVNOMORI FILIVS – 'Drystan lies here, the son of Cunomorus'. *Cunomorus* or 'Great-Hound' is a Latinised version of Cynon.

Drystan son of Cynon, one of Arthur's Enchanter Knights, a famous lover, occasional swineherd and saint, ended his days near the south coast of Cornwall, about as far away from the scene of Arthur's sacrifice as he could get while still remaining in the Island of Britain.

Of those whose hearts broke from bewilderment and grief, one was Caradog Strong-Arm, Arthur's father-in-law and his 'Pillar of the Cymry'. Another was Brânwen, the sister of Brân the Blessed, or – as we know her better – Muirgein.

Writing in the nineteenth century under his pen-name Fiona MacLeod, William Sharpe recounted a strange tale he had heard from a man of Tiree. The story concerned Mary Magdalene and her burial in a cave on the Isle of Iona.

Apparently, after the death of her lord the Magdalene roamed the earth in the company of a blind man until she came to Knoidart in Argyll, where her 'first husband' caught up with her. She attempted to hide the blind man among some pigs, but her pursuer laughingly speared him and then cut off the Magdalene's beautiful hair and left her to die. She was found by one of Columba's monks and her body was conveyed to Iona. Only St Columba knew where she was buried.

At first glance, the tale seems to relate to Gwenhwyfar, whose grave in Perthshire became the site of a daughter cell of Columba's monastery and whose blood possibly ended up in Arthur's burial mound. But the legend, muddled as it is, almost certainly pertains to another powerful woman whose memory was denigrated by the Church.

The story recounted by William Sharpe of the Magdalene and her blind friend compares with the Irish legend of Suibhne Geilt. The character of Suibhne (pronounced 'sweeney') was based on the original Merlin, Myrddin Wyllt. Irish tradition recalls that Suibhne went mad at a battle fought and lost in Ireland by Arthur's nephew. The twelfth-century *Buile Shuibhne* named the female companion who cared for 'Good-cheer the Madman', and whose jealous husband killed him, as Muirghil, the wife of Mongán.

Muirghil ('Sea-Servant') was in fact Muirgein, the mother of Mongán. She had received the remains of her brother Arthur on the island she ruled with her nine maidens, only the island was no longer hers and the beautiful women of Iona had no future there. The Welsh legend of Brân the Blessed reminds us that the final battle arose out of the mistreatment of Brân's sister by the followers of a royal Irishman. Columba and his monks fiercely resented the presence on Iona of Muirgein and her sacred sisterhood, and there is no reason to assume that they would have curbed their hostility in the wake of Arthur's death. If anything, their antagonism probably worsened.

Arthur's half-sister stayed on the Isle of Iona after the burial of the fallen heroes. Her husband still had his fortress on the island, and someone had to take care of the wretched Myrddin. If the local legend that had Mary Magdalene being laid to rest in a cave on Iona was in truth a distant memory of Muirgein's burial, then her cave can still be seen today.

First of all, we need to remember that Muirgein was frequently known as Agna or Anna, a name related to the Irish Eithne ('enya'), the meaning of which was 'fire'. Secondly, we should recall Aneirin's poem of Arthur's final campaign. In *Y Gododdin*, the poet declared that the 'sweet mead' dispensed by the cauldron had turned to 'poison' in the bellies of the Gododdin warriors. This can be seen as a desperate attempt to rationalise the catastrophe. The cauldron was held to blame for Arthur's defeat, and so the fault ultimately lay with the cauldron cult and its mother superior.

At the far end of the machair on the west side of Iona, a short distance to the north of Arthur's grave, there is a little hollow in a rock. It is just large enough to accommodate the body of a small person. To this day, the tiny cavern is known as *Uamh Anna Bhig a' Phuinnsean* – the 'Cave of Little Anna of the Poison'.

The death of Gwenhwyfar's shorter sister was almost certainly hastened by the shock of what had happened. Her cult had been annihilated and her family ruined by a scheming fanatic. Overwhelmed by the insanity of it all, the victims turned to self-destruction. They went from blaming the sacred cauldron for the tragedy to holding the goddess herself responsible.

A curious rhyme was collected by the Gaelic scholar Alexander Nicolson and published in 1881. It was entitled *Tuireadh Brighid* – 'Bride's Lament'. Translated here by Duncan Macleod, it has the authentic sound of a religion in its death-throes:

I call and pray to you, stone,
Release not Brighid,
For she sours the drink.
To many a good warrior without fault
Has she brought death.
Since your thirst now exceeds thirstiness,
May there be an eternal thirst upon you, Brighid.

Whether it was the goddess of the Hebrides who was deemed to have been at fault or her mortal representative, whose Rock of the Weeper stands on the shore near Arthur's grave, the disaster of the battle in Strathmore shattered the Druidic priesthood. The goddess who bestrode the Celtic world as Brigantia and who, as Brìde, shone over her Hebridean islands like the heavenly Venus, was cut down to size and sanitised: she became St Brigid, the 'Mary of the Gael'. Her more potent and fearsome womanly form was buried under a stone on the Isle of Iona, leaving only a sexless virgin to become the 'foster-mother of Christ'.

The same misogynistic impulse which would split Gwenhwyfar in two to create a virgin and a whore, and which denied Brighid her fertile womb and death-dealing qualities, went to work on Arthur's half-sister. She became the witch-queen Morgana or 'Morgan le Fay' – the 'hottest and most lustful woman in all Britain', in the words of the twelfth-century churchman Geoffrey of Monmouth.

She deserved better. Muirgein daughter of Áedán was the 'Beautiful Lady', a gifted healer who brought kings and heroes and saints into the world, and the human avatar of the great goddess who was said to have introduced the art of 'keening' – lamentation – to Ireland.

St Columba died aged 75 on 9 June 597. One of his last acts was to bless the island he had fought so hard to call his own:

> This place, small and mean though it is, will yet be held in great and unusual honour, not only by the kings and the people of Ireland, but by the rulers also of barbarous and foreign nations and their subject tribes, and even by the saints of other churches …

His legacy was tremendous. He would join Patrick and Brigid to form the triumvirate of Ireland's patron saints and is unfairly credited with having almost single-handedly converted Scotland to the Christian faith. His monks would also extend their missionary work into England.

The costs of St Columba's legacy, in terms of both human suffering and historical veracity, are incalculable. His successors sought to portray him as a man of peace – and yet this was the saint who had caused hundreds of deaths at the Battle of the Books in Ireland and many more in Britain, and whose ultimate gift to posterity was the destruction of Britain itself.

The involvement of Columba and other churchmen in the death of Arthur inevitably created a problem for history. The folk memory of the people recalled Arthur's presence in many parts of Scotland, but the monasteries, with their monopoly of the written word, came close to expunging his memory altogether. And while other parts of the British Isles were beginning to lay claim to Arthur, the Scots found it politic to forget all about him. His legends were grafted onto earlier

Irish heroes – such as Fionn mac Cumhail, the Scottish 'Fingal' – and those of his descendants who, like the Campbells, had ambitions to succeed chose to trace their ancestry back to another hero, rather than invite the enmity of the Church.

The voices of Arthur's people could be stifled, but not silenced forever, and they offer a very different view of St Columba from the later portraits. Myrddin called him the 'old-dog' by whose means many a warrior met his death with Arthur. The Welsh tales of the *Mabinogion* remember a slippery Irish 'king' and 'holy bishop' who caused problems for the family of Arthur. And then there was Taliesin.

Three of Taliesin's poems date from around the time of Columba's death. The *Death-Song of Erof* indicates that the saint had broken the human shield which had held back the Picts, while in the *Death-Song of Madog* – a reference, perhaps, to the death of M'Aedóc or St Cadog – the Chief Bard highlighted Columba's cruelty: 'He betrayed Jesus, though he believed.' But it is Taliesin's poem of the *Treasures of Annwn* which best expressed the feeling that lesser men had triumphed through Columba's duplicity:

> Monks howl like a choir of dogs
> Meeting with lords of wisdom.
> We know the way of the wind, the depth of the sea,
> We know why sparks of fire roar fiercely.
> Monks howl like wolves
> From meeting with lords of science.
> They know not what separates midnight and dawn,
> Nor the wind, what is its course, what its duration,
> The place it satisfies, the land where it strikes.
> The grave of the saint – in death he goes
> No farther than the altar.

Taliesin's words cast a fresh light on the Dark Ages. The Church has long argued that it alone was responsible for keeping the lights of learning and civilisation shining softly through the post-Roman era. Taliesin might have begged to differ. It was the Church itself that had brought on the darkness by suppressing every kind of knowledge but its own.

It was not until crusading knights discovered what the Arabs had preserved in the way of ancient knowledge that the Church finally began to lose its stranglehold. With the Renaissance, much pre-Christian thought was rediscovered. Gradually, Europe began to work its way out of the fog of ignorance that had been imposed by men like Columba. But the remarkable wisdom of the Druids was lost forever.

Áedán mac Gabráin never recovered from the horror which had been visited on his people. He remained in power, but his power had been undermined. The death of his eldest son Gartnait, King of the Picts, in 597 merely left the King of the Scots more isolated.

The mighty, Zeus-like lord of the sea had one last battle left in him. It was fought in 603.

Aethelfrith, the grandson of the first Anglian king in Britain, had taken control of Bernicia in 593. It would have been his warriors who supplemented Morgan's forces at the battle in Strathmore. The Britons thought of him as *Fflesawr* – the 'Deceiver'. He became the first true leader of the powerful Anglian kingdom of Northumbria.

Aethelfrith capitalised on the death of Arthur and the British collapse which came with it by extending his territory across much of the Old North. He 'ravaged the Britons more than all the great men of England', wrote the Anglian churchman Bede; conquering more British land and 'either making them tributary, or driving the inhabitants clean out, and planting English in their places, than any other king or tribune.' In 603, being 'very valiant and avid for glory', Aethelfrith marched his warriors into the Scottish Borders region, where he was met by an 'immense and mighty army' commanded by Áedán mac Gabráin.

The battle was known as *Degsastan* and was most likely fought near the Dawston Burn in Liddesdale. Although Áedán's forces inflicted heavy casualties, the battle was a devastating defeat for the defenders. Bede would claim that the Britons suffered so badly at *Degsastan* that they avoided making war on the English again.

Áedán was now in his 70s. He had witnessed the most extraordinary ebb and flow in the fortunes of his people. But this warrior's glory days were gone. As John of Fordun wrote in his *Scotichronicon*:

> King Aidan, after the battle of Degastan, in a state of unbroken grief, was so overcome by his misfortune that, two years after his flight, and being then approaching the age of 80, he died in Kintyre, and is buried in Kilcheran, where none of his predecessors had been buried.

Seemingly, Áedán abdicated in favour of Eochaid Buide, the yellow-haired 'Yew of Battle' whom St Columba had determined would be Áedán's successor. The father of Arthur in fact lived on for another five years after *Degsastan* and died in 608.

Taliesin honoured Áedán with an elegy:

> Am I not he that is called Gorlassar?
> My belt was a rainbow to the enemy ...
> Am I not Arawn who is the protector
> When streaming with the valour of Arthur ...

An old graveyard does exist at Kilkerran, where John of Fordun believed that Áedán was buried. It adjoins Campbeltown at the southern end of the Kintyre peninsula and was one of the very first Irish settlements in Dalriada; it takes its name from a friend of St Columba's. But John of Fordun was wrong about the timing of Áedán's death and he might have been equally mistaken over the place of Áedán's burial.

The Isle of Bute snuggles up against the Cowal peninsula, adjacent to Kintyre. The island was associated with two of Arthur's knights, St Cadog and his nephew St Blane, whose father was said to have been Áedán the Wily. On the east side of Bute, on a hillside just south of Port Bannatyne, a large cairn was broken into in the mid-nineteenth century. The cairn surrounded a stone cist or coffin, which was later incorporated into the gateway at nearby Kames Castle.

Writing in 1893 the minister of Rothesay, James King Hewison, disclosed what he had heard locally about the grave:

> The cairn covered the remains of a great hero. He was wont to wear a belt of gold, which, being charmed, protected him on the field of battle. One day, however, as he rode a-hunting accompanied by his sister, the maid, coveting the golden talisman, prevailed upon him to lend it to her. While thus unprotected he was killed – whether by enemies or mischance the attenuated tradition does not clearly indicate; and this cairn marked the warrior's grave.

'My belt was a rainbow to the enemy,' sang Taliesin in his *Death-Song of Uthyr the Chief*.

Could it have been the grave of Arthur's father that was ruined and plundered in about 1850? Perhaps. The name of the farm where it was found is variously spelled Rullecheddan and Rulicheddan. An eighteenth-century version of the place name – *Realigeadhain* – indicates that the cairn must once have been *Reilig Áedáin*, the 'Grave of Áedán'.

His forefathers, going back at least as far as Fergus Mór mac Eirc, had been buried on the Isle of Iona. Áedán's burial on the Isle of Bute broke with that tradition, and so one of the most important kings of Scottish history was not laid to rest in the sacred isle of his ancestors. No doubt Áedán had his reasons for not wanting to be buried on the island of Columba's church.

There is no record of a Scottish king being buried on Iona for another 250 years. An 'English' King of Northumbria was buried there in 685, and a King of the Picts was interred in *Reilig Odhráin* eight years later. The blessed isle had become the burial place of Arthur's enemies.

It was not until the death of Kenneth mac Alpin in 858 that the practice of burying Scottish kings on Iona, 'where the three sons of Erc were buried', was formally resumed.

According to Jocelin's *Life of St Kentigern*, Arthur's uncle, Cynon son of Clydno, lived to the ripe old age of 185. By dropping the first digit we arrive at a more reasonable estimate. He is said to have died on Sunday, 13 January, in the year 614, when he would have been about 85 years old.

The legend goes that his followers prepared a small vessel filled with hot water and placed him inside it. Cynon died in the bath. His followers then took it in turns to immerse themselves in the hot water, so that they too died. It would appear that the community committed suicide. Presumably, all were buried beneath the hill on which Glasgow Cathedral now stands, or close by at the ford across the River Kelvin, in what would appear to have been known at the time as Padarn's Land.

The *Life of St Kentigern* states that Rhydderch the Generous, King of Strathclyde, then stayed on at his royal hall at Partick, across the river from Cynon's establishment. Rhydderch kept with him a 'certain foolish man', who can be identified as Myrddin Wyllt and who predicted that Rhydderch would die within months of Cynon's passing. The death of Rhydderch is indeed attributed to the year 614. He is rumoured to have been buried near the rocking stone at Clochoderick in Renfrewshire, south of Glasgow.

Rhydderch was possibly succeeded, if only briefly, by Constantine who, as St Constantine, was associated with the settlement of Govan – *Baile a' Ghobhainn*, the 'Town of the Smith' – on the south side of the River Clyde.

Constantine's conversion to Christianity was recorded in the *Annals of Ulster* for the year 588, implying that Constantine was a baptismal name: his real name was probably Cano son of Gartnait, and his conversion caused a deep rift in Áedán's family. He is said to have spent some time living anonymously as a monk in Ireland until he gave away his real identity. According to Geoffrey of Monmouth, it was to his cousin Constantine that Arthur handed the 'crown of Britain' after he was mortally wounded by the River Isla. It should be recalled that in one of his guises – that of Dylan or 'Ocean son of Wave' – Arthur was killed by a blow struck against him by a close relative who was also a smith (Gofannon). The fact that Constantine was obliged to lie low for several years in Ireland suggests that he might have played a key role in the conspiracy against his kinsman Arthur.

In 1855, a gravedigger accidentally unearthed a sarcophagus at Govan Old Parish Church. The sandstone tomb, believed to have held the remains of Constantine, was richly carved and, on one of its sides, showed a Celtic horseman clearly identified by the letter 'A'. Quite why such an elaborate sepulchre should have been hidden away underground is a mystery. But if Constantine did have a hand in Arthur's assassination – and his sarcophagus lends weight to that possibility – then his return from Ireland might have been greeted with dismay by some. This would explain why Cynon and his community chose to kill themselves. It also offers a clue as to why special measures had to be taken to protect the remains of St Constantine.

Even with the support of the Church it would have been impossible for Constantine to have governed Strathclyde in defiance of the warrior caste. Those who remembered Arthur and had fought for the freedom of Britain alongside the emperor would not have tolerated a king who had helped to bring Arthur down – and if Constantine was the mysterious 'Ligessog Long Hand', the lone warrior who had driven the belly-spear into Arthur's loins and was then given sanctuary by the Church, there could not have been a more controversial candidate for the throne of the British kingdom. It would appear that Constantine, the son of Gartnait and foster-son of Rhydderch, renounced the throne so that another prince of Strathclyde could rule in his stead. This was Neithon, the son of Gwyddno Tall-Crane, who had also been King of the Picts since the death of Gartnait mac Áedáin in 597.

The accession of Neithon – or Nechtán, as the Picts knew him – bound the Pictish realms to the kingdom of Strathclyde, forming a strong bloc capable of withstanding the aggression of the Angles.

The deaths of Rhydderch and Cynon son of Clydno in 614 deprived Myrddin Wyllt of his patrons. His own death seems to have followed very shortly.

It is difficult to tell from the legends whether or not Myrddin welcomed his ritualistic three-fold death as a willing sacrifice. He had certainly seen it coming, allegedly telling Cynon (Kentigern) that he, Myrddin, would be stoned to death. On another occasion he predicted that he would be pierced by a stake and, again, that he would be drowned.

The end came for the little hero when he was chased along the banks of the River Tweed by the 'shepherds' of 'King Meldred'. They threw stones at him. One struck him. He slipped down the riverbank, impaling himself on a wooden stake, and drowned in the river.

The Irish legend of Suibhne Geilt, meanwhile, suggests that Myrddin was hiding among some pigs when he was recognised and speared to death. On balance, then, we can take it that Myrddin was murdered.

The River Tweed marked the boundary between the kingdom of Lothian and the Anglian territory of Northumbria. Tradition holds that Myrddin was buried at Drumelzier, the 'Hill of the Medlar-tree', near Merlindale on the banks of the River Tweed. In his *Geographical, Historical Description of Tweeddale*, Alexander Pennecuik wrote in 1715:

> There is one thing remarkable here, which is. The Burn called *Pausayl*, runs by the Eastside of this Church-yeard into *Tweed*, at the side of which Burn, a little below the Church-yeard, the famous Prophet *Merlin* is said to be buried. The particular place of his Grave, at the Root of a Thorn-Tree, was shewn me many years ago, by the Old and Reverend Minister of the place Mr. *Richard Brown*, and here was the old Prophecy fulfilled, delivered in *Scots* Ryme to this purpose.

When *Tweed* and *Pausayl*, meet at Merlin's Grave,
Scotland and England shall one Monarch have.

It is claimed that the Tweed did burst its banks, meeting the Powsail Burn at the grave of Myrddin Wyllt, on the very day in 1603 when James VI became the first king to reign over both Scotland and England.

The accounts of Myrddin's death imply that he was a late casualty of the civil strife which had reached its crescendo at Arthur's last battle. Some said it was King Meldred's queen, whom Myrddin had once accused of adultery, who instigated his ritual murder; others, that it was King Meldred's 'shepherds' who killed him. 'King Meldred' was Morgan the Wealthy – otherwise known as Medrod or Mordred – and the adulterous queen would have been Gwenhwyfar. The terrible death of the enchanter and battle-horseman known as Myrddin Wyllt can be thought of as the last of the slayings associated with Morgan's uprising, carried out by priests loyal to the rebel king.

If the burial of Myrddin in the valley of the River Tweed was intended to create some sort of supernatural defence against Anglian incursions, it failed. Almost immediately after the death of Arthur, the Angles swarmed across the Pennines. Arthur's nephew Owain returned to his kingdom of North Rheged, where he was first attacked by his former allies before being defeated in 595 by Morgan the Wealthy.

With Owain's death – he was reputedly buried in the Giant's Grave at Penrith – the Cumbrian kingdom of North Rheged was effectively finished. Refugees poured from the lands of Rheged into Wales, many settling in Dyfed where they venerated Owain's father Urien as a 'lord' of the Gower Peninsula. By about 616, most of the Old North had been overrun by those same Angles who, just a quarter of a century earlier, had been nearly wiped out by Arthur and his Round Table partners.

It was in 616 that Edwin son of Aelle became King of the Angles of Northumbria. The sons of his predecessor Aethelfrith were forced into exile. Both Oswald and his brother Oswiu were given sanctuary on the Isle of Iona.

Oswald son of Aethelfrith would claim to have been led to victory in a battle of 634 by a vision of St Columba. And so it was with the saint's posthumous support that Oswald was able to destroy a British army and unite the Anglian kingdoms of Bernicia and Deira under his iron rule. He then asked the monks of Iona to send a missionary to convert the Northumbrian Angles. The man chosen for this task was St Aidan, who founded a monastery on the Holy Island of Lindisfarne. Only a few short decades had passed since Arthur's warriors had laid siege to the Angles at Lindisfarne. The island now became the centre of Christianity in the kingdom of the Angles and a major daughter house of Columba's monastery on Iona.

Under Oswald, the Angles finally succeeded in conquering the kingdom of Lothian in 638. Yet more British refugees fled. Those who sailed from their *Leonais* homeland to the 'Lesser Britain' of northern France took with them the tales of those gallant warriors who had battled to preserve the language and culture, the freedom and traditions of the Britons. The legends were dispersed and Arthur rode again in the dreams of the exiles in Brittany.

With the connivance of St Columba's monks the Angles took control of almost the whole of North Britain. Only Strathclyde held out as a British enclave until it was subsumed into the kingdom of Scotland in the eleventh century. But Britain, as a nation, was gone. Not for another 1,000 years would there be a land called Britain.

Oswald was succeeded as King of the Northumbrian Angles by his brother Oswiu, who married a British princess of Rheged. Their son Ecgfrith was the first king for whom burial on the Isle of Iona is a matter of record.

The last of Arthur's knights to die was almost certainly Llywarch, Lord of South Rheged. As the Old North fell, he escaped into Wales and settled at the southern end of Llyn Tegid, once the home of the cauldron cult and the place where Arthur was trained in arms by the ever-loyal Cai. It is possible that Llywarch composed the earliest version of the Welsh poem entitled *Englynion y Beddau* – '*Stanzas of the Graves*' – which names a host of Arthurian heroes and their last resting places.

As for the Chief Bard Taliesin, he simply fades from view. Perhaps he retired to the Welsh coast and ended his days at *Tre Taliesin* ('Taliesin's House'), close to the weir on the River Dovey where he had been fished out of a coracle so many years earlier.

With his death, and that of Llywarch the Old, a light went out in Britain.

It has yet to be rekindled.

21

END OF THE ROAD

THE SUN shone fondly when I stood on the broad, flat summit of *an Sìthean Mór*. The sea to the west sparkled, buffed by the salt breeze. Iona was at her loveliest.

I had come to the end of the road – literally – to climb the Hill of the Fires, the mound in which the long-dead drink mead, listen to sweet music and endlessly replay the death of Arthur. But my journey was not over yet.

A couple of days later, I arrived at the quayside at the same time as the staff: a bearded ferryman and a young woman clutching a cake tin. It was nine o'clock on a Hebridean morning – the sky like an old duvet and no one on the roads.

The ferryman recognised me from a previous reconnaissance and wondered if I had come back for any particular reason. Yes, I said: I wanted to find the cemetery. The path, he told me, was overgrown, but if I kept to the hillside I might just make it.

There are no roads on this island. Such tracks as do exist seem not to have changed since the Middle Ages. I followed the path around the Boathouse – which serves excellent seafood and home-baked confections – and past an old but-and-ben hovel, now a heritage centre. The track then led me round three sides of the main estate, enclosed by stone walls, and through a silent farmyard where vehicles slowly rotted. Cows gazed at me as if surprised to see a human being.

Where the track forked I struck westwards, up a steep incline shaded by trees. The green of their moss was livid, almost luminous. A concrete reservoir held a pool of dark water and an iron gate marked the limits of civilisation. The hinges wailed, and I was out into the open: the heathery moorland of the Isle of Ulva.

The past is ever-present in the Celtic mindset. Battles fought and lost long ago can be recalled as if they happened yesterday.

The Anglo-Saxons, by way of contrast, did not care to dwell on their defeats. Consequently, they left no obvious records of Arthur. Bede, the Northumbrian 'Father of History', made no mention of him in his eighth-century *Ecclesiastical History of the English People*. It was left to a Welsh monk, commonly known as

Nennius, to provide some of the earliest historical references to the 'Duke of Battles' in his erratic ninth-century *History of the Britons*.

Neglected by the nascent English, Arthur lived on in the folklore of Wales, Cornwall and Brittany, and in the Gaelic race-memory of Scotland and Ireland. How then did he come to be so widely thought of as an anglicised king of southern Britain?

The process began with the Norman invasion of 1066 – a crushing defeat which the English would never forget. Twenty years into his reign, William, the first Norman King of England, commissioned a detailed survey of the land he had conquered. The aim was to establish who owned what and how much they should be paying to the royal treasury. More than 13,000 places in England and Wales were swiftly and efficiently itemised and the results were presented to the king in two volumes known as Domesday.

Religious institutions were exempted from paying taxes on land and possessions which had been legally granted to the Church by a king. Many establishments had no deeds to prove that such a grant had ever been made, and so 'charter myths' were hastily invented to explain how the lands were gifted to an earlier saint, often by no less a figure than Arthur himself.

A *Life of St Cadog* was compiled by Lifris of Llancarfan in about 1100. Needless to say, it omitted to go into detail about the saint's betrayal of his friend, although it was happy to paint Arthur in a rather unsavoury light. In it, Arthur happened to be sitting with his companions Cai and Bedwyr when they saw Cadog's father eloping with his intended bride. Arthur's first instinct was to rape the woman, but Cai and Bedwyr talked him out of it. Somewhat later in the story, Arthur is seeking compensation for the deaths of three men at the hands of a murderer whom St Cadog has been sheltering. Cadog assembles a panel of judges and awards Arthur his due but then plays a magical trick on him, after which Arthur begs for the saint's forgiveness and bestows on him a generous gift of land.

Cadog's monastery in South Wales seems to have led the way in making use of Arthur's memory for the benefit of the Church. About thirty years after the *Life of St Cadog* appeared, Caradoc of Llancarfan wrote his *Life of Gildas*, which introduced the notion that Gwenhwyfar was held captive by 'King Melwas' at Glastonbury; allegedly, the clergy intervened to mollify Arthur, who then rewarded the Church with land (the *Life of Gildas* is also notable for its claim that St Gildas was one of the twenty-four sons of Caw of North Britain, several of whom rebelled against Arthur, though it is Arthur who is seen as the aggressor, rather than the turncoats in his company).

Dating from about 1120, the *Life of St Padarn* has Arthur attempting to steal the saint's tunic, even though Arthur was already the owner of the Red-Coat of Padarn. Nonetheless, the saint prays for the earth to swallow Arthur, who promptly disappears up to his chin. He then begs St Padarn to rescue him and gratefully adopts the saint as his 'continual patron'. The *Life of St Illtud* belongs to Llantwit Major in South Wales; written in about 1140, its protagonist is a reformed robber-baron who, it was claimed, was Arthur's cousin. Other saints' lives of the period helped to drag Arthur further away from his Northern roots, routinely portraying him as a brutal hoodlum easily humbled by a clergyman.

Even before these manufactured legends began to appear the Norman over-lords had been hearing about Arthur, thanks in part to the poets of the 'Lesser Britain', Brittany. In 1100, the fourth son of William I came to the English throne. Nicknamed *Beauclerc* because of his scholarly tastes, Henry I became fascinated with Arthur. Henry's wife was Mathilda of Scotland, the daughter of Malcolm Canmore and his Hungarian-born English queen, St Margaret. Queen Margaret was fiercely anti-Gaelic – she and her husband put a stop to the practice of bury-ing Scottish kings on Iona – and at the age of 6 her daughter Mathilda had been sent to a nunnery at Romsey in Hampshire in order to distance her from uncouth Scottish influences. That King Henry I of England developed such an interest in all things Arthurian would suggest that, in spite of her mother's efforts, Mathilda never lost touch with her native traditions.

One of King Henry's illegitimate children married Mathilda's brother, Alexander I of Scotland. Her youngest sibling, David, was granted parts of the border region by his brother but spent much of his adolescence in exile in England where, according to William of Malmesbury (who made no mention at all of Arthur in his twelfth-century history of Glastonbury Abbey), he had 'rubbed off all tarnish of Scottish barbarity'. When Alexander I died in 1124, David received the support of King Henry I of England in pursuing his claim to the Scottish throne and named his son Henry in honour of his benefactor.

Civil war broke out in Scotland when David I was crowned. The leaders of the rebellion were Alexander's son Máel Coluim (or Malcolm – the name means 'Follower of Columba') and Óengus of Moray. Ten years passed before Máel Coluim mac Alaxandair was finally captured and imprisoned, and during that time David relied heavily on his English relations: a Norman fleet cruised the Firth of Clyde and the coast of Argyll, hunting Máel Coluim in Arthur's old stamping ground.

Henry I sired plenty of bastards but had no legitimate male heir, so he named his daughter – another Mathilda – as the next ruler of England. Mathilda's claim to the throne was challenged by Stephen of Blois, who had himself crowned in 1135. The disputed succession resulted in a grim period known as The Anarchy, in which one of Mathilda's staunchest allies was her illegitimate half-brother Robert, first Earl of Gloucester and patron to a certain Geoffrey of Monmouth.

King David I, 'Prince of the Cumbrians', also waged war against Stephen, launching three invasions of England between 1135 and 1138. It was during this very period that Geoffrey of Monmouth completed his fantastical *History of the Kings of Britain*. Clearly, he was influenced by current events. Stephen's usurpation of the throne mirrored that of the tyrannical 'Mordred', while David of Scotland provided Geoffrey with his model for Arthur, the civil war which greeted King David's accession finding its echo in the rebellion which immediately follows Geoffrey's account of Arthur's coronation.

Regardless of the Scottish origins of much of his material, Geoffrey of Monmouth insisted on making his Arthur a man of the south. With the cross-fertilisation of English and Scottish royal bloodlines, Arthur had become the intellectual property of England, although Scottish writers continued to mention him – one of them, John Mair of Haddington, came from the selfsame East Lothian region in which Arthur had been conceived. But Geoffrey of Monmouth led the charge in converting the northern prince into a southern king. Geoffrey undoubtedly intended to flatter his patron, Robert Earl of Gloucester, whose brother Reginald, first Earl of Cornwall, would go on to build the castle at Tintagel, providing the ruins which are much visited by tourists in the mistaken belief that Arthur was born there. Geoffrey also made sure that his Arthur was crowned close to where the elder Queen Mathilda had been raised in an English nunnery.

The younger Empress Mathilda took for her second husband one Geoffrey of Anjou. Their son became the first of the Plantagenet kings of England. Henry II – the 'Lion of Justice' and 'King of the North Wind' – took his grandfather's fascination with Arthur still further by marrying a true aficionado of the legends, the exquisite Eleanor of Aquitaine.

Born in 1122, Eleanor had been raised at the 'Court of Love', where tales of Arthur and his knights were already popular. An itinerant Welshman named Bleddri latimer ap Kadifor had brought the legends to the Count of Poitiers, who was probably Eleanor's grandfather. Referred to by Giraldus Cambrensis as a 'well-known storyteller', Bleddri had been loosely connected with the English court of King Henry I and his Scottish queen. The French struggled with the name Bleddri. They preferred to call him Bleheris, then Blihis, and finally Blaise, the renowned authority on such subjects as Merlin and the Grail.

At the age of 30, Eleanor married Henry II. They were like Arthur and Gwenhwyfar reborn. Indeed, it is probable that Eleanor's fondness for the 'greatest knight that ever lived', William the Marshal, gave rise to the legends of Lancelot's adulterous love for Guinevere, and that the trouble King Henry II had with his sons was revisited in the tales of Arthur's fractious family.

It was the restless King Henry II who encouraged the monks of Glastonbury to go digging for Arthur's grave, thereby instigating one of the greatest hoaxes in history. The ravishing, highly sexed Eleanor meanwhile brought Gallic *élan* and the contemporary cult of chivalry to the romances. Among those who benefited from her patronage were Robert Wace of Jersey (whose *Roman de Brut* versified Geoffrey's *Historia Regum Britanniae* while introducing the Round Table and Arthur's famous sword, Excalibur) and the poet Chrétien de Troyes, who built on the legacy of Bleddri the Welshman to give us the tales of 'Lancelot' (Lleënog), 'Yvain' (Owain), 'Perceval' (Peredur) and the 'Graal'. It is also thought that Queen Eleanor was the mother of Marie de France, whose short poetic stories or *Lais* added much to the romantic idyll of Arthur's court.

By the twelfth century, much of Europe was thrilling to the stories of Arthur. An Arthurian tableau was even carved above the north door of the Romanesque cathedral at Modena in Italy. But if the Church had helped to revive interest in Arthur, through its tales of his clumsy encounters with various saints, it remained extremely ambivalent towards his legends and those of the Grail.

It was as if the man had refused to die. A revealing story was told by a Cistercian monk in 1220: a preaching abbot, realising that his brethren were dozing, exclaimed, 'Listen! I have something new and wonderful to tell you. There was once a king whose name was Arthur ...'

The abbot proved his point when the monks suddenly sat up, wide awake and rapt with interest.

The footpath skittered around rocky hillocks and sprawling bogs. There was a time when the island of Ulva hosted more than 800 people in sixteen settlements, but today the population barely reaches double figures. Most of the dwellings are at the east end of the island, close to the narrow ferry crossing, the rest of the place being more or less abandoned to the red deer and the mountain hair, the eagle and the otter.

The island is twin-backed, like a Bactrian camel. The track I was taking led inland towards the first of those dominant peaks but then lost its nerve, offering a choice of routes around the mountains. I followed the path to the south side.

To my left, the mountains of Mull kept their heads in the clouds while dipping their toes in a looking-glass sea. Away to the south a long arm of land reached across the horizon. Its fist was the Isle of Iona, coyly flashing her sandy petticoats. To the west, a small convoy of islands steamed silently by. A little nearer, the Isle of Staffa was a souvenir fridge magnet stuck on a stainless steel ocean. Other islands were scattered across the water like clumps of moss on a slate roof. The sky was enormous, and I had it all to myself.

The track brought me to what had once been a small village. Only the weathered skeletons of the homesteads remained – tumbledown cottages built sturdy and square but now eyeless in the wind. Most were mere piles of lichen-clad stones, barely recognisable as houses. The settlement, perched on its grassy spur above a ragged bay, was prehistoric in origin. In 1841, fifty-two souls occupied the township, but by the early twentieth century the place was in ruins.

The pathway hugged the flanks of the hills, keeping clear of the bay below. A deserted water-mill crouched in a gully formed by one of the streams which slash the mountainsides. The old millstone lay inside the roofless walls, forgotten like the communities it once served.

Following the path as it trailed like a lazy tightrope between the mountains and the sea, I soon discovered that the ferryman had been right. The footpath was beginning to give up the ghost. At times it disappeared altogether; at others it surrendered to the bracken which grew taller than me, and the way forward meant crashing blindly through the fronds while the ground shifted under my feet. I was 5 miles from the nearest phone or human being: hardly the place to go blundering over the edge of a hillside.

At last, the bracken gave way. The Isle of Iona was now completely hidden by the islet of Little Colonsay. Sunflowers nodded beside the ruins of a vanished chapel, and there below me in the sodden moss above the pale sands of Tràigh Bhàn was the object of my quest. A little graveyard of stone urns and headstones, stonewalled in splendid isolation at the end of the world.

The place is called Kilvikewan or *Cille Mhic Eòghainn* – the 'Chapel of the Son(s) of Owain'. It is the old cemetery of the MacQuarries, the sons and descendants of Gúaire.

There seemed to be no way of approaching the cemetery: not from the land, at any rate. I could not grasp the logic in planting a graveyard at this remote spot. I had found a grave similar to Arthur's at Calgary on Mull – a burial mound sheltered by trees and set back from the shore, its view of the bay blocked by a bank of machair, which in summer was pretty with tiny pink, blue and yellow flowers. The ancient folk who built such cairns had a plan: their dead could sail in the ship of souls towards the everlasting sunset while their bodies lay safe inside earthen mounds which the waves could not reach. The MacQuarrie cemetery, though, has to be one of the most desolate and inaccessible family plots in the whole of the British Isles.

And then it struck me. The Isle of Iona, which is clearly visible from the ruined village on the far side of the bay, cannot be seen from the burial ground of *Cille Mhic Eòghainn*. Little Colonsay stands in the way.

The sons of Owain and Gúaire had been cast out of their earthly paradise. They were no longer welcome on the blessed isle of their ancestors – not unless they were prepared to convert to the faith of Columba – and so they had taken up residence on a wilder, larger island nearby. By its very position the cell or hermitage of the sons of Owain and 'Gweir of Great Valour' bears witness to the painful yearning of the banished. They longed to stay close to the Navel of the sea but could not bear to be buried in sight of Avalon.

Or perhaps they had hoped that Little Colonsay would shield them from the curses of the monks.

If Geoffrey of Monmouth's influential *History of the Kings of Britain* had been inspired, at least in part, by the politics of its day, the same could be said for the *hoole booke of kyng Arthur & of his noble knyghtes of the rounde table* (thankfully, the title was changed by the printer William Caxton to *Le Morte d'Arthur*). Apparently written in prison by a miscreant named Sir Thomas Malory, it is a monumental synthesis of French and English legends along with a few inventions of Malory's own (such as his tale of Sir Gareth).

Malory's epic was compiled in the context of another civil war. Rival branches of the Plantagenet dynasty spent upwards of thirty years tearing each other apart in what became known as the Wars of the Roses. Against such a bloody backdrop, *Le Morte d'Arthur* stood as something more than just a nostalgic fantasy: it was a revisionist history in which the once-and-future king brought order and decorum to a fragmented England. The turmoil of the times cried out for a unifying hero, so that when Malory imagined a fair sword stuck in a stone in a London church-yard and the marble stone engraved with the words 'Whoso pulleth this sword out of this stone and anvil, is rightwise king born of all England' he was dreaming of an end to the factional infighting and the emergence of a true sovereign invested with divine power and endorsed by all his subjects.

Malory's dream was realised within days of his book being printed. Henry Tudor landed on the Pembrokeshire coast and, making the most of his Welsh ancestry, raised a large army with which he defeated Richard III at Bosworth Field. Crowned in 1485, Henry VII was sufficiently eager to invoke an Arthurian heritage that he named his eldest son Arthur. But Arthur, Prince of Wales, died suddenly at the age of 15. England has yet to be ruled by a king named Arthur.

It was Prince Arthur's younger brother who ascended the throne as the latest King Henry – the same Henry VIII who would order the destruction of Glastonbury Abbey and others like it, regardless of such last-minute stories, spun by desperate monks, as the Glastonbury legend of St Collen (Cadog) and Gwyn ap Nudd (Taliesin).

Some thirty years before the last Abbot of Glastonbury was executed on the windy summit of the Tor, the largest battle ever fought between England and Scotland took place at Flodden Field.

James IV was by and large a popular monarch and probably the last of the Scottish kings to speak the language of the Gaels. As he was preparing to invade England in 1513 he went to church in Linlithgow. An account of what happened there was written by George Sinclair, professor of philosophy at the University of Glasgow, in the sixteenth-century.

King James was 'at his Devotions [when] an Ancient Man came in, his Amber coloured Hair hanging down upon his Shoulders, his forehead high, and inclining to Baldness, his Garments of Azure colour, somewhat long, girded about with a Towel, or Table-Napkin, of a Comely and very Reverend Aspect.'

This 'Ancient Man' walked up to the king and addressed him – 'Sir, I am sent hither to entreat you, to delay your Expedition for this time, and to proceed no further in your intended journey: for if you do, you shall not prosper in your enterprise, nor any of your followers. I am further charged to warn you, not to use the acquaintance, company, or counsel of women, as you tender your honour, life, and estate.'

Though he was closely observed by the bystanders, many of whom were eager to speak with him afterwards, the 'apparition' disappeared, 'having in a manner vanished in their hands'.

True or not, this strange tale presents an authentic image of Arthur: the leonine mane of amber hair and the shaved forehead ('high, and inclining to baldness') are suggestive of the Druidic tonsure, while the sky-blue garment recalls the Roman poet Claudian's description of a personified fifth-century Britain – 'her cheeks tattooed, and an azure cloak, rivalling the swell of ocean, sweeping to her feet.' Manifesting as it did in Lothian, the apparition could be thought of as Arthur, still endeavouring, after so many years, to protect his people and addressing King James IV as one Gaelic speaker to another. Even the injunction to shun the company and counsel of women smacks of bitter experience.

But the Ancient Man's entreaties went unheeded. James IV pressed ahead with his invasion of England. Being the chivalrous sort he had given the enemy plenty of advance warning. His army of 30,000 men was routed in Northumberland on 9 September 1513 and the 'rent surcoat of the King of Scots stained with blood' was sent to King Henry VIII.

Mary, Queen of Scots, was the charming granddaughter of King James IV. On 19 June 1566 she gave birth to a son in Edinburgh. He was baptised 'Charles James' at Stirling Castle and hailed as the new Arthur who would one day unite the thrones of Scotland and England. Imprisoned on an island in Loch Leven, his ill-fated mother was forced to abdicate in his favour, so that at the tender age of 13 months the boy became King James VI of Scotland.

On the death of Mary's cousin Elizabeth, the younger daughter of King Henry VIII and last of the Tudor monarchs, the adult James VI was proclaimed the first King James of England – or, as he liked to put it, 'King of Great Brittaine, France and Ireland'.

And so, in 1603, a royal Scot became the first King of Britain since his noble forebear led the Britons into battle over 1,000 years earlier.

I left the sad and lonely graveyard. Retracing my steps through the forest of ferns and past the long-abandoned water-mill, I returned to the empty village. Here, in these ruined houses, the descendants of Gúaire had lived and died, generation after generation, until they were evicted again, victims of the new religion of profit and progress. The MacQuarries had fought 'for the old line of kings' at Culloden, the English having decided by then that they preferred kings who were German (and Protestant) to ones who were Scottish (and Catholic). The clan later lost some of its best sons in Bengal and at Waterloo, their mother receiving a medal from King

George IV inscribed with the words *Màthair nan Gaisgich,* 'Mother of Heroes'. But the clearances came to Ulva in the shape of a new landlord, who tore down their roofs, burned their thatch and smashed their possessions.

A plaque set into a cairn of stones announced that the ghost village of the MacQuarries was called Ormaig. The name is of Norse derivation and meant 'Bay of the Worm' – better rendered as the 'Bay of the Dragon' or 'Serpent Bay'. An odd name: no serpents have ever been found on Ulva which, like Iona, has always been a snake-free zone. Only the limbless lizard known as the slow worm, which does inhabit the island, looks remotely like a snake, although it hardly merits having a township named after it.

Ormaig's claim to fame was its school for pipers. At some date in the misty past, a piper by the name of MacArthur arrived in the village and set up a college to rival the celebrated piping academy run by the MacCrimmons on the Isle of Skye. Both the MacCrimmons and the MacArthurs were experts in the art of *pìobaireachd* and their respective schools vied with each other for supremacy. The students trained for seven years to master the 'Big Music' (*Ceòl Mór*) and practiced, whenever possible, out in the open.

It can be no coincidence that seven years was also the time it took to train a bard, nor that the Chief Bard Taliesin referred in one of his poems to 'the golden pipes of Lleu'. Arthur, it would seem, was a musician, and like the gift of prophecy his skills were handed down to his sons, and to their sons in turn, until one of them settled among the Sons of Gúaire at Ormaig to pass on the tradition of the three Noble Strains – those ancient melodies capable of inducing melancholy, ecstasy and sleep.

How long this extraordinary school for pipers lasted is unknown. A great deal of what constituted Gaelic culture was proscribed in 1609 when King James VI – James I of England – arranged for the Highland chieftains to be taken hostage on board a ship and deposited on the island of Columba's church, where they were made to sign the nine Statutes of Iona. These acts, though slow to be implemented, were designed to impose southern standards of behaviour on the feudal Highlands and Islands. Among their provisions was a prohibition on the bardic arts. The massacre of the Jacobite army at the Battle of Culloden in 1746 dealt a more serious blow to Gaelic culture, and though the playing of the bagpipes was not outlawed in Scotland, warlike weapons and the wearing of tartan were, and as part of the general despondency the pipes were 'laid aside' and the 'music lost'.

The final nail in the coffin of traditional Gaelic society was hammered in by the clan chiefs themselves. Many were lured down to London where, estranged from their dependants, they lost fortunes in loose living and then made fortunes by clearing their tenants from the land to make way for huge flocks of the hardy Cheviot. Sheep replaced people. The Highland glens became practically uninhabited and uninhabitable, a vast playground for sportsmen and millionaires.

The MacArthur school for pipers at Ormaig represented a link with the world of Arthur, which was finally severed when his descendants were driven from their homes by a rapacious landlord. The nature of that link is suggested by the village name – Ormaig, the Bay of the Serpent. There were no snakes on Ulva, but the Druidic *Naddred* or 'Adders' kept their hold on the island long after they had lost Iona to St Columba and his monks. The resident 'serpent' of Ormaig was surely one of these relics of Druidism, and the bardic arts which flourished under the MacArthurs and their kinsmen, the MacQuarrie sons of Gúaire, maintained a lingering continuity with the ways of Arthur's people.

Even the name of the island points to the late survival of the Druidic cult. In Gaelic, Ulva is *Ulbha* (pronounced 'ul-uh-vuh'). It is often translated by way of the Norse *ulfr* as 'Wolf Island'. Alternatively, a local tradition holds that a Viking long-ship once came to the isle; a scout leapt ashore and reported back to his master '*Ullamhdha!*' – 'Nobody home!'

However, *ullamhdha* is not Norse but Gaelic. Munro and Macquarrie, in their history of the Clan MacQuarrie, suggest that the phrase signified that the island was 'ready for occupation'.

There is a simpler and more obvious derivation. *Ullamh* in Gaelic refers to a 'man of learning', such as a doctor or chief poet (*ollam* in Old Irish). The term *ullamh dhà* would imply that the island belonged to just such a sage, literally meaning 'wise man to him'. This would make Ulva the Isle of the Druid or Bard. Perhaps the apocryphal longshipman disembarked from his ship at the Bay of the Boat on the south side of the island, discovered that the main settlement was ruled by a learned *ullamh* and duly named the township the 'Bay of the Serpent' (or 'Dragon').

The Gaelic folktale *Sgeulachd air Sir Uallabh O'Còrn* introduces Arthur as Chief Arthur son of Iuthar, 'King of Ireland'. The son of his sister is called Sir Uallabh or 'Wiseman son of Horn'. Sir Uallabh is a hero and champion who owns a sweet-sounding harp, defeats The Big Lad, 'son of the King of Innean' (i.e. Annwn), and spends a night under a cauldron inside an enclosed cavern in the company of a giant. He is nothing less than the Hebridean answer to the legendary Sir Gawain, formerly known as Gwalchmai son of Gúaire, the nephew and foster-son of Arthur who was also one of the twenty-four horsemen of Arthur's Round Table. The Irish seem to have known him as Mongán, the heroic son of Muirgein and Fiachna, who was killed in Kintyre in AD 625.

Whether we think of him as Mongán ('Little Long-Haired One') or Gwalchmai ('Hair of May'), as Sir Gawain or Sir Uallabh, the smart son of [Brân of the] Horn, we can surmise that he was the first of the sons of Gúaire to lay claim to Ulva, making it the island home of the MacQuarries. The sons of his half-brother Owain set up camp close to his village and buried their dead out of sight of Iona. The families merged, and a piper named MacArthur taught their children to play the Big Music at the Bay of the Serpent.

I made my way back to the boathouse and the jetty. Discarded oyster shells littered the beach. Holiday-makers were arriving to explore the Isle of the Druid.

The ferryman asked if I had found what I was looking for.

Indeed I had. At the dilapidated hamlet of Ormaig, the trail went cold. Arthur's descendants were dispersed like seeds on the wind – and now they are everywhere.

Artuir mac Áedáin
'Duke of Battles'
559–594

Beautiful were the bands of women,
The splendour that used to be about Bran
Melodiously the king would say:
'Though you go, may you come back again.'

Conversation of Bran's Druid & the Prophetess of Febul

APPENDIX

THE GRAIL TODAY

So pass I hostel, hall, and grange;
By bridge and ford, by park and pale,
All-arm'd I ride, whate'er betide,
Until I find the holy Grail.

Alfred, Lord Tennyson, Sir Galahad, 1842

I

IN ORDER to track down the Grail and reveal its present location, we must first of all establish what it is and how it can be recognised.

The first of these questions is in some ways the most difficult to answer, because the Grail has meant different things to different people at different times.

Giambattista Vico (1668–1744) was a Neapolitan philosopher and historian whose great work, *Principi di Scienza Nuova d'intorno alla Comune Natura delle Nazioni* ('*New Science*'), advanced a theory concerning the development of civilisation. According to Vico, civilisations evolve through three distinct phases. The first is the divine age in which, as Thales of Miletus put it, 'All things are full of gods'. The next period is 'heroic' and its institutions are hierarchical and aristocratic. Mankind then enters the human age, which is essentially democratic. Vico argued that these three phases form a recurring cycle (*ricorso*), implying that the human age must somehow or other lead back to the age of the gods: exponential growth and the over-exploitation of resources trigger a breakdown; democracy is undermined, society falls apart – and the cycle begins again.

Vico built his theory around the different ways that language is used in each of the phases of civilisation. Another way of understanding it is by differentiating between the power structures and belief systems that are characteristic of each phase: the divine age is essentially 'magical'; the heroic or aristocratic age 'religious'; and the democratic, human age 'scientific'. The transition from one phase to another requires a renegotiation of mankind's relationship to the universe – from a spirit-haunted world to a God-driven one, and then to a clockwork cosmos – and each transition can be marked by a new development in the history of the written word.

'In the beginning was the Word,' wrote St John in his Gospel, 'and the Word was with God, and the Word was God.' This is as much as to say that in the primitive or magical society of the divine age, the word itself has *power*. The use of language in such a society is metaphorical (Arthur was an 'eagle', he was a 'lion'), in much the same way that a cave-painting is a metaphor for the animal it represents. Ultimately, though, the word and the thing are one – Arthur was not *like* an eagle, he *was* an eagle – and so the word literally captures something of the subject's essence. Magical thinking sees a direct link between subject and image (which is why the primitive Bushman was so loathe to be photographed: his soul was at stake) and so the word has to be handled with extreme caution. The educated elite of Celtic society, whom we know as the Druids, kept the art of writing secret. The written word was an invocation, potentially a curse, and such was its power that a satirical poem could inflict actual physical harm on its target.

The leap from a magical society to an aristocratic and religious one was typified by St Columba. He certainly had one foot in the divine age, but his universe was controlled by one God, rather than a plethora of spirits, and his discourse was typical of the language of the heroic age. This would explain the disagreement between Columba and 'Odhrán' over the nature of hell: Arthur no doubt believed that the soul travels to another place, whereas St Columba thought in terms of a concept (everlasting punishment) for which 'Hell' was a convenient metonym.

To Columba, the word had power, not in itself but as the Word of God. Sacred texts existed to be copied and distributed since they delineated universal laws and were necessary in order to change his society from one in which all things are full of gods to one in which all things are created by God. Such a world is usually doctrinaire, absolutist and polarised (Good versus Evil); it tends towards feudalism and idealises some ('saints') while condemning others ('sinners'). Arthur's greatest achievement during the age of religion was to transform himself from a pagan 'emperor' despised by the Church into something resembling the perfect Christian king.

The widespread dissemination of the written word hastened the move from the magical to the aristocratic-religious age. Still, the transmission of the written word was carefully policed by the Church. Approved texts were copied by hand while others were altered or obliterated. But with the invention of moveable print the Church began to lose its monopoly. Suddenly, information and ideas could be published faster and more widely than ever before. The result was a backlash against the monolithic Church of Rome and, eventually, all hierarchical institutions, such as the monarchy in France.

Thus began the Age of Reason. Rationality replaced the superstition of the magical society and the dogmatism of the heroic age. Galileo's clash with the papacy over the movement of the Earth around the Sun exemplified the shift from the medieval to the modern world. Coupled with the democratic drive towards liberty, equality and fraternity came a new belief-system, that of scientific materialism.

Language continued to evolve through the age of print. Vico noted that the human age uses language ironically (a word can have two meanings). The scientific leanings of the period also meant that words and concepts could be distilled into an equation or formula. It is a measure of how far we had travelled from the divine age, which knew that the name of YHWH should never be uttered, to the human age, which could contemplate $E=mc^2$ without going insane (or maybe it couldn't).

Vico sensed that rationality would lead to what he called 'barbarism of reflection'. We have witnessed that transition. The advent of the internet has allowed the written word to proliferate unchecked, its transmission global and instantaneous. This is changing the very nature of authority: once, the gods were the authors of everything; then it was the Church; then the Establishment – but as the ideological debate over climate change shows, even science is no longer held in high esteem. Everyone is free to broadcast their own opinions. We are all authors now.

The age of anarchy is the digital age: it is virtual and viral. Words are drifting ever further from their meanings or breaking down into text-speak ('lol'). The power of the word exists only in the brand name or logo. It could be argued that one of the most famous of these – the 'golden arches' of a well-known fast food chain – points us back towards the first syllable and the mantra which, in Hinduism, is both the word and the manifestation of god.

DIVINE AGE	HEROIC AGE	HUMAN AGE	CYBER AGE
Theocratic	Aristocratic	Democratic	Anarchic
Magical	Religious	Scientific	Virtual
Ogham/Runes	Script	Print	Digital
Warriors	Knights	Soldiers	Drones

On one level, the Holy Grail has never been anything more than a symbol – of dedication, self-sacrifice and the steadfast pursuit of an elusive, perhaps unattainable goal. What form that symbol takes depends entirely on which societal stage you happen to be in. The questing knight who braves dragons and rescues damsels while preserving his modesty and chastity belongs unequivocally to the heroic age. He is an idealised aristocrat with a religious obsession. Because the Church roused men like him to seek salvation by reclaiming Jerusalem from the Saracens, his notion of the Grail was the cup used by Jesus at the Last Supper.

Moving forward into the human age, the Holy Grail becomes a metaphor for a much-sought-after scientific breakthrough – cold fusion, perhaps, or a cure for cancer. It would be a life-enhancing source of riches, like the philosopher's stone of the alchemists, but it would be discovered in a laboratory, rather than a secluded chapel.

In our digital-anarchic times the Grail can perhaps best be defined as the search for reality. Consumerism preaches the desirability of things, but material acquisitions never seem to do the trick. Meanwhile, we shift ever further into virtual reality while watching so-called reality TV; we ponder alternative realities, talk about 'real life', 'real time', the 'real world'; we claim that we are 'for real' while telling each other to 'get real' and to 'keep it real' – even though we may not be quite sure what 'real' is anymore.

If Giambattista Vico was right, then our current age of anarchy will be short-lived. Our way of life is unsustainable (i.e. unrealistic). Sooner or later, the system will crash. We will be forced, once again, to reassess our attitude towards the universe. The ubiquitous trademark 'M' will revert to being the vibration which reflects absolute reality – 'Om' – if the recurring cycle of civilisation brings us back to the age of magic, and the apple which caused the Biblical fall from grace, inspired Newton's theory of universal gravitation and symbolised the global obsession with consumer electronics will become once again what it was: the golden apple of immortality.

Arthur was reinvented in the heroic age as a knight-in-shining-armour chasing a Christian chalice. Such an image tends to suit the conservative sort who would rather be living in an age of aristocracy, but it has no basis in reality. The real Arthur was a product of the divine age. He was one of the last champions of that society. And in his world the Grail took the form of a cauldron.

2

The use of cauldrons in magical practices is amply documented (we might think of the Weird Sisters in Shakespeare's Scottish play). But the cauldron that was buried with Arthur was no ordinary cooking pot. Judging by the early sources, it would appear that the cauldron was:

> made of gold or silver, or both, and of 'rich workmanship';
> had a 'band around the rim, about the edge';
> tended to fall apart during moments of crisis, and
> had something to do with horses.

A cauldron matching these descriptions was unearthed in a Danish peat-bog in May 1891. It was not all in one piece. What the peat-cutters found was a pile of silver sheets into which fantastical images had been beaten. There were five long rectangular plates, seven shorter panels, a rounded base plate and two pieces of metal tubing. These items had been stacked rather neatly on dry ground and, over the years, the peat had slowly grown around them.

It had clearly been a religious object. The iconography of the designs was Celtic, although the high repoussé workmanship appears to have been Thracian – that is, it had been crafted either in north-eastern Greece or western Turkey (or perhaps the Balkans) or by itinerant silversmiths from those parts. Hundreds of coins – probably Persian – had been melted down to provide the silver (parts of Thrace south of the Danube had been ruled by the Persians around the start of the fifth century BC). The beaten images had been partially gilded and the eyes of the god-like figures might once have been enamelled with coloured glass.

The cauldron originally consisted of eight outer panels (one is missing), which were built up around the circular base plate and held in place by metal strips. The five longer plates formed the sides of the interior, so that the gods depicted on the various panels looked both inwards and outwards. Two bands of tubing circled the base plate and the upper rim. When assembled, the whole thing stood 42cm (16.5in) in height, with a diameter of 69cm (27in), making it the largest surviving example of Iron Age silverwork in Europe.

The cauldron had been dismantled and reassembled many times, and on at least one occasion attempts were made to solder it together. Repairs had been carried out, and it is possible that the base plate was a later addition – it comprises a decorative *phalera* from the bridle of a horse.

The fact that the cauldron could be broken down into its constituent parts would have made it easier to transport from one place to another. More to the point, it meant that the cauldron could cease to be a cauldron when it was not in use. Assembled for a specific ceremony, it could be instantly dismantled afterwards – as seems to have been the case when Taliesin was initiated. Doing so would have ensured that the power of the cauldron could not be abused, especially if different parts were entrusted with different individuals who only came together for the rituals. It would have been important to keep such a unique and sacred object away from the eyes of the greedy and the uninitiated. Reforming the cauldron by piecing it back together would have been part of the ritual occasion, a means of summoning the gods and focusing the latent energy of the gold-and-silver sections. Deconstructing the cauldron allowed that energy to dissipate safely.

Those who were not familiar with the intricacies of the cauldron would have struggled with its assembly, which is perhaps why St Columba was said to have broken the golden cup of truth and to have sent it back to Manannán mac Lir for repair. In two places, the sides had been pierced right through by a sharp object, presumably after its final use, and the cauldron had been roughly pulled apart, causing the plates to buckle (this would be consistent with the forcible destruction of the cauldron at the climax of Brân the Blessed's battle with the Irish king of 'Worship').

Any instrument capable of allowing a shaman to undertake his or her visionary journey was liable to be thought of as a horse. The *phalera* which formed part of the cauldron's base made it especially equine. Hence, in the Welsh tradition we find Pwyll (Urien) sitting on the Mound of Sacrifice and seeing the 'wonder' of the princess Rhiannon (Muirgein) riding on a silver horse. The same mound is identified in the tale of *Culhwch and Olwen* as the 'Measure of the Cauldron'. Aneirin, in his *Y Gododdin* poem, referred to the burial mound as the 'hill of The Horse' (*Eleirch fre*), while Arthur was the 'prime son of Mighty-Horse'. Myrddin, meanwhile, addressed the juvenile Arthur as 'Son of the Cauldron'. And for centuries after Arthur's head had been interred in the mound, the islanders of Iona brought their horses to the hill every eve of St Michael's Day.

The cauldron discovered in the Danish peat-bog fulfils all the criteria: it was made of gold and silver and its workmanship was impressive; it had two bands around it; it could be made to fall apart when necessary and it was very much associated with horses, its base plate incorporating an ornamental horse brass.

So what was it doing in Denmark?

3

At the risk of speculating wildly, we can try to reconstruct the cauldron's travels.

It had come from the ancient world, its skilled Thracian manufacture suggesting that it was perhaps commissioned by the Druids of the *Tuatha dé Danann* when they were based at Thebes (see Chapter 2). One of the plates depicts infantry soldiers being dunked headfirst in a vat by a gigantic figure – a dog also appears to be helping – and then riding off as a phalanx of cavalry. It was said that the Children of Danu revived those warriors of Athens who had fallen in battle against the Persians, which might have meant that the Druids initiated the best Athenian foot-soldiers, who were then reborn as elite horsemen.

Eventually the *Tuatha dé Danann* tired of Greece and returned to their Land of Promise, where the cauldron became one of their magical treasures, the Cauldron of the Dagda (also known as Eochaidh Ollathair – 'All-Father' – a name reflected in the more familiar Uther). Their rivals, the Milesian Druids who worshipped Nechtán, would certainly have found a use for it, no doubt remembering that the last Egyptian pharaoh, Nectanebo II, had staged magical battles in a bowl of water. It is even possible that the legend of Deirdre of the Sorrows recalls the removal of the cauldron to Scotland when the sons of Uisnech migrated there and 'all wisdom flowed out of Ireland'.

The sons of Erc – Arthur's great-great-grandfather Fergus and his brothers – seem to have established Christianity in Dalriada, sixty-five years before the arrival of St Columba. Whether or not they tolerated the use of the cauldron, the marriage of Maelgwyn of Gwynedd (the 'dragon of the island') to Gwallwen daughter of Afallach would have presented the Scottish Christians with an opportunity to rid themselves of the pagan vessel. The cauldron, therefore, found its way to North Wales, where it came to be associated with the sow-goddess Ceridwen ('Blessed Song'). Maelgwyn's twenty-four bards would have received its wisdom, as did Taliesin of course, and it is probable that the twenty-four 'sons' of Brychan of Manau were also initiated (if they weren't in fact the same as Maelgwyn's bards).

When war broke out between Gwynedd and Strathclyde in the 550s, the cauldron returned to the North, perhaps carried by Creirwy and Taliesin to Lothian and then smuggled back to Iona by Áedán. It was hidden away in a lake when St Columba stormed the isle in 563 but brought back into use when Áedán secured the support of Columba's superior for his bardic cult in 575. The cauldron became a source of tension between the followers of Áedán and those of Columba and led to the conspiracy to assassinate Arthur. The warriors of the Gododdin drank its 'pale mead' before setting sail with Arthur in 594. It was then broken up and placed inside his grave.

As for what happened next, we must turn to a tale told by Arthur's enemies – specifically, to an Old English poem first sung by the Angles within a century or two of Arthur's death.

The tale is known as *Beowulf*, after its hero (like the name of Arthur, Beowulf meant 'Bear' – literally, 'Bee-wolf'). Initially, Beowulf comes to the aid of another king whose hall is being terrorised by a monster called Grendel. Beowulf kills Grendel by tearing off his arm, after which Grendel's mother attacks the hall. Tracking her back to her lake dwelling, Beowulf confronts the monster's mother in a cavern containing several bodies, including that of her son, and decapitates her. Beowulf then returns to his Swedish home and becomes king of his people. He reigns peacefully for fifty years but is dragged out of retirement to fight a fearsome dragon.

The dragon had been roused by the theft of a golden cup from a burial mound. The 'high barrow' stood on 'flat ground where the breakers beat at the headland', and inside it the last survivor of a warlike race had laid the 'gold of the earls', bemoaning as he did so: 'Who shall polish this plated vessel, this treasured cup?' Years had then passed. Men no longer knew of 'the way underground' into the burial chamber, but a servant hiding from his angry master found a way in. 'There were heaps of hoard-things in this hall underground which once in days gone by gleamed and rang.' The slave took the plated treasure from the mound and presented it to his master as a peace-offering.

The guardian of the mound and its treasures was a fire-breathing dragon or 'worm'. On finding that the 'dear drinking vessel' had been stolen, the 'barrow-keeper' had begun to scour the land, incinerating everything in sight. Beowulf attacks the dragon and slays it, but is himself killed in the process.

The action of *Beowulf* is set in Scandinavia, but the poem is Anglian. As we know, there were 'Englishmen' among Columba's servants on Iona when Aethelfrith the Deceiver was King of the Northumbrian Angles. When Aethelfrith died in 616, Edwin son of Aelle became King of the Angles. Oswald and Oswiu, the sons of Aethelfrith, were given sanctuary on the island of Columba's church – even though their father had recently killed 'multitudes of holy men' in a battle he fought against the Britons at the 'City of the Legion'.

Just a few short years later, in 623, the *Annals of Ulster* and the *Chronicon Scotorum* record the 'storming of Ráith Guala' by Fiachna mac Báetáin, Arthur's brother-in-law. The *Annals of Inisfallen* record the same event for 624. The *Annals of the Four Masters* date it somewhat earlier – in 618 – and state that Fiachna declaimed:

Fire took the Fort of Guala
When the dear little treasure was taken;
Remarkable was the vigour of the abbot,
Hot-footing it into jeopardy.

Fire took the Fort of Guala
When the dear little treasure was taken;
Eagerly did evil from within the mother-church
Bring fire to the Fort of Ead of the Belly.

Ráith Guala might have been a 'Fort of the Shoulder [of Land]', although it is more likely to have been the 'Fort of Aelle'. The first Anglian King of Deira had also been the father of Edwin or Eadwine, and so the 'Fort of Aelle' and the 'Fort of Ead' were probably the same place.

Fiachna was one of the last survivors of Arthur's gallant team. He had taken on the defence of Manau in 584 and therefore he would have defended Arthur's former headquarters – the 'City of the Legion' at Camelon – against Aethelfrith's Northumbrian warriors. Now, in an extraordinary act of vengeance, he had stormed Edwin's stronghold and burnt it to the ground because a 'dear little treasure' had been stolen.

In the *Beowulf* poem, it is a 'luckless slave' who steals the 'plated vessel' in order to appease his master. Fiachna's own poem points the finger at the 'mother-church', for it was an 'evil' element within the Iona community which had provoked the torching of the Anglian fortress. The presence of Aethelfrith's sons on Iona would suggest that Arthur's grave was robbed and the 'dear drinking vessel' sent as a peace-offering to Edwin of Northumbria.

Fiachna took his revenge by swooping down on the Angles like a true champion, assisted by the outraged Abbot of Iona. The Angles were stunned by his fury. Many years later, one of their storytellers would recall the 'fiery dragon's flames' which 'blasted all the land by the sea' and devastated 'the fortress of the people'.

Within a couple of years, both Fiachna and his son Mongán were dead. Fiachna was slain in battle in 626. The year before, Mongán had been one of four men executed in a churchyard in Kintyre, his head stoved in with a stone by a Briton of Strathclyde whose name was Arthur son of Bicor (or *bicar* – an old Welsh word for 'vicar').

The Angles must have suspected that the cauldron had something *Wyrd* about it. Like the beautiful Deirdre, it brought only sorrow and destruction. Whether it was stolen, traded or sent as tribute, it found its way to the original homeland of the Angles – the Angeln peninsula in Jutland – the legend of the fire-breathing dragon going with it. It was then transported a little way up the coast to Himmerland, where it was deposited, neatly and unobtrusively, on a patch of ground near the hamlet of Gundestrup. But its capacity for causing trouble was undiminished: the peat-cutters who discovered it in 1891 quarrelled bitterly over their reward.

It is now on display in the National Museum of Denmark in Copenhagen. A replica can be seen at the National Museum of Ireland in Dublin.

Finding the Grail is not the culmination of the quest. That comes when the seeker yields to the 'terrible desire' – *sannt grathail* – for wisdom. It is only by shedding our fears and insecurities, baring our inmost selves and listening patiently to what the gods might be trying to tell us about the planet and our place in the universe, that we can hope to banish moral ignorance.

The cauldron is merely a marvellous vessel that reflects back at us whatever we see in it.

Selected Bibliography

Primary Sources

The internet allows the researcher to access many early documents online. Two resources in particular are worthy of note: Celtic Literature Collective (maryjones.us) and CELT Corpus of Electronic Texts (celt.ucc.ie).

Aberdeen Breviary
Aided Díarmata Meic Fergusa Cerbeoil
Amra Columb Chille
Anales Toledanos (*Annals of Toledo*)
Annales Cambriae (*Welsh Annals*)
Annals of the Four Masters
Annals of Inisfallen
Annals of Tigernach
Annals of Ulster
Black Book of Taymouth
Bonedd y Gwyr Gogledd
Bonedd y Seint
Book of Deer
Book of the Dean of Lismore
Buchedd Collen
Buile Shuibhne
Carmina Gadelica
Chronica Gentis Scotorum (John of Fordun)
Chronicon Scotorum
Cognatio de Brachan
Compert Mongáin
Confessio (St Patrick)
De Excidio et Conquestu Britanniae (St Gildas, *Of the Ruin and Conquest of Britian*)
Félire Oenguso
Fiachairecht & Dreanacht
Gein Branduib maic Echach 7 Aedáin maic Gabráin
Hanes Taliesin
Historia Brittonum (Nennius)

Historia Gentis Scotorum (Hector Boece)
Historia Regum Britanniae (Geoffrey of Monmouth, *History of the Kings of Britain*)
Imacallam Choluim Chille ocus ind óclaig I Carn Eolairg
Immacallam in Druad Brain ocus inna Banfháitho Febuil
Immrama curaig Mail Dúin
Immram Brain
Inmain tir in tir ud thoir
Lebar na Núachongbála (Book of Leinster)
Leabhar Baile an Mhota (Book of Ballymote)
Leabhar Buidhe Lecain (Yellow Book of Lecan)
Lebor Gabála Érenn
Llyfr Aneirin (Book of Aneirin)
Llyfr Coch Hergest (Red Book of Hergest)
Llyfr Ddu Caerfyrddin (Black Book of Carmarthen)
Llyfr Gwyn Rhydderch (White Book of Rhydderch)
Llyfr Taliesin (Book of Taliesin)
Mura cecinit
Navigatio sancti Brendani abbatis
Oidheadh Chloinne Tuireann
Orygynale Cronykil of Scotland (Andrew of Wyntoun)
Scél asa mberar co mbad hé Find mac Cumaill Mongán
Senchus Fer nAlban
Sgeulachd air Sir Uallabh O'Corn
Táin Bó Cúailnge
Tochomlod mac Miledh a hEspain I nErind
Trystan ac Essyllt
Urien a Modron
Vera Historia de Morte Arthuri
Vita Columbae (Adomnán of Iona)
Vita Columbae (Cumméne the White)
Vita Gildae (Caradoc of Llancarfan)
Vita Kentigerni (Jocelin of Furness)
Vita Merlini (Geoffrey of Monmouth)
Vita Sancti Cadoci (Lifris of Llancarfan)
Vita Sancti Kentigerni Imperfecta
Vita Sancti Paternus
Vita Sancti Servani
Ymddiddan Arthur a'r Eryr
Ystoria Taliesin

Arthurian Legend & History

Most of the quotations from the *Mabinogion* in this book are taken from Lady Guest's original translations, although I have modernised some of the spellings.

Anon. *Mabinogion* translated by Jeffrey Gantz (London, 1976)
Anon. *Mabinogion* translated by Lady Charlotte Guest, facsimile of 1877 edition (Cardiff, 1977)
Anon. *Mabinogion* translated by Gwyn Jones and Thomas Jones, revised edition (London, 1993)

Anon. *The Quest of the Holy Grail* translated by P.M. Matarasso (London, 1969)

Ardrey, Adam *Finding Merlin* (Edinburgh, 2007)

Ashe, Geoffrey *The Discovery of King Arthur* revised edition (Stroud, 2003)

Ashe, Geoffrey (ed.) *The Quest for Arthur's Britain* (London, 1968)

Ashley, Mike *King Arthur, The Mammoth Book of* (London, 2005)

Barber, Richard *The Figure of Arthur* (London, 1972)

Barber, Richard *King Arthur: Hero and Legend* third edition (London, 1986)

Béroul *The Romance of Tristan* translated by Alan S. Frederick (London, 1970)

Bromwich, Rachel *Trioedd Ynys Prydein* third edition (Cardiff, 2006)

Burgess, Glyn S. & Keith Busby *The Lais of Marie de France* (London, 1986)

Chrétien de Troyes *Arthurian Romances* translated by William W. Kibler and Carleton W. Carroll (London, 1991)

Cox, George & Eustace Jones *Arthurian Legends of the Middle Ages* reprinted edition (London, 1995)

Day, David *The Quest for King Arthur* (London, 1995)

Dixon-Kennedy, Mike *A Companion to Arthurian & Celtic Myths & Legends* (Stroud, 2004)

Eschenbach, Wolfram von *Parzifal* translated by A.T. Hatto (London, 1980)

Geoffrey of Monmouth *The History of the Kings of Britain* translated by Lewis Thorpe (London, 1966)

Gidlow, Christopher *The Reign of Arthur* (Stroud, 2004)

Giles, J.A. (translator) *The Works of Gildas and Nennius* (London, 1841)

Loomis, Roger S. *Celtic Myth and Arthurian Romance* (New York, 1967)

Lupack, Alan *The Oxford Guide to Arthurian Literature and Legend* (Oxford, 2005)

Malory, Sir Thomas *Le Morte d'Arthur* new edition (Ware, 1996)

Matthews, Caitlín *Mabon and the Mysteries of Britain* (London, 1987)

Matthews, John (ed.) *An Arthurian Reader* (Wellingborough, 1988)

Matthews, John *Merlin: Shaman, Prophet, Magician* (London, 2004)

McCall, Alexander and William *Artur, Gwenwhyvawr and Myrddin, Ancient Brythons of the North* (Bishop Auckland, 1997)

Mersey, Daniel *Arthur: King of the Britons* (Chichester, 2004)

Skene, William F. *The Four Ancient Books of Wales* (Edinburgh, 1868)

Strassburg, Gottfried von *Tristan* translated by A.T. Hatto, revised edition (London, 1967)

Tolstoy, Nikolai *The Quest for Merlin* (London, 1985)

Williams, Gwyn A. *Excalibur: The Search for Arthur* (London, 1994)

British Folklore & History

Adomnán of Iona *Life of St Columba* translated by Richard Sharpe (London, 1995)

Aitchison, Nick *Scotland's Stone of Destiny* (Stroud, 2000)

Alcock, Leslie *Arthur's Britain* revised edition (London, 1989)

Anon. *Beowulf* translated by Michael Alexander (London, 1973)

Ashe, Geoffrey *Mythology of the British Isles* (London, 1990)

Balfour, Michael *Mysterious Scotland* new edition (Edinburgh, 2003)

Barber, Chris *More Mysterious Wales* new edition (London, 1987)

Barber, John & Jim Killgore *Saint Columba* (Blairgowrie, 1998)

Barber, Richard *Myths and Legends of the British Isles* (Woodbridge, 1999)

Bartlett, Robert *England Under the Norman and Angevin Kings 1075-1225* (Oxford, 2000)

Bede *Ecclesiastical History of the English People* translated by Leo Sherley-Price, edited by D.H. Farmer (London, 1990)

Blundell, Nigel *Ancient Scotland* (London, 1996)

Selected Bibliography

Clancy, Thomas Owen & Gilbert Márkus *Iona: The Earliest Poetry of a Celtic Monastery* (Edinburgh, 1995)

Crookston, Peter (ed.) *Island Britain* new edition (London, 1993)

Darling, F. Fraser & J. Morton Boyd *The Highlands and Islands* reprinted edition (London, 1969)

Davies, John *A History of Wales* (London, 1993)

Finberg, H.P.R. *The Formation of England 550-1042* new edition (London, 1976)

Fry, Plantagenet Somerset *Roman Britain* (Newton Abbot, 1984)

Laing, Lloyd and Jenny *The Picts and the Scots* (Stroud, 1993)

MacArthur, E. Mairi *Columba's Island: Iona from Past to Present* (Edinburgh, 1995)

MacDougall, W.B. *Chronicles of Strathearn* (Crieff, 1896)

Maclean, Charles *The Isle of Mull: Placenames, Meanings and Stories* (Dumfries, 1997)

Macleod, Fiona *Iona* new edition (Edinburgh, 1992)

Macleod, John *Highlanders: A History of the Gaels* (London, 1996)

Macnab, P.A. *Mull & Iona* (Newton Abbot, 1995)

Macquarrie, Alan & E. Mairi MacArthur *Iona Through the Ages* second edition (Coll, 1992)

Maine, G.F. (ed.) *A Book of Scotland* (London, 1950)

Marsden, John *The Tombs of the Kings: An Iona Book of the Dead* (Felinfach, 1994)

Massie, Allan *The Thistle and the Rose* (London, 2005)

McHardy, Stuart *Scotland: Myth, Legend & Folklore* (Edinburgh, 1999)

McNeill, F. Marian (ed.) *An Iona Anthology* new edition (Iona, 1990)

Menzies, Lucy *Saint Columba of Iona* reprinted edition (Felinfach, 1992)

Moffat, Alistair *The Sea Kingdoms* (London, 2002)

Morris, John *The Age of Arthur: A History of the British Isles from 350 to 650* (London, 1973)

Prebble, John *The Lion in the North* new edition (London, 1974)

Pryor, Francis *Britain AD: A Quest for Arthur, England and the Anglo-Saxons* (London, 2004)

Ralls-MacLeod, Karen *Music and the Celtic Otherworld: From Ireland to Iona* (Edinburgh, 2000)

Ralls-MacLeod, Karen & Ian Robertson *The Quest for the Celtic Key* (Edinburgh, 2002)

Reid, Alexander George *The Annals of Auchterader and Memorials of Strathearn* (Crieff, 1899)

Ritchie, A. & E. *Iona Past and Present* third edition (Edinburgh, 1934)

Ross, Anne & Don Robins *The Life and Death of a Druid Prince* (London, 1989)

Salway, Peter *The Oxford Illustrated History of Roman Britain* (London, 1993)

Senior, Michael *Myths of Britain* (London, 1979)

Smith, Lesley M. (ed.) *The Making of Britain: The Dark Ages* (London, 1984)

Smith, Robin *The Making of Scotland* (Edinburgh, 2001)

Tacitus *Agricola* translated by H. Mattingly, revised by S.A. Handford (London, 1970)

Thompson, Francis *The Supernatural Highlands* new edition (Edinburgh, 1997)

Watson, William J. *The Celtic Placenames of Scotland* new edition (Edinburgh, 1993)

Weir, Alison *Eleanor of Aquitaine* (London, 1999)

Westwood, Jennifer *Albion: A Guide to Legendary Britain* (London, 1987)

Westwood, Jennifer & Sophia Kingshill *The Lore of Scotland: A Guide to Scottish Legends* (London, 2009)

Whitelock, Dorothy *The Beginnings of English Society* revised edition (London, 1972)

Wood, Michael *In Search of England* (London, 1999)

Wood, Michael *In Search of the Dark Ages* (London, 1981)

Young, Simon *A.D. 500: A Journey Through the Dark Isles of Britain and Ireland* (London, 2005)

Magic, Myth, Religion & Ritual

Bates, Brian *The Real Middle Earth: Magic and Mystery in the Dark Ages* (London, 2003)

Bulfinch, Thomas *The Age of Chivalry* new edition (New York, 1995)

Bulfinch, Thomas *The Age of Fable* new edition (New York, 1995)

De Martino, Ernesto *Primitive Magic: The Psychic Powers of Shamans and Sorcerers* (New South Wales, 1972)

Fierz-David, Linda *Women's Dionysian Initiation* (Dallas, 1988)

Frazer, Sir James *The Golden Bough* abriged (London, 1922)

Gardiner, Philip & Gary Osborn *The Serpent Grail* (London, 2005)

Grigsby, John *Warriors of the Wasteland* (London, 2003)

Hesiod *Theogony* translated by Dorothea Wender (London, 1973)

Kondratiev, Alexei *Celtic Rituals* (Cork, 1998)

Lincoln, Bruce *Death, War, and Sacrifice: Studies in Ideology and Practice* (Chicago, 1991)

Matthews, John *Taliesin: Shamanism and the Bardic Mysteries in Britain and Ireland* (London, 1991)

Nicholson, Shirley (ed.) *Shamanism: An Expanded View of Reality* (Wheaton, 1987)

Perera, Sylvia Brinton *Descent to the Goddess* (Toronto, 1981)

Piggott, Stuart *The Druids* (London, 1968)

Rolleson, T.W. *Celtic Myths & Legends* new edition (London, 1994)

Rutherford, Ward *Celtic Mythology* (Wellingborough, 1987)

Rutherford, Ward *The Druids: Magicians of the West* (Wellingborough, 1978)

Somé, Malidoma Patrice *Of Water and the Spirit* (New York, 1994)

Spence, Lewis *The Magic Arts in Celtic Britain* reprinted edition (Van Nuys, 1996)

Spence, Lewis *The Mysteries of Britain* reprinted edition (London, 1994)

Thompson, C.J.S. *Mysteries and Secrets of Magic* reprinted edition (London, 1995)

Versluis, Arthur *The Philosophy of Magic* (Boston, 1986)

Wright, Harry B. *Witness to Witchcraft* new edition (London, 1958)

Young, Dudley *Origins of the Sacred* (New York, 1991)

Miscellaneous

Bamford, Christopher & William Parker Marsh *Celtic Christianity: Ecology and Holiness* new edition (Edinburgh, 1986)

Cahill, Thomas *How the Irish Saved Civilization* (London, 1995)

Chadwick, Nora *The Celts* (London, 1979)

Childe, Gordon *What Happened in History* revised edition (London, 1964)

Clancy, Thomas Owen (ed.) *The Triumph Tree: Scotland's Earliest Poetry AD 550-1350* (Edinburgh, 1998)

Ellis, Peter Berresford *Celt and Greek* (London, 1997)

Evans, H. Meurig & W.O. Thomas *Y Geiriadur Mawr* new edition (Dinefwr, 1989)

Gardner, Laurence *Bloodline of the Holy Grail* (London, 1996)

Hamilton, Claire *Tales of the Celtic Bards* (Alresford, 2003)

Harding, M. Esther *Woman's Mysteries* (London, 1989)

Haswell-Smith, Hamish *The Scottish Islands* revised edition (Edinburgh, 2008)

Hern, Gerhard *The Celts* (London, 1976)

Herodotus *The Histories* translated by Aubrey de Sélincourt, revised by A.R. Burn (London, 1972)

Homer *The Odyssey* translated by E.V. Rieu, revised by D.C.H. Rieu (London, 1991)

Selected Bibliography

Jaynes, Julian *The Origins of Consciousness in the Breakdown of the Bicameral Mind* new edition (London, 1993)

Johnson, Samuel & James Boswell *Journey to the Hebrides* edited by Ian McGowan (Edinburgh, 1996)

Koestler, Arthur *The Sleepwalkers* (New York, 1959)

Lane Fox, Robin *The Classical World* new edition (London, 2006)

MacLennan, Malcolm *Faclair Gàidhlig* new edition (Edinburgh & Stornoway, 1979)

MacNeill, Nigel *The Literature of the Highlanders* edited by John MacMaster Campbell (Stirling, 1929)

Nicolson, Alexander (ed.) *A Collection of Gaelic Proverbs and Familiar Phrases* new edition (Edinburgh, 1996)

Ó Corráin, Donnchadh, Liam Breatnach & Kim McCone (editors) *Sages, Saints and Storytellers* (Maynooth, 1989)

Ovid *Metamorphoses* translated by Mary Innes (London, 1955)

Rees, Alwyn & Brinley Rees *Celtic Heritage: Ancient Tradition in Ireland and Wales* (London, 1961)

Ritchie, W.F. & J.N.G. *Celtic Warriors* (Aylesbury, 1995)

Seyffert, Oskar *Dictionary of Classical Antiquities* revised and edited by Henry Nettleship & J.E. Sandys (New York, 1957)

Southworth, John *Fools and Jesters at the English Court* (Stroud, 1998)

Various *A Celtic Miscellany* translated by Kenneth Hurlstone Jackson (London, 1951)

Vico, Giambattista *New Science* translated by David Marsh (London, 2001)

INDEX

314